RURAL RHYTHM

RURAL RHYTHM

The Story of Old-Time Country Music in 78 Records

★

TONY RUSSELL

OXFORD
UNIVERSITY PRESS

OXFORD
UNIVERSITY PRESS

Oxford University Press is a department of the University of Oxford. It furthers the University's objective of excellence in research, scholarship, and education by publishing worldwide. Oxford is a registered trade mark of Oxford University Press in the UK and certain other countries.

Published in the United States of America by Oxford University Press
198 Madison Avenue, New York, NY 10016, United States of America.

Library of Congress Cataloging-in-Publication Data
Names: Russell, Tony, 1946– author.
Title: Rural rhythm : the story of old-time country music in 78 records / Tony Russell.
Description: New York City : Oxford University Press, 2021. |
Includes bibliographical references and index.
Identifiers: LCCN 2020042458 (print) | LCCN 2020042459 (ebook) |
ISBN 9780190091187 (hardback) | ISBN 9780190091200 (epub) |
ISBN 9780190091194 (pdf) | ISBN 9780190091217
Subjects: LCSH: Old-time music—History and criticism. | Popular music—United States—1921–1930—History and criticism. | Popular music—United States—1931–1940—History and criticism. | Country music—To 1951—History and criticism. |
Old-time music—Discography. | Popular music—United States—1921–1930—Discography. |
Popular music—United States—1921–1930—Discography.
Classification: LCC ML3477 .R87 2021 (print) | LCC ML3477 (ebook) |
DDC 782.42164209041—dc23
LC record available at https://lccn.loc.gov/2020042458
LC ebook record available at https://lccn.loc.gov/2020042459

In memoriam
John Cohen
Nolan Porterfield
Mike Seeger

Contents

Acknowledgments

I am indebted to my colleague and friend Patrick Huber, both for his meticulous reading of the manuscript, which saved me from making many careless errors, and for his enthusiastic support. I am also grateful to family members and friends: Sharon Banoff, Tony Engle, Sally Feldman, and Ricky Russell read parts of the manuscript, suggested many improvements, and gave me generous encouragement.

I owe a great deal to my late friends and teachers Bob Pinson and Charles K. Wolfe, and to my late colleagues and correspondents George C. Biggar, Archie Green, Clarence H. Greene, Jr., W. K. McNeil, Guthrie T. Meade, John P. Morgan, Donald R. Nelson, Nolan Porterfield, John I. White, Gene Wiggins, and Joe Wilson.

I received invaluable assistance from Mary Katherine Aldin, Tony Barker, Ray Bellande, Kerry Blech, Harry Bolick, Bob Bovee, Sarah Bryan, John Burton, Joyce Cauthen, the Center for Popular Music, Kevin Coffey, Norm Cohen, Les Cole, Bob Cox, David L. Crisp, Guy Cundell, Charlie Dahan, Frank Dalton, Wayne Daniel, Eric Dawson, Wade Falcon, Ben Franklin, Dave Freeman, Cary Ginell, Fred Hoeptner, Hunter Holmes, Peter Honig, Brody Hunt, Ola Jean Kelly (Union County Library, Union, SC), Chris Kimmer, Christopher King, Trev King, Joe LaRose, Lance Ledbetter, Bob and Lee Linn, Kip Lornell, Bill Malone, Frank Mare, John Marsden, Wayne and Margaret Martin, Barry Mazor, The Mudcat Café, Dean Mullaney (www.libraryofamericancomics.com), Jim Nelson, Rich Nevins, *The Old-Time Herald*, Ted Olson, Peter Paeth, Anthony Pearson, Jerry Pevahouse, Hal Pugh, Ronnie Pugh, Thomas Quinn, Bradley Reeves, Rich Remsberg, Margaret Riddle, Kinney Rorrer, Michael Rosen, Howard Rye, Nathan Salsburg, Ben Sandmel, Paul Shoffner, Dave Sichak (hillbilly-music.com), Zach Sigall, Chris Smith, Paul Solarski, the Southern Folklife Center, Jack Spence, Dick Spottswood, Christian Stanfield, Chris Strachwitz, Allan Sutton, John Tefteller, Ivan Tribe, Guido van Rijn, Malcolm Vidrine, Gaylon D. Wardlow, Steve Weiss, Richard Weize, Win Wiacek, and Marshall Wyatt.

I have profited from the expertise and collegiality of numerous members of these Facebook groups: Black & White Hillbilly & Blues Music; Dedicated to Old Time Music; Oldtime Country, Hillbilly, Rockabilly & Bluegrass 78s; The Rarest 78s; 78 rpm In The Wild; and 78 rpm records & cylinders fan group.

Many musicians and their families were generous enough to share their memories and memorabilia with me, among them the late Maggie Bivins, Donna and Joyce Butler Blake, Dottie Blankenship, Daniel Bowling, Virginia Brown, the late Cliff Bruner, Kenneth Butler, the late Claude Casey, the late Homer Christopher, the Clark-Vaughn-Skelton family, Sybil Garner Crow, Cathy Skiles Culver, Jerry Culver, Terry Culver, Anita Davis, Terresa and Mildred Dutton, Terry Ford, the late John Foster, the late Ausie B. Grigg, the late Dixie Landress, Peggy Lawhon, the late Kathleen Lockamy, Tom Lockamy, Mary Lockamy Loy, the late Lewis McDaniel, Donna Meng, Sue Mize, Odessa (Dot) Wilson Moss, Dale Murphy, R. D. Murphy, the late Marshall Nations, Victoria O'Connell, Barbara Campbell Plumley, Beth Preddy, the late Leo Raley, the Reeve family, Cathy Meng Robinson, the late Olive Boone Roesink, the late Mack Sievers, Laurah Sims, David Sloan, Ethel Garland Slusher, the late Bernard C. Smith, Dale Snyder, Betty Tudor, the late Clayton Tyler, Vivian Hall Wall, Jane and Ed Weldon, Chris Williams, Rick Wilson, and Vonda Yeary.

At Oxford University Press, I have deeply appreciated the support of my editors, Suzanne Ryan, who commissioned the book, and Norman Hirschy, who guided it to publication, and the expertise of Joellyn Ausanka, Farzie Razak, India Gray, and Mary Horn.

Sales Figures

Columbia sales figures were compiled from company papers by David Freeman. Champion data were researched by Kinney Rorrer and T. Malcolm Rockwell and published online by *The Old-Time Herald* at www.oldtimeherald.org/champion/index.html. Superior data were gathered from Gennett files by George W. Kay and published in *Record Research*. Sales data on Victor records were derived from research in RCA archives by myself and by Michael Brooks. I am grateful to all those named for access to their findings.

Label-scans

The majority of the label-scans are from records in my own collection, but some were kindly provided by Bear Family Records, John Heneghan, Chris Hood, Gregg Kimball, Music Memory, Big Boy Woods, and Marshall Wyatt. Further thanks to Marshall for skillfully restoring some imperfect images.

★

Introduction

The literature of recorded old-time music is a broad field, but surprisingly little of it has been given over to the cultivation of songs and their contexts. The barn is stacked with histories and biographies, but the gleaners have brought in less of the actual stuff of songs: the words, and the stories within, or behind, the words.

Fine work has been done on songs about coal mines, railroads, and textile mills. But the subjects and meanings of early country music as it is represented on record are immensely varied, and many have passed without commentary. In this book, I identify some of those subjects and meanings, and explore what they tell us about the musicians who expressed them, the listeners who absorbed them, and the development of the genre, old-time music, in which they found a home. So too with the context: I look at the circumstances in which these songs and tunes were recorded, the intentions and interventions of the companies that commissioned those recordings, and their fates once they were issued.

In these pages the reader will meet songs, and stories of songs, about home and family, love and courtship, marriage and separation, childhood and schooldays, old age and death, crime and punishment, farms and floods, chain gangs and chain stores, wagons and automobiles, dogs and mules, drink, disasters, jokes, journeys, money, memories, and much more.

The title has a double meaning. "Rural rhythm"—which, lexically at least, is almost a synonym for "country music"—suggests the tempos and styles of rural and small-town music-making and hints at the gearshift that accelerated country music from the barn-dance pace of the 1920s to the hyperdrive of late '30s proto-bluegrass and Western Swing. This is exactly the period the book spans, and "rural rhythm" in that sense is a continuous underlying theme. But I have also tried to acknowledge a larger rural rhythm: of life in these years in the South, Southwest, and Midwest, with its recreations, its rituals, and its oddities.

The focus falls on those territories because it was from them, and often in them, that the record companies of the 1920s and '30s gathered almost all their material. In fact, old-time music was made in many parts of the nation, and the standard narrative of country music's history has not adequately acknowledged the music and musicians of, for example, the Northeastern states, or much of the Midwest, largely because the record business ignored them. But rewriting that narrative requires looking beyond records: a task for another day, and another writer.

By "records" I mean the original objects, the black shellac discs that in the 1920s, '30s, and '40s were the current best medium for capturing music and redistributing it. Each of these seventy-eight essays is devoted to a single 78rpm record—sometimes just one of the songs or tunes on it, sometimes both—and attempts to describe and contextualize it; to extract a story, or to tell one.

I have been fascinated by these records and their makers for many years, and I own copies of most of the 78s, but this is not an anecdotal tour of my record shelves, and, apart from occasional asides, it is not a conversation with other collectors. There is a larger plan.

Rural Rhythm is episodic and chronological, the order of the essays being determined by recording date. The intention, as with my previous book *Country Music Originals*, is that anyone who chooses to read it in a straight line, so to speak, will gain some sense of the music's historical development. For a more step-by-step account of how old-time country music took shape, and of the media that helped it to do so, I have constructed a Timeline (pages 263–70).

From the start, the book calculatedly introduces the reader to the characteristic properties of old-time music of the period. The first essay is on Fiddlin' John Carson's "The Little Old Log Cabin in the Lane," generally accepted to be country music's first recorded song. The second, on the Hill Billies, ushers in the hillbilly band, since this was the first recorded group playing old-time music to make its mark *as* a group. The third and fourth pieces, on "Woman's Suffrage" and "The Death of Floyd Collins," raise the curtain on the topical song, the latter piece being a twentieth-century equivalent of a broadside ballad. "When the Work's All Done This Fall" beckons the reader to the Old West and the songs of the cowboy. The next essay focuses on fiddlers' contests as a social as well as musical phenomenon. Another deals with the vast audience for Southern sacred music, as revealed by the sales of one disc. A waltz record by McMichen's Melody Men finds country players ambitious for musical legitimacy, for finding a way to exchange wool shirt and neckerchief for tux and tie; it also allows us to peep into record-company accounts and see what kind of money an astute operator could earn from hillbilly music.

Subsequent essays deal with topics like the Darwinism debate ("You Can't Make a Monkey out of Me") and Prohibition ("When the Roses Bloom for the Bootlegger"). Crime and scandal are aired in "The Bluefield Murder" and "The Fate of Rhoda Sweetin," and events of the moment in "Eleven Cent Cotton Forty Cent Meat," "Henry Ford's Model A," "I've Got the Chain Store Blues," and "Got the Jake Leg Too." Readers can follow the dramatization of rural life in recorded sketches ("A Corn Licker Still in Georgia," "Tennessee Coon Hunt") and by traveling vaudeville troupes ("Who Broke the Lock on the Hen-House Door?"). They can view the relationship between old-time music and the textile industry from the different angles of "Walk Right in Belmont," "Cotton Mill Girl," and "Cotton Mill Blues." Their reading will frequently be disturbed by collisions and collusions of white and black music, as in "Blue Yodel," "I've Got the Chain Store Blues," "Feels Good," "V-8 Blues," or "Hello Stranger."

There are also instrumental tunes here that have a special resonance in old-time music. "Seneca Square Dance," "Combination Rag," and "The Lost Child" exemplify how regional fiddling styles and repertories—in these instances, from Missouri, east Texas, and northern Alabama—were disseminated on nationally distributed phonograph records. "Carbolic Rag" suggests connections between the banjo- or mandolin-fronted stringband and earlier stringed-instrument clubs. "Gray Eagle" and "Forked Deer" are uncommon instances of a racially mixed group being recorded making music together.

I chose some records partly for the mystique that, thanks to collectors, drapes them like Spanish moss: the hypnotic "Wimbush Rag," the impressionistic "Flat Wheel Train Blues," the near-unique copy of "That's My Rabbit—My Dog Caught It." Others were picked for their reverse mystique: records that many enthusiasts are bewildered by, or disdain, or perhaps just don't know, such as "Handy Man," "Rye Waltz," "The Roamin' Musician," "That's the Blue Heaven for Me," or "Salvation Is for All."

Sales figures survive for some (unfortunately not all) of these recordings, and are duly provided, but this is not a catalog of old-time best-sellers. Nor is it confined to what are customarily considered historically important recordings (some of which I have already written about). Several of the records discussed here were huge hits, wayside markers on the long road of sociocultural history. Others sold in only moderate quantities, some in mere hundreds, and their impact on the history of country music was often negligible and sometimes invisible. Why write about them, then, if they are so little known? (Though nearly all of them are accessible to anyone with a computer.) Because their obscurity is very often unmerited, and besides, they contain what I believe to be valuable information about their period and milieu, information that has not always found a place in the official narratives of American social history. Furthermore, many of these songs and tunes, both well known and obscure, have caught the imagination of later musicians and taken on new lives in different places and different times, including our own.

Two-thirds of these recordings were made between 1923 and 1929, a period of optimism and self-assurance for many Americans, though perhaps less so within the region that produced hillbilly records. It would be reasonable to inspect these communiqués for signs of that confidence, and sometimes, to be sure, we find them, such as a glad hand for a new Ford car. But these recordings were not made by businesspeople, and if they respond to the world around them, it is not with go-getting triumphalism so much as suspicion or mistrust of the prosperity it promised, if not outright disbelief. In that respect, the writers and singers of these songs, though they are several generations away from us, often seem like contemporaries, for many of their troubles have returned to trouble us or never went away.

Record-making in that period was not a straightforward means of making a social comment, let alone a political statement. The artists might not be businesspeople, but the record company staff were, and the industry could not help but be implicated in the big-business world that a discontented farmer or millhand might feel like criticizing. We have little evidence of out-and-out censorship, of a recording director telling an artist, "You can't say that on a record." But it is sensible to recognize that the recording process could act as a filter, removing crumbs of criticism, particles of protest, the silt of social unrest.

Some of these songs express attitudes about race or gender that we now consider deplorable. I have chosen not to editorialize about this, since I don't personally find it a useful way of approaching, let alone understanding, the past. The songs were what they were, in a time that was as it was, and it is the commentator's job, as I see it, to look squarely at them and report what he sees to the reader, unapologetically, always alert to their context.

"Hillbilly" is a word that bothers some people, so I should make it clear how I use it. In this book, the terms "hillbilly music" and "old-time music" are more or less interchangeable. It might be argued that because, as a marketing tool, "hillbilly" was not widely used until the mid-'30s, applying the word to music made years earlier is anachronistic; but in fact, outside the record industry, it was a descriptor at least as early as the mid-1920s. So I employ it without compunction, but also, I hope, without offense.

Some of these performers were included, and a few of these songs briefly mentioned, in *Country Music Originals*, but in writing about them again I have concentrated on fresh, and often overlooked or undocumented, aspects of the musicians' life and work, and on providing more detail about the songs. That said, more than a third of the musicians and almost two-thirds of the songs and tunes are written about here for the first time. The books, articles, interviews, correspondence, and other materials that lie behind each essay are listed in mini-bibliographies (Sources, pages 271–85). I have also made extensive use of contemporary newspapers, and those references are cited in the text.

Many essays touch upon musicians, themes, or topics that surface elsewhere, and are duly cross-referenced, so that, for example, (➤75) directs the reader to essay 75.

The majority of the recordings I discuss have been reissued on CDs that present the music sounding as I believe its makers, the musicians and the recording executives, intended it should. In giving details of these CDs, I am acknowledging the expertise of the label owners, collectors, and remastering engineers who have collaborated to produce them, such as Richard Nevins (Yazoo Records), David Freeman (County Records), Richard Weize and Christian Zwarg (Bear Family Records), Chris Strachwitz (Arhoolie Records), Marshall Wyatt (Old Hat Records), and Christopher King (Tompkins Square Records and others). Regrettably, their work has sometimes been transferred (to put it as neutrally as possible) to online entities that give them no credit. That said, however, since the majority of the recordings written about here can be heard online, and some readers may prefer to find them there, I have noted their presence on Spotify and YouTube (YT), which are free sites as of this writing.

★ ★ ★

No doubt, great music was made by practitioners who never recorded. Some of it, to judge from written accounts, was as exciting or profound as the music I have chosen to write about here. But it is all gone, and there is nothing we can know about it beyond what witnesses have told us, and nothing much we can feel about it beyond regret. The recordings, at least, are *there*. They may have flaws or deficiencies; we may sometimes wish they had been better made, whether by the musicians, by the men producing and engineering the records, or by the factories pressing them. What they contain—tune, words, allusions, the spirit of a moment—may not mean to us what it meant to their makers. They are messages from another time, and sometimes reach us in code. To understand them, we must decipher them, which in many cases is what this book tries to do. So recorded music, like any history, comes with problems of meaning and context, and its story is littered with "possibly"s and "what if?"s. But, in the end, it is unarguable. This is how it was done by *these* people, in *these* places, in *those* times, preserved forever by a fortunate collaboration of industry and enterprise.

Tony Russell
London, England
October 2020
tonyrussell@bluetone.uk

User Notes

Each essay is preceded by a headnote including

- essay number
- song/tune title(s)
- artist(s)
- original 78rpm release
- place and date of recording
- date of original release
- sales figure (if known)
- reissue(s) on CD
- availability (at the time of publication) on the online sites Spotify and YouTube (YT)

During the period covered by this book, songwriters and composers were generally not named on record labels. When I know who they were and consider it valuable to identify them, I do so.

Birth and death dates are generally shown in an abbreviated form, e.g., (1892–1958), but if the information is being published for the first time, I frequently give the dates in full.

RURAL RHYTHM

1

"THE LITTLE OLD LOG CABIN IN THE LANE"

Fiddlin' John Carson
Okeh 4890

Recorded in Atlanta, GA, probably June 14, 1923
Released in July 1923

Reissued on *Fiddlin' John Carson Vol. 1 (1923–1924)* (Document DOCD-8014)

Online: Spotify, YT

This was the first vocal recording in the genre we call old-time music made in the South by a Southern artist. The phonographic ancestry of the country song begins here.

★ ★ ★

The log cabin is a core image of old-time music. You might call it one of its founding myths.

Its first appearance in American song may be in "The Log Cabin," "A Patriotic Ballad" of 1840 that hymns "a hardy and an honest class, Of freemen in their prime," who "with their axes on their shoulders . . . sallied for the west." But this is a partisan and particular piece, promoting the presidential candidacy of William Henry Harrison (who took office in 1841 and died a month later).

Three decades pass, and the image generates very different songs: first, "The Little Old Cabin in the Lane" (1871), composed by William Shakespeare Hays, a Louisvillean who originated many songs sung by old-time musicians; then "The Old Log Cabin in the Dell" (1875) and "The Little Old Log Cabin by de Stream" (1880). In these post-emancipation compositions, as the artwork of their sheet music immediately informs us, the narrator, the resident of the log cabin, is not an axe-carrying pioneer but a hoe-wielding African American: an elderly ex-slave, fondly recalling a past that will never return, and looking trustfully toward the day when "the angels they will lead me when my time has come to go." (But an early pastiche of the genre, "I've Mortgaged That Old Cabin in the Lane" [1875], described as an "Answer to 'The Old Log Cabin in the Lane,'" finds the narrator in a less hopeful, indeed a sullen, disbelieving mood: "When I tink de angels comin', oh, dey fool this ole man sure.")

Songs like these, redrawing the history of slavery with the airbrush of sentiment, distancing and perhaps absolving guilt, were instruments of comfort and reassurance for the white audience for which they were written. But why were they still being sung half a century later? The historian Patrick Huber argues that "The Little Old Log Cabin in the Lane" "suggested a nostalgic rural alternative to the troubling and often alienating modern urban world of Atlanta. . . . In Carson's rendition, [it] became a metaphor for the disintegration of rural southern communities and, by extension, the erosion of bedrock traditional values in the modern South." But did this idealized vision of an old black man sitting outside his cabin, quietly living out his days, also serve to obscure the real and unsettling perspective of a present in which his descendants, unshackled by loyalties to old masters, might look instead to new leaders and argue for new rights?

★ ★ ★

We don't know when Fiddlin' John Carson learned "The Little Old Log Cabin in the Lane." He is reported to have got it from "an old almanac." By the beginning of the twentieth century, it was what we would now call a standard. It was recorded by popular interpreters like Len Spencer, who delivered it in aural blackface around 1900, and by the actually black Carroll C. Clark about a decade later. Carson was singing it in public at least as early as 1915.

On September 9, 1922, the forty-eight-year-old fiddler played on Atlanta's six-months-old radio station WSB. Reviewing the program the next day, the *Atlanta Journal* (which owned WSB) chortled,

"Fiddlin' John Carson . . . is an institution in himself and his singing of 'The Little Old Log Cabin in the Lane' and the playing of 'Turkey in the Straw,' 'Old Joe Clark,' and 'The Old Hen Cackles' . . . was enough to put any program over with a rush."

Nine months later, in an improvised studio on Atlanta's Nassau Street, Carson sang "The Little Old Log Cabin in the Lane" for a recording team from Okeh Records.

The June 1923 Atlanta recording trip has sometimes been described as if recording Carson was its primary motive. The story has often been told of how Polk C. Brockman, the sales manager of Jas. K. Polk, Inc., a furniture store on Atlanta's Decatur Street that was also the city's chief outlet for Okeh Records, saw a newsreel about a fiddlers' contest, was prompted to think of Carson, and conceived the idea of getting him on record. But Brockman was already aware of Okeh's interest in other Atlanta talent. Warner's Seven Aces, an orchestra on station WGM, which was owned by the *Journal*'s rival the *Atlanta Constitution*, had proved popular in many parts of Georgia, Alabama, and the Carolinas. Okeh had booked the band for recording in New York in mid-May (*Constitution*, April 22,

(OTM Collection)

1923), but something prevented this, and the company decided instead to take the unprecedented step of sending its equipment to Atlanta. This may have been Brockman's cue to propose adding Carson to the recording team's worksheet; or the thought may have come to him later, when the engineers were on the job, and there was time to spare in the recording schedule.

The Seven Aces spent much of Wednesday and Thursday, June 13–14, in the Nassau Street studio space. Between their two spells at the microphone, time was found for a quartet from the African American Morehouse College to record a couple of spirituals, and for Carson's log cabin song and its destined reverse side, "The Old Hen Cackled and the Rooster's Going to Crow."

★ ★ ★

The story of this first recorded country song's first release is a tangled one. We know that Okeh squeezed production time down to a month and shipped copies to Brockman in Atlanta in time to be sold at a fiddlers' convention on July 13. From here, the received narrative runs like this: Carson's record was merely expected to satisfy a local demand; Okeh's recording manager Ralph S. Peer, who was disappointed by its sound quality, had no intention of promoting it elsewhere. So this initial pressing of "The Little Old Log Cabin in the Lane"—500 copies, according to Brockman; 1,000, according to Peer—was treated as a one-off "special" and given no catalog number. It was only when Brockman reported a swift sell-out and placed another order that Peer realized he was stuck with this hillbilly oddity, shrugged, and assigned it a number. The record was advertised as Okeh 4890 in the *Constitution* on August 3.

This account of an unnumbered pressing came from Peer himself, in an interview held more than thirty years later. Some collectors are suspicious of

(OTM Collection)

the tale, since in almost a century no one has discovered one of these unnumbered copies. If there had been 500 of them, let alone 1,000, then the odds on at least one surviving would be reasonably good. Numerically rarer records have been recovered (➤64, 66): why not this?

So there may be grounds for skepticism about the no-number story. Very likely Peer did hesitate over listing the record in the Okeh catalog and making it nationally available. It was, after all, a step in the dark. There had been records of fiddling before, though not fiddling like this, and of "The Little Old Log Cabin in the Lane," but not done like this. The musical architecture of Southern songs recorded in the first two decades of the twentieth century was solid and familiar: military-style bands, perhaps a minstrel banjo, accented but always carefully articulated vocals. Beside such edifices, Carson's solo recording of "The Little Old Log Cabin" was *like* a little old log cabin: primitive in design, crooked in construction, full of chinks and irregularities. His free-meter singing, crosshatched with the strokes of his bow, was a sound of the South never heard on a record before. When it was given catalog status in October 1923, it was under the heading "Okeh Novelty Record."

★ ★ ★

Nine months later, *The Talking Machine World* reported approvingly on an Okeh dealer in Van Alstyne, Texas, whose son had created

> an unusually attractive window display . . . featur[ing] one record [which] centered the entire attention of passers-by on that particular number and materially increased the chances of making sales. . . . [The window] happened to feature "The Little Old Log Cabin in the Lane," played by Fiddlin' John Carson, a popular Southern fiddler. . . . [It] is actually a vizualization [*sic*] of the title. There is the little old log cabin, the tumble-down barn and the old well. There is something in this type of display to intrigue the imagination and to make the song desirable. (July 15, 1924)

Even without such ingenious marketing, Carson's record continued to sell, went through many repressings, and remained in catalog until the early '30s. It was covered for rival labels by Uncle Dave Macon, Fiddlin' Powers, Riley Puckett, Ernest Stoneman, Bradley Kincaid, and others. Carson himself revived it at his last session, for Bluebird in 1934, when it was retitled "I'm Old and Feeble."

The folklorist Archie Green discerned in the song "a joint pattern of rejection as well as sentimentalization of rural mores. We see the eroded land with its rotting cabin; at the same time we cover it in rose vines of memory." Such perceptions were largely confined to white musicians: the log cabin beckoned only feebly to African Americans. True, Trixie Smith's "Log Cabin Blues," probably written by the African American composer Tom Delaney, and recorded about three months before Carson's debut, had told the pathetic story of a woman who had traveled north for a better life, only to find it elusive, leaving her with "the blues for my log cabin home"; but this response was seldom echoed by other blues singers. Many of them, like their listeners, had quit a log cabin, even if only to exchange it for a sharecropper's or itinerant worker's shack. (Years later, the singer and pianist Mercy Dee Walton would vividly evoke such a refuge in his 1949 hit "Lonesome Cabin Blues.") But at least it was movement, and blues is about moving on, not staying put.

The old log cabin's secure place in the topography of '30s hillbilly songs is attested by titles like "In an Old Log Cabin" by W. Lee O'Daniel and His Hillbilly Boys, "Just a Little Pine Log Cabin" by J. B. Whitmire's Blue Sky Trio, "An Old Log Cabin for Sale" by Whitey and Hogan, "There's a Little Pine Log Cabin" by Lulu Belle and Scotty Wiseman, and "Little Poplar Log House on the Hill" by the Callahan Brothers and the Carter Family. A popular radio duo of the mid-'30s, Freddie Owen and Frankie More, called themselves the Log Cabin Boys, their bill matter conferring authenticity by asserting that they "have really lived in log cabins a part of their lives."

The potency of the image would be sustained through further generations by bluegrass, whose landscape is crowded with signifiers of antiquity. Travelers pass the old crossroads, the weeping willow, the lonesome pine, and the little white church, as they make their way back to the little old log cabin on the hill.

2

"SILLY BILL"/ "OLD TIME CINDA"

The Hill Billies
Okeh 40294

Recorded in New York, NY, January 15, 1925
Released in February/March 1925

Reissued on *The Hill Billies/Al Hopkins and His Buckle Busters—Vol. 1 (1925–1926)* (Document DOCD-8039) ["Old Time Cinda"]

Online: YT

"The Okeh library has been enriched recently," announced *The Talking Machine World* in its April 15, 1925 issue,

> by several records made by the Hill Billies, an organization that has attained considerable popularity in the South. A banjo, fiddle and guitar plus the exceptional ability of the pianist gives [*sic*] the true mountaineer music, and throughout the South the Hill Billies are welcomed wherever they appear.

The article was accompanied by a line drawing (derived from a photograph) showing the four members with their instruments: banjoist John Rector, pianist Al Hopkins, guitarist Joe Hopkins, and fiddler Elvis "Tony" Alderman, each man dapper in suit, vest, collar, and tie. The first coupling from the band's January session, "Silly Bill" coupled with "Old Time Cinda," had been presented to the trade in February and put on sale probably in March; a second record was scheduled for April.

The Hill Billies' debut release was not the first record to exploit the idea of the hillbilly. Uncle Dave Macon had recorded a "Hill Billie Blues" for Vocalion in July 1924; it was issued in January 1925, the month the Hill Billies recorded for Okeh. Nor was the group the first to make records of Southern stringband music. In March or April 1924, Okeh had recorded Fiddlin' John Carson's Virginia Reelers (two fiddles, banjo, and guitar), and in July, Henry Whitter's Virginia Breakdowners (fiddle, banjo, and guitar). The same day as the Hopkins crew recorded in New York, the Tweedy Brothers (fiddle and piano) from western West Virginia were cutting tunes for Gennett in Richmond, Indiana, not for the first time: they had made their debut sides in June 1924.

What "Silly Bill" and "Old Time Cinda" *can* claim to be are the first recordings by musicians who *called* themselves hillbillies.

"Silly Bill" is a comic song about marriage, put in the mouth of a young woman. A young man comes to court her, but she regards him with impatience: "I thought to my soul the blockhead would never go away." As for marrying him . . . "I hardly think I will!" "Old Time Cinda" is a lively dance tune with a few

(OTM Collecrion)

lines sung. Bascom Lamar Lunsford called it "a crackerjack party tune."

This coupling of rustic romance and rural rhythm amounted to a composite definition of old-time music exactly matching what the record business was discovering it wanted. Which is not to say that the Hill Billies were cynical, but simply that they knew their audience. "Silly Bill" and "Old Time Cinda" gave those listeners a whistle-stop visit to Hiramville; six minutes' immersion in the recapturing of a landscape and a past that seemed to many to be fading.

The Hill Billies offer a model of successful Southern music presentation. Unlike, say, Henry Whitter, also on Okeh, they had a vaudeville name, were beginning to make one on radio, and were known outside the South. This reputation their records now validated. Yet compared with other Okeh acts of the mid-1920s, such as Whitter, Carson, or Ernest V. Stoneman, their sales seem not to have been considerable. It was only when they moved to Brunswick's Vocalion label in 1926 that they became significant record-sellers.

Something that may strike us today as odd about the Hill Billies is the presence of a piano. Probably, on acoustic recordings, it came through louder than a guitar and so provided a stronger rhythmic base; once the group began making electric recordings, the piano sank a little lower in the mix. Or perhaps it was just that the piano player was the bandleader.

But the piano was already a common accompanying instrument for fiddlers, and it was so used on early or mid-1920s recordings by Eck Robertson, William B. Houchens, Allen Sisson, John Baltzell, Uncle Jimmy Thompson, and others, as well as many Irish-American fiddlers. Archie Green asserted that Al Hopkins "turned the piano into a country music instrument—a precedent infrequently followed by subsequent string-bands," but in fact it played a role in many of them, as we can hear on records by the Tweedys, the Shelor Family, Herschel Brown, Theron Hale, Smith's Garage Fiddle Band, the Blue Ridge Ramblers, the Walter Family, Sharp, Hinman and Sharp, and others.

★ ★ ★

A turning-point in the Hill Billies' professional career, Tony Alderman later recalled, was a huge fiddlers' convention held in Mountain City, Tennessee, on May 8, 1925. The band drew more fans than other participants did and discovered it was due to their broadcasts from WRC in Washington, DC, where the Hopkinses had moved from Ashe County, North Carolina, in their youth. So they began to travel further in the South, following the WRC audience.

A couple of months later, their touring schedule brought them to the high school auditorium in Kingsport, Tennessee, a two-night engagement arranged by the local branch of the Modern Woodmen of the World. (This was just one of many engagements the band filled in the second half of the 1920s and is submitted simply as a snapshot.) A preview in the *Kingsport Times* on July 12 mentioned the band's broadcasts and records and said they would offer "old-time melodies, string band music, piano, vocal music and also 'Vaudeville Acts.' They present an absolutely clean performance which no one can afford to miss." They would be joined by Uncle "Am" Stuart of Morristown, who was something of a local celebrity; indeed, when the paper reviewed the shows on July 19, they declared him "easily the favorite each night," while another local figure, fiddler Charlie Bowman, who had recently joined the Hill Billies, was judged "an efficient leader of the band." Evidently untroubled by this not wholly tactful promotion of the homeboys, the Hopkins brothers, having played a gig in town at a tobacco warehouse, gracefully donated 10 percent of the proceeds to the Community Chest.

★ ★ ★

In March 1926, the band, now augmented by two more Hopkins brothers, John on ukulele and Elmer on harmonica, was the subject of an article in *Radio Digest*, the most extensive coverage that national journal had yet given to hillbilly music. Under the headline "'HILL BILLIES' CAPTURE WRC—Boys from Blue Ridge Mountains Take Washington With Guitars, Fiddles and Banjos; Open New Line of American Airs," the *Digest* described these

> keen-eyed, ruddy-cheeked youths who have captured the rhythms of the hills, and who, with fiddles and other stringed instruments, present the classics of the country entertainments.
>
> There isn't a bar of jazz in the Hill Billy music. There isn't a note of weird modern harmony or anti-harmony, nor is there a single skip-stop syncopation. . . . It is the folk music of America, to

A Johnson City paper advertises a Hill Billies engagement in the city, 1927. "Wilson and Williams" are Frank Wilson and Frank "Dad" Williams. (Author's Collection)

> which the backwoods youth and the farmer boys "hoe it down" on rough-plank dance floors.

Note the separation line drawn between hillbilly music and jazz, a theme we shall meet again (➤4, 35). Unusually, the article recognized that musicians have lives outside the radio studio and off the touring circuit:

> When they aren't on the road, the Hill Billies melt into the ordinary industrial lives of their communities like the snows in spring. Albert and Joe Hopkins are salesmen; John and Elmer are first-class mechanics. Alderman is a motion picture camera man. Bowman paints barns and houses or what-have you.

But what enchanted the *Digest*'s reporter was their versatility.

> They can sing a negro spiritual to suit the longest-faced deacon, or they can turn it into a "can't-keep-still-your-foot" country dance. . . . If John gets tired of singing baritone in the quartet he just grabs Elmer's second tenor part, and Elmer can shift to baritone or get out of the race. Bowman and Alexander [*sic* Alderman] present a stunt in which each bows the other's fiddle and fingers his own.
>
> Some evil day one of the boys is going to pick up a loose saxophone, take ten or fifteen minutes to learn to play it, and the party will be ruined. Heaven postpone that day, for when the sax supplants the mouth harp and the trap drummer drowns the banjo (one string at a time if you please) America will lose an organization that represents all that is best in the music of its hills—the real simon-pure "leider" [*sic*] of our country.

The Hill Billies, ca. 1929. Back row: Charlie Bowman, "Tony" Alderman, Al Hopkins; front row: Frank Wilson, Walter "Sparkplug" Hughes, John Hopkins. (Bob Cox Collection)

Committed to his narrative of musical purity, the journalist nowhere suggests that the Hill Billies' mastery of variety and stunts might have owed anything to vaudeville. Yet before they ever made a record, the Hopkinses had had years of opportunities to visit Washington's theaters and absorb lessons in musical presentation and entertainment skills. Surely their exposure to vaudeville practices shaped, or at least lent color to, their performances on stage or in the studio?

★ ★ ★

During 1927–28, the group—now sometimes billed as Al Hopkins and His Buckle Busters, the name used on their Brunswick records—added Frank Wilson, "King of the Steel Guitar" (➤13), and "Spark Plug, The 16-Year-Old Boy Wonder In His Original Songs" (Walter Hughes from Avery County, North Carolina), while Bowman was replaced by fiddler Ed Belcher. The Hill Billies were becoming less a band than a franchise, the consistency of the product assured by the constant presence of at least one Hopkins. Around the time of their last recording session, in December 1928, they made a Vitaphone short, which survives, though unfortunately only as silent film.

By now, there was stiff competition in the rustic vaudeville stakes from the Blue Ridge Ramblers and several other aggregations (➤35), some of them no doubt inspired by, if not actually modeled on, the Hill Billies. Perhaps for that reason, the group made fewer appearances in the press in the early '30s. Al Hopkins's death in October 1932, following a car accident, ended the career of what Archie Green resonantly called "the band that named the music."

3

"WOMAN'S SUFFRAGE"

George Reneau
Vocalion 14999

Recorded in New York, NY, February 24, 1925
Released in (probably) April 1925

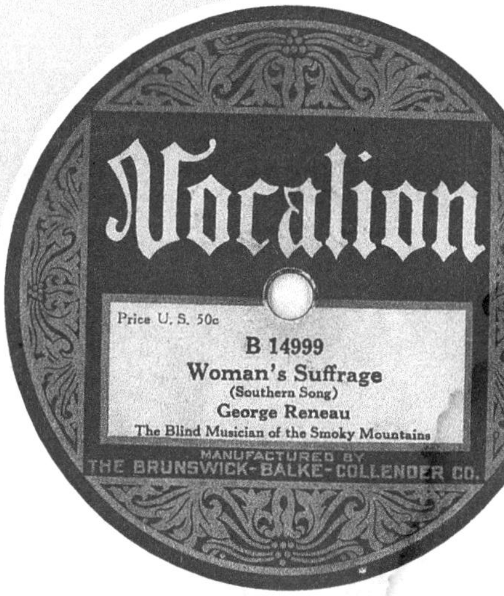

The idea of women having the right to vote exercised the comic imagination of journalists, songwriters, and other male contributors to public discourse for more than half a century, from Elizabeth Cady Stanton's suffrage proposal of 1848 to the anxious 1910s, when there were suffrage parades in New York and Washington, the first woman was elected to Congress, and the National Woman's Party picketed the White House, leading to hundreds of arrests. Then, in 1920, the Nineteenth Amendment to the Constitution decreed that a citizen's right to vote "shall not be denied or abridged by the United States or by any State on account of sex."

But the legions of mordant misogyny were too entrenched to give up the fight.

> Some fine morning, we'll all awake,
> To find the stand that the women will take.
> They'll change this world all upside down,
> We'll have a lady mayor in every town.
> They'll spend all the money we poor men make,
> To run the country they'll undertake . . .

—the opening lines of "Woman's Suffrage" as sung by George Reneau, the first appearance of this composition on a hillbilly recording. Three years later, it was recorded again, by Lester McFarland and Robert A. Gardner. Like Reneau, both were Knoxville residents and blind; as boys, Gardner and Reneau had been fellow students at the Tennessee School for the Blind in Nashville. The piece (whose author has not been traced) may have originated as a set of verses printed in a newspaper. It was in fact published (but probably not uniquely) in the *Sand Mountain Banner* in Albertville, Alabama, on April 17, 1924, ten months before Reneau recorded it.

★ ★ ★

George McKinney Reneau (1902–38) was one of the success stories of the young hillbilly recording business. He was a one-man band, and one-man bands, perhaps because they look complicated and interesting, have always been popular with the public. In the days of pre-electrical recording, they were popular too with the record companies; little enough of one instrument's sound made the perilous journey through a recording horn and onto a finished disc, so it helped if the performer was playing several. In practice, "several" generally meant two, most commonly guitar and harmonica, the latter held on a rack around the musician's neck. This was the modus operandi of not only Reneau but also the Virginian Henry Whitter; Walter C. Peterson, "the Kentucky Wonder Bean with His Double Barrel Shotgun," who broadcast from Chicago on the WLS National Barn Dance; Ernest Thompson of Winston-Salem, North Carolina, another blind man; and the African American performers Stovepipe No. 1 and Daddy Stovepipe. All of them began recording in the early light of old-time phonography, in 1923–24, and most of them sold carloads of records.

Reneau also benefited from a business connection. Born in Jefferson County, Tennessee, he had moved to Knoxville in his late teens or early twenties and there made an important contact. The story was told in a leisurely fashion in a 1924 Vocalion Records press release.

> George Reneau, Blind Musician of Tennessee, . . . [is] about 23, a tall clean-cut young mountaineer, who came from a tiny settlement of a half-a-dozen crude huts in the mountains of

George Reneau. (OTM Collection)

> Tennessee to earn what he could with his music on the street corners of Knoxville.
>
> Day after day the crowds collected around the young musician, who twanged on his combination guitar and mouth-harp, singing an occasional verse of the folk-melodies of his native mountains.
>
> Among those who daily elbowed their way thru Reneau's impromptu street audiences was G. A. Nennstiel, record manager of Sterchi Brothers, new Southern distributors of Vocalion records. It was he who recognized the unique talent of the young mountain boy and suggested . . . to have his playing reproduced on Vocalion records.

Sterchi Brothers had furniture stores in many Southern cities, and their music departments were major outlets for phonograph records. Gus Nennstiel joined the company in 1923; he had previously worked for a Brunswick Records store in Louisville, and he maintained the connection after his move to Knoxville. In April 1924, he sent Reneau to New York and the studios of Brunswick–Vocalion. (A couple of months later, he dispatched fellow Tennesseans Uncle Dave Macon and Uncle "Am" Stuart in the same direction, and in 1926, McFarland and Gardner.) The record company's executives liked Reneau's harmonica and guitar well enough, but they judged that his voice did not record well and his timing was uncertain. So at his first two sessions, in 1924, he just played his "combination," while the vocals, mostly opportune cover versions of recent old-time hits on other labels, were handled by the popular singer Gene Austin. By the following year, however, perhaps because he was more at ease in a studio, Reneau was allowed to sing most of his numbers himself. One of these was the lengthy text (six eight-line verses) of "Woman's Suffrage."

> The men the house will have to fix,
> While their wives talk politics.
> They're going to the legislative halls
> And say they're going to make the laws.
> The old maids will be in power then;
> They'll try to marry all the single men.
> The man that refuses to take a wife
> Will have to go the pen for life . . .
>
> Now ever since the world began,
> The women have tried to rule the men.
> She made man commit the first offense,
> She's been after him ever since.
> God made the world and he rested then;
> Then he made man and he rested again;
> Then he made a woman for man's expense,
> And God nor man has never rested since.

That concluding thought was echoed a few years later by a great soapbox orator of old-time music, Blind Alfred Reed: "We can plainly understand, Woman was made after man—And she's been after man ever since."

★ ★ ★

Street musicians make good copy, and we may spot Reneau in a piece by Rosa Naomi Scott for the *New York Times Magazine* on December 8, 1929, with the headline "IN OLD KNOXVILLE MARKET: Mountain People of Strange Old-Fashioned Ways Come There to Gossip and to Trade."

> There are minstrels on quaint old Market Square. All day a blind mountaineer with flaxen

(OTM Collection)

> hair and a guitar walks slowly down the market sidewalk, keeping close to the walls of the stores. He sings wistful hymns, or occasionally an old English ballad that has gained a novel twist by centuries in the Appalachians. He is not incongruous in the welter of flowers and vegetables and bargaining.

Reneau was still singing on the street in 1929, but, although he recorded over fifty sides for Vocalion, the label had abruptly dropped him in 1925. (A couple of years later, he had cut some duets with Lester McFarland for budget labels, but they were poorly recorded and pseudonymous.) Perhaps he had come to realize that the music he had helped kick-start was now speeding past him, too fast to catch up with. As the Knoxville historian Jack Neely wrote, "The Jazz Age didn't bode well for what Reneau did best. It was the era of the crooner, like Gene Austin. [Some irony there. TR] By the time he turned 27, George Reneau's day as a recording artist had come and gone."

When Vocalion sent recording crews to Knoxville in 1929 and 1930, Reneau was not on their to-do list. But perhaps, from his familiar spot on Market Square, the blind man listened to passers-by talk about the crowd of musicians outside the St. James Hotel, where the sessions were being held, and wondered what kind of music was being transacted within. Some of it he would have recognized, for he had recorded those songs himself, like "Little Rosewood Casket" and "The Bald Headed End of the Broom" (➤56), a song of marital woe that shares some of the snickering misogyny of "Woman's Suffrage." Could Reneau, even at this date, in a world accustoming itself to emancipated women, raise a laugh with jests about wives having the right to search their husbands' pockets?

All too likely he could. Several years later, hillbilly singer Bill Cox—actually five years older than Reneau, but a performer in a more modern mold, who would have a far longer career—was still able to woo his radio audience on WCHS in Charleston, West Virginia, and the buyers of his many records, with humorous diatribes like "Alimony Woman" and "Rollin' Pin Woman." "Woman's Suffrage" was just his kind of song, and he duly acquired it, probably from Reneau's record or McFarland and Gardner's. In 1933, he took it to ARC, and it was circulated all over again, on half a dozen dime-store labels, as "When the Women Get in Power."

> The men will have to take back seats,
> While the women police the streets.
> Then you dare not smoke or chew,
> For you'll catch it if you do.
> They'll be running the courts, you see,
> Judge and jurors they will be.
> What the shes say will have to go,
> And we poor hes won't stand no show.

4

"THE DEATH OF FLOYD COLLINS"/"LITTLE MARY PHAGAN"

Al Craver [Vernon Dalhart]
Columbia 15031-D

Recorded in New York, NY, May 27, 1925
Released in July/August 1925
Sold 306,044

Online: Spotify [both] • YT ["Little Mary Phagan"]

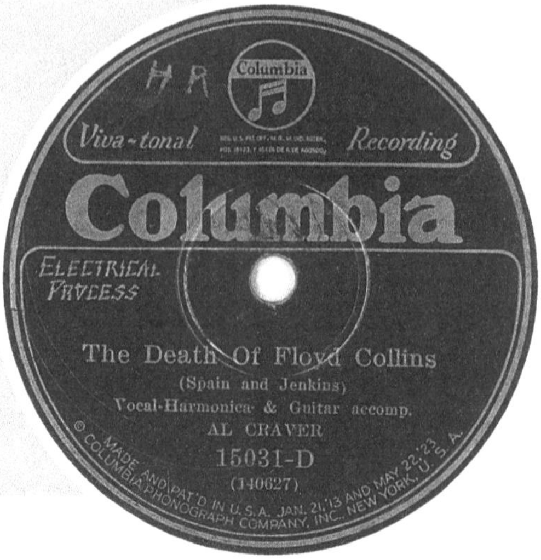

On Friday, January 30, 1925, a thirty-six-year-old explorer named Floyd Collins, investigating subterranean systems in the Mammoth Cave area of south-central Kentucky, was trapped near Sand Cave when a boulder fell on his left foot, pinning him in a narrow passage. His cries for help were eventually heard and a group of friends and other locals began to consider ways of freeing him. Outsiders started to arrive—potentially useful ones like coal miners and geologists, merely troublesome ones like gawping tourists—and the area around the cave mouth turned into a campsite. Within a week, there were hundreds there; by Sunday, February 8, thousands.

The reason was publicity. Collins and his predicament were splattered across the national consciousness by newspapers, radio, even motion pictures. The affair was one of the century's greatest explosions of ballyhoo.

It was sparked by William B. "Skeets" Miller, a young reporter for the Louisville *Courier-Journal*, who was slim enough to negotiate the passage down to Collins and get close enough to speak to him. He arrived on the scene on Monday morning, February 2, straightaway descended to see Collins's plight for himself, and, shaken, filed his first story. The *Courier-Journal*'s coverage caught the attention of the Associated Press, and that day stories about Collins appeared on front pages all over the country. On Tuesday evening, Miller went underground again, taking coffee, milk, and whiskey, to conduct what has been called "the most unusual interview in the history of American journalism." "I've faced death afore," Collins reportedly told the newspaperman. "It don't frighten me none. But it's so long—so long." A rescue crew, led by Miller, descended that night with jacks and crowbars but was frustrated by the difficult conditions.

A week in, experts were doubting whether Collins was still alive. Further rockfalls had blocked parts of the passage, and it could not be determined whether he was answering his rescuers when they called out to him. Soon afterward, rumors began to spread that

"Skeets" Miller. (Author's Collection)

he was not there at all, but had been extricated earlier, and that the whole thing was a publicity stunt for the sake of local interests. The nearest town, Cave City (population around 700), was experiencing a boom of Gold Rush proportions.

Nevertheless, the rescue operation continued, now overseen by the National Guard. The original passage having become unusable, a shaft was drilled and dug out alongside it, and on Monday, February 16, rescuers finally broke through to where Collins lay. He had been dead for perhaps three or four days.

★ ★ ★

The story more or less died with him, so far as the press were concerned, but it lived on in other media. Floyd's younger brother Homer went on the vaudeville circuit to describe his part in the rescue attempt. Then, sometime in March or April, a notion came to Polk Brockman, the Atlanta entrepreneur who had instigated the recording career of Fiddlin' John Carson (➤1). His experience in the phonograph business had no doubt alerted him to the public's interest in songs about tragedies, and he decided that the Floyd Collins affair deserved such a song. He duly commissioned Rev. Andrew Jenkins, a local versifier and radio singer whom the *Atlanta Journal* had dubbed "the newsboy-evangelist-poet," to write one, for $25, and Mrs. Irene Spain Futrelle, Jenkins's stepdaughter, to arrange music for it. "After listening to the radio so much," Ms. Futrelle remembered, "we knew the entire tragic horror of it, so, after getting the telegram [from Brockman], Daddy took his guitar out to the front steps and went to singing. . . . Mr Brockman received it in a few hours." Brockman copyrighted the composition on April 20, and Carson's record of it, made in Atlanta a few days earlier, was the first on the market, officially released in June.

The same brainwave had rolled into the mind of George E. Hunt, a salesman for the Vocalstyle piano roll company in Cincinnati. Moving faster than Brockman, on March 13 he filed copyright on a "mountain ballad" called "Sand Cave." On April 30, a Cincinnatian named George Ake, accompanied by a stringband identified as the "Jolly Four Orch.," recorded the song for Gennett, and it was in stores by mid-July.

Vernon Dalhart's Columbia recording of Jenkins's song, with accompaniment by the singer's harmonica and Carson Robison's guitar, was made in late May, scheduled for release in August, and being advertised by music stores in mid-July. The company soon knew they had a hit on their hands: advance orders during June–July totaled nearly 70,000. By mid-August,

THE EVENING TRIBUNE

VOLUME XXVIII. ALBERT LEA, MINNESOTA, MONDAY, FEBRUARY 16, 1925 NUMBER 39

FLOYD COLLINS FOUND DEAD

JUDGE M'GEE IS FOUND DEAD IN OFFICE VAULT

Daughter Discovers Body With Pistol at Side—Note Explains Fear of Ill Health—Jurist Noted for Fearlessness on Bench.

Cave Explorer Who Was Trapped Jan. 30

68TH CONGRESS PLANS FOR FINAL ACTION ON BILLS

Senate to Resort to Night Sessions In Order to Clear Up Business—Fate of Postal and Farm Relief Measures Watched by Law Makers.

LIQUOR, 'DOPE' CASES CAUSE OF JUDGE'S DEATH

At Mouth of Sand Cave Shaft

This picture was taken at the mouth of the shaft dug to reach Floyd Collins at Sand Cave, Kentucky, just as workers were changing shifts. The rope shown in the center of the photo was used to haul stone and shale to the surface.

PHYSICIANS ARE TAKEN DOWN TO EXAMINE BODY

Discovery of Trapped Cave Explorer Comes Hours Earlier Than Expected When Roof of Cavern Collapses—Body to Be Brought Out as Soon as Possible.

(By Associated Press.) Cave City, Feb. 16 at 3:15 p. m.—Floyd Collins was reached and found dead at 2:45 o'clock this afternoon is an official announcement made after rescuers had penetrated into what they believed was the original Sand cave where Collins was caught.

No medical examination was made, it being impossible for physicians to reach the victim.

Mr. Carmichael and M. E. S. Posey, executive secretary of the state highway department and personal representatives of Gov-

(Author's Collection)

a record store in Gulfport, Mississippi, had already sold over 700 copies. By January 1926, sales had topped 200,000.

The response was promptly noted by other companies. In early September 1925, Edison called the singer in to record it for them, and the following month the company reported to *The Talking Machine World* (*TMW*)

> a strong demand . . . for the series of records being made by Vernon Dalhart and company, representative of the type of songs apparently favored by the Southern mountaineers, and which appeal to record purchasers in other localities. Such songs as "Little Rosewood Casket," "The John T Scopes Trial" (The Old Religion's Better After All) and "The Death of Floyd Collins" may not make a strong appeal to jazz hounds on Broadway, but the sales indicate that they are distinctly popular in the so-called "sticks."

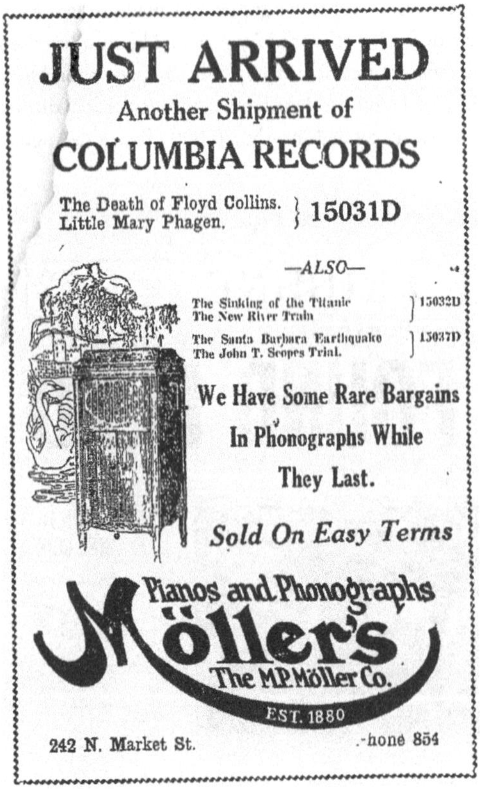

Ad in *Frederick* [Maryland] *News*, October 14, 1925. (Author's Collection)

In December, a *TMW* writer went further:

> The advent or revival or whatever you choose to call it of what are described as the "hillbilly" songs signifies more than the mere vogue of such publications. The "Death of Floyd Collins," "Wreck of the Shenandoah," "At My Mother's Grave," and other such songs which have had fairly widespread popularity may mark the initial move in the passing of jazz. . . . It must be remembered that these weird funereal musical offerings have been preceded by several months by other offerings, the outstanding feature of which was that they were in most simplified song form. In fact, some of the outstanding record sellers to-day and for the past few months have been solo numbers with minor accompaniment. . . . Probably we have had an over-production of songs of the fox-trot order and in self-defense the public has revolted and turned to . . . the sob songs of several generations ago, brought up to date and made into a pathetic song on some current topical event or catastrophe.

A less amiable response appeared in *Variety*, where, under the heading "'HILL-BILLY' MUSIC," Abel Green identified the audience for such effusions.

> The "hillbilly" is a North Carolina or Tennessee and adjacent mountaineer type of illiterate white whose creed and allegiance are to the Bible, the chautauqua, and the phonograph. . . . Illiterate and ignorant, with the intelligence of morons, the sing-song, nasal-twanging vocalizing of a Vernon Dalhart or Carson Robison on the disks, reciting the banal lyrics of a "Prisoner's Song" or "The Death of Floyd Collins" (biggest hillbilly song-hit to date), intrigues their interest. (December 29, 1926)

By then, Dalhart had cut "The Death of Floyd Collins" for Victor, Plaza, Pathé, and Gennett. In February 1926, he waxed it for Okeh, and over the next couple of months several labels commissioned a "Floyd Collins Waltz," mostly an instrumental for fiddle, harmonica, and guitar, with a single establishing verse.

In February 1927, the syndicated columnist Gilbert Swan commented:

> These dolorous ballads, I am told, are ground out by the yard and mile in the phonograph record factories. . . . [S]ale reports indicate that through the farm belt and in the backwoods of the south and northwest there is a terrific sale of [these] numbers. . . . One concern was said actually to have figured on selling two and three discs of the same record to certain of the backwoods boys and girls who play them so much they wear the records out. . . . [T]he Floyd Collins disaster song still carries a big sale in certain parts of the south, they tell me. The story went round the phonograph belt that in one southern town a dealer had to stop playing the record because the crowds about the store were so great. (*Athens* [Ohio] *Messenger*, February 1, 1927)

A feature writer for the *Charleston Daily Mail* sourly observed:

> A man can't get killed these days or do a great deed without being dressed up as a clown by the song writer and made to dance upon the piano[,] stagger from the phonograph, or rival the static of the radio. Floyd Collins perished in a cave in Kentucky. "The Death of Floyd Collins" leaped feverishly from the brain of some composer who needed money and needed it bad. It gave every Charlestonian a chance to exercise his chords and if Floyd Collins had been only dead before that, he was well buried afterward. (July 24, 1927)

And *still* the song would not die. In May 1928, Gennett brought Dalhart back into the studio to remake electrically the acoustic recording he had done for them two and half years earlier, presumably because there was still a market for it. Toward the end of that year, two further hillbilly acts, singing teachers Claude and Clarence Ganus from Alabama and a group called the Ozark Warblers, recorded a new addition to the folio, "Memories of Floyd Collins."

★ ★ ★

Interviewed by the New York columnist James Haswell for an article syndicated in the summer of 1926, Dalhart had candidly described his modus operandi. The song, he said

> has to be slow and very sad, or quick and devilish. . . . The end must carry a moral, even tho the moral has nothing to do with the story. The tune is simple. The notes repeat over and over again, and there can be as many verses as needed. The accompaniment is slight. . . . The important thing is to tell the story. (*Lima* [Ohio] *News*, June 25, 1926)

He had added, *à propos* "The Death of Floyd Collins": "A preacher in Atlanta wrote [it]. I sang it for Kentuckians, thinking it would go only in the rural districts of that state. And it sold nearly a million records."

That figure may well be accurate. The Columbia record alone achieved a final sales total of over 300,000, making it by some distance the best-selling record in the company's "Old Familiar Tunes" series, and probably one of the bigger phonograph hits of the period in any idiom. Victor's recording, which was as efficiently distributed as Columbia's, surely made it into six figures. And there were something like twenty other Dalhart recordings in circulation.

Rev. Jenkins's original text was long, but Dalhart's Columbia recording cut it down to five verses: the set-up; a predictive dream Collins was supposed to have recounted to his mother not long beforehand ("I dreamed I was a prisoner, my life I could not save"); two stanzas about the rescue attempts; and the closing "take warning" verse that, as Dalhart had told Haswell, was a staple of this kind of song: "Get right with your Maker before it is too late." The Victor version offered a somewhat different text, with two introductory stanzas and only one about the rescue; it also added a mournful fiddle.

What the song, as recorded, signally fails to do is *explain* the event. Why was Collins underground in the first place? To discover an attraction to rival Mammoth Cave and make its finder's fortune—but this hard-headed motive could have no place in Jenkins's soft-hearted tale of an unfortunate victim. Without background, the event is reduced to what insurers call an act of God: Nature admonishing an over-adventurous man by dropping a big rock on him. Hard to see how getting right with one's Maker could have prevented *that*.

★ ★ ★

No doubt many, perhaps most, of the people who purchased this record did so because they had been intrigued or horrified by the fate of Floyd Collins, but when they turned the disc over, they could enjoy a frisson of a different kind.

The case of Mary Phagan is one of the most notorious in Southern criminological history. On April 26, 1913—Confederate Memorial Day, a public holiday—this thirteen-year-old girl from Marietta, Georgia, went to her place of work, the National

Pencil Factory on Atlanta's South Forsyth Street, to collect $1.20 in back pay. She never returned home. The following day, her dead body was found in the factory's basement, bruised, strangled, and possibly raped. The factory's superintendent, twenty-nine-year-old Leo Frank, who had grown up in New York and moved to Atlanta in 1908, becoming a well-regarded member of the city's Jewish community, was tried for her murder in an atmosphere reeking with sexual titillation and antisemitism. He was found guilty and sentenced to death, though this was commuted in June 1915 to life imprisonment. Two months later, he was abducted from the state prison at Milledgeville by an organized lynch mob, driven to a quiet spot a couple of miles outside Marietta, and hanged.

Three quarters of a century later, inquiring too closely about Frank's captors was still discouraged: the old-time music historian Gene Wiggins, investigating the matter for his biography of Fiddlin' John Carson, told me he had been warned to let it drop. The lynchers' names have since been published, for example by David Oney in his outstanding study of the case, *And the Dead Shall Rise* (2003). They included numerous solid citizens of Cobb County who later enjoyed successful careers in Georgia's political and legal circles.

Carson, also a Cobb Countian, constituted himself the balladeer of the anti-Frank party. During

Fiddlin' John Carson and Rosa Lee Carson

From *The Talking Machine World*, August 15, 1925. (OTM Collection)

the trial, Wiggins suggests, "he probably was in the large crowd outside the courthouse, perhaps already singing an uncompleted version of the ballad." At some point, he had a version printed on song sheets, which he sold. Then, on June 13, 1915, the *Atlanta Constitution* reported on a public meeting outside the state capitol protesting the commutation of Frank's sentence: "The meeting was brought to a clamorous end when the crowd cheered for an encore from Fiddlin' John Carson, the native musician, who fiddled and sang an original song dedicated to Mary Phagan."

On August 18, in its lengthy coverage of the lynching, the paper took a longer look at the musician. Frank's body having been cut down and taken away.

> The hundreds of morbidly curious then being deprived of the hideous spectacle, withdrew and congregated around "Fiddlin' John" Carson, who has turned up with his fiddle at every Frank development within a radius of thirty miles of Marietta since the day Mary Phagan's body was discovered, as he stood in front of the courthouse and fiddled a symphonic jubilee. . . .
>
> "Fiddlin' John" is a lanky mountaineer, who lacks a number of teeth, which doesn't seem to impair his vocal aspirations.
>
> In his repertoire of folk songs, he has one that is adapted to a quaint, rural hymn, and has for its words a narrative of the murder of Mary Phagan "by Leo M. Frank, the president of the pencil factory."
>
> "Fiddlin' John" would fiddle and sing his song in a typical nasal twang, and he could be heard to the center of the square, around which were grouped hundreds of automobiles, buggies and mountain transports. . . . The crowd would cheer and applaud him lustily and, inspired by this show of appreciation, he would repeat his song, over and over again. Presently, when his hearers began to tire of the same tune, he deserted it, and replaced it with such well-known selections as "Little Old Log Cabin by the Lane." . . . [T]he troubadour of the mountains, [he] basked in "reflected glory," and it was not until the court-house crowds began to tire of his songs and fiddle that he departed, reluctantly.

★ ★ ★

A decade after Carson performed his song on the steps of the state capitol, his daughter Rosa Lee made a recording about Mary Phagan, in the middle of John's June 1925 Okeh session in New York. She was just short of thirteen years and eleven months—almost exactly the same age as Mary Phagan had been when she died. (The *Constitution* missed a story there.) Her impassive sixteen-stanza tale of the murder and Leo Frank's conviction (but not his lynching) is textually very similar to the version of "Little Mary Phagan" that Polk Brockman (again) had copyrighted, on May 22, on behalf of John and Rosa Lee as writers and Irene Spain Futrelle as arranger. Since Rosa Lee was less than two years old at the time of Mary's death, we must wonder how far the 1925 text she is supposed to have co-written resembled the song her father had sung a decade earlier. John himself never recorded the piece. Six months after his daughter's recording, he waxed "The Grave of Little Mary Phagan," but this was a memorial piece, based on an older song, "Over the Mountain," rather than a documentary one.

Within five days of copyrighting "Little Mary Phagan," and about a month before Rosa Lee Carson recorded it, the text fell into the hands of Vernon Dalhart, in time to provide what was evidently considered an appropriate B-side for "The Death of Floyd Collins." His Columbia recording of "Little Mary Phagan" was the first into the stores, ten years after Frank's lynching. His text, similar to Rosa Lee's, though abbreviated from sixteen stanzas to ten, is marked with references to the scene of the crime (the pencil factory, the metal room where Mary worked, night watchman Newt Lee) and to the trial; yet, unlike Rosa Lee, Dalhart does not name either Frank—the murderer is merely a "villain" or "brute"—or the disgruntled

(Author's Collection)

On a 1950 ten-inch LP, *A Treasury of Immortal Performances*, RCA Victor corralled Vernon Dalhart and Gene Austin, with Jimmie Rodgers, as "Folk Singers." (Author's Collection)

employee Jim Conley, who fatally implicated him, and is now considered by many historians Mary Phagan's likeliest murderer. And there is still not a word about the lynching. But many of those who bought this record would have remembered the case and would long ago have reached their own conclusions about the rights and wrongs of it. What were their thoughts as they listened to Dalhart's final verse?

> Now come all you good people, wherever you
> may be—
> Supposing little Mary belonged to you or me?

★ ★ ★

Most collectors do not care for Vernon Dalhart. When out hunting, if they come across his records, they may leave them where they found them. And come across them they do, because very often Dalhart outsold everyone in the old-time field—frequently by a factor of ten or more.

Today, lovers of old-time music value more highly singers like G. B. Grayson or Charlie Poole, but, on the evidence of sales, many record-buyers of the 1920s did not. For some enthusiasts, this fact is unsettling. If the taste of the original purchasers was so debased that they preferred Dalhart to, say, Dock Boggs, how did some of the records we now cherish get made at all?

Such a reaction probably stems from ideas about authenticity—Grayson, Poole, and Boggs "the real thing," Dalhart a professional recordist for hire, a mere mediator—that had little or no currency at the time the records were made. These ideas were developed chiefly by collectors and other interested parties responding to recorded vernacular music, many years later and in a very different cultural climate. This new congregation created an aesthetic orthodoxy that sanctified some records and excommunicated others, often for reasons that a record-buyer in 1925 would have found incomprehensible.

But unless we lift our eyes from this record-collector's rulebook, we shall fail to grasp an important fact about record-buying in the 1920s: It was primarily driven by the content, not by the providers—by songs and tunes rather than by the people who recorded them. And especially by songs that were also stories: wrecks at sea or on the iron road, homes left or returned to, lessons learned or forgotten, murders impulsive or repulsive, comic mishaps, poignant fates. Listeners craved storylines, and, as "The Death of Floyd Collins" and "Little Mary Phagan" demonstrate, it didn't much matter if they were tenuous or straggly or none too skillfully told. Even a crudely fashioned key can unlock memory and imagination, turning dead news into living stories.

5

"WHEN THE WORK'S ALL DONE THIS FALL"

Carl T. Sprague
Victor 19747

Recorded in Camden, NJ, August 5, 1925
Released in September 1925
Sold 152,661

Reissued on *Cattle Call: Early Cowboy Music and Its Roots* (Rounder CD1101), *Western Cowboy Ballads & Songs 1925–1939* (Frémeaux FA034)

Online: Spotify, YT

This is a song about cowboys—but with no six-guns, no OK Corrals, no Deadwood stage. It is drawn from the actual working life of a Western cowhand.

The first line transports us to a cattle camp and "a group of jolly cowboys, discussing plans at ease." One reminisces about his home in Dixie. He hasn't seen it for many years, but when the present job is over, he'll go back and visit with his mother. That night, while he is guarding the herd, they stampede. He tries to turn them, his horse falls, and he is crushed beneath the panicking hooves. Gazing at the friends gathered around as he slips away, he faces the truth: "I'll not see my mother when the work's all done this fall."

This was not the first recording of a cowboy song. Charles Nabell, a blind Georgia-born street singer who had moved to Joplin, Missouri, had recorded "The Great Round Up" for Okeh in November 1924 and "Utah Carl" a few months later. It was not even the first recording of *this* cowboy song. Fiddlin' John Carson had sung it, also for Okeh, a year earlier, under the title "Dixie Cowboy." But Carl Tyler Sprague's "When the Work's All Done This Fall" was unquestionably the first cowboy hit. It's sometimes claimed that it sold over 900,000 copies, and that pebble of misinformation has lodged in historians' horseshoes ever since. According to Victor's written records, the original release actually sold about a sixth of that number, but that was itself a remarkable total for a first record by a new artist, in what, so far as Victor was concerned, was a virtually new idiom.

The folklorist John A. Lomax, who printed the song in his *Cowboy Songs and Other Frontier Ballads* (1910), noted: "D. J. O'Malley of the S. A. ranch, near Miles City, Montana, claims to be the author of this song. On October 6, 1893, the *Stock Growers*['] *Journal* of Miles City published the words with the caption, 'After the Round-up,' giving the author as D. J. White." There's a whiff of mistrust about the way Lomax phrases this, but it was unwarranted. O'Malley's father died when he was very young; D. J.'s stepfather was Charles White and, in his twenties, he took that surname; "After the Round-Up" was published when he was twenty-six. He had written similar verses for the *Stock Growers' Journal* before and would do so again. The cowboy singer and historian John I. White, who corresponded with O'Malley for years, had no doubts about his authorship, though he added that he had failed to convince another celebrated Texas folklorist, J. Frank Dobie. "To him, a cowboy song as genuine as 'When the Work's All Done This Fall' could have originated in only one place—Texas."

"Genuine" is a slippery word to use when discussing the cowboy songs recorded in the 1920s and '30s. Only a few originated in the great trail days of the 1870s. According to the cowboy recordist Jules Verne Allen, in the preface of his book *Cowboy Lore*, the trail finally closed in 1895, two years after the first appearance in print of "When the Work's All Done This Fall." Within a generation, the old occupational cowboy songs became historical, transformed from newsreels of actuality into costume dramas. Much of the cowboy repertoire we know from records was written in a spirit less of observation than of obsequy. The same spirit permeates the depictions of cowboy life by the artist Frederic Remington. Men like Allen (b. 1883) and Sprague (b. 1895) learned their cowboy songs as cowboys themselves were beginning to hang up their saddles, and by the time they came to perform them professionally, they were engaged in a process of preservation, cowboy curators.

★ ★ ★

As originally conceived, "After the Round-Up" was to be sung to the waltz melody of Charles K. Harris's huge success of the 1890s, "After the Ball," and indeed its chorus began, "After the round-ups are over . . ." This is how John Carson rendered the song, but Sprague's version was set to a different tune and dropped the chorus. He also omitted one verse and added another that O'Malley didn't write (the final stanza about the cowboy's burial and epitaph), but otherwise he was essentially faithful to the O'Malley–Lomax text. He accompanied himself on guitar in what would become almost a default style for singers of cowboy songs, the alternating bass notes mimicking the step and sway of the singer's notional horse.

Born near Houston, Carl Sprague had grown up with cowboy songs. "My uncles and I used to sit around the fire at night and sing the very same songs that cowboys sang many years before. I used to go on cattle drives with them, and we'd make camp right there on the open prairie where there wasn't anything but cattle, horses, and stars."

In 1915, he enrolled at Texas A&M. After a break for war service, he graduated in 1922 and joined the college's athletics department, where he would stay for fifteen years. In the summer of 1925, he made a trip to New York to pitch himself to Victor Records as a cowboy-song recordist, was taken on, and waxed six issuable numbers. Back in Texas, with "When the Work's All Done This Fall" racking up sales across the nation, he was soon juggling his college post and a radio career. In December 1925, he was singing on KPRC in Houston, and the following February he headlined a three-day radio special on WFAA in Dallas, accompanied by violinists Harold McKinzie and Charles Dockum, students at Texas A&M (*Galveston Daily News*, February 20, 1926). In June, the three men, accompanied by Sprague's new wife Lura Bess Mayo, headed off to New York for another Victor recording date, playing concerts en route (*Corsicana Daily Sun*, June 9, 1926). "O Bury Me Not on the Lone Prairie (The Dying Cowboy)" coupled with "The Cowboy's Dream," both made at this session, gave Victor another substantial seller.

Meanwhile, "When the Work's All Done This Fall" was stirring up executives throughout the record business. Within a month of its release, it had received its first cover version, done for Vocalion by George Reneau. Over the next decade, there would be some two dozen recordings competing with Sprague's, on every label in the business, by Ernest V. Stoneman, Vernon Dalhart, W. C. Childers, Marc Williams, the Cartwright Brothers, Pie Plant Pete, Bradley Kincaid, Frank Luther, and others. In 1929, Victor even had it recorded by another singer on their cowboy roster, Jules Verne Allen.

Carl T. Sprague, with an early wood-bodied National Triolian. (Richard Weize Collection)

For Sprague, cowboy songs were never a career option—after his time at Texas A&M, he worked for years selling insurance—but he did carry on singing into his seventies (he died in 1979), and he was one of the small company of artists who, having first recorded in the early 1920s, lived long enough to do so again in the LP era. In March 1972, he stood at a recording microphone to recall the songs he had sung almost half a century before. Perhaps recognizing how he would best be remembered, he placed first on his list "When the Work's All Done This Fall."

6

"SENECA SQUARE DANCE"/ "ECHOES OF THE OZARKS"

Fiddlin' Sam Long of the Ozarks
Gennett 3284

Recorded in Richmond, IN, February 1926
Released in May 1926

Reissued on *Echoes of the Ozarks Volume One* (County CD-3506) [both] • *The Return of the Stuff That Dreams Are Made of* (Yazoo 2203) ["Seneca Square Dance"]

Online: Spotify ["Seneca Square Dance"] • YT [both]

When recording gave a voice to the vernacular music of white rural and small-town America, the first sounds to emerge from the phonograph horn were of old-time fiddling. Country music, as a recorded medium, was born out of fiddling, and its cradle was the fiddlers' contests. These regional tourneys, a venerable tradition before the phonograph was invented, were the stages where all the early recorded fiddlers made their names: Eck Robertson and Henry Gilliland in Texas and Oklahoma, John Carson and Gid Tanner in Georgia, Dix Hollis and Y. Z. Hamilton in Alabama, Uncle Jimmy Thompson and Uncle "Am" Stuart in Tennessee, Fiddlin' Cowan Powers and Charlie La Prade in Virginia....

These are the old-time fiddlers whose names may spring most readily to mind because they fit the standard South-centric narrative of country music history, but fiddlers' contests were an all-American phenomenon, making local—and sometimes, briefly, national—heroes out of Mellie Dunham from Maine, Uncle Joe Shippee from Connecticut, Jasper Bisbee from Michigan, and John Baltzell from Ohio. And then, as now, the contests enjoyed particular popularity in the Midwest. In March 1926, *The Talking Machine World* reported on a fiddlers' contest held in January in Joplin, Missouri, that was "probably the largest of this kind ever held." This was of interest to *TMW* because of its outcome:

> The Starr Piano Co., Richmond, Ind., maker of Gennett records, is now recording a series of "Old Time Mountain Tunes," played by Sam Long, "Fiddlin' Sam" of Oklahoma, champion fiddler of the Ozarks. "Fiddlin' Sam" has just won first prize in the Old Time Fiddlers' Contest held in Joplin's New Memorial Hall, Joplin, Mo. . . . There were ninety-one other fiddlers competing for a great variety of prizes, among which was a free trip to the Starr recording laboratory for the fiddler and accompanist. . . . The Memorial Hall, seating four thousand, was filled to capacity on both nights. . . . The champion fiddler has been booked for vaudeville and he is being backed by the Ozark Playground Association, which is taking a great interest in the sale of his records. . . . There seems to be a great demand for old time tunes, played in the characteristic old time mountain style.

At the time of his victory, Samuel W. Long was a fifty-year-old zinc miner, living just over the state line in Commerce, Oklahoma. "He has played for barn dances and the like all over the district," wrote the *Joplin Globe*. He now began to appear in vaudeville theaters such as Joplin's Electric, where he and the second-prize winner, "Gentleman" George Morris, were featured on the bill alongside "The Original Indian Jazz Revue, with Chief Howling Wolf."

The Joplin papers also carried stories about, and advertising for, Long's records. Sometime in the first half of February, the champion fiddler and his guitar accompanist Floyd Kastner, a twenty-year-old fellow miner and resident of Commerce, had journeyed more than 600 miles to Richmond, Indiana, where they made half a dozen recordings, of which four were issued, each appearing on several labels owned by or affiliated with Gennett. The first Gennett coupling, "Sandy Land" (i.e., "Sally Ann") and "Listen to the

Fiddlin' Sam Long and Floyd Kastner, 1926. (Author's Collection)

Mockingbird," released in April 1926, is the earliest known record of fiddling from the western Midwest. (The pedantic definition is necessary because earlier records of old-time fiddling were made, in 1922–24, by musicians from, or in, the eastern Midwest, such as the Ohioan Baltzell, or the Illinois-born, Ohio-based William B. Houchens. Kansas, where Long and Kastner were born, and Missouri are in what is defined as the West North Central Division of the Midwest.)

The first tunes Long and Kastner recorded, which Gennett held over for their second release, were versions of two pieces familiar to fiddlers then as now, "Shoot the Turkey Buzzard" and "Yellow Rose of Texas," but these were not the titles printed on the record labels. "Buzzard" became "Seneca Square Dance," after a town on the Missouri–Oklahoma state line, about twenty miles south of Joplin, while "Yellow Rose" was called "Echoes of the Ozarks." These may have been Long's names for the tunes, but it's also possible that this was an early instance of the strategy, quickly developed by the record business, of disguising familiar tunes, which the potential buyer might already own, by giving them new, often regional, titles. Both tunes are rendered with great vigor, but the reason I focus on them is that, unlike contemporary recordings by Houchens and Baltzell, they have lost all their Old World accent. This is indisputably *American* fiddling.

Back in Joplin, April 17, 1926, was declared "Fiddlin' Sam Long Record Day" at McMillan's Music Store: "Sam Long records are the most popular records in this community," said the *Globe*. The *Joplin News Herald* reported that Long and Kastner "signed a contract to make many more," and that "the heads of the phonograph company pronounced their efforts a unique musical attraction, and made arrangements for another series of records in three months." But, so far as we know, neither man ever returned to the Gennett studios.

The Joplin press continued to follow Long, with the *Globe* reporting that at the January 1927 Old Time Fiddlers' Contest he "will take part . . . but will not compete for prizes. The winner of the coming contest and Long will hold a dual contest on the closing night. Twenty-five dollars in gold will be awarded the winner." The *News Herald* revealed that, following Long's win the previous year, "it has been announced by the sponsors that 15,000 phonograph records of a selection recorded by [him] . . . have been sold throughout the United States and Canada."

Fiddlin' Sam Long, 1928. (Author's Collection)

In March, Long became fiddling champion of Oklahoma, receiving $100 in cash and "a medal, set with a diamond." In February 1928, he appeared again at the Joplin contest, evidently permitted to compete this time, and duly won again, over seventy-six contestants. Soon afterward, he moved to Tulsa and began broadcasting over KVOO, as noted in *Radio Digest*'s "Who's Who in Broadcasting" in March.

When the 1929 Joplin contest was announced, Long was again barred from competition, along with four other past prizewinners. The *Globe*'s advance notice of the event, a month beforehand (January 16, 1929), specified that it was open "to all white fiddlers," a restriction that may have been routine at fiddlers' contests in those days but was rarely spelled out. No such limitation applied to Native Americans, and the second prize that year went to Chief Bacon Rind of Muskogee, Oklahoma.

The 1931 Joplin contest elicited an interesting editorial in the *Globe*, encouraging its readers to support the event: First, because its proceeds were to go to the city's Health and Welfare Association. Second, because

> these annual fiddlers' contests bring a lot of visitors to Joplin. It is expected that there will be close to 100 contestants and many of them will come from a considerable distance.... It is not merely that the contestants themselves make a trip here, but most of them come by automobile and bring members of their families or friends with them. It is a worthwhile activity from a civic and commercial standpoint.
>
> Finally, an old fiddlers' contest affords fine, clean entertainment. It's a good chance to study psychology, if you like that. Or it is an interesting throw-back into a bygone era. Among the entries for the coming contest are two women of near 70 and a full-blooded Cherokee Indian. A large majority of the contestants are highly interesting personalities. (February 22, 1931)

Evidently these "highly interesting personalities" did not include Sam Long, who in any case may not have been fit enough to play; he died in Wichita, Kansas, in May of that year. By then, the library of records of old-time fiddling to which he had been an early contributor had swollen to hundreds.

7

"WISH TO THE LORD I HAD NEVER BEEN BORN"

Luther B. Clarke Accomp. by Blue Ridge Highballers Columbia 15096-D

Recorded in New York, NY, March 24, 1926
Released in October/November 1926
Sold 15,974

Online: Spotify

Anyone in the winter of 1926 who handed over 75 cents for a record called "Wish to the Lord I Had Never Been Born" might have expected some sort of existential lament. And, for a verse, they would have got it.

> Wish to the Lord I had never been born,
> Died when I was a baby;
> Wouldn't been left to shed a tear
> And eat so much old gravy.

It seemed to be shaping up as a version of the old-time song "Hard to Love," gravely accompanied by a stringband of fiddle, banjo, and guitar. But, from the second stanza, the song took a new and strange direction. Instead of the familiar story of irksome life and unsatisfied love, listeners were treated to a highly localized satire.

> Wish I'd never been a co-op,
> [But] listened to J. H. Wilson,
> I'd have been ridin' in a Ford sedan,
> Payin' my bills and a-whistlin'.
>
> Never sow on an open floor,
> You just wait till Fall.
> I'm gonna drive in Banner Warehouse
> And hear old Sam Robertson call.
>
> I want to hear Sam Robertson say,
> "Drive to the White Oak Mountain.
> You've been a durn fool long enough,
> You can drink right at this fountain."
>
> Henry Payne carries the mail,
> Sometimes drives a mule.
> Ain't got time to cuss no more,
> He's busy with that pool.

What was the point of this farrago of gossip and in-jokes? Who were J. H. Wilson and Sam Robertson? What was the significance of White Oak Mountain? What was a "co-op," and why was Henry Payne busy with a pool?

★ ★ ★

To answer these questions we must set our historical GPS to Pittsylvania County, Virginia, in the 1920s the heartland of Bright Leaf tobacco and of one type in particular. In the early nineteenth century, a grower on White Oak Mountain had devised a new method of heat-curing the leaf that avoided the bitterness of smoke-curing. "From then on," according to Pittsylvania County historian Larry G. Aaron, "White Oak tobacco became the popular standard."

The business hub of this region was Danville, described in its 1927 city directory as "one of the greatest tobacco trading centers of the world." It had "large brick buildings for the storage of tobacco . . . [such as] the Holland Warehouse, . . . the Planters', the Graves', and the Central," and

> a system has gradually been evolved whereby the farmer brings his tobacco to market and delivers it to the warehouse, where buyers of different manufacturing or exporting companies compete for its purchase. The Warehouse owners who handle the sale of the leaf do their best to obtain the best price possible, and after the sale, pay the farmers the price agreed upon by the purchaser, the latter making his settlement with the warehouseman.

That was how it had been done for decades, but lately there had been changes. "Within the past few years," the directory continues,

> a co-operative society has been organized among some of the farmers, who through their representatives now deal directly with the manufacturers. This, of course, has somewhat lessened the amount of tobacco which is cleared through the Danville market, but . . . it is argued by members of the co-operative organization, business in Danville is actually increased, for the farmers are more prosperous and have more money to spend.

However the business was conducted, it was massive: in 1926, almost 39 million pounds of tobacco were sold in Danville.

Perhaps trying to be even-handed, the directory writer gives the impression that the co-op movement and the established warehouses enjoyed a peaceful coexistence. In fact, in the mid-1920s, the co-operatives constituted a serious threat to the interests of the warehouse owners, men like James H. Wilson, manager of the Central Warehouse on North Union Street, and Sam Robertson, manager of the Banner Warehouse on Craghead Street. Wilson was described by the Danville *Bee* on his death in 1938 as a "jovial figure" whose "death saddened the community which was aware of solid work he did years ago in the development of the Danville tobacco market." Back in 1924, however, he was accused of instigating an anti-co-op movement, a charge he vigorously denied.

On April 24, 1926, a month after this recording was made, the *Bee* reported that a meeting on the future of the co-operative "pool" would be held in May that would "virtually spell the fate of the method of delivering tobacco during the next season. . . . [U]pon the response will depend whether or not the growers shall deliver their crop or go back to the auction system." There was evidence that many growers

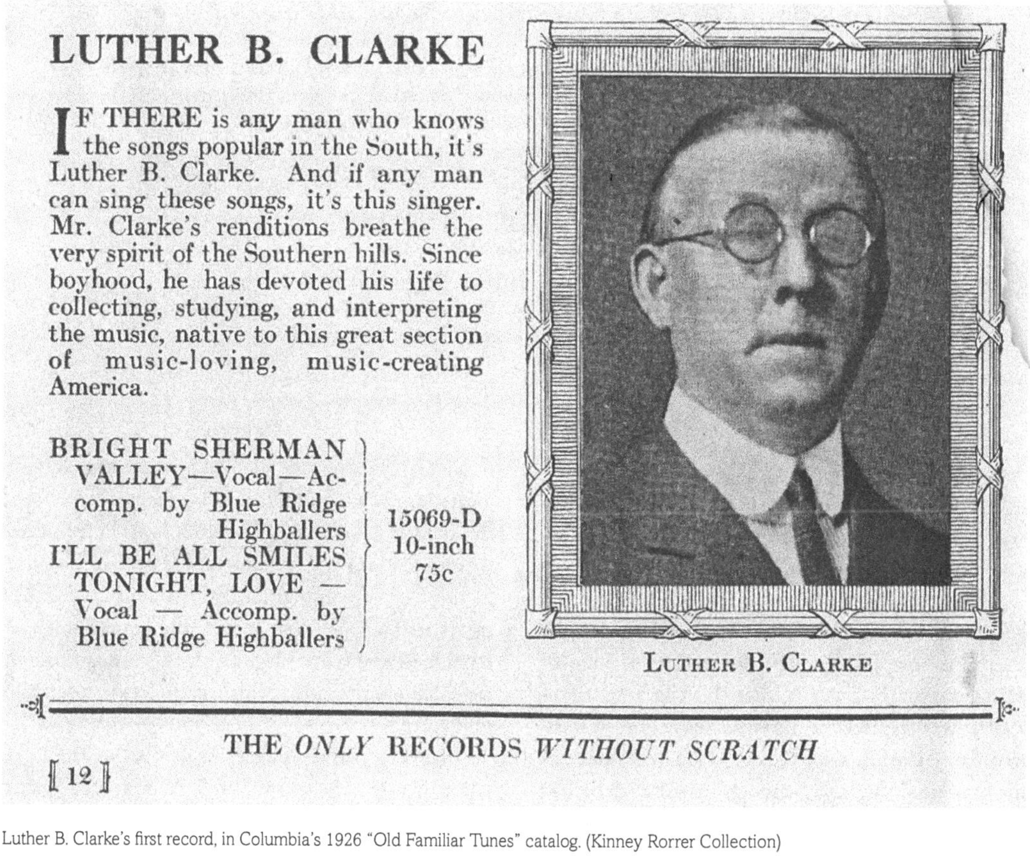

Luther B. Clarke's first record, in Columbia's 1926 "Old Familiar Tunes" catalog. (Kinney Rorrer Collection)

THE BLUE RIDGE HIGHBALLERS

(Led by CHARLEY LA PRADE, *Fiddler)*

HERE they are — the Blue Ridge Highballers from the highlands of the South! When it comes to playing the mountain dance music and the tunes, melodies and marches famous in the Southern hill country, the Highballers take nobody's dust. Charley La Prade, fiddler of note in a country critical of this type of music, is the organization's leader.

THE BLUE RIDGE HIGHBALLERS

SOLDIER'S JOY — Mountain Dance Music. SKIDD MORE—Mountain Dance Music	15168-D 10-inch 75c
DARNEO—Mountain Dance Music DARLING CHILD—Mountain Dance Music	15132-D 10-inch 75c
GOING DOWN TO LYNCHBURG TOWN—Intro.: Don't Let Your Deal Go Down—Mountain Dance Music WISH TO THE LORD I HAD NEVER BEEN BORN—Vocal—Luther B. Clarke, Accomp. by Blue Ridge Highballers	15096-D 10-inch 75c
SANDY RIVER BELLE—Mountain Dance Music ROUND TOWN GIRLS—Mountain Dance Music	15089-D 10-inch 75c
FLOP EARED MULE—Mountain Dance Music FOURTEEN DAYS IN GEORGIA—Mountain Dance Music	15081-D 10-in. 75c 75c
GREEN MOUNTAIN POLKA—Mountain Dance Music UNDER THE DOUBLE EAGLE—March Medley—Mountain Dance Music	15070-D 10-inch 75c

All of the Blue Ridge Highballers' Columbia releases, in the 1927 "Old Familiar Tunes" catalog. (OTM Collection)

preferred the pool, so long as it was competently managed, but, within a few years, the co-operative system collapsed and left the warehouses in their old command of the market.

Whether we read this song as heartfelt or humorous, it's clear that the singer sides with the warehouse owners. Perhaps some were friends or acquaintances because Luther B. Clarke (1880–1950) was himself a Pittsylvania County businessman. Sightless since the age of six, a graduate of the Staunton, Virginia, School for the Blind, he had advanced from freelance piano tuner to manager of the music department of Benefield, Motley & Co., located on Main and Craghead Streets, not far from the Banner Warehouse. The store dealt in furniture, stoves, pianos, and phonographs, and it boasted, in the face of competition from at least two other stores in Danville, that it had "the largest stock of records in southern Virginia." It was a major outlet for Columbia records, which it tirelessly advertised in the *Bee*.

In 1928, Clarke opened his own store, the L. B. Clark Music Co., located at "205 Main St. Facing the Bridge . . . handl[ing] Columbia, Brunswick and Victor machines and records," as well as various brands of pianos and radios. (He had evidently settled on the e-less spelling of his name, which is almost always how it is written in public records.) The store was described in an ad in the *Bee*, the following year, as "A Progressive Music Center in a Progressive Town," and he ran it until his death.

The description of him in Columbia's 1926 "Old Familiar Tunes" catalog as an expert on "the songs popular in the South" is borne out by his other two recordings, the evergreens "Bright Sherman Valley" and "I'll Be All Smiles Tonight, Love," but it was his topical song "Wish to the Lord I Had Never Been Born" that sold the best.

★ ★ ★

His accompanists were a natural choice: The Blue Ridge Highballers were Pittsylvania County's most famous stringband. Fiddler Charlie La Prade (1888–1968) and guitarist Lonnie Griffith (1905–74) lived on the same block in Schoolfield, a community a little outside Danville, built as the mill village for Riverside & Dan River Cotton Mills, one of the largest textile operations in the South; both men were employed by the mill throughout their working lives. Banjoist Arthur Wells (1904/5–?) also lived in Schoolfield and worked for the mill, but in later life became a Pentecostal minister, based in North Carolina, though he often returned to Danville to hold revivals.

The Highballers—whom Clarke, as a music-store man, may have recommended to Columbia—recorded eleven issued sides at this March 1926 session, among them "Flop Eared Mule," "Soldier's Joy," "Going Down to Lynchburg Town" (the reverse side of "Wish to the Lord I Had Never Been Born"), and "Green Mountain Polka." "If you go to a fiddlers' convention around here," observed the old-time music historian Kinney Rorrer, himself a Pittsylvania County resident, "and ask, 'Where did you learn to play "Green Mountain Polka"?,' they'll say from La Prade or from his records. . . . He had a tremendous impact on fiddlers in this region. He specialized in mountain dance music, but he was very versatile. And years ahead of fiddlers in his style."

"When he played some of these old slow pieces," remembered Lewis McDaniel, a Pittsylvania Countian who played guitar with La Prade in later years, "he'd make it sound like about *three* violins. . . . 'The Old Rugged Cross,' he can make cold chills run all over you with that, he can really do it."

The Highballers' records were successful, each of their first two releases selling well over 20,000 copies. The band played at square dances and for functions throughout the Virginia–North Carolina Piedmont, and, in the '30s, La Prade played over WBTM Danville during the tobacco sales season.

And what of Henry Payne? A lifelong resident of Pittsylvania County, when he died in 1954 his obituary in the *Bee* stated that he had served as a rural mail carrier for thirty-three years. By then, probably no one turning the leaves of the paper knew that, along with his fellow townsmen J. H. Wilson and Sam Robertson, he was also commemorated for all time on a long-gone record about a dispute over another kind of leaves.

8

"WHERE WE'LL NEVER GROW OLD"/"PICTURES FROM LIFE'S OTHER SIDE"

Smith's Sacred Singers
Columbia 15090-D

Recorded in Atlanta, GA, April 23, 1926
Released in October 1926
Sold 277,199

Online: Spotify ["Pictures from Life's Other Side"] • YT [both]

> Who of us does not appreciate the old "Camp Meeting" Sacred Songs; and who of us does not appreciate those hymns most when they are sung by a "close-harmony" quartet and sung so clearly that we can follow the high tenor and deep base [*sic*] throughout the selection?
>
> The Smith's Sacred Singers are making just such records for Columbia and if you haven't heard them, you'll find them at their best in these selections. (*Burlington* [North Carolina] *Daily Times*, April 8, 1927)

There followed half a dozen discs that the newspaper's readers could find downtown at M. B. Smith's furniture store, among them "Where We'll Never Grow Old" and "Pictures from Life's Other Side," the first release by Smith's Sacred Singers, recorded in Atlanta almost a year earlier. "This record proved so popular," the group's local paper reported in November 1926,

> and enjoyed such a large circulation that over fifteen thousand were sold through the Atlanta office within 60 days from date o[f] release. The New York officials claimed the record has made the largest sale since its release of any sacred record ever released by their company.
>
> The success of this group as recording artists is assured and from time to time [they] will record and release new selections made exclusively for the Columbia people.

By the end of 1926, "Where We'll Never Grow Old"/"Pictures from Life's Other Side" had sold over 80,000 copies. During 1927, it added a further 120,000. At the close of its catalog life in 1931, it was the second-best seller in Columbia's "Old Familiar Tunes" list, and almost certainly the era's best-selling record of Southern white sacred music.

★ ★ ★

These were not new songs. "Pictures from Life's Other Side" is credited (not without debate) to the songwriter Charles E. Baer and was copyrighted by the prolific author and publisher Henry J. Wehman in 1896. It could have been learned from one of Wehman's multitudinous "songsters." It is not strictly a sacred piece—its title may have been inspired by Hamlet's "Look here upon this picture, and on this"—but it prompts moral reflection:

> In this world's mighty gallery of pictures,
> Are the scenes that are painted from life;
> Are scenes of much grief and of pleasure,
> The picture[s] of love and strife.
> The picture[s] of youth and of beauty,
> Old age and a blushing young bride,
> All hang on the wall, but the saddest of all
> Are the pictures from life's other side.
> 'Tis a picture from life's other side,
> Somebody has fell by the way.
> A life has gone out with the tide
> That might have been happy some day . . .

"Where We'll Never Grow Old" was composed in 1914 by Rev. James Cleveland Moore, a singing-school teacher in Paulding County, Georgia. Based on Revelation 21:4—"and there shall be no more death, neither sorrow, nor crying, neither shall there be any more pain: for the former things are passed away"—it is an affirmation of belief in an afterlife that will be joyous and endless:

> I have heard of a land on the faraway strand,
> 'Tis a beautiful home of the soul;
> Built by Jesus on high, where we never shall die,
> 'Tis a land where we'll never grow old.

The record thus conveyed two quite different spiritual messages. In "Never Grow Old," it showed the listener the sunny upland of spiritual reassurance: if we live right, we shall earn eternity. But in "Life's Other Side," it revealed a less sure terrain: see what happens when things go wrong. How can we evade the misfortunes that befall others? Where shall *we* be when that first trumpet sounds?

★ ★ ★

The men who made this momentous record were J. Frank Smith (1884–1937), who sang lead; Clarence Cronic (1902–90), tenor; Cronic's uncle Clyde B. Smith (1886–1965), baritone; and Marion Luther Thrasher (1885–1953), bass. The Smiths and Cronic lived around Braselton and Hoschton in Jackson County, Georgia, some fifty miles northeast of Atlanta; Clyde Smith and Cronic farmed, while Frank Smith worked as a barber. He had attended rural singing schools as a boy, and when grown up he taught them himself. Sometime in the 1920s, he formed a quartet

Columbia *"New Process"* Records
REG. U. S. PAT. OFF.

SMITH'S SACRED SINGERS

J. FRANK SMITH, the leader of this group of inspired sacred singers, is widely known in the Southern States for his courageous work among the masses. Smith's Sacred Singers travel, by car, to every section of the South where they feel that good can be done. By them the word of God is taught in song. A preacher, capable of delivering a sermon, or, when necessary, doing his share of the singing, always goes on these trips.

SMITH'S SACRED SINGERS

ARE YOU WASHED IN THE BLOOD OF THE LAMB JESUS DIED FOR ME—Vocals—Violin and Piano Accomps.	15430-D
MEET ME THERE—Guitar Accomp. WORKING FOR THE CROWN—Vocals—Violin and Piano Accomp.	15401-D
WHEN THE HAPPY MORNING BREAKS—Violin and Piano Accomp. I AM GOING THAT WAY—Vocals—Piano Accomp.	15389-D
LORD I'M COMING HOME WHEN JESUS COMES—Vocals	15371-D
THE UNCLOUDED DAY KEEP ON CLIMBING—Vocals	15351-D

MADE THE NEW WAY—ELECTRICALLY

[40]

From Columbia's "Old Familiar Tunes" catalog, 1929. This seems to be the original 1926 lineup, with J. Frank Smith, far right, and Rev. M. L. Thrasher, center. (Kinney Rorrer Collection) to sing in local churches. Thrasher was a minister, originally from Lawrence County in northern Alabama, but based in the late 1920s in Braselton.

"Never Grow Old" was arranged for a trio of lead, baritone, and bass, but on "Life's Other Side" Frank Smith sang the verses alone, with the other three joining in the refrain and using the device of "echoing" repetition: "'Tis a picture from life's other side (other side), Somebody has fell by the way (by the way)."

* * *

By the winter of 1926, "Never Grow Old"/"Life's Other Side" was a hit record, and therefore worth copying. It was duly copied by the Old Southern Sacred Singers, a group put together by Vocalion, probably for this very purpose, consisting of Lester McFarland and Robert Gardner, the Knoxville duo Vocalion had signed a couple of months earlier, with Vernon Dalhart and another experienced studio singer, Wilfred Glenn. In the following year, McFarland and George Reneau, as the Gentry Brothers, replicated the Smith record for a handful of Plaza labels, while Dalhart and Carson Robison did so for the Pathé group. As late as 1934, there was enough mileage in the paired anthems for the Frank Luther Trio to sing them into a Decca microphone.

There were also recordings of "Never Grow Old" by Alfred G. Karnes, the McCravy Brothers, the Carter Family, and others. "Life's Other Side" was recorded less assiduously in the 1920s–'30s, but in later years it would accrue versions by Hank Williams (in his narrative persona of Luke the Drifter), Woody Guthrie, and the Blue Sky Boys.

* * *

"Where We'll Never Grow Old"/"Pictures from Life's Other Side" was more than a hit record; it had a lasting impact on the marketing of Southern music.

Until the mid-1920s, sacred songs and hymns were typically recorded either unaccompanied or with a piano. On "Never Grow Old," the pianist's role was taken by Maud (Mrs. T. C.) Llewellyn, a schoolteacher's wife from Braselton. But for "Life's Other Side" Frank Smith diverged from record-business practice and gave the accompanist's role to guitarist Clarence Cronic. Perhaps Smith reflected that, since "Life's Other Side" wasn't exactly a sacred song, it could be less formally clothed, but once he had broken the conventional mold there was no going back, and for the rest of its life the group gave its recordings a variety of settings: fiddle and guitar, fiddle and piano, solo piano, solo guitar.

It was more than its instrumental setting that set the record apart. Earlier recordings of sacred songs by quartets and quintets were more disciplined in diction and harmony, more musically "correct," "straighter." This formality was embodied in the singing of the Vaughan Quartet, assembled by the publisher James D. Vaughan of Lawrenceburg, Tennessee, who began circulating his compositions on records in 1921. When Frank Smith first arranged his men around a recording microphone, Vaughan had released some forty discs on his eponymous label. In contrast to the cathedral solemnity of the Vaughan quartets, Smith's Sacred Singers offered the restrained fervor of the little country church, a sound immediately and heart-touchingly familiar to every rural and small-town community in the South.

And the South responded. According to the old-time music historian Charles Wolfe, Smith's hometown of Braselton "was so small that [it] had no mail truck, and the post office soon found that it had to deliver Smith huge sacks of fan mail in a wagon." Smith, he concluded, "more than anyone else, convinced the big commercial record companies that white gospel music had a place in their catalogues [*sic*] of old time and country music."

* * *

Impressed by the sales of their debut release, Columbia summoned Smith's Sacred Singers to Atlanta again in November 1926. While in the city, they presented on WSB "an hour of vocal and instrumental selections, together with two splendid piano selections by Mrs. T. C. Llewellyn," which, this local paper's report loyally added, "was one of the best ever heard over WSB's microphone."

At a third session in April 1927, however, the only original member of Smith's Sacred Singers was Frank Smith himself. About that time he had moved to Lawrenceville in Gwinnett County, where he opened a barbershop in the courthouse square. The re-formed Smith's Sacred Singers reportedly included Joe Day, Willie Fowler, and Will Brewer, but others were also involved, so identifying the group's personnel at any given session remains problematic.

Marion Thrasher, still in Braselton, formed his own recording group, reportedly with Clarence Cronic. Between 1927 and 1929, generally using Smith's template of a small singing group

Smith's Sacred Singers

Familiar Tunes—Old and New

The Southern mountaineer musicians are one of America's chief sources of genuine folk music. In the past, this priceless heritage has been passed down without recorded notes, often to the loss of many airs. In this field, Columbia now both helps and makes history.

15201-D 10 in. **75c.**
A Corn Licker Still in Georgia—Parts 1 and 2.
Featuring Clayton McMichen, Riley Puckett, Gid Tanner, Lowe Stokes, Fate Norris, Bob Nichols and Bill Brown.

15204-D 10 in. **75c.**
Big Ball in Town.
Old McDonald Had a Farm.
Gid Tanner and His Skillet-Lickers with Riley Puckett and Clayton McMichen.

15207-D 10 in. **75c.**
When the Roll Is Called Up Yonder.
What Shall We Do with Mother?
Rev. M. L. Thrasher and His Gospel Singers.

15202-D 10 in. **75c.**
Aloha Oe (Farewell to Thee).
The Missouri Waltz. McMichen's Melody Men.

15203-D 10 in. **75c.**
He Pardoned Me.
Saved By His Sweet Grace. Sacred Music.
Bush Brothers.

15209-D 10 in. **75c.**
Ladies on the Steamboat.
Billy in the Low Ground. Dances.
Burnett and Rutherford.

15205-D 10 in. **75c.**
The Old Hat.
Monkey in the Dog Cart. Leake County Revelers.

15210-D 10 in. **75c.**
Old Aunt Betsy.
Fly Around My Pretty Little Miss.
Frank Blevins and His Tar Heel Rattlers.

15208-D 10 in. **75c.**
Gospel Waves.
He Bore It All. Smith's Sacred Singers.

15206-D 10 in. **75c.**
Red River Valley.
When You Wore a Tulip. Vocal Duets.
Hugh Cross and Riley Puckett.

Columbia

Columbia new releases, February 1928. (Author's Collection)

accompanied by piano or by fiddle and guitar, he made sixteen discs for Columbia, among them versions of "When the Roll Is Called up Yonder" and "Where the Soul Never Dies." They were well received but did not match the sales of the older group. In 1930, Thrasher left Georgia for Covington

This photograph was used to promote the group's Bluebird releases. J. Frank Smith is second from left. (Author's Collection)

County, Alabama. He must have expected to continue recording, since in April 1930 he advertised for a "1st tenor singer . . . for recording with Columbia Phonograph Co." (*Andalusia* [Alabama] *Star*, April 4, 1930), but evidently the company's call never came.

Smith's Sacred Singers, however, basked in the warm regard of Columbia Records for four and a half years, making thirty-two discs and achieving total sales of almost 700,000. Among the well-loved sacred songs they put on wax were "He Will Set Your Fields on Fire," "Life's Railway to Heaven," "Climbing up the Golden Stairs," "Hold to God's Unchanging Hand," "The Unclouded Day," "The Church in the Wildwood," and many more.

★ ★ ★

No doubt encouraged by their good fortune with Smith's Sacred Singers, Columbia recorded many other Southern quartets. The Deal Family from Burke County, North Carolina, and the Bush Brothers from Jones County, Mississippi, were the most successful, with ten releases each, but neither came anywhere near to matching the sales of the Georgia quartet. The company's policy was cautious: typically, an act that failed to make its mark with its first recordings was given no second chance. Such was the fate of estimable groups like the Albertville Quartet from Alabama, the Copperhill Male Quartet from Tennessee, the Garland Brothers and Grinstead from Kentucky (➤33), and the Spindale Quartet from North Carolina. Nevertheless, when Columbia's "Old Familiar Tunes" series ended in 1932, Southern sacred selections accounted for almost 20 percent of its nearly eight hundred releases. Other companies' hillbilly catalogs offer similar figures. Arguably, if it had not been for Smith's Sacred Singers, most of this music would have gone undocumented.

★ ★ ★

In 1934, someone at Bluebird remembered how well Smith's Sacred Singers had done before the Depression. I suspect it was Dan Hornsby, a Columbia staffer back then, now working for Bluebird. When the group returned to an Atlanta studio, the lineup reportedly consisted of Smith, Day, and Fowler, with Bob Coker to sing bass and play guitar, and Mildred Cowsert as piano accompanist. Over two sessions in 1934–35, they made a further thirty-eight recordings. Some recalled their past successes, such as "Never Grow Old" and "Life's Other Side" (though this time not coupled), "Let the Lower Lights Be Burning," and "You Can't Do Wrong and Get By," but many had been newly sourced. In the summer of 1935, the group had a fifteen-minute radio program that was heard as far away as Utah.

J. Frank Smith died in September 1937. His simple grave marker in Lawrenceville's Shadowlawn cemetery—name, dates, no more—gives no clue that this was a man who spread the gospel message throughout the South on almost a million records.

9

"LET ME CALL YOU SWEETHEART"/"SWEET BUNCH OF DAISIES"

McMichen's Melody Men
Columbia 15111-D

Recorded in Atlanta, GA, November 4, 1926
Released in February 1927
Sold 99,368

Reissued on *The Legendary Fiddler* (BACM CD D 081) ["Sweet Bunch of Daisies"]

Online: Spotify ["Sweet Bunch of Daisies"] • YT [both]

"McMichens' [*sic*] Melody Men, famous in the mountains of the South for their dance music, have just been signed up exclusively by the Columbia Phonograph Co., Inc.," reported *The Talking Machine World* in January 1927. "Their first record couples 'Let Me Call You Sweetheart' and 'Sweet Bunch of Daisies.'"

It doesn't seem like a riveting news item. Both of these slow waltzes were chestnuts: "Let Me Call You Sweetheart" (Friedman–Whitson) had been published in 1910, and Anita Owen's "Sweet Bunch of Daisies" in 1894. Clayton "Mac" McMichen and his Melody Men had made the recordings two months earlier, during Columbia's winter trip to Atlanta. They had been waxed by old-time artists before, "Sweetheart" by Riley Puckett and by Jimmie Wilson's Catfish String Band from Oklahoma, "Daisies" by the Hill Billies and by an earlier McMichen lineup, the Home Town Band. (Mac evidently liked the tune because he also recorded it in a fiddlers' convention sketch in 1931 and with his Georgia Wildcats in 1937.)

But if the tunes were unsurprising, the band playing them was not. It consisted of McMichen on fiddle, Riley Puckett on guitar and vocals, and a young man lately arrived in Georgia from Kentucky by way of Florida, seventeen-year-old Kasper Delmar "Stranger" Malone—playing clarinet.

"[McMichen] liked a lot of slow ballad things," Stranger recalled in interviews many years later. "His idea was to have a harmony line [with] the violin [playing] the higher notes and the lower-register clarinet more or less like alto in a choir." Mac had first tried out this idea in 1925 with the Home Town Band, but his young clarinetist Robert Stephens, Jr. had since died. Hearing about Stranger, who was then playing with an orchestra for silent movies at the Rivoli Theater in Rome, Georgia, Mac conscripted him for his new band.

When recording with the Melody Men, Stranger remembered, recording director Frank Walker's "friendly, sandy to red haired, Jewish assistant would give the three of us, me included, a good shot of very fine whiskey, just before the recordings were to be cut; possibly that was to prevent microphone fright. With two or three shots of that great whiskey, I wouldn't have been scared of anything, not even Toscanini."

The Melody Men in this lineup—McMichen, Puckett, Malone—existed only to make records. In public, Stranger's place was taken by McMichen's brother-in-law Bert Layne on harmony fiddle.

★ ★ ★

"How come you didn't record popular numbers?" Fred Hoeptner asked McMichen during his and Bob Pinson's 1959 interview. Mac explained.

> They'd already been recorded. And that's a funny thing: I'm gonna tell you exactly what the man [Frank Walker] said. "Mac, I wonder why you think that we bring all this equipment, comin' down here from New York to Atlanta, to get this music you fellows play, instead of just getting them fellows up there in New York to play it and be done with it?" He says, "They don't know this music." Says, "There's millions up there can play that there popular tunes that come out." I said, "Yes, but I still think people'd like them better played on string music and hear them words."

> And we tried a few of it and it didn't mean a thing. He said, "Go ahead, cut 'em. I'll release 'em." He did, he give 'em a fair shake. But it didn't mean nothin'.

This is puzzling. If we assume, as I think we must, that by "popular numbers" Hoeptner meant new or recently published pieces, then indeed only one McMichen-associated recording of this period fits that description, the Melody Men's peppy version of "Ain't She Sweet," cut in 1927, the year of its publication. But it did quite well, selling over 14,000.

That tune apart, the Melody Men—as Hoeptner would have known—recorded almost nothing *but* "popular numbers," in the sense of published compositions from Tin Pan Alley. They just weren't new. "Lonesome Mama Blues," a number popularized by Mamie Smith, and "Wabash Blues" were from the very early 1920s, and the rest of the group's recorded repertoire came from one, two, or even three decades earlier. Certainly, many of them had "already been recorded." But in the light of the Melody Men's sales totals, the rest of McMichen's reply makes no sense at all.

Following the near-six-figure score by "Sweetheart" and "Daisies," the next release by the Melody Men, "House of David Blues"/"Down Yonder," sold over 67,000; "Aloha Oe"/"The Missouri Waltz," over 28,000; "My Carolina Home"/"Fifty Years Ago," over 19,000; and "When You and I Were Young Maggie"/"Silver Threads Among the Gold," over 15,000. Apart from "My Carolina Home," composed by McMichen and Layne, all of these were time-proven popular tunes. Four other Melody Men couplings, similar in character, scored lower totals, but a record by the group almost always sold about twice as many copies as an average release in the "Old Familiar Tunes" series.

Possibly what McMichen had in mind when he said, "We tried a few of it and it didn't mean a thing" was a couple of other outlets Columbia gave him for his concept of hillbilly–pop string music. One was Lowe Stokes's North Georgians, with whom McMichen usually sang, and whose records likewise drew from a well-thumbed folio of popular tunes, such as "Everybody's Doin' It" (introduced in 1911), "Sailing Down the Chesapeake Bay" (1913),

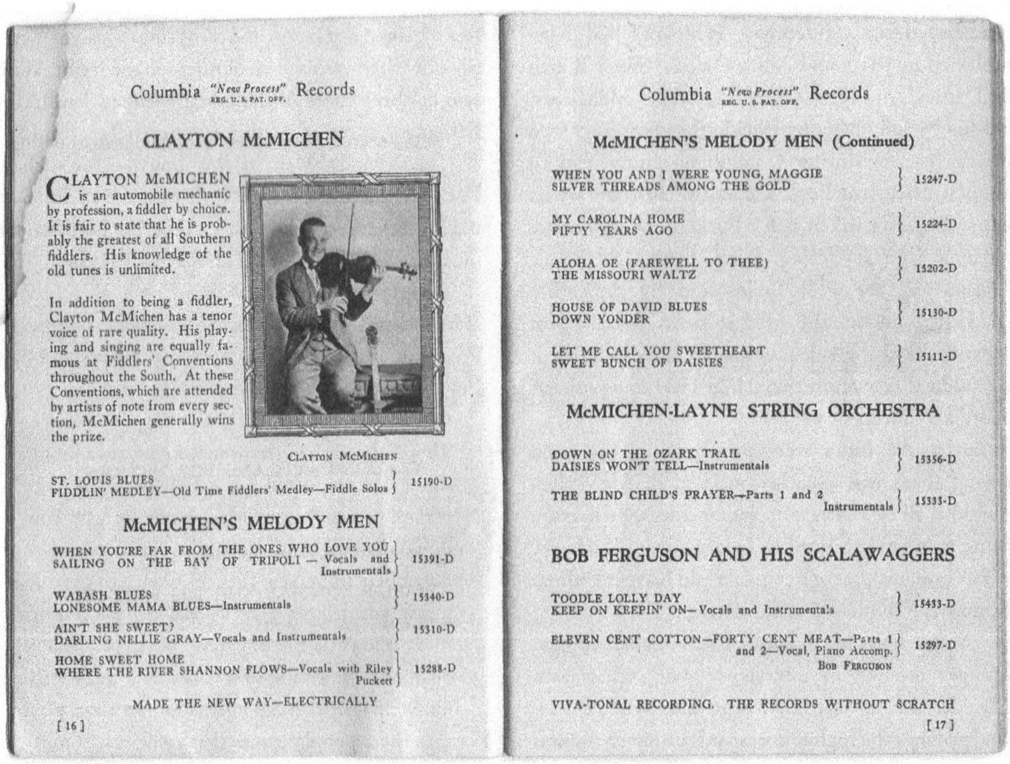

Columbia "*New Process*" Records
REG. U. S. PAT. OFF.

CLAYTON McMICHEN

CLAYTON McMICHEN is an automobile mechanic by profession, a fiddler by choice. It is fair to state that he is probably the greatest of all Southern fiddlers. His knowledge of the old tunes is unlimited.

In addition to being a fiddler, Clayton McMichen has a tenor voice of rare quality. His playing and singing are equally famous at Fiddlers' Conventions throughout the South. At these Conventions, which are attended by artists of note from every section, McMichen generally wins the prize.

CLAYTON MCMICHEN

ST. LOUIS BLUES FIDDLIN' MEDLEY—Old Time Fiddlers' Medley—Fiddle Solos	15190-D

McMICHEN'S MELODY MEN

WHEN YOU'RE FAR FROM THE ONES WHO LOVE YOU SAILING ON THE BAY OF TRIPOLI — Vocals and Instrumentals	15391-D
WABASH BLUES LONESOME MAMA BLUES—Instrumentals	15340-D
AIN'T SHE SWEET? DARLING NELLIE GRAY—Vocals and Instrumentals	15310-D
HOME SWEET HOME WHERE THE RIVER SHANNON FLOWS—Vocals with Riley Puckett	15288-D

MADE THE NEW WAY—ELECTRICALLY

[16]

Columbia "*New Process*" Records
REG. U. S. PAT. OFF.

McMICHEN'S MELODY MEN (Continued)

WHEN YOU AND I WERE YOUNG, MAGGIE SILVER THREADS AMONG THE GOLD	15247-D
MY CAROLINA HOME FIFTY YEARS AGO	15224-D
ALOHA OE (FAREWELL TO THEE) THE MISSOURI WALTZ	15202-D
HOUSE OF DAVID BLUES DOWN YONDER	15130-D
LET ME CALL YOU SWEETHEART SWEET BUNCH OF DAISIES	15111-D

McMICHEN-LAYNE STRING ORCHESTRA

DOWN ON THE OZARK TRAIL DAISIES WON'T TELL—Instrumentals	15356-D
THE BLIND CHILD'S PRAYER—Parts 1 and 2 Instrumentals	15333-D

BOB FERGUSON AND HIS SCALAWAGGERS

TOODLE LOLLY DAY KEEP ON KEEPIN' ON—Vocals and Instrumentals	15433-D
ELEVEN CENT COTTON—FORTY CENT MEAT—Parts 1 and 2—Vocal, Piano Accomp. BOB FERGUSON	15297-D

VIVA-TONAL RECORDING. THE RECORDS WITHOUT SCRATCH

[17]

From Columbia's "Old Familiar Tunes" catalog, 1929. (Marshall Wyatt Collection)

and "Take Me to the Land of Jazz" (1919). Another, more experimental lineup was the McMichen–Layne String Orchestra, consisting of Mac, Stokes, and Layne on fiddles, sometimes Malone on clarinet, Puckett singing and playing guitar, and a bass player. Half a dozen records were released by these two groups in 1928–30, and two of them sold over 10,000, but perhaps to McMichen, accustomed by then to the Melody Men's sales, such modest numbers really "didn't mean nothin.'"

★ ★ ★

The strong market for the Melody Men's records proved that McMichen's instinct had been right: offered a stringband arrangement of a well-known popular tune, many record-buyers would favor it over, or no less than, a danceband version. Was this because some of those listeners had an innate preference for fiddles and guitars rather than orchestral instruments? Or because Riley Puckett did such a good job with the vocals?

McMichen himself might have ascribed their success to the fact that they were string music without, in Stokes's term, "foolishments"—chitchat, hollering, Gid Tanner's falsetto—all the things Mac disliked in the music of the Skillet-Lickers. They had arrangements; they had class. The Melody Men were the first lineup to realize McMichen's lifelong vision of an uptown string music, an ambition he would develop throughout the next decade, broadcasting and recording with the talented younger musicians who composed his Georgia Wildcats.

★ ★ ★

Success in terms of record sales was largely irrelevant to McMichen because he received no royalties from them. "In that day and time," Bert Layne recalled, "we knew nothing about royalties. We played for whatever we could get and keep our mouth shut because we thought that was a devil of a thing, somebody hear us on records. Which it was."

However, McMichen was in the unusual position, in the hillbilly business, of being on a record-company retainer, whereby he received a sum on each of Columbia's biannual expeditions to Atlanta. For this, he agreed to provide his services in any capacity: recording fiddle tunes; accompanying Riley Puckett and other singers; participating in the Skillet-Lickers' band sides and sketch recordings, and in other groups such as the Melody Men, North Georgians, and the McMichen–Layne String Orchestra; plus talent spotting. Between 1926 and 1928, his fee was $300 per Atlanta trip, with a guarantee of $600 per year, though in 1927 he also earned $100 for "talent" and a bonus of $150, as well as expenses. The retainer was increased in 1929 and 1930 to $1,000 per expedition, with a guaranteed minimum of $2,000 per year: equivalent, in 2020 money, to around $30,000—and all for no more than three or four weeks' work. In 1931, Columbia made only one Atlanta trip and recorded fewer masters; McMichen was involved in just twenty, and not all of those were issued, yet according to his contract he received $1,000 that year, paid monthly.

It's commonly believed that in the 1920s and '30s, no one but Jimmie Rodgers and the Carter Family made any real money out of hillbilly music, but Clayton McMichen's documented income over five years proves that others could make a very good living.

10

"I'M A STERN OLD BACHELOR"

Chubby Parker
Silvertone 5012

Recorded in Chicago, IL, c. February 26, 1927
Released in c. May 1927

No sales figures are available for Silvertone 5012, but the same recording was released on Champion 15247, selling 13,790, and on five other issues

Online: YT

The joys of single life are an enduring theme in old-time music, and nowhere more jubilantly expounded than in "I'm a Stern Old Bachelor."

> I am a stern old bachelor, my age is forty-four;
> I do declare I'll never live with women any more . . .
>
> When I come home late, I have no fear, I smile and walk right in;
> I never hear a voice yell out, "I say, where you have you been?"
>
> I go to bed whene'er I please and get up just the same,
> I change my socks three times a year with no one to complain.

(Just so the Norwegian bachelor farmers of Lake Wobegon, by whom you can tell when spring has arrived because they hang out their bedsheets. And burn their socks.)

The artist who first put this song across to the hillbilly market was Chubby Parker, who sang whiskery songs from years gone by in a high, clear voice and plucked a banjo and was one of the earliest exponents of old-time music to become famous through the power of radio.

His base was WLS, the Chicago station founded in 1924 by the mail-order giant Sears, Roebuck. (WLS stood for "World's Largest Store.") The station's focus was the Midwestern farm home, the men and women who tilled the wheat fields of Iowa and Nebraska or wrestled with Nature in smallholdings in Wisconsin and Minnesota, and it was sharpened when Sears sold the station, in September 1928, to Prairie Farmer, a company with many spoons in the agricultural pie and weekly access to the farming community through its eponymous magazine. Within a few years of its founding, WLS and its audience turned the station's artists into household names. They are mostly forgotten now, but at one time, every listener in the Midwest knew the Maple City Four, the pop duet of Ford Rush and Glenn Rowell, one-man-band Walter Peterson, contralto Grace Wilson, organist Ralph Waldo Emerson—and Chubby Parker.

He was born Frederick R. Parker in 1876 in Lafayette, Indiana, about a hundred miles southeast of Chicago. A young man with the same name graduated from Purdue University, a few miles away in West Lafayette, in 1898 with a B.S. in electrical engineering, an appropriate background for the Frederick Parker who turns up in Chicago a few years later and works successively as patent attorney, inventor, and electrician.

Music was perhaps no more than a hobby for this ingenious man, but he was proficient, or keen, enough to win a place on WLS's Saturday-night National Barn Dance program, launched on April 19, 1924. He appeared on the show frequently, usually as a solo act but sometimes in an old-time danceband with fiddler Tommy Dandurand, a streetcar motorman from Kankakee, Illinois, who had lately moved to Chicago.

Charles Wolfe, who believed that Parker was a Kentuckian, asserted that he "left WLS abruptly in 1926, reportedly upset at the greater success young Bradley Kincaid was having with the same kind of material." On the contrary, in 1926 Parker could not have been more secure at WLS. In December, the *Hammond*

The cast of the National Barn Dance, photographed by Louis Paeth in the WLS studio, Hotel Sherman, Chicago, May 31, 1929. Third from left, front row, Tom Corwine, MC of the WLS Barn Dance and Show Boat; fifth from left, singer Grace Wilson. The young couple with cowboy hats behind the microphone is the Hawaiian guitar duo Cecil and Esther Ward. Right, behind the pumpkin, are fiddlers Tommy Dandurand and Rube Tronson, with Chubby Parker. (Photograph © Peter Paeth.)

[Indiana] *Times* described him as "one of [WLS's] leading acts . . . at present the most popular entertainer of that station, who has, for the last month, led Ford and Glenn in the number of requests for encores."

In September 1927, WLS's director Edgar Bill took a team to Atlanta, where a Sears store had recently opened, and the company's Agricultural Foundation sponsored several shows on WSB, such as Dinner Bell R.F.D. Bill's purpose was to recreate a typical week of WLS programs on the Atlanta station, and for this he selected Parker as the sole old-time artist. The week culminated with a two-hour presentation of the National Barn Dance, in which the visiting banjoist shared the stage with Fiddlin' John Carson and other local musical celebrities. The *Atlanta Journal* described him as "without doubt the premier old-time radio entertainer of the northern states."

By 1928, Parker's bill matter was even more enthusiastic. In April, when he played the Rialto theater in Hamilton, Ohio, he was advertised as the "World's Most Popular Radio Artist In Person. . . . 'Chubby' Has Charmed Millions Of Radio Listeners All Over The World." (WLS was among the most powerful stations in the US, and on a clear night could be picked up in Canada and Hawaii, but "all over the world" may be something of an overstatement.) The *Hamilton Evening Journal* (April 7, 1928) reminded its readers that Chubby was "the fellow that sings the quaint humorous songs to the tune of his little banjo from the WLS station every Saturday night," and quoted a Chicago paper as reporting, earlier that year, that "from October 2, 1926, to July 15, 1927, Chubby received 24,000 pieces of radio mail and telegrams. . . . In one single week [in February 1927] he received 2,853 pieces." These were believed, at the time, to be world records.

In May, the *Rushville* [Indiana] *Daily Republic* claimed—or reprinted a publicist's claim—that Parker was "the highest paid entertainer in the world. . . . Recently 'Chubby' signed a contract with Kenneth Hackley Enterprises for a weekly salary of more than ever paid to one man for theatre appearances."

★ ★ ★

Parker, or his employer, had been swift to capitalize on his popularity. Within days of that heavy mail week in February 1927, he was in a Chicago studio waxing not only "I'm a Stern Old Bachelor" but the ancient nonsense songs "Nickety Nackety Now Now Now" and "Bib-A-Lollie Boo." The company that recorded him was Gennett, but most of his sales were on Silvertone, a low-priced label that Gennett manufactured for Sears, which promoted it aggressively through its mail-order catalogs. (According to Fred

Ad in Richmond [Indiana] *Palladium Item*, May 3, 1928. (Author's Collection)

Gennett's son Robert, "There were more Silvertone pressed than either Gennett or Champion.") Between 1927 and 1931, Parker would produce more than fifty issued sides, though the repertoire is only about half that size because he recorded many songs twice or three times. Early sides like "I'm a Stern Old Bachelor," "Oh Susanna," and "Little Brown Jug" were so successful that three years later Gennett commissioned him to remake them, perhaps because the original metal stampers had worn out.

Parker claimed he wrote "I'm a Stern Old Bachelor," and had sheet music printed to validate it, but at least some of the verses were much older. A text published in a Kansas newspaper in 1887 under the title "The Old Bachelor," by one A. L. Stokesberry, contains three verses almost identical to Parker's. The essential idea can be traced back even further to the song "O I'm a Jolly Bachelor" (Super–Holmes, ca. 1860), with its refrain

O I'm a jolly bachelor,
With heart and fancy free;
And evermore my song shall be,
A single life for me.

Whatever the age of the old bachelor, Parker's song folio was stuffed with antiques like "Whoa, Mule, Whoa," "Darling Nellie Gray," "Uncle Ned," and "Oh Dem Golden Slippers," pieces known to every second or third American from the "songsters"—little books of minstrel-show ditties, comic songs, and read-'em-and-weepies—that were printed in millions from the 1870s to the 1910s. Many of these songs had been recorded before, in the 1900s and 1910s, by artists like the banjo-playing Harry C. Browne, and some of Parker's interpretations were in a similar minstrel idiom, with its burnt-cork talk such as "I'se gwine" and "'kaze" (for 'cause). But the older recordings were typically made with orchestral accompaniments. What gave Parker's versions their appeal was his jaunty solo banjo playing, his high but unstrident voice, which cut through the discs' murk of surface noise, and the choruses of whistling he often threw in.

Minstrel songs, banjo—are we, perhaps, approaching Uncle Dave Macon country? The two men were close in age, both born in the 1870s, and, though they shared only a couple of songs on record, they surely knew many of the same pieces. The banjo connection is a little harder to make. In the best-known photograph of Parker, he holds a five-string, but the evidence of his recorded playing suggests that he used a four-string plectrum banjo or, possibly, a five-string model with the fifth string absent.

★ ★ ★

In 1930, Parker told a census taker he was a "radio broadcasting artist," implying that he was making a living out of his radio work, records, and personal appearances. But in February 1931, *Radio Digest* reported that he "is not on WLS any more. . . . He is living in Chicago, with his family"—the propagandist for bachelordom had been married for two decades to Frances Kischel, and they had a daughter, Claudia—"but is not connected with any station." Nonetheless, his name was still potent, and in October 1931 he made a last batch of recordings—for Conqueror, another Sears label—again reprising some of his earlier hits, among them "I'm a Stern Old Bachelor," which finally lent credibility to that "all over the world" claim by being released in the UK.

Yet Parker was fondly remembered by the WLS audience, and when the station celebrated its twelfth anniversary in April 1936, he was one of the old timers invited back for the occasion, where, according to a newspaper report, he "will revive 'Nickety, Nackety, Now, Now, Now,' which he made famous in his radio days. He is now a Chicago business man." (*Wisconsin State Journal* [Madison, Wisconsin], April 18, 1936)

Chubby Parker died in 1940, but he was resurrected, at least for music lovers, in 1952, when Harry Smith included his "King Kong Kitchie Kitchie Ki-Me-O," a sprightly version of the children's song "Froggie Went a-Courting," in the hugely influential six-LP collection *Anthology of American Folk Music*. This brief flash of attention did nothing to illuminate Parker's life, and the few historians who subsequently attempted to do so shone their torches in the wrong direction. Charles Wolfe looked for him in Kentucky; Rick Kennedy, historian of Gennett Records, not only followed that wrong turn but then drove off the road with his assertion that Parker "exploited the stereotype of the backward hillbilly," a misreading of his repertoire, style, and appeal. In fact, Parker's old-time comic songs and banjo playing recall the long-gone merriment of the minstrel stage, where grandfather's clock stands in one corner and a wooden rocker in another, and a jolly fellow with a banjo fends off old maids and ornery mules and exults in being "from matrimony free."

11

"GOING SLOW"/ "SPARTANBURG BLUES"

Homer Christopher and Raney Van Vink

Okeh 45117

Recorded in Atlanta, GA, March 18, 1927
Released on July 5, 1927

Online: YT ["Spartanburg Blues," and the Victor recording of "Going Slow"]

It's a curious fact that many of the musicians who recorded in the old-time field in the 1920s and '30s had unusual names. To be sure, there were numerous Smiths, Browns, and Johnsons, but they were balanced by a considerable array of men with names like Haskell Wolfenbarger, Clarence Cronic, Mumford Bean, Leonard C. Fulwider, or Zandervon Obeliah Lam. Even in this company, there is a luxuriant improbability about a moniker like Raney Van Vink, especially when it's attached to that rare character in early country music, a piano accordion player. But neither his name nor his choice of instrument is the oddest thing about him. Raney Van Vink was—and I think we may say this with some confidence—the only old-time recording artist who was also . . . Belgian.

About this, more in a moment. But first, the piano accordion: not an instrument many would think had a place in old-time country music. Actually, hillbilly records captured the big box on several occasions: played by Fred Shriver with the Middle Tennessee fiddler Blind Joe Mangrum (Victor, 1928), by Fran Trappe with the Bowman Sisters (Columbia, 1929), by the songwriter and singer Bobby Gregory (Okeh, 1929), by the Dallas musician Roy Rodgers with fiddler Hugh Roden (Okeh, 1930), by Charles Magnante in the various Fields–Hall groups of 1930–32 (➤63), and by Frank Novak, a musician much employed in the late 1920s and early '30s by Bob Miller, Carson Robison, and Frank Luther, juggling accordion with half a dozen other instruments.

Piano accordionists were featured in several early West Coast cowboy ensembles, such as the Beverly Hill Billies and bands fronted by "Mac" McClintock or Charlie Marshall, and, from the late '30s onward, in Western Swing groups like the Tune Wranglers, the Light Crust Doughboys, and Jimmie Revard's Oklahoma Playboys. During the '40s, when country music was progressively Westernized, the flavor lent by the piano accordion—as played, for instance, by Paul Sells on the early '40s records of Gene Autry—became an almost essential ingredient of the product.

★ ★ ★

But for the first piano accordionist to make a mark in old-time music, we need look no further than Raney Van Vink (1899–1972). During 1927, he made three sides for Victor and a dozen for Okeh, partnered with the guitarist Homer Christopher (1905–77). (Writing about these musicians hitherto, I mistakenly assigned their instruments the other way round. Christopher did take up the accordion later, playing it with the WBT Briarhoppers in the '30s and '40s.) At the time, both men were living in Greenville or Spartanburg Counties, South Carolina. Honore Ray Van Vink (correctly Van Vynckt or Vanvynckt) was born in Ghent and came to the US in 1907 with his parents and siblings. Within a few years his father, Peter, and older brother Kamiel were employed in Greenville County textile mills. Raney initially followed them but then became an electrician with Southern Power and later Duke Power, a trade he followed all his life.

In October 1927, Van Vink won a piano accordion contest at the Egyptian Theatre in Greenville, and a few days later his local paper in Greer ran a story on this "musical prodigy" whose "talent of music is secondary with him, as his profession is electrical

Greer Musicians Sign With Record Concern

GREER, March 3—(Special)—Raymond Van Vink, one of the South's foremost piano-accordion players, and Homer Christopher, an expert guitar player, have just returned from Atlanta, where, upon invitation of the OKeh Record company, they made a number of records. While there they broadcasted their music. These Greer musicians have signed a two-year contract with the Okeh records.

Mr. Christopher resides at Suber, near Greer, and is engaged in farming. Mr. Van Vink is an electrician, and is the operator for the substation of the Piedmont and Northern railway, at this place. He was born in Ghent, Belgium.

Greenville [South Carolina] *News*, March 4, 1927. (Author's Collection)

operator of the sub-station for the Piedmont and Northern railway, at Greer."

> "Rainey," as he is called by his friends and admirers, had played an accordion all of his life, but four years ago he saved up $300 and purchased the great desire of his heart, a piano-accordion, and it is on this instrument that he plays the entrancing music that is usually rewarded with cash prizes (reprinted in *Greenville News*, November 3, 1927).

During 1927–28, Van Vink played several times at the Egyptian as an "Added Attraction De Luxe" to the movie program. From phrases in the ads like "He's Hot" and "Jazz Jazz," we might speculate that his repertoire was broader than the selection of marches, waltzes, and rags that he committed to record. "Going Slow," which he cut for both Victor and Okeh, was an ironic title, because it belted along, while "Spartanburg Blues" was a misleading one, since it was not a blues but a jolly ragtimey number, in which the ostensible lead and backup instruments merged into a duet of equals. (Okeh also issued "Spartanburg Blues" in its Mexican series, retitled "El Payaso"—"The Clown.")

★ ★ ★

Van Vink may be unique among recorded old-time musicians in his country of origin, but he was by no means the only one to have been born outside the United States. Some were English, like Arthur Bishop (➤21), or George Pickard, who sang bass in the Calhoun (Georgia) Sacred Quartet; or Scottish, like the Ohio-based Hawaiian guitarist James Brown. Damon Champagne, who played harmonica with the Rodeo Trio in El Paso, was from Ontario, Canada, as was the Atlanta-based actor Harold Selman, who recited "The Face on the Bar Room Floor" for Okeh's old-time series in 1928. The singing evangelists Perry Kim and Einar Nyland, who delivered attractive duets for Homer Rodeheaver's Rainbow label in the early 1920s, were from the Netherlands and Norway, respectively.

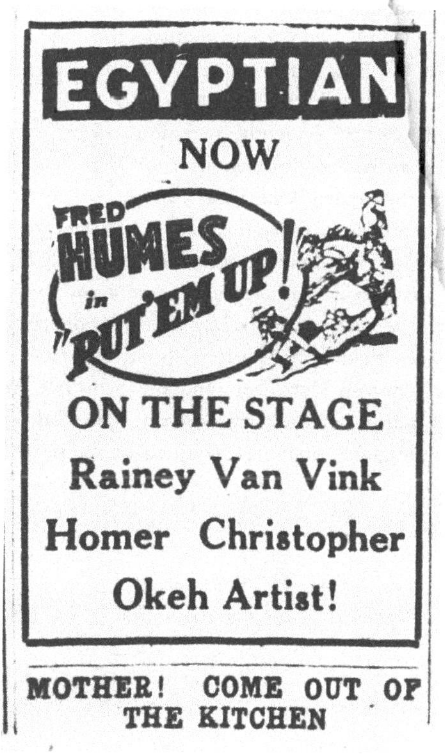

Ad in *Greenville* [South Carolina] *News*, May 5, 1928. (Author's Collection)

Okeh catalog of "Old Time Tunes," April 1927. (OTM Collection)

Also Dutch was Christine Endeback, who (without her surname) was popular on the WLS National Barn Dance in the '30s; also Norwegian was the singer and mandolin-player Carl Swanson, of the '30s act Jake and Carl (see *Country Music Originals*).

This rollcall takes no account of studio musicians who contributed to hillbilly records, such as the Italians William Carlino, who played banjo on numerous Vernon Dalhart sessions, and Alfred Cibelli (mandolin, cello); the German-born pianist Sam Jospe, who accompanied fiddler Don Richardson; and Meyer Gorodetzer, from Kiev in Russia, a theater violinist in Philadelphia whom Victor once called in to play with Kelly Harrell.

★ ★ ★

What are we to make of the music of Raney Van Vink? Where can we locate it on the spectrum of what we call old-time music? Okeh issued "Going Slow" and "Spartanburg Blues" amongst records by the Georgia fiddler Earl Johnson, the West Virginia singer-guitarist Frank Hutchison, and the Scottdale String Band (➤12), evidently regarding all these artists as representative of the genre they called "Old Time Tunes." To some enthusiasts today, this generous classification is puzzling. What have stringbands and hillbilly blues guitarists to do with ragtime piano accordionists? But what may seem to us like significant differences between them—in repertoire, in style, in the fact that Johnson, Hutchison, and the Scottdale crew were native Southerners, whereas Van Vink was an immigrant—may have counted, at the time, for very little. "Old Time Tunes," "Old Familiar Tunes," "Native American Melodies": these terms were deliberately big, baggy nets, intended to scoop up a mixed catch. If we attempt to define old-time music on the basis of cataloging decisions made almost a century ago, we shall be led inexorably to an equally baggy answer. So far as the record businessmen were concerned, old-time music was whatever they said it was.

12

"CARBOLIC RAG"/"STONE MOUNTAIN WOBBLE"

Scottdale String Band
Okeh 45118

Recorded in Atlanta, GA, March 21, 1927
Released on July 15, 1927

Reissued on *Old Folks Better Go to Bed* (Arhoolie CD7054) [both] • *Serenade in the Mountains* (JSP JSPCD7780) ["Carbolic Rag"]

Online: Spotify [both] • YT ["Stone Mountain Wobble"]

In the halcyon age of recorded country music, from the mid-1920s until the early '30s, not all instrumental groups were fiddle bands. Combinations of mandolins, banjos, and guitars were well represented on records too. Generally trios or quartets, some may have been drawn from, or connected with, the larger ensembles of stringed-instrument players found all over the country, often sponsored by instrument manufacturers, like Gibson or C. F. Martin, but seldom recorded. (A group called the Carolina Mandolin Orchestra played "Georgia Camp Meeting" and "Red Wing" for Okeh in New York in 1927; what one hears is a strongly recorded mandolin or two and a piano, over a background ripple of subsidiary mandolins.) Among the smaller recording bands, playing a wide repertoire of ragtime tunes, popular songs, waltzes, breakdowns, and blues, were the Proximity String Quartet from North Carolina (➤31), the Aiken County String Band from South Carolina, the Gibson String Trio from Cincinnati, and the Collier Trio from Leake County, Mississippi. But one such group stands out for its extensive and diverse legacy of sparkling performances: the Scottdale String Band.

During the 1920s, a sure sign of popularity for musical acts in and around Atlanta was an appearance on WSB. On January 29, 1927, the *Atlanta Journal* trailed a program that evening of "old-time fiddlin' selections, presented by a quartet of two guitars and two mandolins," identifying the players as Marvin Head and Ed Freeman, mandolins, and Eunice and Bonnie Pritchard, guitars. "The quartet has been heard at gatherings, clubs and fraternity meetings in Atlanta, and many of the selections which have proven so popular with their listeners will be repeated before the microphone for the invisible audience."

This, though the *Journal* did not tell its readers so, was the Scottdale String Band. They took their name from the cotton-mill village of Scottdale in DeKalb County, some eight miles northeast of downtown Atlanta. The first Scottdale mill, named after its founder, Col. George W. Scott, opened around 1901, and a village was built around it to house its employees and their families. With some 350 looms and 10,000 spindles, Scottdale Mills became a significant player in the north Georgia textile industry.

All the members of the band named by the *Journal* (or misnamed: "Ed Freeman" and "Bonnie Pritchard" were actually Belvie Freeman and Barney Pritchard) were Scottdale residents. John Marvin Head was the senior man, a native Georgian, born in 1889, and a longtime textile worker who spent a decade or more at Scottdale Mills. Belvie Freeman was born in 1904 in Gwinnett County and put in many years at Scottdale Mills, working as a doffer and rising to spinning-room overseer. Barney Lindsey Pritchard was also born in 1904, in Cliffside, North Carolina, another new cotton-mill town. After his mother died in the influenza epidemic of 1918, the family seems to have dispersed, and Barney is next heard of in South Carolina, where he married Eunice Roddy and fathered Barney, Jr., in 1922. The family then moved to North Carolina and, around 1925–26, to Scottdale, where Barney, Sr., worked as a plumber and in later years as a radio repairman.

When the band next appeared on WSB, on July 9, 1927, the *Journal* gave them their title: "The Scottdale

Barney Pritchard, Belvie Freeman or Charlie Simmons, Marvin Head. (OTM Collection)

String Band of Scottdale, Ga., O-keh [*sic*] recording artists of old-time and novelty numbers." The lineup was now a trio of Belvie Freeman on banjo-mandolin and Barney Pritchard and Marvin Head on guitars. The *Journal* also stated: "Included among the numbers to be given are two that will be recorded at an early date, the 'Carbolic Rag' and the 'Italian Glide.'"

The writer was behind the times. The Scottdale String Band had already recorded twice for Okeh, in October 1926 and March 1927, when they cut both "Carbolic Rag" and "Italian Glide" (renamed "Carolina Glide"). As record-collectors can testify, the releases from that second session were above average sellers. "Carbolic Rag" and its coupling "Stone Mountain Wobble" define the band's approach to peppy instrumentals, the melodic lead on banjo-mandolin buttressed by a fast-moving guitarist with a talent for double-time flatpicking.

On their next visit to Atlanta, in October 1927, Okeh had the band in to record again, but they may have undergone a personnel change. From the Okeh photograph and the press notices cited above, we deduce that the first two sessions were by the Freeman–Pritchard–Head trio, but Head's widow Eva, writing to researcher Bob Pinson in 1977, revealed that some of the band's recordings had a Charlie Simmons on mandolin. "Belvy [*sic*] Freeman," Eva Head wrote, "was the one that slipped around behind my husband & the other two men and let Gid Tanner & His Skillet Lickers have the tune 'Down Yonder,' but my husband, Charlie Simmons, [and] Barney Pritchard had already recorded it at the time so that's why Belvy Freeman wasn't in the band any more." Quite how Freeman could have "let Gid Tanner . . . have the tune 'Down Yonder'" is hard to say: he didn't write it, and the Scottdale String Band's recording was not the first in the old-time field.

Throughout their 1927–28 sessions, the band gave many of their tunes verbal decoration, often dance calls like "Peavine!," sometimes spur-of-the-moment comments like "Shake that thing!," "Step on it, boy!," "Watch him now!," or "Black bottom, do your stuff!" Such informality may owe something to black music. Scottdale, unlike some mill villages, was (and remains) a racially mixed community.

For a few years, the Scottdale String Band held one of the leading names in Okeh's catalog of "Old Time Tunes." Their success was noted in other quarters. Victor, talent grabbing in Atlanta in February 1928, recorded four sides by a Fulton County group consisting of banjo-mandolin, banjo, and two guitars, playing old-time dance tunes, an old popular song, and a rag. The Watkins Band echoed the Scottdale crew in repertoire, in instrumentation, and in peppering their tunes with dance calls, exhortations, and other chitchat, but their record sales did not match their rivals,' and they did not record again.

The Scottdale String Band made the trip to WSB's studio in the Biltmore Hotel at least twice in 1929, in January and May. The *Journal*, previewing the latter appearance, didn't identify the members, but the

Barney Pritchard (guitar) and probably Willie Sellers (banjo-mandolin). (Bill Rattray Collection)

WSB logbook names Marvin Head as their contact. The paper described them as "one of Georgia's best old-time fiddlin' units and recorders." As we know from earlier reports, the *Journal* was prone to using "fiddlin'" as a descriptor for old-time music regardless of whether any fiddles were involved, but at a March 1929 recording session the lineup was in fact expanded with two fiddlers. Eva Head thought they might have been Owen McDearis and Luke Talton, both men with a background in cotton-mill work and a connection with Scottdale.

At their final Okeh session, in December 1930, the band fielded two banjo-mandolins. Possibly the rift had been mended, and they had re-enlisted Belvie Freeman, who was living next door to Barney Pritchard on Stone Mountain Highway.

The last traces of the Scottdale String Band on record are two discs made at the Paramount studios in Grafton, Wisconsin, in the spring of 1932, which included a remake of "Stone Mountain Wobble," taken at a faster lick. The only certain member of the group is Pritchard, who is named on one of the records' labels. The discs, one issued late in the Paramount old-time series, the other late in the parallel Broadway series, were cast before an audience that had more important things to do with its money than buy phonograph records and are consequently almost impossible to find.

The group played on into the later '30s, sometimes augmented by Barney, Jr., and by Pritchard's brother-in-law John Roddy. But time was running out for the old gang. Marvin Head died in 1943 and Belvie Freeman in 1946. The last of the original Scottdale boys, Barney Pritchard, Sr., died in 1963. The Scottdale mill closed in 1982 and was destroyed in 2010–11. But the Scottdale boys are remembered, and today "Carbolic Rag" and "Stone Mountain Wobble" have secure places in the repertoire of country ragtime.

(Jim Bollman Collection)

13

"CHAIN GANG SPECIAL"/ "WALK RIGHT IN BELMONT"

Watts and Wilson
Paramount 3019

Recorded in Chicago, IL, c. early April 1927
Released in May/June 1927

Reissued on *My Rough and Rowdy Ways Vol. 1* (Yazoo 2039) ["Chain Gang Special"] • *Times Ain't Like They Used to Be Vol. 4* (Yazoo 2048), *Gastonia Gallop* (Old Hat CD-1007) ["Walk Right in Belmont"]

Online: Spotify, YT

Victor and Gennett got into old-time music in 1922, Okeh and Edison in 1923, Columbia and Vocalion in 1924. So in delaying its first serious engagement with this music until 1927, Paramount was arriving late at the station, with many of the trains long gone.

Not that it was a latecomer in the world of vernacular music: it had been assiduously recording African American singers like Alberta Hunter, Ida Cox, and Ma Rainey since 1922–23. This was profitable business, and the men who ran it from the offices of the Wisconsin Chair Company, Paramount's owners, may have seen no reason to diversify; but by mid-decade they would have been aware that their competitors were amassing considerable sales with white Southern artists like Fiddlin' John Carson, Henry Whitter, Uncle Dave Macon, and Riley Puckett. They released some recordings in their popular series, including a batch by Arthur Tanner and Earl Johnson in 1925, but there was no sense of a strategy. So when one of their regular suppliers of black talent, Harry Charles, a salesman for the E. E. Forbes & Sons Piano Company in Birmingham, Alabama, and freelance talent scout, expressed an interest in recording hillbilly music, they would have been disposed to trust his instinct.

Charles began to assemble a roster of recordable acts, which encouraged Paramount to initiate, as Columbia, Okeh, and Vocalion had already done, a catalog devoted to "Old Time Tunes," introduced in the spring of 1927. The first releases were by two of Charles's Alabama discoveries, the Edgewater Sabbath Singers from near Birmingham, and the Hugh Gibbs String Band from Huntsville. Next up was a duo, Watts and Wilson, whom Charles had test-recorded some months earlier and sent back to Chicago for a second session in April. Their first releases did considerably better than the Alabama acts: Paramount's recording manager Art Satherley remembered "Chain Gang Special"/"Walk Right in Belmont" as an above average seller.

Wilmer Watts was born in Mount Tabor, Columbus County, North Carolina, in 1896 or 1898, and in his boyhood learned to play fiddle, guitar, banjo, and other instruments. In his early twenties, he moved to Gaston County to participate in the expansion of employment opportunities in the textile mills. He would spend much of his life there, but he also lived for spells, and farmed, in Horry County, South Carolina, across the state line from Columbus County.

Alphonso Percy "Frank" Wilson was born in Virginia in February 1900. By the age of twenty, he was living in Burlington and employed as a twister in a cotton mill, and in that year he married a fellow cotton-mill worker and Burlington resident, Edna Totten. During the 1920s, he and Edna lived at various addresses in and around Burlington, where, in addition to mill work, he ran laundry and pressing businesses, and taught piano, violin, and guitar. He and Watts probably began playing together while both mill workers in Gaston County or, possibly, according to one account, in Charlotte. They were almost certainly spotted in one location or the other by Harry Charles, who was based in Charlotte for several months in 1926–27. Watts sang lead and played banjo on the recording, while Wilson sang tenor harmony and played steel guitar.

"Chain Gang Special" and "Walk Right in Belmont"—versions of two enduringly popular old-time songs, "Buddy, Won't You Roll Down the Line"

Frank Wilson. (OTM Collection, from Dot Moss)

and "Midnight Special," respectively—were rooted in Gaston County, specifically in Belmont, a community that owed its existence to cotton mills. The first to be built there, Chronicle Mills in 1901, was followed by Imperial Yarn Mills in 1905 and another two years later; by 1910, Belmont was the third-largest city in Gaston County, exceeded only by Gastonia and Bessemer City. Ten years on, it stood second after Gastonia, and it continued to hold that rank.

"A lively musical scene blossomed in Gaston County's working-class neighborhoods and textile towns," the historian Patrick Huber notes. "[C]rowded mill villages offered millhands greater opportunities to form string bands . . . and perform for appreciative audiences." To catch the ears of this rapidly growing community and coax coins from their pockets, Watts and Wilson scattered both songs with local allusions. In "Chain Gang Special," the narrator, identified by racial epithets as black, warns, "You lay around old Belmont, Call yourself a sport, In fifteen minutes they'll arrest you, And bind you over to court." "Walk Right in Belmont" begins: "Oh, when you go to Belmont, Well, you better walk right, And you better not gamble, And you better not fight." Ignore this advice and you'll be "chain gang bound." So this is in effect a companion song to the other, though not explicitly about a black experience.

★ ★ ★

The importance of these recordings is not merely that they sold well enough to justify Paramount's venture into the old-time market, but that they were the earliest recordings of songs shaped by the Southern textile industry. Wilmer Watts and Frank Wilson were not the first cotton-mill workers to make records: Fiddlin' John Carson and Henry Whitter had done so four years before, to be followed in 1925–26 by Kelly Harrell, George Walburn, Emmet Hethcox, and Charlie Poole. In later years, there would be dozens more, among them several featured in this book.

But Watts and Wilson were the first to make unmistakable references to mill culture. Anyone from their neck of the woods, catching the allusions to Belmont, would have known the kind of place the musicians were describing and the kind of people who lived there. They might have recognized the kind of people Watts and Wilson were, too: young men originally from the sticks, now citywise, alert to the risks and rewards of a rapidly growing urban culture. "Chain Gang Special" and "Walk Right in Belmont" are songs from the streets. You might argue that they are early examples of hillbilly rap.

A curious coincidence arises here. Around the time they initiated the "Old Time Tunes" catalog, Paramount's owners created a similar list on the Broadway label, devoted to "standard and Southern selections." Though a budget line (35 cents against Paramount's 75, and later even cheaper), Broadways were "Guaranteed To Play 500 Times!—250 times on each of the two sides or 500 times in all. Such a daring guarantee demonstrates our absolute faith in the quality of these records," trumpeted an ad placed by the St. Louis Music Co. mail-order company in the farm magazine *Southern Ruralist* (February 13, 1930). Many couplings from the Paramount old-time catalog were also issued on Broadway, but often with the artists' names replaced by made-up aliases. Two of the three discs from Watts and Wilson's April 1927 session came out on Broadway (though not "Chain Gang Special"/"Walk Right in Belmont," which is odd, if it had been a good seller for Paramount), and the pseudonym chosen for them was "Weaver and Wiggins." Fairly common Southern last names, beginning with the same letters as the originals: a neat enough artifice, often employed by record companies.

But it happened that both names were widespread in Gaston County, and one would soon have

Frank Wilson, ca. 1928. (Bob Cox Collection)

great resonance in that section. Ella May Wiggins, a twenty-nine-year-old spinner at the American Mill in Bessemer City, was a union activist, songwriter, and singer who took part in a dispute between the owners of the Loray Mill in Gastonia and the National Textile Workers' Union (NTWU). In the spring of 1929, this led to strikes in Gastonia and other mill towns, described by the historian W. J. Cash as "the first genuinely serious labor revolt the South had ever known." In September, turned back from a NTWU rally, Wiggins was ambushed by strikebreakers, shot, and killed.

And as for Weaver: what else were many of the men and women who worked alongside Watts and Wilson in the mills of Belmont?

★ ★ ★

Watts recorded again in late October 1929, when Harry Charles set up a session for Paramount in New York. He was now playing with guitarist Charles Freshour and steel guitarist Palmer Rhyne, as Wilmer Watts and The Lonely Eagles. The story of their song "The Fate of Rhoda Sweetin" is told on page 170.

Another song from that session, "Cotton Mill Blues," made explicit what "Chain Gang Special" and "Walk Right in Belmont" had touched upon obliquely. It is based on a poem, "A Factory Rhyme," written by the anthologist George D. Stutts of Alamance County, North Carolina, and published in a songbook around 1919 by his son John C. Stutts of Haw River, himself a cotton-mill worker. Watts adapts the opening stanza, moving Stutts's Greensboro narrator to Belmont but similarly describing it as "a lively town." The remaining verses are slightly reworded but do not dilute Stutts's disapproval of "uptown people" who dismiss mill workers as "the ignorant factory set."

October 1929 was a highly relevant time to be recording cotton-mill songs. All summer, the nation had been watching the Carolina Piedmont, some with approval, others with horror. The Loray Mill strike had been going since April, and there had been a large rally of the strikers and their supporters in mid-September. Mill workers in East Marion, North Carolina, also left their looms through July–September. In those days, the local response to strike action was swift and concerted: newspapers, respectful to the interests of the mill owners, represented it as Communism on the march, which it was the duty of law officers, hired strikebreakers, and often the National Guard to repel. They did so enthusiastically, almost always violently, and sometimes murderously. On October 2, about two weeks after the death of Ella May

(Author's Collection)

Wiggins, six strikers were killed at a demonstration in Marion, all shot in the back. Less than four weeks later, a few days before Watts recorded "Cotton Mill Blues," the West Virginia team of Frank Welling and John McGhee spent some of their time in Paramount's New York studio commenting on the strike and its bloody aftermath in a coupling, issued under the pseudonym "Martin Brothers," of "The North Carolina Textile Strike" and "The Marion Massacre." It is one of only two hillbilly records of the period to explicitly commemorate a strike; the other was Earl Shirkey and Roy Harvey's "The Virginian Strike of '23," about a walkout by railroaders (➤23). By an odd coincidence, the two recordings were made just days apart.

★ ★ ★

Wilmer Watts later moved to Bessemer City, where he formed a quartet with some of his daughters that sang on radio in Charlotte and Spartanburg, South Carolina. His last years were spent in St. Paul, North Carolina, where he ran a tourist home and gas station, and died from stomach cancer in 1943.

Frank Wilson pursued a musical career more assiduously. During 1928–29, he toured the vaudeville circuit and made records with the Hill Billies; he also recorded in his own name, with banjoist Jack Reedy, and with Charlie Bowman and His Brothers. Willie Sievers Wiggins of the Tennessee Ramblers (➤24) remembered meeting him in Ashland, Kentucky, in February 1928, by which time, she said, he was famous for having been in movies. (This probably refers to Vitaphone's short film about the Hill Billies [➤2].) Later the Ramblers played engagements with him in Tennessee, Florida, and possibly elsewhere. But because of Wilson's continual absences from home, his wife sued for divorce, which was granted in 1931. He may have kept in touch with the Hill Billies: Tony Alderman of the group said that the last time he saw him was in about 1935, evidently in Washington, DC.

"That sighting apart," I wrote in 2013, when I was annotating these Watts and Wilson sides for a gigantic Revenant/Third Man Records set devoted to Paramount Records, "Frank Wilson vanished from country music history, and indeed altogether: neither his ex-wife nor his daughters ever heard from or of him again." Reluctantly, for one never wants to give up on an investigation, I thought I was writing the last sentence in the story of Frank Wilson.

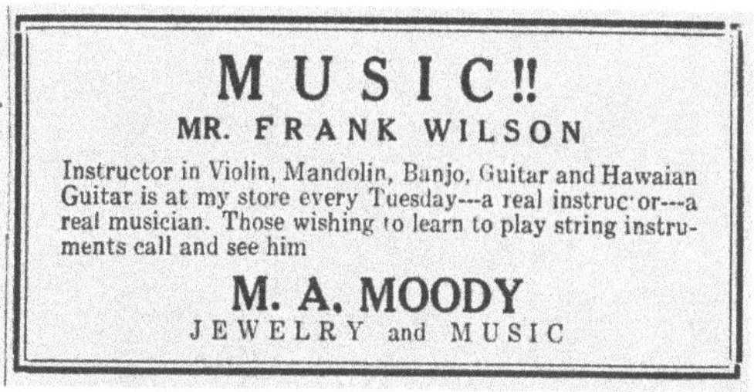

Ad in *Guntersville* [Alabama] *Advertiser & Democrat*, July 1, 1936. (Author's Collection)

In fact, there was a whole other story to be told.

★ ★ ★

Albertville, Alabama, 1936. Frank Wilson, who has been playing with a group—quite possibly the Tennessee Ramblers—in the small towns of southern Tennessee, Alabama, and Georgia, meets a young woman named Ellen Ardell Elliott. Ellen persuades her mother Letha to accompany her to the show. When Wilson appears, Ellen nudges Letha and says, "There is my husband on stage." The announcement doesn't go down well with her parents—he's seventeen years older and a traveling musician, for heaven's sake—but Ellen has her way and they are married. Wilson leaves the show and the couple move first to Georgia, then, in 1947, to Washington County, Florida, where they build a home south of Chipley, near Wausau, and raise a family.

"Dad started teaching private music lessons," Rick Wilson, their youngest son, told me.

> He would teach in the student's home, our home, or in churches, and built up a large number of students. He taught in Chipley, Wausau, Lynn Haven and Panama City, Florida, and in Dothan, Geneva, and Brantley, Alabama. The instruments he taught were piano, acoustic guitar, Spanish guitar, steel guitar, accordion, mandolin, banjo, organ, xylophone, and violin. He really didn't like to teach violin but if he had a student that wanted to learn the instrument he taught them. I remember him saying, "The violin played alone sounds like a cat having its tail pulled." He never taught classical nor rock 'n' roll. He said both types were noise not music.

His second family were well aware of Frank's musical past, since he reminisced about Al Hopkins, Wilmer Watts, and other former colleagues. But

Frank Wilson, 1947. (Courtesy of Rick Wilson)

there were subjects he was vague about. When he was called upon to give his birthplace, for instance when filling out birth certificates for his children, he might put down Butte, Montana, or Québec. In census years, Ellen would give the rest of the family's details but leave Frank out. He seemed to be doing his best to cover his tracks. Why the mystery? What did he have to hide?

"We often wondered if he had lost everything in the stock market crash in 1929 and was so devastated he never recovered," says Rick Wilson. "Then one day my brother Jim said, 'Do you think Dad could have been involved in criminal activity?'" Frank did talk about Al Capone, almost as if he had been acquainted with him and known about his activities. "It was as if Dad wanted to live a life of obscurity," Rick muses. "We grew up in poverty. He would not be employed by anyone. He never had a bank account. Here is a brilliant man and musician with unending talent that chose to live in this condition. . . ."

Frank Wilson died in Ellen's arms on August 10, 1972, while watching a rerun of *The Virginian*. It was one of his favorite TV programs, reminding him, perhaps, that he was a Virginian himself, back in that former life he had left so far behind.

14

"GRAY EAGLE"/ "FORKED DEER"

Hill's Virginia Mountaineers [Taylor's Kentucky Boys] Silvertone 8183

Recorded in Richmond, Indiana, April 26, 1927
Released c. August 1927

Reissued on *Kentucky Mountain Music* (Yazoo 2200)

Online: Spotify, YT

Offered a time machine and the chance to visit one occasion in old-time musical history, many enthusiasts would consider a trip to April 26–27, 1927, and the Gennett studio in Richmond, Indiana. Among the men who showed up to record on these two momentous days were the banjo player Marion Underwood (1882–1939), singer-guitarist Aulton Ray (1909–82), and fiddler Jim Booker (c. 1869–1940), assisted by guitarist Willie Young and singer Sam Deatherage (probably 1900–71), alias Sam Harris. Most, if not all, of these men were from the adjoining counties of Madison, Garrard, and Jessamine in east-central Kentucky. In different combinations, they made eleven remarkable recordings, with which the record company was so satisfied that it issued them on up to eight labels. Some of these, like the cheap Challenge and Silvertone releases advertised in Sears, Roebuck catalogs, sold quite well, with the happy consequence that collectors today can acquire, without undue financial stress, exceptional performances like Ray's "The Dixie Cowboy" or the pair of stringband trio performances by Booker, Underwood, and Young, "Gray Eagle" and "Forked Deer," which have been described by the collector and reissue producer Richard Nevins as "the most captivating single record of the period."

These trio sides are notable not just for the music: Underwood and Young were white, but Booker, then in his late fifties, was African American. Of the few recordings of old-time music made by a racially mixed group, these may be the earliest. (They precede by four months the African American fiddler Andrew Baxter's collaboration with the Georgia Yellow Hammers, "G Rag.") Arguably they are also the best.

What distinguishes all the recordings made at this session is how *odd* they sound. It had been recognized very early in recording history that banjos recorded loud, and if banjoists recorded with other musicians they needed to be placed much farther from the microphone. Raymond Hundley of Fieldale, Virginia, who recorded on banjo with the singer Kelly Harrell a month before the Kentuckians' session, told me how the Victor engineers placed him four or five feet back from the other musicians: "If I'd have been on the same level as the rest, they wouldn't have heard nobody but me."

No doubt Gennett's engineers did likewise: Underwood comes across clearly, but not at the expense of Booker, though Young is inaudible. But the acoustics of the studio itself lent the recordings an extraordinary character, hard, hollow, and resonant, as if the musicians were playing in a steel shipping container. It wasn't something specific to this occasion: six days earlier, recordings by a group of African American musicians from St. Louis, Henry Johnson's Boys, had had the same airy, not to say eerie, echoing acoustics.

"Gray Eagle" and "Forked Deer" are among the most exhilarating recordings of their era: intricate melodies, flawlessly executed, yet with an energy that elevates them above mere skillful demonstrations of tunes. Disconcertingly, "Gray Eagle" suddenly ends halfway through a strain, the musicians responding too hastily to a "wind it up" light from the control room. "Forked Deer" finishes more neatly. Alan Lomax, entering it in his *List of American Folk Songs on Commercial Records* in 1942, described it as a "fine piece of square dance music."

Gennetts of Old Time Tunes

Taylor's Kentucky Boys

TAYLOR'S KENTUCKY BOYS

FORKED DEER—*Old Time Playin'*
GRAY EAGLE—*Old Time Playin'* } 6130 .75

Marion Underwood (banjo), Aulton Ray (guitar), and possibly Dennis W. Taylor, sitting in for the African American fiddler Jim Booker. From a 1927 Gennett catalog. (OTM Collection)

Later that day, Booker and Underwood accompanied the teenaged Aulton Ray on a couple of songs, and Underwood recorded a pair of vocal duets with the stentorian Deatherage/Harris. The following day, Ray recorded two more numbers, and Underwood played an astonishing version of a local tune, "Coal Creek March."

★ ★ ★

During the Kentuckians' second day at the microphone, the Gennett engineers made time for a couple of "personal" recordings. Into the studio came William Ryley Rhinehart, a forty-four-year-old mechanic from Muncie, Indiana, and his pianist Hattie Fletcher Buckles. What Gennett's ledger clerk meant when he or she logged these as "personal" wasn't that they were vanity recordings (though Gennett did that kind of work) but that they were custom-made for a specialty label. In this case, the label was called 100%. The selections were "The Pope's Warning" and "Klansman's Round-Up."

For Gennett, this was business as usual. Rhinehart had been dropping into the studio regularly since 1924, the year in which he co-authored the songbook *The Klansman's Friend*. The Ku Klux Klan, which in the early 1920s was stronger in Indiana than anywhere else in the nation, and effectively the state's political masters, had seized upon the phonograph as a medium for disseminating its message. Rhinehart was one of a group of singers who specialized in recording Klan-friendly songs and parodies that were issued for the delectation of Klan members on Gennett-manufactured labels like 100% or KKK. Rhinehart advertised in the Muncie paper that "Klan records and piano rolls" were available from his home address.

Major record companies such as Victor and Columbia had no truck with this trade. Thomas Edison listened to one of Gennett's Klan recordings and noted, "Don't bother with this trash." Gennett did bother because, unlike its contemporaries, it was an all-purpose manufacturer. The Richmond studio might as well have had a sign over its door: "We Record Anyone." Among the individuals and organizations for whom they made recordings to be issued on private labels were the James D. Vaughan gospel music publishing company of Lawrenceburg, Tennessee, which commissioned more than fifty discs for the Vaughan label; the O'Byrne de Witt Irish music stores in New York City and Boston; the Chicago-based Nazarene evangelist and mandola-player E. Arthur Lewis, on the Lewis label; and the gospel-singing Garner brothers, on the Jubilee Gospel Singers label. George and Robert Garner must have been acquainted with Rhinehart, since they too were from Muncie (the subject, unidentified at the time, of Robert and Helen Lynd's celebrated sociological work of 1929, *Middletown: A Study in Modern American Culture*) and were busy propagandists for the Klan, traveling with the evangelist Lewis King of Toledo, Ohio, whose anti-Catholic rants caused riots in several Midwestern cities in the 1920s.

Though a familiar figure in the Gennett studios, Rhinehart may not have known that the engineers who recorded his Klanthems had been similarly occupied, a couple of days earlier, with an African American blues singer and guitarist, Sam Collins.

Marion Underwood and the band he took to the World's Fair in Chicago, 1933. (Courtesy of Sue Mize)

Today, we may find it morally satisfying that, although the recordings of Booker, Underwood, and company were bookended in time and space by a black bluesman and an apologist for white supremacy, Collins's recordings, like theirs, are both valued by collectors and alive in modern media, whereas the legacy of W. R. Rhinehart (who committed suicide in 1936 by swallowing carbolic acid) is all but forgotten, and, if his records are collected, it's by people who don't talk about it.

★ ★ ★

Booker, Underwood, Young, and the rest of the group did not roll up in Richmond by chance. They had been introduced to Gennett by Dennis Woodson Taylor, a well-to-do farmer in Madison County, Kentucky, who had been connecting local talent with Gennett since 1925, when he sent to Richmond the fiddler Doc Roberts, guitarist Edgar Boaz, and singer Welby Toomey. Roberts would become a mainstay of Gennett's hillbilly catalog. Over the next few years, Taylor would add to the roster of his informal agency the singer-guitarist Asa Martin, from Clark County, who made scores of records both solo and with Roberts, as well as numerous other guitarists, singers, and fiddlers, some of whom made a good deal of money for Gennett—and, thanks to his agreement with the record company, a fair amount for Taylor, too.

Taylor was also aware of local African American music and sent several exponents to Gennett: "Big Boy" George Owens of Lancaster, in Garrard County (where Underwood also lived), who recorded a "Kentucky Blues"; Jim Booker and his brothers, who recorded as the Booker Orchestra; and the aforementioned Sam Collins, who may have lived in Madison County at the time. Another industry fixer of the period, Harrison Smith, recalled "finding" Collins in Kentucky and introducing him to Gennett, but Taylor was the strongest link in this chain. Collins's recordings, the royalties for which Gennett paid directly to Taylor, were always made at sessions alongside those by other artists he managed. Evidently, every few months, Taylor organized troupes of recordable musicians, black and white, and dispatched them to Richmond. We shall detect his hand again in recordings made a couple of years later by Leonard Rutherford, John Foster, Byrd Moore, and Melvin Robinette (➤37).

Talent spotters, such as Dennis Taylor, filled a vital role in identifying and promoting regional music in the 1920s, by creating lines of communication with the record companies and supplying them with musicians who fulfilled the needs of their catalogs, whether they were blues singers, old-time stringbands, or gospel quartets. These men were seldom altruists: most of them were in it for their commission. But without their intermediacy, much of the music we now value would never have been preserved.

15

"THE PICTURE ON THE WALL"/"MY CAROLINA GIRL"

Georgia Yellow Hammers
Victor 20943

Recorded in Charlotte, NC, August 9, 1927 ["Picture"]/August 10, 1927 ["Girl"]
Released in October/November 1927
Sold 115,881

Reissued on *The Georgia Yellow Hammers and Associates Vol. 2 (1927–1928)* (Document DOCD-8068) [both] • *Old Mountain* (ASV Living Era CD AJA5577) ["The Picture on the Wall"]

Online: Spotify, YT

Like "The Little Old Log Cabin in the Lane," "The Picture on the Wall" is a song about remembering and what prompts it: the trigger that fires the synapse that sets off the process of creating or retrieving a memory. Here it is that simplest of mementos, "an old and faded picture on the wall, that's been hanging there for many, many years."

Around 1927, brooding upon one of these venerable objects, George "Bud" Landress of Gordon County, Georgia, wrote what would become his most enduring composition. As the journalist Lloyd Gulledge told the story years later, Bud

> was inspired to write the song one night after he had plowed corn all day. After going to bed, he became fascinated with a picture hanging on the wall in his bedroom and the idea to make a song about it was born. The picture, however, was not one of his mother, about whom the song was written. He got out of bed, wrote the words and "sawed out the tune" on his old fiddle. Several hours later when the composition was finished, he awakened his wife and sang it to her for an opinion. . . .

The title phrase was already in the public domain, attached to a poem by Henry C. Work, published in 1864, though there too the image is not of a mother but of a son who perished in the Civil War.

★ ★ ★

On August 4, 1927, the *Calhoun* [Georgia] *Times* carried this story:

> Calhoun Talent Making More Records. The Georgia Yellow Hammers, Gordon county's own breakdown music makers[,] will be at Charlotte, North Carolina, all next week making more Victor records. This organization has made a big hit on records and the Victor Company call it their best break-down orchestra. A number of new fiddling and singing numbers will be put on record by this outfit next week. Members of the organization going to Charlotte are: Bud Landress, fiddler; Ernest Moody, banjo-uke; Clyde Evans, guitar, and Phil Reeve, steel guitar. Phil Reeve and Ernest Moody will also make a number of yodling [*sic*] records and several southern melodies in duet form with guitar and ukulele. The boys will have a big time "High high high up in the hills."

The Georgia Yellow Hammers had made their debut for Victor six months earlier, in Atlanta and a different lineup, without Moody and Evans, but with Bill Chitwood as fiddler rather than Landress, who played banjo. Chitwood would figure in most of the Yellow Hammers' subsequent recordings, so his absence in August is puzzling. However, between the two Victor sessions, there had been one for Okeh, billed as by "Bill Chitwood and His Georgia Mountaineers," and Chitwood may have been (or thought he was) contractually bound to that company.

The Yellow Hammers offered something different, a blend of stringband music and quartet singing, a provocative alliance of the Saturday night hoedown and the Sunday singing convention. It was not a sound that had been common on hillbilly records, but after the Yellow Hammers, and perhaps because of them, it began to be heard from groups far away, like the Leake County Revelers in Mississippi or Dr. Smith's Champion Hoss Hair Pullers in Arkansas.

Both "The Picture on the Wall" and "My Carolina Girl" were arranged by Moody, who may also have written the words of "My Carolina Girl"; the tune is one known to old-time fiddlers as "Merry Widow Waltz." The verses of "Picture" were sung by Landress, joined by the other three on the chorus, over a steady two-beat rhythm; it was a nice touch to have the last chorus sung partly sotto voce. "My Carolina Girl" sounds like a trio of Moody, Reeve, and Evans. Coupled on Victor 20943, this pair of songs would rewrite the band's future.

★ ★ ★

The Charlotte-bound crew was an interesting blend of personalities. Landress (1882–1966) was a farmer, Moody (1891–1977) a hymn writer and church choir director; Reeve (1897–1949) and Evans (1906–74) worked in Calhoun stores. J. Max Barnette, who came along to play organ on the gospel songs, was a public-school teacher. The five men made the trip, as Moody recalled twenty-five years later, in a Model T Ford containing them and all their instruments, including the organ. Their stay in Charlotte yielded stringband sides by the Yellow Hammers, duets by Reeve and Moody, and a gospel quartet coupling under the billing "Turkey Mountain Singers," named after the peak in nearby Floyd County.

Traveling separately were two other Calhoun musicians, the African American fiddler Andrew Baxter (1874–1955) and his son Jim (1898–1950), who played guitar. Andrew would play, uncredited, on one of the Yellow Hammers' sides, "G Rag."

The Calhounians' two days' work in Charlotte on August 9–10 may be the best contemporaneously documented recording session of the period. An article describing the Yellow Hammers' session on August 9 appeared in the *Charlotte Observer* and was promptly reprinted by the *Calhoun Times*. A week later the *Times* talked to the musicians, now back in Calhoun, and ran its own piece. But as well as these accounts of the music, we know something of the contractual and financial background from papers kept by Phil Reeve, the band's business manager. He worked at a Calhoun music store, Moss Music, owned by his stepfather Lawrence Moss, and was responsible for the phonograph record side of the business. No doubt he used this insider position to make the initial contact with Victor's recording director Ralph Peer and pitch the idea of recording Calhoun musicians.

On August 10, Reeve, Landress, and Moody, representing the Yellow Hammers (Evans was evidently regarded as an employee rather than a partner), signed a one-year recording contract with Peer as "Manager" for $50 per selection plus travel expenses. They also signed a contract in respect of the eight pieces they had just recorded, for a royalty of 45/100 cent per selection on all records sold, plus 2 cents per copy on sheet music sales. Reeve and Moody had similar contracts for their duet recordings.

Bud Landress and his teenaged son Roy, late 1920s. (Author's Collection, from the late Dixie Landress)

Phil Reeve (standing, third from left) played cornet in the orchestra of the Calhoun Methodist Church in the early 1920s. His wife Jewell (seated, third from left) played piano on the 1927 recording of the Calhoun Sacred Quartet, which included both Phil and Ernest Moody. Fiddler Gus Boaz (seated, far right) also recorded with Reeve and Moody. (OTM Collection)

It was as well that the band had someone with inside knowledge to negotiate these business arrangements, for they were about to make a good deal of money. "The Picture on the Wall"/"My Carolina Girl," the second release from the Charlotte session, opened its sales log in the last quarter of 1927 with a respectable 7,324, in the first quarter of 1928 more than doubled that figure to 15,562, dipped slightly in the next to 13,304, then rose in the last two quarters of 1928 to 16,943 and 15,948, yielding a total for the year of 61,757. Through 1929 and 1930, the record continued to outsell all the band's other discs put together. In the fall quarter of 1930, for example, it registered sales of 970; the band's next biggest seller achieved only seventeen. By that point, Victor 20943 had sold over 115,000 copies, putting it in the same sales sector as the Skillet-Lickers and the Carter Family.

There would—or should—have been more money coming to Bud Landress from other people's versions of "The Picture on the Wall": it was recorded by Posey Rorer and the North Carolina Ramblers, McGhee and Welling, and Walter Smith and Buster Carter, though theirs was retitled "I Know I'll Meet My Mother After All," probably so that the company could evade paying the (uncredited) writer. But the Carter Family's 1932 Victor recording bore Landress's name, as did its reissues on Bluebird and Montgomery Ward, the latter selling over 30,000 copies, one of the store label's biggest hillbilly hits. In 1936, Mainer's Mountaineers recorded it as "The Old and Faded Picture," and in 1940, the Blue Sky Boys did too. "The Picture on the Wall" can fairly be called a standard of old-time country music.

★ ★ ★

Clyde Evans. (Courtesy of Anita Davis)

Ernest Moody, stringband musician and hymnographer. (OTM Collection)

In the context of a song about memory, it's interesting how some of the band chose to recall their own pasts. To the end of his days, Bud Landress would cheerfully talk about his career in music, which, if he'd had his way, he would never have quit. Ernest Moody reported to Lloyd Gulledge in 1952, with some bemusement—since most of his music-making had been for God rather than Victor Records—that "I made more money on that record ["The Picture on the Wall"/"My Carolina Girl"] than with any other single musical enterprise." Phil Reeve, however, though he continued to handle the band's royalty statements, and as late as 1942 wrote to Peer, "If ever you need any hill billy records again we would like a trial on them," shared little of his musical backstory with his family, and his grandchildren grew up knowing nothing about it.

Then, one day, his grandson Robin told me, someone found a copy of Phil's duet record with Moody "Down Where the Watermelon Grows," and Robin asked his father, C. P., to explain it. The story, as C. P. had heard it from *his* father, was that Phil was driving to Charlotte one day when he met three men on the road and gave them a ride. It turned out that they were musicians on the way to make records. During the trip, Phil said, he and Moody wrote the song, and they recorded it, and then he was invited to join the band.

It was an ingenious fiction. In fact, "Watermelon" was recorded at the Calhounians' first session, in Atlanta, the song was a minstrel composition from twenty years earlier, and Phil Reeve already knew the other Yellow Hammers. Yet for some reason his five years of productive involvement in local music—his many other records with the band, his administration of their finances, his managerial involvement with the Baxters and other artists—all of that, for his descendants, was to be a picture with its face turned to the wall.

16

"YOU CAN'T MAKE A MONKEY OUT OF ME"

Eva Quartette with W. J. Smith Gennett 6239

Recorded in Birmingham, AL, August 11, 1927
Released on October 15, 1927

Online: YT (*Robert Crumb Old Time Radio Show*)

You can't make a monkey out of me,
You can't make a monkey out of me.
I am human through and through,
All my aunts and uncles too,
And you can't make a monkey out of me.

The lines are by the celebrated hymnographer J. R. Baxter, Jr. (1887–1960). They are not among his best remembered. Modern collections of his work ignore the song, and online folios of yesteryear's melodies offer several different compositions under that title.

These songs were all published in 1925–26, when the phrase "You can't make a monkey out of me" achieved currency because of a major cause celèbre: the case of the *State of Tennessee v. John Thomas Scopes*, a twenty-four-year-old substitute teacher at Rhea County High School, concerning the teaching, then illegal in state-funded public schools, of Charles Darwin's theory of evolution by natural selection. "In the Tennessee mountains," the *Boston Herald* helpfully explained to its readers, "R. F. D. does not mean Root for Darwin." Because the author of *The Origin of Species* had argued (not, originally, in early editions of that epoch-making work, but in the later *The Descent of Man*) that *Homo sapiens* had evolved from ape ancestors, the journalists watching the proceedings at the Rhea County courthouse in Dayton, Tennessee, during July 1925—among them prominent figures like H. L. Mencken of the *Baltimore Sun* and Joseph Wood Krutch of *The Nation*—dubbed it the "monkey trial."

Three weeks before the trial commenced, a columnist in an Iowa paper had remarked:

> [T]he trial will serve two purposes. It will stimulate interest in Darwin and what he really wrote, and likewise, in the heretofore obscure biology teacher. Mr. Scopes will undoubtedly vie with Harry Snodgrass [a pianist in a Missouri prison orchestra who had brief radio fame in the early 1920s—TR] in receiving the adulations of vaudeville fans. Very shortly we may look for a popular song entitled, "You can't make a monkey out of my grandpop," or some equally enlightening caption. (*Sumner Gazette*, June 25, 1925)

The journalist was probably just being flippant, but in fact the Scopes affair sent a clear message to songwriters and record-company managers: monkey trial = money trial. In the "Old Familiar Tunes" sector, Columbia were quickest off the mark, with Vernon Dalhart—of course—singing "The John T. Scopes Trial," written by Carson Robison under the name Carlos B. McAfee, and recorded on July 10, the day the trial opened. It was coupled with a Robison song about the Santa Barbara earthquake of June 29 to make a hotly topical two-header that sold almost 80,000 copies.

At the end of the twelve-day trial, Scopes was found guilty, but the Tennessee Supreme Court overturned the verdict on a technicality. It hardly mattered: the case was not about an individual but about a doctrine. As Mencken said to the defense counsel Clarence Darrow, "Nobody gives a damn about that yap schoolteacher. The thing to do is to make a fool out of Bryan." William Jennings Bryan, the distinguished old statesman and Christian fundamentalist, had volunteered his service for the prosecution. It was his last public appearance, for he died five days after the trial ended.

(Center for Popular Music)

Actually, the case was just as much about boosterism, for the whole thing was set in motion by local businessmen, in collaboration with the American Civil Liberties Union and the accommodating Scopes, as a means of publicizing their city. "Dayton," they declared, "would be woefully remiss in her duty to herself not to grasp this hour of her lime-light incandescence." But when the limelight was switched off, the city remained much as it had been, and so did the law: teaching evolution in Tennessee public schools remained illegal until 1967. The Dayton boosters' business plan was finally vindicated nine decades later when the Rhea Heritage Preservation Foundation instigated an annual Scopes Festival and Trial.

★ ★ ★

Less than a month after Dalhart's recording, Vocalion responded with a version by the blind street singer Charles Oaks, coupled with an appropriate memorial piece, "The Death of William Jennings Bryan." (At the same session, Oaks plucked twice more at Dalhart's coattails, covering his Floyd Collins and Mary Phagan songs [➤4] for a back-to-back release.) In October, another blind street singer, Charles Nabell, recorded for Okeh a more detailed account of the proceedings, "Scope's [*sic*] Trial." Meanwhile, Dalhart recorded his song for several other labels.

The following year, more singers and songwriters pitched into the debate. The Nazarene evangelist E. Arthur Lewis recorded his composition "If I Came from a Monkey" for his own label, while Uncle Dave Macon gave his opinion on the matter in "The Bible's True" (Vocalion):

> Evolution teaches man came from a monkey,
> I don't believe no such a thing in the days of a
> week of Sundays.
> God made the world and everything that's in it,
> He made man perfect and the monkey wasn't in it.
> For the Bible's true, oh, yes, I believe it!
> I've seen enough and I can prove it.
> It's what you say, what you say,
> It's bound to be that way.

A few months later, Charlie Poole, riding high on the success of his first two Columbia releases, revived a twenty-year-old comic song recorded by the pioneer phonographist Cal Stewart, "Monkey on a String." According to the Stewart version, "Some say one time we all was monk's, Some say the other way: That a monk' was made from odds and ends On the great creation day." Poole garbles some of this, but then strikes out into extratextual country, turns Darwinism on its head, and proclaims that monkeys are descended from humans, specifically Irishmen.

It was also in 1926 that Baxter wrote "You Can't Make a Monkey out of Me," fulfilling the Iowa columnist's prediction almost to the letter. In the same year, he joined the Texan singer and music teacher Virgil O. Stamps to found the Stamps–Baxter Music & Printing Company, which helped to uncage his monkey song into the world of gospel quartet singing. It was recorded by the Eva Quartette in 1927, the Gentry Family from Nashville (Victor, 1928), the Hodges Quartet from Corbin, Kentucky (Columbia, 1928), and the Ashford Quartette from West Virginia (Brunswick, 1929).

The first of these recordings was probably the most successful, certainly the most widely disseminated. The Eva Quartette were the Morgan brothers, Frank (1903–92) and Fred (1895–1955), from Eva in Morgan County, Alabama, and Wyatt Judson Smith (1878–1962) and Otis Self (1896–1970), from adjacent Cullman County. Smith's son Ossie

The Eva Quartette. Below left, Wyatt J. Smith. (Author's Collection)

played the organ accompaniment. They journeyed to Birmingham twice in the summer of 1927 while Gennett was conducting recordings in the city. The company evidently thought well of their performances, issuing them not only on Gennett and Champion but also on the Sears labels Silvertone, Supertone, and Challenge, often cross-coupled with numbers by the Woodlawn Quartette (from a district in northeast Birmingham), so that the Eva Quartette's six issued sides ultimately appeared on twenty-eight discs. "Monkey" itself was on seven. Surprisingly, the company never called them back for further recordings.

★ ★ ★

Monkeys had scampered down Tin Pan Alley before. Pieces like "In Monkey Land" (1907) or "Moving Day in Jungle Town" (1909) belong to a time when explorers and big-game hunters were filing reports to the US press from faraway places populated by exotic animals and bringing some of them back to stock American zoos. Greetings-card versifiers, book illustrators, and writers of popular songs, always ready to make animals behave like humans, hastened to equip the monkey for the New World. But there was also a dark side to Jungle Town. In an acute article on music inspired by Darwinism, Vassiliki Betty Smocovitis writes:

> Obsessed with African themes and primitivist motifs that played on attitudes about race, gender, and ethnicity, popular audiences were entertained by fantasy worlds like "Monkeyland," where anthropomorphic Africanized monkeys frolicked, canoodled and spooned, or otherwise engaged in sexualized "monkey business" under the bamboo, coconut, or banyan trees. . . . Such simian motifs were so heavily used that the mere mention of Darwinian monkeys became coded for a racist attitude that gained widespread acceptance among . . . audiences who avoided more explicit slurs. . . . [T]he monkey and jungle themes were also used heavily against evolutionists by moralists and religious leaders . . . who called evolution "the jungle theory." The same Darwinian monkeys were featured again in musical-comedic form during and after [the Scopes trial] . . . and contributed to the carnivalesque or circus-like atmosphere associated with it.

Dr. Smocovitis instances Dalhart's trial song and the several "You Can't Make a Monkey out of Me"s before tracing an evolutionary line, down to the present day, of songs about Darwinism—perhaps the only common theme to have inspired the Incredible String Band, Elvis Costello, Bruce Springsteen, and Weird Al Yankovich.

A song that eluded Dr. Smocovitis is "My Evolution Girl," recorded in 1931 by the Carolina Buddies: singer and songwriter Walter Smith, fiddler Odell Smith, and guitarist Norman Woodlieff. The

Left, Wyatt and Ossie Smith. (Author's Collection)

singer encounters a young woman with red cheeks, sparkling eyes, and chestnut-brown hair, and learns to "love her well." But unfortunately this paragon has two strikes against her: "She believes in evolution and she lives in New York town." Alarmed, he attempts conversion (though not relocation), appealing to old-time religion rather than to science. "Be a better girl, and prepare to meet the Savior in a bright and better world. . . . Don't believe in evolution, or the Devil will get your soul." Since he has told us that the young woman doesn't believe in the Savior or Hell, this may not be an effective argument. But logic is perhaps not always at a premium in this debate.

★ ★ ★

Present-day listeners for whom Darwinism is a done deal may be disposed to find "You Can't Make a Monkey out of Me" amusing and to assume that Baxter intended it to be. They would be mistaken. It was written expressly to support "the blessed Bible plan," the biblical account of divine creation, and to paint any other explanation as both irreligious and absurd. It even attempted a quasi-scientific rebuttal of evolution, albeit one that betrayed some confusion about what Darwin had proposed: "If a man ever came from a monkey, as some say, They'd be coming now, and would ever be; But mankind is the same in all ages and today . . ." Such an affirmative message, delivered by a quartet of upstanding community members, very often in church, would be taken as seriously as any other didactic or cautionary song in the gospel repertoire.

That message would no doubt command respect from many congregations today, though perhaps less effectively when couched in verse of antique simplicity. Yet, though the song may have passed out of general use, the phrase has not. In 2012, Andrew F. Babick, a children's writer from Michigan, published "a fun book that teaches children the basic biblical principles that will help them . . . work through the confusing teachings about creation taught in today's schools." His title was *You Can't Make a Monkey out of Me*, which I suppose you might call a natural selection.

17

"A CORN LICKER STILL IN GEORGIA"— PARTS 1 AND 2

Clayton McMichen, Riley Puckett, Gid Tanner, Lowe Stokes, Fate Norris, Bob Nichols, and Bill Brown
Columbia 15201-D

Recorded in Atlanta, GA, November 1, 1927
Released in February 1928
Sold 160,693

Reissued on *Gid Tanner and His Skillet Lickers: A Corn Licker Still in Georgia* (Voyager VRCD303)

Online: Spotify, YT

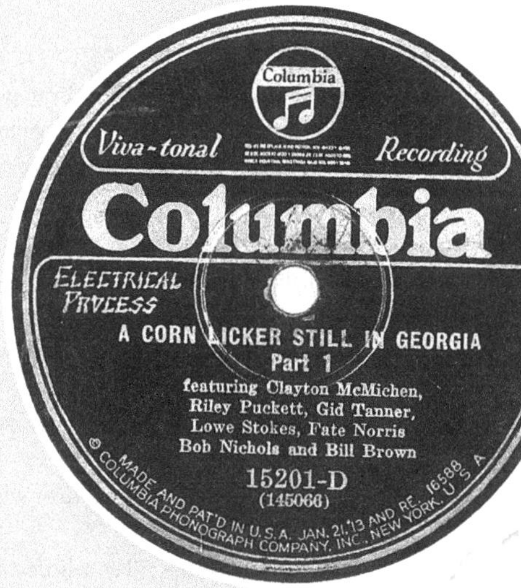

In 1927, Prohibition was eight years old. Described by Herbert Hoover at its outset as "a great social and economic experiment, noble in motive but far-reaching in purpose," it had been curiously unsuccessful in imposing temperance upon the American people. As Bert Layne would observe in a song he wrote and recorded three years later, "Prohibition is a failure, most anyone can see, For whiskey's sold in every town in the good old U. S. A."

"If anything was needed to suggest how ubiquitous was the illicit still," argued the historian Frederick Lewis Allen, "the figures for the production of corn sugar provided it. Between 1919 and 1929 the output of this commodity increased *sixfold*, despite the fact that as [a report] put it, the legitimate uses of corn sugar 'are few and not easy to ascertain.' Undoubtedly corn whisky [*sic*] was chiefly responsible for the vast increase."

It was against this backdrop that six men gathered in Atlanta, one winter day, to perform a comic sketch. (The other name in the lineup, Bob Nichols, was an alias of Clayton McMichen. The dialogue has been slightly edited.)

ACT 1. *Somewhere in the woods of north Georgia.*
Riley sings "Rye Whiskey" with the band.
Sound effect.

MAC: Here, here, we can't have all this fuss around here. If we're gonna make this liquor, why, let's make it and get through with it.

He assigns jobs to Riley, Gid, Lowe, and Fate.

All right, let's have a little tune now, Fate.

He and Fate play "Soldier's Joy."

All right, that's a good tune.

He checks with Riley, Gid, Lowe, and Fate that they've done their jobs.

All right now, there's no use to be in no hurry, because we don't want to scorch this liquor. And if you fellows want to take a little drink, why, we'll take it *after* the liquor starts—'cause I know you, if you get started drinking liquor, why, we won't have no music. So we'll have another little tune.

RILEY: How about us takin' a drink first?

MAC: No, I know you too well . . .

Riley sings "Whoa Mule" with the band.
Sound effect.

Hey, hey—who's that comin' through the gap down there? Who is that feller, you know him?

ACT 2. *The same. Sound of a car horn.*

MAC: Ah, that's old Slim, ain't it? Hello there, Slim!

STOKES: Hello, Mac, how are you? . . . Seems like you got a bunch of good music 'round here.

MAC: Yeah, I got lots of it. There's a bunch of my boys I got hired 'round here, good stringband too. Fine, yeah.

STOKES: What do you get for your stuff, Mac?

MAC: You want the best, I guess. Well, I can give you sweet mash for two and a half a gallon, I can give you sugar liquor for two dollars—that is, if you've got your own cans with you.

STOKES: Heh-heh. A little high, ain't you, Mac?

MAC: Aaaah, high enough . . . you fellows get twenty-two pints to a gallon down there in Atlanta, and want me to *give* you my liquor, don't you?

STOKES: Heh, heh, heh. Pretty good for you, Mac. How about settin' me up?

MAC: How'd you like to hear a little tune while the boys is fittin' you up?

STOKES: Yeah, that'll be fine. Play a little tune while I'm waitin'.

The band plays "Black-Eyed Susie."
Sound effect.

REVENUE OFFICER (BILL BROWN): Right, you boys, stick 'em up there, we've got you covered. Watch that big boy over there by the bushes, Tom, he's tryin' to get away. What are you boys startin' 'round here? Who's runnin' this place?

MAC: (*He sounds drunk.*) I—I—I'm runnin' it myself . . .

BROWN: What kind of a run you got started?

MAC: We, we got about five, five hundred gallons . . .

BROWN: I'm sorry, I'm gonna have to bust you up and take you down to Gainesville.

MAC: Look like there's some way to get out of this now . . . here, taste it.

BROWN: Well, that is pretty good liquor, I'll admit. What's all these instruments doin' round here? Can they fiddle? I'd like to hear a little music if they can play . . .

MAC: All right, boys, come on, play him a little tune now. Whoop it on up—it's either play or go to jail.

Riley sings "Pass Around the Bottle and We'll All Take a Drink" with the band.

BROWN: Well, they're fiddlin' fools all right, aren't they? That's fine whiskey. I'll tell you what I'm gonna do, Mac. You seem to be a pretty decent boy.

MAC: I . . . try to be.

BROWN: We'll let you off this time, if you give me about ten of those cans. Can you do that?

MAC: Man, I'll give you a hundred if you want—and the still and all. All right, boys, fix him up a hundred of them there.

BROWN: I want you to keep quiet from here on. Keep quiet.

MAC: Ah, we sure will.

BROWN: Good luck to you, boys.

ALL: Goodbye!

This vignette so tickled record-buyers that it sold almost as well as the first, hugely successful, discs of old-time songs that this circle of musicians had made a year and a half earlier, under the name of Gid Tanner and His Skillet-Lickers. In April 1928, the cast was summoned back to record a follow-up, and, over the next two and a half years, they added a new two-part disc to the "Corn Licker Still" series every time Columbia Records' location-recording team came to Atlanta. The actors now included Dan Hornsby, like Bill Brown an Atlantan and a Columbia employee. The saga ran to fourteen parts, the longest serial in old-time recording history. (Jimmie Rodgers's blue yodels reached thirteen.) The seven discs together achieved sales in excess of 300,000. Whenever a "Corn Licker Still" installment was issued, it sold twice as many as most of the releases around it in Columbia's "Old Familiar Tunes" catalog.

The later sketches were faithful to the format of the first, with plenty of musical breaks, and frequent namechecks to familiarize listeners with the cast. McMichen, always the central figure, set the tone of each episode. In Parts 3 and 4, he oversaw a series of brief but exciting musical passages, and, when Brown deserted his job as a revenue officer, he enrolled him on the team. In Parts 5 and 6, he urged his crew to load a shipment that Brown had brokered for them, only to be confounded when Brown arrived in a hail of gunshots, a turncoat again, and arrested them. Mac was doleful in Parts 7 and 8, since they were all in jail, but turned optimistic in Parts 9 and 10, where, out on probation, they went back to making liquor ("for our own use") and opened a fried chicken restaurant in Atlanta, the Hen Cackle Inn, which burned down on the opening night. Parts 11 and 12 discovered them depressed and drunk, but in Parts 13 and 14 they were cheerful again, since they sold $300 worth of liquor to an Atlanta nightclub owner, were introduced to roulette, and won a pile of

COLUMBIA Familiar Tunes

Another . . .

Corn Licker Still in Georgia

Parts 11 and 12

Record No. 15618-D

By

Clayton McMichen · Riley Puckett · Gid Tanner · Lowe Stokes · Fate Norris · Tom Dorsey ·

GID TANNER AND HIS SKILLET-LICKERS

VOCAL SELECTIONS

15612-D 10" 75c. { Georgia Wagner. / Sugar in the Gourd. — Gid Tanner and His Skillet-Lickers with Riley Puckett and Clayton McMichen

15605-D 10" 75c. { Waitin' for the Evening Mail. / Ramblin' Boy. — Riley Puckett

15613-D 10" 75c. { My Little Home in Tennessee. — Hugh Cross / If I Had Only Had a Home Sweet Home. — Mr. and Mrs. Hugh Cross

Parts 11–12 of the "Corn Licker" saga were issued at the end of 1930 and sold 3,439 copies—considerably more than contemporary releases in the "Old Familiar Tunes" catalog by the Skillet-Lickers, Riley Puckett, and Hugh Cross. "Tom Dorsey" was Dan Hornsby. (Author's Collection)

money. "Well, see you again," said Mac at the end of the sketch. But the saga stopped there.

Alongside the "Corn Licker Still," the participants fulfilled Columbia's recording director Frank Walker's demands for more "rural dramas," producing a further ten double-sided playlets. Occasionally, they gave a countryman's view of national issues, as in "Prohibition—Yes or No" or "Taking the Census," but mostly they were about rural recreations: a possum hunt, a bee hunt, a medicine show, a county fair.

According to Lowe Stokes, Walker even envisaged a movie based on the "Corn Licker Still." "He was a money-maker," said Stokes, adding approvingly, "He knew the music."

* * *

The success of these sketches was noted by the Victor producer Ralph Peer, and he asked one of his top artists, Ernest V. Stoneman, who had some of Mac's entrepreneurial skill, to devise and cast similar rustic theatricals. They had already conceived a piece called "Old Time Corn Shuckin'," recorded in July 1927. Stoneman opened it like this:

> Now, folks, you know it's the custom in these here mountains to shuck old people's corn when they're old and can't work. So we've shucked Uncle Joe Stutes's corn, and we will begin now with what we call a reg'lar old corn-shuckin' ceremony. We want everyone to take part in it, for everyone in these here mountains can play some kind of music.

Whereupon the members of the Blue Ridge Corn Shuckers, one by one, showed their stuff. What Peer and Stoneman clearly had in mind was not a comic strip, such as the "Corn Licker Still" would prove to be, but a colored lithograph, "Customs in These Here Mountains," a portrayal of ancestral Southern folkways still practiced in the hills and hollows of Appalachia. In the same ensemble's "Possum Trot School Exhibition" (1928), old-time music is interspersed with displays of spelling, recitation, and oratory, with "Uncle" Eck Dunford applying his matchless mountain brogue to lines like "What a beautiful bird the frog are!"

But by now the moonshining Georgians were inexorably tugging the Virginians in their direction, and the smoky aroma of the "Corn Licker Still" wafts from the Stoneman company's "A Serenade in the Mountains": "Where you boys been so long? I ain't seen you in a coon's age." "Oh, we've been up in the mountains a-makin' a little run of corn liquor and had stayed kind of hid, you know." So too in "Going up the Mountain After Liquor," a dialogue between Stoneman and Dunford over the banjo playing of Bolen Frost. All these two-part productions have a charming ambience, but the performers seem awkward beside the boozily confident Skillet-Lickers.

* * *

To an unsympathetic observer, "Corn Licker Still" and the Georgia group's other sketches might seem like galleries of hillbilly stereotypes, offensive to the men and manners depicted in them as the minstrel show was to African Americans. ("Men" is strictly accurate: women's voices are seldom heard in hillbilly skits, and when they are, they are almost always men's impersonations.) But just as minstrel performers, and some of the writers of minstrel songs, were often themselves African American, so the cast of the Atlanta sketches were mostly north Georgia hillbillies, though some might not have cared for the term. They were parodists poking fun from the inside, and if they were indeed being diminished to stereotypes, they were complicit in the process.

But would they have seen it as diminishment? The hillbillies in these comic turns may not appear to know much about anything except fiddling and making liquor, but, like the countryman in the venerable crosstalk of "The Arkansas Traveler," they're smarter than the stranger in their midst, the revenue man, census taker, or Prohibition booster (usually played by Brown or Hornsby) who irritates them with his impertinent interventions. In Part 12, Hornsby pretends to be a lightning-rod salesman looking for a bed for the night, but the skeptical musicians realize he's a revenue officer and drive him off. In "Prohibition—Yes or No," he plays a proponent of abstinence, whose every point Mac robustly rebuts.

"I'll have to bid you gentlemen goodbye," says the frustrated Hornsby eventually. "I hardly think it'd be worthwhile to make a talk on temperance in this neighborhood."

"Well, I guess we read him a page out of the right book that time, boys," says Mac, and the band resumes playing—what else but "Pass Around the Bottle and We'll All Take a Drink."

Beneath the skin of these sketches runs a vein of anti-establishment contempt: the contempt of small farmers for banks and, by extension, for perceived representatives of authority or power. Or just people

Gid Tanner. (OTM Collection)

who aren't from round here. As Mac states firmly in "Corn Licker Still" Part 9: "No outsiders."

★ ★ ★

The naming of the participants in the "Corn Licker Still" saga extended to the other sketches and sometimes too the apportioning of tasks. This may simply have been a way of giving everyone on the record something to do and say. But it also embodies what the cultural historian Elizabeth Stevenson identified as a constant in American life, "the husking-bee habit . . . when people of a community worked hard together to do quickly a complex thing that had to be done, enjoying the meshing of effort and the accomplishment of many hands and purposes all directed to one end, as in the assembly line . . ."—or the making of liquor.

From such angles we may be able to view what the participants thought they were doing in these sketches. But what of their purchasers? Did they spot subtexts, read between the lines, or just enjoy the unraveling saga of music and moonshine? In 1928, many of them would not have owned a radio, but even those who did could hardly have developed a taste for serial drama, since the concept had only just been devised; radio's first dramatic serial is considered to have been the NBC comedy Snow Village Sketches, which debuted, like the "Corn Licker Still," in February 1928, while the daytime soap, as we would recognize it, began in 1930 with a domestic drama called Painted Dreams.

So for its purchasers, a recorded comedy sketch would be like a play performed in their own home, the whole set an unfolding sequence, a Rube's Progress through hard times toward prosperity, or at least good luck. The conclusion of the "Corn Licker Still" series finds the cast not in the mountains where they started out but in a joint in the big city surrounded by money. Urbanites now, they need lick skillets no more. A beguiling fantasy in those hard times.

But we need not assume that the audience for the "Corn Licker Still" was entirely composed of folks like the performers, of fellow—sometimes drunken—sailors in the same boat. In New York, a lawyer and amateur musician named Edward Abbe Niles, who had lately begun reviewing new releases of jazz, blues, and old-time music in *The Bookman*, commended the Skillet-Lickers to readers of that literary journal. Can we imagine a group of baggy-trousered Northern collegians and their flapper girlfriends gathered round a Victrola, enjoying

Bert Layne in the 1930s. (Margaret Riddle Collection)

hillbilly humor as we know many of them did hot jazz?

★ ★ ★

Who wrote these sketches? In 1966, Mac told Lou Curtiss and Ken Swerilas that the "Corn Licker Still" was "mostly made up on the spot by Riley and myself, with maybe some help from Fate Norris and Ted Hawkins. We'd go over them once or twice and turn on the record machine. . . . It was never written down or anything. . . . We'd adlib the whole thing." Some years earlier, though, talking to Bob Pinson and Fred Hoeptner, he gave a much more credible account. The "Corn Licker Still," he said, was dreamed up by fellow Skillet-Licker Bert Layne and himself.

> We had a brother-in-law down there in Georgia that did actually make liquor, and we'd go up there to help him distill, you know, and if they'd caught us they'd have sent us to jail—I mean, to sure-enough jail. We got to thinkin' about it, and Bert spoke up one day and said, "You know, Mac, the conversation that we carry on down there at that liquor still, over in them Georgia mountains, you know," he says, "we're gonna make a record of that, call it 'Corn Licker Still in Georgia.'" And I says, "Let's do." And we got down there [Atlanta], got the producer to help us write it out and fix it all up, you know, and the producer was Bill Brown. And he helped us write it out and get it in shape, and rehearsed it about, I guess, an hour or an hour and a half, and went ahead and made it.
>
> We wasn't pitchin' no fun at nobody. It was amusing to us—we thought it was. We'd done got up into the production end of the thing by then, gettin' to be old seasoned heads, findin' out what was sellin' and what wasn't. To us it was just another phonograph record.

We know Brown was adept at rural dialogue, since spoken exchanges between him and other musicians are scattered over numerous recordings he supervised (➤56). In the later "Corn Licker Still"s (Part 7 onward), he was replaced by "Tom Dorsey," alias Dan Hornsby, who may also have contributed to the scripts. (Frank Walker claimed a hand in them too.)

Despite his role in creating the "Corn Licker Still," Bert Layne featured only once, on the last of the seven discs. He was compromised by his name having appeared on Okeh and Victor, in collaborations with the singer and guitarist Claude Davis. "What knocked me out of the 'Corn Licker Still' was that," he told Margaret Riddle, "and I originated the darn name of it and everything."

He found a way to get his own back. In June 1928, not long after the release of "Corn Licker Still" Parts 3 and 4, Layne, Davis, and Stokes gathered round a microphone at the Gennett studio to record the two-part sketch "The Fiddlin' Bootleggers." The storyline was slight—the gang loads the liquor into their Ford (sneaking a drink first) and attempts a delivery, disarming "Squire Murphy" with a $10 bribe—but there were several passages of sturdy fiddle-and-guitar music, ending, appropriately, with "Done Gone."

It seems to have sold well, and in February 1929 Gennett sent a copy to one of their leading hillbilly artists, Doc Roberts, with a request, repeated at intervals through that spring, that he devise something similar. He never did, and in April Gennett created their own two-part skit, issued as "The Smoky Mountain Boys at the Still" on Gennett or "The Coon Hollow Boys at the Still" on Champion. Rather than call on musicians like Layne or Roberts, the engineers economically selected extracts from recordings on their shelves by the Red Fox Chasers, a stringband from northwestern North Carolina, and other acts, and interspersed them with dialogue delivered by characters named Slim, Red, Ike, and Joe—probably company employees. It's an interesting early example of phonographic montage, but the "performance" lacks the élan and the inside knowledge that the Skillet-Lickers brought to such work.

Perhaps reaching the same conclusion, Gennett commissioned the Red Fox Chasers to write and record, in June 1929, a moonshine sketch of their own, "The Red Fox Chasers Makin' Liquor," Parts I–IV. Stillhouse terms like "condenser barrel" and "swabstick," and plot devices such as a bribable revenue officer and the musicians' fondness for sampling their own product, showed the care with which the group followed the Skillet-Lickers' model.

* * *

Fittingly, some of the last rural sketches, like some of the first, were performed by Gid Tanner, at his final session in 1934. Perhaps finding himself in a recording studio again with Puckett, Hornsby, and mandolinist Ted Hawkins—who had always been in the Skillet-Lickers' orbit, and acted, uncredited, in the "Fiddlers' Convention" sketches—stirred memories of the "Corn Licker Still," though, with the end of Prohibition, moonshine was no longer a hot subject. But the Depression was, and in "Prosperity and Politics" the group discussed, and vehemently approved, the new president, Franklin D. Roosevelt. Topicality satisfied, they then reproduced a "Practice Night with the Skillet Lickers."

After that, the rural sketch virtually disappeared from records. The only artist who continued to employ the format—in its primal form, in two parts and with multiple voices and instruments—was the versatile professional hillbilly Carson Robison. "The Back Porch" and "Making a Record" (Zonophone, 1932) and "An Evening on the C R Ranche [*sic*]" (Rex, 1936), all recorded in London during UK tours, were broadly similar to their forerunners and imply that Robison was acquainted with the "Corn Licker Still." In "The Back Porch," between the arrival of a hooting car and a chorus of farewells, the musicians chat, joke, whistle, and play music. But these sketches were released only in the UK and Australia; the record companies presumably reasoning that listeners there would find them intriguing novelties.

For most of the new generation of country musicians, however, the sketch format must have seemed old-hat, the jokes corny, the hick characterizations backward-looking. Ensembles like Mainer's Mountaineers and the Tobacco Tags performed skits and olios as part of their act, but neither they nor the record companies were interested in putting these on record. (Fragments of the Tags' gender-swapping routines do survive in recordings like "Courtin'" [➤71] and "Tall and Handsome Comedy.") And we can be sure that jukeboxes would have had no use for anything like the "Corn Licker Still." They required quick-impact records, strong in melody and rhythm, with evocative titles and catchy hooks. The business of the jukebox was providing instant public entertainment; the sketches, with their quilt-patterns of talk and music and their rambling storylines, were essentially domestic diversions.

18

"BLUE YODEL"

Jimmie Rodgers

Victor 21142

Recorded in Camden, NJ, November 30, 1927
Released on February 3, 1928
Sold 400,000+

Reissued on *The Singing Brakeman* (Bear Family BCD15540), *First Sessions, 1927–1928* (Rounder CD1056), *RCA Country Legends* (RCA/BMG Heritage 07863 65129 2)

Online: Spotify, YT

During the fall of 1927, Victor's recording director Ralph Peer had time to think about an artist he had signed that summer: a thirty-year-old singer and guitarist named Jimmie Rodgers.

A former railroader from Meridian, Mississippi, Rodgers had quit that work because of tuberculosis and moved to Asheville, North Carolina, for its healthy mountain air. There he worked at various jobs—taxi driver, cop, private investigator—and in his spare time played with some young friends from Bristol, Tennessee, Jack and Claude Grant and Jack Pierce. In August 1927, the four of them found their way to a location recording session that Peer was conducting for Victor in Bristol. As things worked out, the Grants and Pierce recorded as a stringband, and Rodgers on his own with his guitar. He cut two well-worn numbers, "The Soldier's Sweetheart" and "Sleep Baby Sleep," and this debut single sold moderately well.

What impressed Peer about his discovery was not his material but his natural gift of a warm, communicative voice and an ingenious trick of following each verse with a yodel—not the virtuoso vocal contortions of the Alps, but a countryman's yodel, the voice rising and falling, swerving and twisting, like a lick on a Hawaiian guitar.

In 1927, country music (though it wasn't called that then) was still rooted in the past. The Southern singers who had had success on records so far, men like Fiddlin' John Carson, Riley Puckett, Uncle Dave Macon, or Ernest V. Stoneman, had relied chiefly on old songs, stories people already knew. Seeking to describe this music, the record business devised phrases like "Old Time Tunes," "Old Familiar Tunes," or "Songs from Dixie." But Rodgers, despite the repertoire choices he had made at his first session, had little interest in being old-time. He saw a different path ahead of him.

Immediately after the Bristol session, he had moved, with his wife and daughter, to Washington, DC, to be available when the record company next needed him, as he was sure it would. In November, he impulsively drove to New York, checked into a hotel, placed a call to Peer, told him he was in town, and suggested they make some more records. Peer was agreeable.

So, on November 30, 1927, Jimmie Rodgers went to church. Not for a service: it was a Wednesday afternoon, and besides, Trinity Baptist Church in Camden, New Jersey, now served an earthly purpose rather than a divine one, as Victor's chief recording studio. He sang a railroad song and an old Tin Pan Alley weepie, then, loosened up, he played a brief guitar figure and launched into a new number. Within a few minutes, he had produced a song that would change popular music—with just a guitar, some jokes, and a yodel. "T for Texas, T for Tennessee—T for Thelma, that gal that made a wreck out of me-ee. O-lay-ee-o, lay-ee-ay, lay-ee . . ."

And so for six verses: a ragbag of blues couplets about women and liquor and guns, each jaunty verse tagged with that mocking yodel. So, naturally, they called it "Blue Yodel."

Victor released it the following February, coupled with another new number, "Away out on the Mountain," written by the old-time singer Kelly Harrell in the same pastoral-fantasy vein as the hobo song "Big Rock Candy Mountain." It's an

(OTM Collection)

intriguing song, and in retrospect the disc seems like a formidable two-header, but at the time all the attention went to the A-side. In three months, the record's sales climbed into six figures, an extraordinary achievement for a virtually new artist. "'Blue Yodel' just swept the country," Peer recalled. In May, a record reviewer for the *Wichita Sun Times* commented: "Jimmy Rogers"—misspelling his name was endemic from the start—"seems to be going over big now with his vocal and guitar records. They are reminiscent of Kentucky and Tennessee mountain folk songs." In fact, there was nothing of the mountain folk song about "Blue Yodel." What it *was* was something quite different and, in its way, revolutionary. "Blue Yodel" gave country music a white approach to the blues.

★ ★ ★

White entertainers had been appropriating African American repertoire and performance styles for decades, from the blackface minstrels of the mid-nineteenth century to vaudeville singers like Sophie Tucker, Mae West, and Lee Morse, and radio acts like the Boswell Sisters. But what Rodgers produced for Ralph Peer that winter day at Trinity Church was something new: a white version of black country blues, an intrinsically solo and personal idiom that dealt with life and its vagaries in the rural and small-town South.

"Blue Yodel" differed from the African American model in its sound—the white intonation, the steady 2/4 of the guitar, the yodel—but borrowed some of its attitude. "I'm gonna buy me a pistol, just as long as I'm tall—I'm gonna shoot poor Thelma, just to see her jump and fall . . ." In Rodgers's easygoing delivery, this is comic-book violence, a guy strutting his stuff. The guy who in the previous verse had boasted that he could get more women than a passenger train could haul. Such grandstanding would have been instantly recognizable to the black Memphis singer Furry Lewis (an almost exact contemporary of Rodgers), who sang lines like "Mama, get a hatchet, kill a fly on your baby's head."

But then Rodgers seems to become more serious. He'd rather drink muddy water, he says, and sleep in a hollow log, than to be in Atlanta, treated like a dirty dog. Here we draw nearer to what many people over the years have felt to be the real point of the blues: a fist shaken, whether angrily or impotently, at the injustice of life. Maybe that is how some of Rodgers's audience understood it. Today we have a more nuanced view of the blues, have learned to read them less as pleas for pity or manifestos of resentment than as the original black humor: dry, sardonic two-liners. Set-up: I'm going, the singer says, where the water drinks like wine. Why? Punchline: Because the water round here tastes like turpentine.

We don't know how many of Rodgers's listeners interpreted "Blue Yodel" that way, but some contemporary observers certainly did. In New York, the music reviewer Abbe Niles, three years Rodgers's senior, warmed to him straightaway, greeting "Blue Yodel" in his July column in *The Bookman* as "engaging, melodious and bloodthirsty." He followed his career on record with interest, but after a while he found his attention slipping. Rodgers's "singing and guitaring," he wrote in November of "Blue Yodel No. 3," "are as easy and lazy as ever, but [he] needs a gag-writer, for he's running short of verses."

The public's appreciation of "Blue Yodel" had been so swift that at his next session, on February 15, 1928, less than two weeks after the release of the original piece, Rodgers had recorded both a "Blue Yodel—No. 2," all about his "lovin' gal Lucille," and a "No. 3": "She's long, she's tall, she's six feet from the ground—she's tailor-made, she ain't no hand-me-down." "Blue Yodel" wasn't just a song, it was a franchise, and it continued until its thirteenth episode, recorded at his final session in 1933, eight

(OTM Collection)

Frank Marvin spent all his session time in June 1928 recording cover versions of Rodgers songs for four record companies. (OTM Collection)

days before he died, and released posthumously as "Jimmie Rodgers' Last Blue Yodel." (Actually, as "Jimmie Rogers' Last Blue Yodel." Even his record company couldn't always spell his name right.)

All the "Blue Yodel"s were cut from the original cloth, being mostly twelve-bar blues, collages of stanzas about troublesome or tantalizing women, with yodel trimmings and generally one or two guitars, though there were exceptions: "Blue Yodel No. 4 (California Blues)" was accompanied by a small danceband, while "Blue Yodel No. 9" (exceptionally, an eight-bar "Blue Yodel") was a remarkable biracial collaboration between Rodgers and jazz cornetist Louis Armstrong, with Louis's wife Lillian Hardin Armstrong on piano.

The cover versions were not long in coming. In April 1928, as music-store tills rang country-wide with sales of Rodgers's original disc, Columbia commissioned a "Blue Yodel" from their most popular old-time singer, Riley Puckett. In June, a young singer and guitarist lately arrived in New York from Oklahoma—not Gene Autry, but a talented contemporary who would become his sidekick, Frank Marvin—copied Rodgers's hit for four companies, which issued it on seventeen different American labels and even one in the UK. Autry himself would hitch a ride on the Rodgers bandwagon, covering several of the later-numbered "Blue Yodel"s.

There were reactions, too, from African American musicians. In October 1928, on a record by Jimmy Wade and His Dixielanders out of Chicago, cornetist and singer Punch Miller chucked a Rodgersian verse into a thrown-together song called "Gates Blues:" "T for Texas, T for Tennessee—T for Tempe, who thought the world and all of me." There was even a response from the Mexican department of the industry: Rodgers's "Blue Yodel" had been on the market a mere few weeks when the Martinez brothers, Valentin and Pedro, broke off from their customary music and sang—in English, with a swooping slide guitar—a two-part "Yodel Blues."

In 1930, another admirer, Cliff Carlisle, recorded "Blue Yodel" under its alternative name, "T for Texas." Singer and guitarist Roy Gonzales waxed a version in Cajun French, "Un Fussie Qui Brille"—Rodgers's "shotgun with a great long shiny barrel." From 1928 until well into the '30s, many of Rodgers's releases were rerecorded by one or another of a cadre of copyists, singing and yodeling guitarists like Hoke Rice, Jess Hillard, and Howard Keesee, while the general sound of "America's Blue Yodeler" permeated the work of Jimmie Davis, Jack Jackson, Fred Richards, Daddy John Love, and "Ramblin' Red" Lowery—and those are just the ones we know from records.

But if we step back and take a panoramic view of hillbilly blues, we see that it was more than simply

Membership card for the Jimmie Rodgers Society, 1950s. (OTM Collection)

an extended tribute to Jimmie Rodgers. There were things intrinsic to the blues, beyond his particular take on it, that fascinated white musicians and their audiences alike. Performing the blues allowed a hillbilly musician to appropriate the black blues singer's presentation of self. Wearing that mask, he (rarely she) could become a swaggering, devil-may-care, self-absorbed solipsist, an atomized modern human. Insulated by his disguise, he could tell stories no Godfearing family man would utter outside the poolhall or barbershop. Look at some of the material Jimmie Davis got away with in the early '30s: bear cat mamas, red nightgowns, the "Tom Cat and Pussy Blues," and the insatiable Corrine.

More than that, the blues-enabled hillbilly singer could loosen, even break free of, the bonds of narrative that had defined both the ballad and the nineteenth-century popular song. A blues did not have to tell a story, or at least not in conventional narrative installments. It did not have to offer a moral. (The blues singer would have approved the guiding principle, according to one of its creators, of the TV show Seinfeld: "No hugging. No learning.") A ballad is a fine thing, and a tearstained letter from Victorian Tin Pan Alley is another, but sometimes you just want to sing, or have someone sing to you, a song about hum-dum dingers from Dingersville.

The point of a hillbilly blues lies less in where the wagon is heading than in who's driving it and how they use their whip: a fast slideshow of images, an audacious guitar figure, a quirky yodel. The singer juggles witticisms, wry reflections, shifts of tone—for behind the mask he can speak in any voice.

★ ★ ★

When Rodgers died, every record company tried to fill his place. None succeeded, but the sound persisted. Throughout the '30s, almost every country band with its sights on fame would have a member who could sing and yodel like Rodgers.

His "suave, rueful vernacular songs," wrote Bob Coltman, made him "the first real people's popular singer, stylistically ten years ahead of his time, breaking the long dominance of golden voice and stage manner." Ralph Peer saw it more simply: "A fellow like Jimmie Rodgers appealed to a much wider audience because he had a popular version of hillbilly."

Look at his legatees. Ernest Tubb. Hank Snow. Lefty Frizzell, whose versions of Rodgers songs are among the best things he did. And of course Hank Williams, a man haunted by Rodgers's music who explored its darker side, looking beyond the clown's smile to the skull's grin.

Now past its ninetieth birthday, "Blue Yodel," or "T for Texas," is a vehicle in excellent shape, undiminished, maybe strengthened, by attempts to redesign or repurpose it. It has been heard from Johnny Cash, Waylon Jennings, Willie Nelson, Merle Travis, the Everly Brothers, Doc Watson, Lynyrd Skynyrd, and Dwight Yoakam. Yoakam's was on the 1997 collection *The Songs of Jimmie Rodgers: A Tribute*, whose other contributors, such as Bob Dylan, Van Morrison, Steve Earle, and Aaron Neville, testify to Rodgers's rock-solid stature as a country music original—a stature based upon that one song. T for timeless, T for 'ternity.

19

"COMBINATION RAG"

East Texas Serenaders
Columbia 15229-D

Recorded in Dallas, TX, December 2, 1927
Released in May 1928
Sold 19,099

Reissued on *Old-Time Texas String Bands Volume Two: Dallas Bound* (County CO-CD-3525), *East Texas Serenaders (1927–1937)* (Document DOCD-8031), *Old Mountain* (ASV Living Era CD AJA5577), *Texas Hillbillies* (JSP JSPCD77213)

Online: Spotify, YT

Ragtime is the soundtrack of early-twentieth-century urban America: the music of progress, the tempo of hustle. The 1973 movie *The Sting*, and the brief but intense vogue for piano ragtime that followed it, made it seem decorative, perky, yet with an essential orderliness. Early ragtime recordings, however, even by normally staid studio orchestras, sometimes reveal a frenzied, riotous music, a fit accompaniment not so much for dancing as for burning down the dancehall.

Ragtime's provocative vigor was a potent energy source for early country music. In the 1900s and '10s, much of the ragtime committed to records was played on the banjo, the instrument not only embodying the music's brightness and gaiety but ringing out loudly enough to record well. Thanks to the influence of discs by banjoists like Vess L. Ossman and Fred Van Eps, we hear country ragtime first in recordings of small groups using banjo or banjo-mandolin, such as the Scottdale String Band (➤12). But there was no reason why the music should not be translated to the format of the hillbilly fiddle band—if a fiddler could be found with the technique to make the speed and negotiate the changes on the ragtime railroad, together with accompanists to stoke the engine.

You might expect such a crew to turn up in Atlanta or Memphis or Louisville, some city where musicians were numerous, seasoned, and competitive. In fact, country music's first recorded ragtime fiddle band was made up of men from a couple of small towns in northeast Texas: fiddler Daniel Huggins Williams and guitarist Cloet Hamman from Lindale in Smith County, and banjoist John Munnerlyn and cellist Henry Bogan from Mineola, a dozen miles north in Wood County, the next stop on the railroad line to Dallas. These four became the core of the band, but Hamman was sometimes joined by another guitarist, such as Jack Hopper of Mineola, who appears in the best-known photographs of the group, or Carl Jeffus of Lindale. Freeman Patton, also from Lindale, is known to have played with them too, probably on guitar or banjo.

Williams, interviewed in 1959 by Bob Pinson and Fred Hoeptner, and Hamman, talking to Bill Malone almost twenty years later, both remembered that they chiefly played for local functions: house parties, dances, church entertainments. Hamman enjoyed all-night serenading: "I got more pleasure out of it than a feller could ever imagine." One of the first references to the band's members in the Mineola paper finds two of them playing for a community get-together. This somehow prompts its reporter to show off his memory of Dryden's translation of Virgil's *Aeneid*:

> "With crackling flame the caldron fries" spoke Mr. Dryden on one occasion and had he been along with some of the fellows Monday night at Lindale Country Club Lake he would have revisioned [*sic*] an enactment of the finest fish fry ever staged.... Fresh water channel catfish and an even dozen pounds at that, french fried potatoes, onions, black coffee, pickles, bread and everything that goes to make a fish fry complete. Add to this setting a guitar played by Henry Bogan and fiddle played by Huggin [*sic*] Williams, and you have the best music to be found for an outing. (*Mineola Monitor*, April 7, 1927)

The East Texas Serenaders, probably 1928. Standing: Cloet Hamman (guitar), Huggins Williams (fiddle), John Munnerlyn (banjo); seated: Jack Hopper (guitar), Henry Bogan (cello). (Dave Freeman Collection)

The Serenaders received their first namecheck in the paper in January 1928, when Williams, Bogan, Jeffus, and Patton went to Dallas to broadcast on WFAA—the second time they had done so, the reporter notes. Then, two months later, the *Monitor*, too breathless to care about punctuation, gave its readers more momentous news.

> Several weeks ago the East Texas Serenaders an orchestra composed of Mineola and Lindale talent went to Dallas at the request of The Columbia Phonograph Company to make two records of their playing. . . . [This week] Henry Bogan manager of the orchestra who lives in Mineola received a record . . . together with a check for a good amount of money . . . . According to those who have heard the records the music is par excellent. The selections which are original with this orchestra are entitled Sweetest Flowers, a waltz, and Combination Rag. (March 22, 1928)

The "orchestra" was now identified as Bogan, Williams, and (allowing for misspellings) Hamman, Jeffus, and Munnerlyn.

The idea of recording came, Williams recalled, from a local record retailer who heard them at a dance and recommended them to Columbia's regional salesman. When a Columbia team came to Dallas—the company's first recording trip there—in December 1927, the Serenaders were on the work-sheet for the first day of record-making. (Four days later, Columbia captured another effervescent rag-time performance, the African American Dallas String Band's "Dallas Rag.") For Hamman, the acoustics of the room, which was padded with rugs, made it "the hardest playing that I ever done in my life. It just sounded dead." Williams remembered they had some difficulty making a successful recording of "Combination Rag." "I believe you boys need a little drink," the recording manager remarked and produced a bottle from his pocket. The band nailed it on the second take.

A pair of ragtime tunes meet in "Combination Rag," and the listener is tossed, in the confluence of these dashing streams, like a raft on white water. The exhilarating recording sold well, yet Columbia did not call the Serenaders back, probably because the band offered themselves elsewhere. After receiving Columbia's check for $400, Hamman said, "we decided that maybe that wasn't as much as we was worth, and we wrote Brunswick, and they accepted us on contract." They were summoned to Dallas again in October 1928, now with Jack Hopper rather than Jeffus on second guitar. The first Brunswick release, "Acorn Stomp"/"Shannon Waltz," was a strong seller, and over the next three years the company released six more couplings by the Serenaders, mostly waltzes and rags. In 1929, Brunswick's house magazine for their hillbilly catalog, the *Dixie Flyer*, gave the band an imaginative write-up:

> This group of former Texas Rangers go after their music like a bunch of stampeding steers. It is the sort of music to pull one out of the doldrums and keep a party moving merrily into the wee sma' hours. And they play waltzes as waltzes were intended to be played and danced. We know you'll like their stuff and will give you their life's history next time, unless the Jones' Law gets 'em for putting too much stimulation into their records. (Quoted in the *Mineola Monitor*, July 25, 1929)

For most of the men who played as the East Texas Serenaders, music was a spare-time pursuit. Henry Bogan worked for the postal service, John Munnerlyn for the United Gas Pipe Line Company, Cloet Hamman on his father-in-law's farm. Jack Hopper was an insurance agent, Carl Jeffus a farmer, Freeman Patton a restaurant owner. Huggins Williams was the only one to give his occupation as "musician." He and Hamman remembered that, in the early '30s, they had a chance to go on the vaudeville circuit with H. M. Barnes, the promoter of the Blue Ridge Ramblers (➤35): "He had one orchestry," said Hamman, "and needed another."

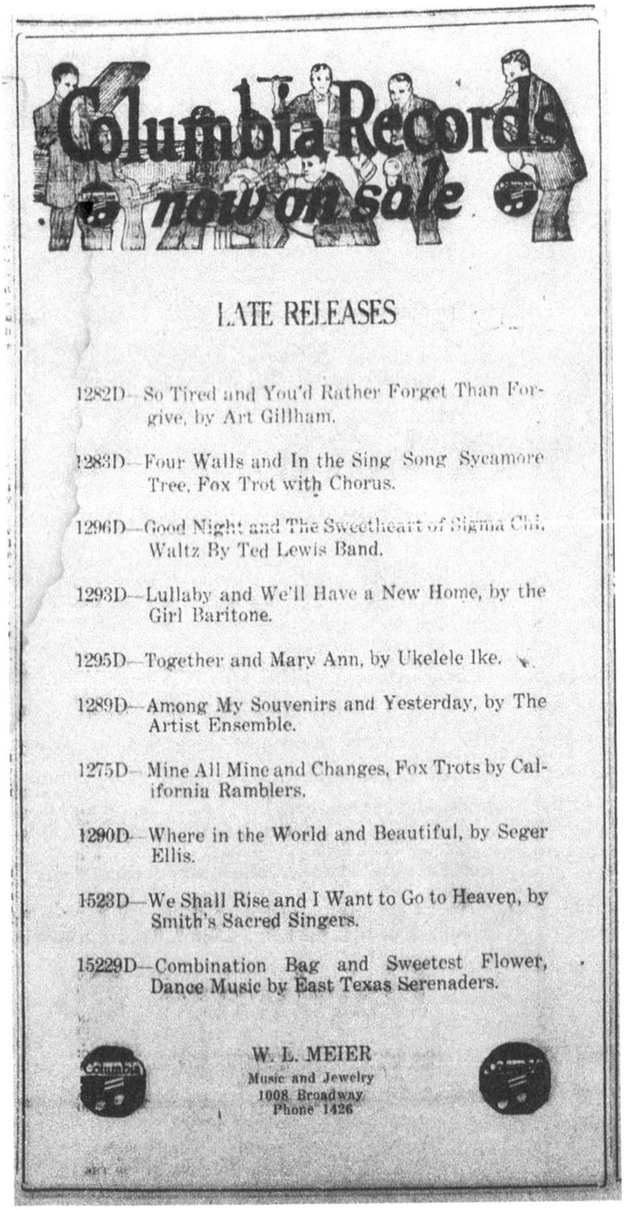

Ad in *Lubbock* [Texas] *Avalanche Journal*, April 1, 1928. (Author's Collection)

Brunswick promptly commissioned a photograph of the band wearing overalls. Nothing came of it: the Serenaders weren't interested in the traveling or the prospect of becoming full-time musicians. Yet they enjoyed playing and knew they were good, so they continued to fill engagements locally, though without Munnerlyn, whose job took him out of Texas.

★ ★ ★

In March 1937, the Mineola paper reported that the Serenaders, "after years away from the microphone and the recording disc, have returned to the wax plate. . . . Last week the group journeyed to Dallas there to tune up their instruments and whang them with gusto [for] the Decca record people." Decca's hillbilly recording was in the hands of Dave Kapp, whose brother Jack had signed the Serenaders to Brunswick nearly a decade before, but the band's new contract was not a gesture for old times' sake. Decca was deeply committed to the new sound of Texas Swing and was busily signing up hot acts like Milton Brown's Brownies (➤67) and Cliff Bruner's Texas Wanderers. An expert fiddle-fronted band like the Serenaders fit comfortably into that sales strategy, but to emphasize their kinship with the new sound the band added a second fiddler, Henry Lester. From Hall County in West Texas, he was visiting in Lindale, sat in with the Serenaders at a party, and sounded so good that they drafted him into the lineup, along with his younger brother Buster "Shorty" Lester on tenor banjo.

The East Texas Serenaders are often described as harbingers of Western Swing, and Bob Wills is supposed to have said that, when he was starting out, they were the only significant competition. Nancy Fly Bredenberg, annotating an LP of their recordings, claimed that, in blending regional dance fiddling with fast Northern ragtime, "they set the pace for all the other western and Texas bands that were to follow," creating "a wholly new indigenous style which was later jazzed up and elaborated" to become Western Swing. Hoeptner agreed that they "probably . . . prepared the way for the change," but insisted that they "never played in western swing style." Even their latest recordings, the 1937 Decca sides, bear him out: a characteristic mixture of waltzes, blues, and up-tempo tunes, they show little of the daring improvisation or jazz feel that spilled out of the recordings of Bob Wills or Milton Brown. Huggins Williams did later put in some Western Swing time, working with Lew Preston's band, and he was an early mentor of the Western Swing fiddler Johnny Gimble.

But though the East Texas Serenaders may own only a small niche in the Western Swing columbarium, they can lay claim to another distinction, one they earned with their debut record. "Combination Rag" is the first stringband instrumental in the hillbilly catalog to be played at an unabashed, supercharged, dance-if-you-dare speed: a crackling display of instrumental virtuosity for its own sake.

20

"DAVY"/"GREENBACK DOLLAR"

Weems String Band
Columbia 15300-D

Recorded in Memphis, TN, December 9, 1927
Released in November 1928
Sold 6,800

Reissued on *Rural String Bands of Tennessee* (County CO-CD-3511) [both] • *Times Ain't Like They Used to Be Vol. 6* (Yazoo 2064) ["Davy"] • *Down in the Basement* (Old Hat CD-1004), *Times Ain't Like They Used to Be Vol. 5* (Yazoo 2063) ["Greenback Dollar"]

Online: Spotify, YT

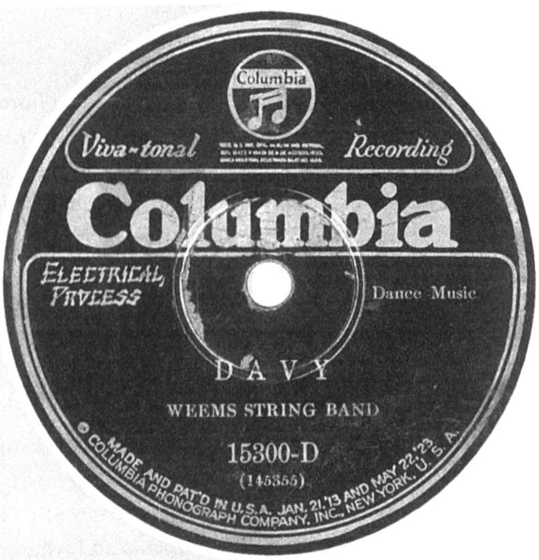

Collectors rhapsodize about this record. If Adam and Eve had owned a fiddle and a banjo (you almost imagine them saying), this might have been the music of Eden.

These sober, dignified performances do seem to belong to a time long before they were recorded, an age before there were recordings at all. In part this is because they are played by a stringband anchored by a cello, a format that had once been common, as may be seen in many band photographs from the late nineteenth and early twentieth centuries, but by 1927 was rapidly disappearing. In its stately unhurriedness, this family band evokes the sylvan quiet of Perry County, Tennessee, before the railroad and the automobile.

The core of the band was three brothers, fiddlers Dickson (Dick) Weems (1886–1965) and George Franklin (Frank) Weems (1879–1967), and Jesse Weems (1875–1948), who played cello, with their sister Ella's son Alvin Conder (1898–1945) on banjo. There had been Weemses in Perry County since the early nineteenth century, if not before, and fiddling went a long way back in the family: the brothers' father, William Thomas Weems, was a fiddler, and so was his father Augustan (Gus) before him. Dick, according to his son Harold, "tried to play exactly like Gus," so he was modeling himself on a man born in 1821. "Dad," said Harold, "was the best fiddler of the bunch." Dick always played the lead, while Frank generally played a tenor or baritone harmony part. The band, which might also include Harold on guitar and his brother Dean on banjo (and later another brother, Aubrey, on cello), played for square dances in Perry and Decatur counties, ferrying themselves around by horse and wagon.

Harold also remembered there were "some women folks played in that band way on back. They played the same thing Nonnie's playing." "Nonnie" was Nonnie Smith Presson, who lived nearby, and with her brother Bulow constituted the area's other recorded stringband, the Perry County Music Makers. The "thing" she played—uniquely on old-time records—was a zither.

In the winter of 1927, Columbia Records invited the Weems band to Memphis to make a record. The company might have been alerted by a Perry or Decatur County music-store contact, who could have mentioned that Dick Weems and Al Conder had played on WSM's Saturday-night barn-dance program, the Grand Ole Opry in all but name, six months earlier. On that trip to Nashville, the *Perry Countian* reported,

> after they had played Arkansas Traveler they were asked to sign on the dotted line, which they did, and a program was arranged for . . . April 30. Monday . . . they were invited out to the Capitol to make music for the members of the Legislature who managed to stop the "Law Mill" for a period of thirty minutes and enjoy some real old time "heel tickling" music, and according to [Conder] some of the senators sure can dance. . . . [S]o far as we know [these musicians] are the first Perry Countians to make string music over the radio.

Dick Weems, Frank Weems (fiddles), Harold Weems (guitar), probably Dean Weems (banjo), Jesse Weems (cello), Al Conder (banjo). Pope, according to Perry Countian Jerry Pevahouse, was "not a town, just a place on Highway 100. . . . This photo was taken on the front porch of their home at Mousetail Landing, July 4, 1930. That night they performed at a square dance to commemorate the opening of the Alvin C. York Bridge. The dance was held on the bluff overlooking the Tennessee River." Al Conder later worked as a toll collector on the bridge. (Big Boy Woods Collection)

They had made a second trip to WSM more recently (Murfreesboro *Daily News-Journal*, October 28).

Also traveling to Memphis with the Weems brothers and Conder was the teenaged Harold Weems, though he seems not to have played on the record. But he did contribute to it.

★ ★ ★

For many listeners, these seemingly archaic recordings epitomize what they mean by "old-time music." Yet, as so often with old records, we must be careful how we interpret them. Jerry Pevahouse, who grew up in Perry County and knew the Weems and Conder families, observed:

> "Davy" and "Greenback Dollar" were not typical of their music. . . . They mostly played tradition[al] breakdown tunes for local square dances and singing was not usually part of their music. . . . [But] Columbia was hesitant to record the band, saying they wanted songs with vocals. [The musicians] had been waiting at the hotel all week to record, were almost out of money and desperate to finish and get back to Perry County. [So the lyrics for] "Davy" and "Greenback Dollar" were written by Mr Dick and Harold Weems in Memphis a day or two before they recorded. . . . There were many rhymes about Davy Crockett that circulated from the days [he] lived. The family . . . [that] owned the old Howard store near the Weems home had an old ledger entry where Davy Crockett bought a jug of whiskey. . . . He was known in that neighborhood and no doubt remembered.

"Davy" and "Greenback Dollar," mesmerizing though they may be, are constructs: old-time music as reshaped by the record industry.

There are many similar stories about bands being told by record-company representatives that their tunes were of no interest unless they could be fitted out with lyrics, even if they were brief (➤47) or, as in the case of the Carter Brothers and Son, more or less nonsensical. Whether this belief that purely instrumental music was unappealing was based merely on producers finding it boring or upon actual market research, it quickly solidified into a virtual rule; hence the fashion for decorating instrumentals with faux-impromptu commentaries (➤54, 56). Of the best-sellers in Columbia's "Old Familiar Tunes" catalog between 1925 and '30, only two were instrumental dance music (by the Leake County Revelers and the Cartwright Brothers). Much the same was true of Victor.

The Weemses' record sold reasonably well, but Columbia never returned to Memphis and did not call them back. Two months later, however, Al Conder was in that city with an older partner, William Addison Lindsey of Henderson County (west of Decatur County), to make a few highly flavored recordings, for Victor and Okeh, of old minstrel songs like "Turnip Greens," Lindsey singing and playing guitar, Conder doubling on banjo and harmonica. It was said that Conder made the head for his banjo from the skin of a catfish caught in the Tennessee River: a detail that, for me, perfectly characterizes the otherworldliness of the Weems String Band.

21

"HANDY MAN"/ "I TICKLED 'EM"

New Arkansas Travelers Victor 21288

Recorded in Memphis, TN, February 4, 1928
Released in April/May 1928
Sold 6,384

Reissued on *Serenade in the Mountains* (JSP JSPCD7780), *My Bonnie Lies Over the Ocean: British Songs in the USA* (Nehi NEH3X1)

Online: Spotify

Saturday, February 4, 1928, Memphis. The Victor engineers, on location at the City Auditorium, had spent the day recording the African American blues singers and guitarists Tommy Johnson and Ishman Bracey, a six-piece jazz band, the Memphis Stompers, and a piano-accompanied sacred quartet from Crockett County, Tennessee, the Friendship Four. Their last job, before they turned off the equipment, retired to their hotel, and enjoyed a Sunday's rest, was a small group with a couple of comic songs. Sitting at the controls, the technicians first heard a jaunty instrumental chorus of harmonica and guitar music. Then the singer began.

> Now I'm a very handy man.
> To save a bit of oof's my plan.
> One day last week I said to my wife,
> "The yard wants a whitewash, upon my life.
> I'll try and do the job,"
> And I did, so help me, Bob.
> Bought a pail of whitewash, set to work,
> And the old girl hung in like a Turk.
> With a slap-dab, slap-dab, up and down the brickwork,
> Slap-dab all day long,
> In and out the corners, round the Johnny Horners,
> We were a pair of fair clean goners;
> Slap-dab-slap with the whitewash brush,
> And talk about a fancy ball,
> But I put more whitewash on the old woman
> Than I did upon the garden wall . . .

I see the engineers exchanging mystified glances. "Oof"? "Johnny Horners"? "So help me, Bob"? What was the guy on about? And was that an English accent?

Yes, because he was English. Arthur Robert Bishop (1880–1962) had lived in Memphis for almost twenty years, but his voice still declared his origins, in the county of Kent, where he was born in the village of Snodland. Applying for naturalization in 1911, he stated that he had entered the United States in 1907, returned to Kent the following year to marry Martha, and sailed back to the US in July to settle in Memphis. He worked, as he had in England, as a brick mason, his father's trade.

As a young man in Kent, he must have visited music halls (there were several nearby in Maidstone and Chatham) or bought the sheet music of music-hall songs because what he produced for Ralph Peer and the Victor engineers was a pair of songs straight out of that milieu.

"Handy Man" is an almost perfectly remembered version of "The Amateur Whitewasher," written by Fred Murray and Fred Leigh and first published in 1896. It was sung in English music halls in the early years of the twentieth century by a fairly well-known performer, Frank Seeley, but never recorded. Several generations have enjoyed the piece, and folksong collectors could still find Southern English pub singers delivering it as late as the '70s.

(Glossarial note: "So help me, Bob" is the Christian expression "So help me, God," bowdlerized somewhat in the manner of "Jeepers Creepers" or W. C. Fields's "Godfrey Daniel." "Johnny Horners" is Cockney rhyming slang for "corners." "Oof," originally

Arthur Bishop. (Author's Collection)

"ooftish," from the Yiddish *auf [dem] Tische*, "on the table," means "money.")

★ ★ ★

An amateur with a whitewash brush would have been an appealing subject in late Victorian England, where DIY was regarded as intrinsically funny. Two English comic novels published in the late 1880s have beguiled generations of readers with stories of domestic ineptitude: in George and Weedon Grossmith's *Diary of a Nobody*, their hero Charles Pooter, *Homo habilis suburbanus*, paints the bathtub red, with embarrassing results, while in Jerome K. Jerome's *Three Men in a Boat*, Uncle Podger makes a terrible mess of trying to hang a picture.

Not long after Arthur Bishop left England with "The Amateur Whitewasher" lodged in his luggage or his head, the comic singer Billy Williams scored a great success there with a similar tale of unskilled home maintenance, "When Father Papered the Parlour" (1909). Five years later, a couple of American songwriters came up with what it would be tactful to call a close imitation, "When Father Put the Paper on the Wall." (It would be recorded for Okeh's "Old Time Tunes" catalog in 1929 by Lloyd Yarbrough, a Fort Worth railroader and entertainer who went by the name of Captain Appleblossom.) But despite the funny songs, in the US, DIY had become a serious business. Home ownership rose rapidly in the early twentieth century, and interest in the practical aspects of domestic life was fanned by mass-circulation magazines like *Popular Mechanics* and *House Beautiful*. Sears, Roebuck published a regularly updated booklet called *How to Paint*. In 1905, the mail-order company's catalog advertised a mantel that "[would] not require the services of a brick mason." With his livelihood thus under threat, Arthur Bishop probably took some delight in a song about amateurs tackling professionals' jobs and coming to grief.

★ ★ ★

The piece on the other side of the record had been called by its author, the music-hall composer T. W. Connor, "Tickle-ickle-um."

> I've got a very funny way with me,
> I want to tickle everybody I see.
> I'm all over 'em if I get a chance,
> It's a quid to a coconut I make 'em dance . . .

Tickling had a peculiar appeal for turn-of-the-twentieth-century songwriters and the old-time singers who chose from their folios. The droll narrative of "Ticklish Reuben" ("I've been tickled by a feather, I've been tickled by a wasp, I've been tickled by a yellow bumblebee"), first recorded in 1902 by its composer Cal Stewart, was adapted in the 1920s by Uncle Dave Macon and several other hillbilly artists; with its choruses of helpless cackling, it belongs to the once popular but now almost forgotten genre of laughing songs. "I Tickled Nancy" (also recorded by Macon) and "I Tickled Her Under the Chin" (Emry Arthur), on the other hand, are mildly naughty courtship pieces. "Tickle-ickle-um" is gender-neutral: the narrator tickles members of both sexes, always purely in fun.

It was not the only composition by Connor to cross the Atlantic. "I Can't Change It" (1894), a comic catalog of poor but irreversible decisions, turned up in the repertoire of Otto Gray's Cowboy Band in Oklahoma, and, probably from there, was picked up in the '30s by a hillbilly swing band, the Tune Wranglers—a Victorian comic song finding a distant echo in San Antonio, Texas.

★ ★ ★

Although Bishop sang his songs more or less as the music-hall artists of his youth did, their accompaniments were something else entirely. In Britain, a music-hall song was typically performed with a pianist or a theater pit orchestra. In Memphis, "Handy Man" and "I Tickled 'Em" were backed by guitar and a pair of harmonicas, one almost certainly played by the singer. This accompaniment lends the

(Tony Barker Collection)

recordings a flavor of American old-time music, further evoked by the group name New Arkansas Travelers. Perhaps, as Arthur Bishop recalled the songs of his boyhood, he felt he was acknowledging his presence in a musical New World by employing American ways of accompanying them. For some years after the recording, the Arkansas Travelers played on radio, the group now including Arthur's daughter Margaret (born in 1917), who sang and played piano and banjo, and is remembered by her family for tunes like "Danny Boy" and "Ballin' the Jack."

★ ★ ★

You might expect dealers and customers alike, hearing this quixotic release, to have first scratched their heads and then shaken them, but, for reasons we can hardly begin to guess at, it sold quite well. Peer had recorded two more songs by Bishop and his associates a week later, and a follow-up release would surely have been a reasonable investment, but it never happened, and admirers of the New Arkansas Travelers were denied the chance to hear two more songs from the English music-hall stage, "Glorious Beer" (1895), popularized by singer Harry Anderson, and "Burglar Bill," originally written as a recitation by F. Anstey (Thomas Anstey Guthrie), another prolific humorous writer of the 1880s.

★ ★ ★

Thanks to Arthur Bishop, Ralph Peer, and Victor Records, we have a unique document of quintessentially English urban songs from the 1890s, transplanted to an American setting. For Bishop himself, we may imagine there was the satisfaction of creating something tangible and audible to remind him and Martha of the Old Country, and to provide their children with proof of their heritage. But might he also have been amused by the thought of his American friends—his soon to be fellow-American friends, for he was finally naturalized in 1933—listening to these songs of slap-dab and tickling and not being able to make heads or tails of them?

22

"HOG EYE"

Pope's Arkansas Mountaineers
Victor 21295

Recorded in Memphis, TN, February 6, 1928
Released in April 1928
Sold 7,955

Reissued on *Echoes of the Ozarks Volume One* (County CD-3506)

Online: YT

> Chicken in the bread patch, peckin' up dough.
> Sally, will your dog bite? No, child, no.
> Sally's in the garden, sifting sand,
> Sally's upstairs with the hog eye man.

The hog eye man is a disreputable character who lurks in the dark corners of text collections of folksongs, particularly Vance Randolph's treasury of "unprintable Ozark folksongs and folklore." Because of its shape, the hog's eye was a euphemism for the vagina. In his 1928 Okeh recording "Boe Hog Blues," the African American blues singer Texas Alexander sang, "My gal's got something that looks like a boar hog's eye." According to Randolph, a hog eye man "was an inveterate wencher . . . a man obsessed with women and sex."

As the reader may guess, placing such a character upon the stage of a recorded old-time song could have presented certain problems. (The South Carolinian humorist Chris Bouchillon had got halfway there in his 1926 Columbia recording "Talking Blues," where he referred to "eatin' hog eye," but ventured no further.) So the musicians who made this record half-concealed the hog eye man in what, to a careless listener, might seem like a random collection of folk verses and children's rhymes. Chickens, dogs, hogs . . . all just bucolic fun.

"Hog Eye" was done by Pope's Arkansas Mountaineers, the first stringband from that state to make records. The record companies, having found rich harvests of old-time music in Georgia, North Carolina, and Virginia in 1926–27, had begun to look for similar music further afield and were investigating the Mid-South and Southwest. Arkansas, western Tennessee, and northern Mississippi all looked promising, and in early 1928 both Okeh and Victor dispatched recording crews to the city where it made most sense to congregate musicians from those territories: Memphis.

None of the five men who came to Memphis to record for Victor in February as Pope's Arkansas Mountaineers was a Pope. Their nominal leader, John D. Pope (1865–1951), owned a music store in Searcy in White County, Arkansas, but he played no part in the music-making and didn't even attend the session, sending his young nephew Milton instead. The band consisted of fiddler John Chism (1877–1967); his son Wallace (1905–94) and John Wesley Sparrow (1897–1978) on guitars; and the McKinney brothers, Joseph Washington (1883–1958), who picked the banjo, and Lee Finis Cameron (1898–1984), who played guitar and mandolin and did the singing on the records together with Sparrow and Chism, Jr.

In 1974, Lee "Tip" McKinney recalled the session for Julia Hager and Jim Olin of the Missouri Friends of the Folk Arts.

> I was down here in town [Searcy] one day and of course we'd dealt with the Popes a whole lot, you know, and my brother'd bought a Victrola from him. And so J. D. Pope told him . . . there's a feller comin' now pretty soon from Camden, New Jersey, over here to see if he could find some string band music here.

This "feller," though McKinney couldn't recall his name, would have been Ralph Peer. So the word went round, and some musicians gathered at Pope's store.

"Tip" McKinney playing at the Mississippi Valley Folk Festival, St. Louis, Labor Day Weekend, 1977. (Photo by Joe Wilson, from the OTM Collection)

So Mr. Pope told us, he said, "I'd like for you fellers to get together—a bunch of you fellers that play, sing, and all." So . . . we went over there [Memphis] and made those records and they give us so much for what time we was over there . . . something like nearly a half a day. They paid our way—our expenses and everything. They tried to get us to stay, but there's three of the fellers had wives. . . . They wanted us to broadcast at the Peabody Hotel over there that night, but none of the three wanted to stay. . . . Well, it wouldn't a done no good if we all couldn't a been there, you know, to broadcast it. We put out six pieces [recordings] over there and they paid us off. They said they didn't never pay a royalty for the first time.

The setup sounds fortuitous, and was. "We'd knowed one another for a long time," said McKinney, "but we had never all played together as a band." Yet this hastily assembled quintet would make remarkable music. Some of the pieces they recorded, like "Jaw Bone" and "George Washington," McKinney said they made up, though "made up" in this context means something like "put together from bits and pieces of older songs." "Jaw Bone" was distantly connected to at least two different but related songs, "Old Jaw Bone" and "Walk Jaw Bone," that were circulating on the minstrel stage and in sheet music as early as the 1840s. Others were simply old: "Get Along Home, Miss Cindy" McKinney knew as "an old-time tune; it was played way back during the Civil War, and 'Cotton Eyed Joe' was too. That 'Hog Eye' is an old song—a hundred and thirty years or older."

Abbe Niles greeted "Hog Eye" enthusiastically in the September 1928 issue of *The Bookman*, calling it "an intensely rhythmical reel with interesting blue sevenths, but quite different from [Carl] Sandburg's tune of the same name," published in 1927 in *The American Songbag*, a book Niles revered and wrote about at length in his column. In fact, the tune the Pope boys used was "Fire on the Mountain."

"Hog Eye," as we have seen, mines a deep vein of rustic innuendo. "George Washington," treading more carefully, uses the venerable device of promising a scandalous rhyme and then cheating the listener of hearing it:

I take my gal a walking down on the flowery dell,
And when the old folks find that out, you bet
they give us—
Hallelujah, hallelujah, hallelujah, got glory in my
soul.

"You know," said McKinney, "when that feller recorded that record, he said, 'That one'll go over, I know!'"

"After them records was made," he continued, "well, I got a telegram from Kansas City, a Victrola house [distributor] up there—wanted to know when Pope's Arkansas Mountaineers was going to make some more records. Said they was excellent." And indeed J. D. Pope was ready to send the band to Victor's studios in Camden, New Jersey, for another session—except that some of the musicians made the mistake of trying to follow the money.

McKinney met John Sparrow and Wallace Chism on the street one day. "We're going to find out how much Pope got out of this," they said and tried to persuade McKinney to accompany them to the People's Bank, where they were going to quiz the president. He thought they would get nowhere and refused to go with them. He was right. The banker wouldn't talk to them, but he did talk to Pope, and that was it for the Arkansas Mountaineers: even though only two of them had stepped out of line, Pope would have nothing more to do with the band. He turned instead to another White County group, the Reaves brothers from around McRae, whom he connected with Brunswick–Vocalion, but the records sold much less well, and that, as far as we know, was Pope's last venture into musical fixing. As for the hog eye man, after his brief exposure by Victor, he retreated into the cultural underbrush and made no further appearances on hillbilly records.

23

"THE BLUEFIELD MURDER"

Roy Harvey and The North Carolina Ramblers Brunswick 250

Recorded in Ashland, KY, February 16, 1928
Released on September 13, 1928

Reissued on *People Take Warning!* (Tompkins Square TSQ1875)

Online: Spotify, YT

Bluefield, West Virginia, Saturday afternoon, January 9, 1926. Walter W. Palmer, twenty-three, a truck driver, takes a taxi to 432 Union Street, the home of C. V. Foland, a well-to-do president of a printing company, and his wife Ethel, a music teacher. He is not making a social call.

Nursemaid to the Folands' twin sons is the teenaged Ethel May Sullivan, who lives next door to Palmer on Railroad Avenue, a less prosperous part of town, with her widowed mother and three younger sisters. About a year before, she was his girlfriend, but since then, he will claim later, she has "spurned his love."

Palmer knocks at the Folands' back door, and Ethel lets him in. There is a quarrel, a slap is heard, and then he shoots her three times, in the neck, chest, and leg, killing her. He flees the scene, "holding passersby at bay with his smoking gun," according to a press report, "as he mounted the taxi and ordered the driver to speed away." Soon afterward the taxi crashes, and Palmer surrenders himself to the police, claiming, "She has wrecked my life."

When he was brought to trial in February, Palmer's lawyers attempted to show that he was insane, arguing that several members of his family had been mentally disturbed, and suggesting that his own mental state might have been affected by gonorrhea, for which he had been treated for the past two years. Shortly after his arrest, questioned about his motive, Palmer had told reporters, "When you have had as much dealing with women as I have you will understand." It was also alleged that he was addicted to the barbiturate drug Veronal and "would sit staring at objects for long spaces of time . . . his head hung low as though he were downhearted."

The court heard details of the couple's relationship. "Love letters, identified . . . as written to Walter by Ethel Sullivan, were introduced. They were of a mushy character and established the fact some time or other Ethel and Walter had really had some sort of love affair. . . . Ethel was sixteen years old when the letters were written."

In fact she was younger—perhaps considerably younger. The newspaper reports consistently described her as seventeen at the time of her death, but her death certificate gave her age as sixteen years, eight months, and nineteen days, implying a birthdate of April 20, 1909. In the January 1920 census, however, she was reported to be nine, suggesting a birthdate in 1910, making her fifteen when she died, so her "sort of love affair" with Palmer may have begun when she was fourteen.

"As the testimony grew somewhat obscene," the *Bluefield Daily Telegraph* reported, "a few of the women [in the courtroom] retired, but most of them seemed to feel they could listen it out." This may not refer to Palmer and Sullivan's relationship but to personal details about Palmer that the paper said were unfit to print.

The jury rejected the insanity plea and found Palmer guilty of murder in the first degree but recommended life imprisonment rather than the death penalty. He greeted the verdict, it was reported, with the inexpressive demeanor he had maintained throughout the trial. After sentence had been passed, he asked if he might visit Ethel Sullivan's grave—to "make sure she was dead."

★ ★ ★

Walter Palmer as he appeared in newspapers. (Author's Collection)

As a Bluefield resident, Roy Harvey (1892–1958) would undoubtedly have heard or read about this case. Though born in Monroe County, West Virginia, he later moved with his parents and sisters to Mercer County. Since his early teens, he had worked on the railroad: first for the C&O, then for the Virginian, initially as a clerk, later as a fireman. In 1916, he married Mary Cleo Farley and in that year was promoted to locomotive engineer, "which position he held," he wrote in the *Raleigh* [West Virginia] *Register* some twenty years later, "until November 8, 1923, when he was one of 556 railroad men who left the service—on strike. He is still on that strike, which was instituted in an effort to secure justice for union labor."

He and Cleo were then living in the Princeton–Bluefield area, where he found work with the Princeton Power Co. as a motorman. While driving his trolley between Bluefield and Princeton, one day in 1925, he met three men with instrument cases: Charlie Poole and his companions Posey Rorer and Norman Woodlieff. A guitarist himself, Harvey began playing with them, and the following summer, when Poole and Rorer were thinking about a forthcoming recording session, they decided to enlist their new acquaintance. They found him at his home (now in Beckley, West Virginia), rehearsed, and set off for New York. For the next four years, Harvey's association with Poole would place him in one of the hottest acts in old-time music.

Harvey appears to have known many of the popular songs of the late Victorian and Edwardian eras, which constituted a large part of the repertoire of old-time musicians in the 1910s and '20s. Also, in the second half of the 1920s, he worked at the Beckley Music Store, where he could observe what kinds of sheet music and records were selling. He would have been familiar with other recordings about murders, such as the stories of Mary Phagan (➤4) and Naomi Wise, and would have known how popular they were with record-buyers. So it may have been Harvey who wrote "The Bluefield Murder"—or, to put it more accurately, grafted some of the facts of the case onto the rootstock of the venerable bad-man song "The Boston Burglar."

"The Bluefield Murder" is cast, like many an eighteenth- or nineteenth-century broadside, in the mold of the gallows confession, though the scaffold is replaced by the looming Gothic of the State Penitentiary at Moundsville. In keeping with such compositions, the condemned man and narrator identifies himself—not in his true name but as "Walter Summers"—and lays claim to a sound upbringing by "honest parents," though Palmer hardly knew his father, who had died when he was three. He confesses to the crime—Ethel, at least, retains her own name—and is arrested. His friends all desert him. (In fact, there were attempts to move the trial from Bluefield, since it was feared he would not get a fair hearing in his hometown.) The jury finds him guilty, the judge gives him ninety-nine, and now, speaking from his cell, he is sad and lonely—"how sad nobody knows . . . the only song that cheers my heart is 'The Convict and the Rose.'"

All the customary pieties of the genre, in fact—except for the reference to "The Convict and the Rose." In this song, a prisoner on death row remembers his true love and promises her that, when he goes to meet his end, he will carry next to his heart the rose she sent him. That the song should turn up here seems a little too good to be true, a sprig of melodramatic fancy—yet why would Harvey, or whoever wrote "The Bluefield Murder," plug somebody else's composition?

Because it really was, as you might say, a document in the case.

In its report of the trial on February 17, 1926, the *Charleston* [West Virginia] *Daily Mail* revealed:

> In an effort to show that Palmer was mentally unbalanced, the defense introduced witnesses to prove that Palmer carried about with him a phonograph record, "The Convict and the Rose," and that he was in the habit of playing the tune over and over and brooding at the same time. The record was played on a portable phonograph for the court this afternoon and proved to be on [*sic*] the ancient variety of moany songs that were popular a generation ago.

The prisoner's sister Nannie testified that Palmer had one of these disc-spinning sessions at the family home the day before the murder, and that, at his request, "[her] little son cranked the victrola and restarted the record as it would finish."

"The Convict and the Rose" was actually a new composition, published in 1925. Within that year, it had been recorded for eight companies, to be issued on some fifteen labels, by that industrious specialist in the ancient and moany, Vernon Dalhart. Almost certainly, it was one of Dalhart's discs that so beguiled Walter Palmer. A witness stated that he had offered Palmer a dollar for the record, which he wanted for the other side, "The Dream of the Miner's Child." Four of Dalhart's recordings of "The Convict and the Rose" were coupled with that piece. One of them, the Columbia disc under the pseudonym "Al Craver," was advertised in the Bluefield paper during the trial. Palmer's record collection, which his brother Charley attested was considerable, numbering fifty to seventy-five discs, also included "The Prisoner's Song," probably in one of Dalhart's many versions. Dalhart may not be held in high regard by many of today's record-collectors (➤4), but few, perhaps, would maintain that obsessive listening to his records was evidence of insanity.

★ ★ ★

Two years later, Roy Harvey, who by then had made records in his own name for Columbia, Paramount, and Gennett, besides his touring and recording work with Poole's North Carolina Ramblers, secured a deal with Brunswick for himself and *his* North Carolina Ramblers, fiddler Posey Rorer and banjo-mandolin-player Bob Hoke. At a location session in Ashland, Kentucky, in February 1928, where they cut ten estimable sides, they chose to lead off with "The Bluefield Murder," sung by Harvey with Hoke contributing the tenor harmony. Rorer's fiddle traced the line of another desperado song, "The Highwayman," which he and Harvey had recorded with Poole over a year before.

Some murder songs caught the national imagination and were taken up by singers all over the country; some remained local stories. The only other artist to record "The Bluefield Murder," a year and a half later, was Emry Arthur from Wayne County, Kentucky, who sang it for Paramount as a duet with his wife Della Hatfield. He must have got it from Harvey's disc, because not only did he follow the text almost exactly, but the very next thing he and Della did at that session was sing the ancient Old World ballad "George Collins"—the song on the other side of Harvey's record.

★ ★ ★

Walter Palmer was paroled in about 1941 and returned to Bluefield, where he got a job at a grocery store. He was arrested in August 1944 for violating parole, and again on the same charge in January 1945, when, officers said at the time of the arrest, he was carrying "a long butcher knife." By 1948, still in Bluefield, he was working as a truck driver and living with his mother, Maggie. After her death in 1951, he appears to have quit Bluefield, and his subsequent history is uncertain.

24

"A FIDDLER'S CONTEST"

The Tennessee Ramblers

Brunswick 257

Recorded in Ashland, KY, February 17, 1928
Released on October 18, 1928

Sometime in the mid-1920s, the Sievers family of Clinton, Tennessee, near Knoxville, turned themselves into a semiprofessional stringband. William (1875–1954), the paterfamilias, by day a barber, played fiddle, his son Mack (1904–88) banjo (though he could also play fiddle and guitar), and daughter Willie (1909–98) guitar. They played around eastern Tennessee and southwestern Virginia, and at Willie's suggestion, they called themselves the Tennessee Ramblers.

Thus far, a commonplace story, but the Tennessee Ramblers were not a commonplace group.

In February 1928, they were invited by Brunswick to Ashland, Kentucky, to make records. It was the company's first venture into recording in the South, and the choice of location is suggestive: Ashland, in the northeast of the state, is just a few miles up the Ohio River from Huntington, West Virginia, which, as Brunswick executives may have been aware, had proved to be fertile ground for both old-time and African American music, harvested for Gennett Records by the talent scout and Huntingtonian W. R. Calaway.

Calaway, who would later work for ARC-Brunswick, may have suggested some of the acts who were booked for this session, though the company would have needed little guidance from him to approach already recognized Appalachian musicians like Bascom Lamar Lunsford or Roy Harvey. The Tennessee Ramblers were a new name, but Brunswick had evidently heard good things about them, possibly through the company's connection with Sterchi Brothers of Knoxville, who distributed Brunswick and Vocalion records (➤3). In correspondence before the session, the company made it clear what they wanted. "Kindly have your organisation thoroughly prepared on various selections we specified in recent communication to you," wrote James O'Keefe, "so that we may execute this job with a maximum of efficiency in a minimum amount of time." The company required twelve numbers (six records) and offered $100 a record plus traveling expenses.

"We stayed at the Hanshaw Hotel," Willie remembered. (She had married a few weeks earlier and was now Willie Sievers Wiggins.) Owned by Jack Hanshaw, also a musician, it was either next door to, or just across Sixteenth Street from, Waverly Carter's Phonograph and Music Shop, where the Brunswick crew had set up their equipment. "And we met this famous steel guitar player that had been in movies that later went to Florida with us, but we met him up there and he was recording too. And so we got together kinda on it and each one knew some of the pieces that the other group knew." The "famous steel guitar player" was Frank Wilson (➤2, 13), there with banjoist Jack Reedy's Walker Mountain String Band. Also in town for recording, a week or so earlier, were Warren Caplinger's Cumberland Mountain Entertainers, a band formed round the Sieverses' good friends, and fellow Anderson Countians, George Rainey and his sons Albert and Willie. The Tennessee Ramblers were scheduled for just two days' record-making, but the lure of meeting old friends and making new ones kept them in Ashland, Willie said, for about ten days.

★ ★ ★

The first piece the Ramblers performed for the recording microphone was "A Fiddler's Contest." Brunswick had presumably commissioned this as one of their "specified selections" because of the

James Sievers, Willie Sievers Wiggins, Mack Sievers. (OTM Collection, from Mack Sievers)

success of "A Fiddlers' Convention in Georgia," done for Columbia the year before by a group drawn from the Skillet-Lickers. Willie may have chosen a ragtime piece for her guitar solo because Riley Puckett did for his in the earlier sketch.

But, unlike that earlier confection, this was a nuanced and even prophetic vignette. Though the Ramblers were in Kentucky to record, they staged "A Fiddler's Contest" at the Market House in Knoxville. The spoken introduction saying so was by Mack and Willie's cousin Walter McKinney, who frequently played guitar and Hawaiian guitar with them, and had joined them for the session. The Market House, a large hall in downtown Knoxville, had been home to fiddlers' contests for decades, and the Ramblers played there often, winning so regularly that, according to Charles Wolfe, "friends jokingly accused them of rigging the contest." But by 1928, fiddling contests were perhaps not quite the bastions of musical tradition they had once been, and the Ramblers' record dramatized this. "Fiddlin' Bill" played the old-time fiddle tune "Old Joe Clark," but Willie chose the "Silver Leaf Rag," while Mack rapped out on banjo the "Mean Man Blues."

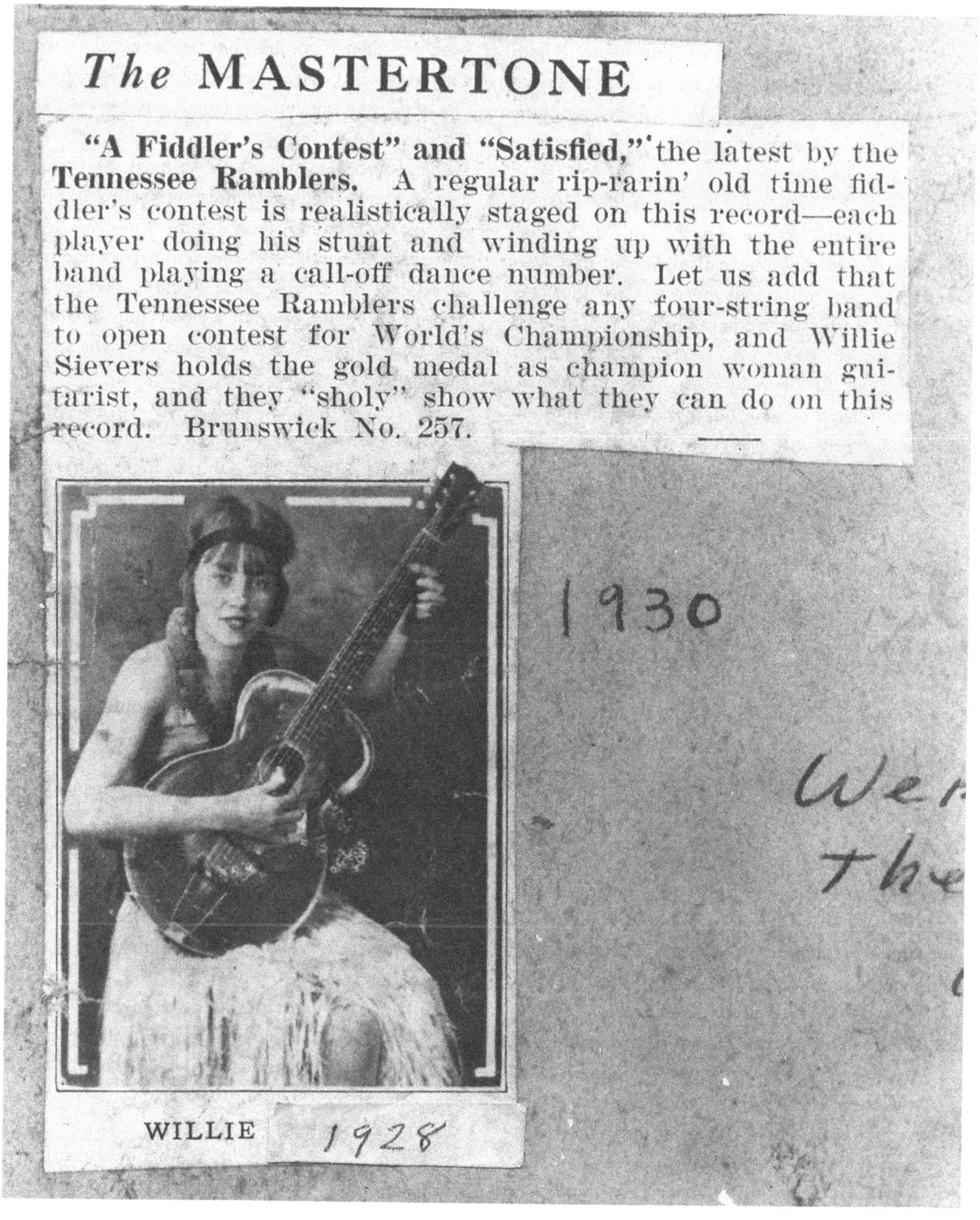

The MASTERTONE

"A Fiddler's Contest" and "Satisfied," the latest by the **Tennessee Ramblers.** A regular rip-rarin' old time fiddler's contest is realistically staged on this record—each player doing his stunt and winding up with the entire band playing a call-off dance number. Let us add that the Tennessee Ramblers challenge any four-string band to open contest for World's Championship, and Willie Sievers holds the gold medal as champion woman guitarist, and they "sholy" show what they can do on this record. Brunswick No. 257.

"A Fiddler's Contest" reviewed in the Gibson Company's house magazine *The Mastertone*. (OTM Collection, from Mack Sievers)

"I learned that," he told Wolfe, "from a Negro named Charley Bolin [possibly Charles Bolling, an Anderson County railroad worker—TR] from the Foley Hill area of Clinton. They did stuff nobody could play. You could put your fingers just like theirs . . . but it wouldn't sound the same. They had stuff in their songs you don't even hear today, all these diminished chords and all. Willie tried to copy some of their stuff on the guitar."

After the blues, the three united to raise the dust with "Bile Them Cabbage Down," but the point had been made: Dad's tunes were on the way to being ousted by the kids'. So, although this recording came quite early in the history of country music, there was already an elegiac note.

This was no fiction for the recording session. Willie would later explain that she and Mack liked their father's old-time music all right, but they also liked what they considered more modern music—the first music they played in public together, as kids, was a Hawaiian guitar piece—and, as they toured the country in the Depression, they found that their audiences liked the new numbers too. Eventually they came to play little else. As Mack recalled,

> When Dad passed away, that part of the music went too. We had always liked this Polynesian music, so about a year after he died we renamed ourselves and went to it exclusively. Every now and then, people will say, "Mack, you're gettin' above your raising, you used to play all kinds of good country music." And I say, "Wait a minute—we had a fiddler then. We don't do those bits any more because you don't just pick up a fiddle overnight."

★ ★ ★

The fiddle-contest format had enough steam in it to generate a few more recordings. In March 1930, a group of north Georgians assembled in Atlanta under the baton of guitarist and raconteur John Dilleshaw, "Seven Foot Dilly," to record the two-part sketch "A Fiddler's Tryout in Georgia" (➤54). In December, more than three and a half years since they first staged "A Fiddlers' Convention in Georgia," Clayton McMichen and company returned to the theme for Parts 3 and 4. In 1931, during a lengthy ARC session in New York, Tom (Clarence) Ashley MC'd "The Fiddler's Contest," featuring himself and the rest of the Blue Ridge Mountain Entertainers in brisk, brief examples of music from fiddle or guitar solo to full band.

Compared with these dramatizations by casts of five or six musicians, the Ramblers' sketch for four actors might seem rather low budget—and oddly titled—for it presented only one performer on each instrument, so no contest. But "A Fiddler's Contest" was notable for another reason. Eighteen-year-old Willie Sievers Wiggins, whose debut recording it was, and the only one on which she played a solo, was not merely a talented guitarist but also an equal claimant with Maybelle Carter (a very different player) for the title of the first outstanding female instrumentalist in recorded country music.

Brunswick saw the story at once. In October 1928, when "A Fiddler's Contest" was released, a photograph of the band appeared in the *Brunswick Record Edition of American Folk Songs*, a four-page pamphlet advertising the label's "Dixie Records." Willie, who in the photograph sported a glossy Louise Brooks-style bob, was presented to the reader in the style of a circus barker:

> Girl Plays Guitar With Her Feet. Ladies and what you brought with you: Right this way for the Girl Guitar-Playing wonder of the world. Plays with the Guitar held behind her—plays the instrument with her feet. Right this way to hear Willie Seivers [*sic*]—Champion Woman Guitarist of the World.

It needs to be emphasized how rare it is, in the promotional literature of old-time music, to find a spotlight falling on a female musician. It is obviously relevant that Willie Sievers Wiggins offered an appealing image. With her fashionable crop, a refutation in coiffure of Blind Alfred Reed's preachments against bobbed hair, she represents, better perhaps than anyone else in the photo gallery of recorded old-time musicians, that iconic female figure of the 1920s, the flapper. It was an intriguing splash of modernist color on the old-time canvas. But in the next decade, as we shall see (➤70, 76), the image makers of country music would encourage female performers to adopt older, less sexualized fashions, and conform to more demure archetypes.

Willie Sievers Sharp (as she became) continued to make music in her own way and with enormous skill and brio, well into her eighties.

25

"RYE WALTZ"/ "MEDLEY—SCOTTISCHE"

Bob Skiles Four Old Tuners
Okeh 45211

Recorded in San Antonio, TX, March 13, 1928
Released on May 5, 1928

This was a band from somewhere else that happened to be in San Antonio in 1928 when Okeh were making location recordings there. The chance meeting preserved a form of old-fashioned dance music unlike anything that was being documented on records. Indeed, the old-time catalogs of the late 1920s offer few recordings that so explicitly challenge the aesthetic of most present-day collectors and reissue producers—which is a good reason to take a look at them.

Late in 1927, a Midwestern couple took a winter vacation in San Antonio. But, as a newspaper there was soon to report,

> Even a vacation cannot take a man or a woman away from their work—if they really like it. . . . Mr. and Mrs. Robert Skiles of Kansas City, Mo., cannot get away from their work.
>
> Twice a week they follow their profession for the enjoyment of fellow members of the Conopus club tourist headquarters at 513 North St. Mary's street. For, assisted by two other tourists whom they met here, Mr. and Mrs. Skiles form the tourist club orchestra, and they play for all the tourist club dances.
>
> When they are not on vacation they do the same thing in their home city, and during the past few years they have broadcast from twenty-five broadcasting stations throughout the Middle West.
>
> Although all the most modern dance pieces find a place on their program, they specialize in the old tunes.
>
> Assisting Mr. and Mrs. Skiles on the tourist club orchestra are A. L. Phares of Burlington, Kan., who plays the drums, and J. L. Williamson of St. Paul, Minn., banjoist and singer. Mrs. Skiles plays the piano, and Mr. Skiles plays the violin and a group of novelty instruments. (*San Antonio Light*, January 2, 1928)

Three weeks later, the *Light* reported that "[t]he Victor phonograph company will make records by 'The Conopus Tourist Club Orchestra of S. A.'" "Victor" was an error for "Okeh," for on March 11 the *Light* ran a photograph of Skiles signing a contract with Okeh officials Polk C. Brockman and Thomas G. Rockwell, and four days later the paper announced:

> The first three records produced by the Conopus Tourist club orchestra under their two-year contract . . . have been transferred to the wax in the recording rooms of the company in the real estate building, according to Robert Skiles, orchestra leader.
>
> The numbers on the three records are: Burton's Rye Waltz, Medley Scottishe, Uncle Bob's Favorite Polka, Tourists' Special Vesuvianne, Wagner's Quadrille, and Casey Jones descriptive.

Allowing for title variations and misspellings, these were the half-dozen numbers the band had recorded two days earlier. Despite the mention of drums in the first article about the band, photographs showed a brass bass instrument, evidently a sousaphone, perhaps played by Phares, and this is heard on the recordings by "Bob Skiles Four Old Tuners."

The first release coupled "Rye Waltz," the well-known Scots tune "Coming Thro' the Rye," with a

CONTRACT GIVES S. A. PUBLICITY

When guests at the Conopus Tourists' club here formed their own orchestra they didn't know what they had started. Left to right are Robert Skiles, one of orchestra members, and P. C. Brockman and T. G. Rockwell, officials of the Okeh Phonograph company, signing contracts for records that will boost S. A.

San Antonio Light, March 11, 1928. (Author's Collection)

Bob Skiles. (Courtesy of Cathy Skiles Culver and Jerry Culver)

schottische medley combining "Jenny Lind Polka" and "Nightingale Clog." Bob Skiles's fiddling is uninflected by blues slurs, jazz improvisation, or hillbilly wildness, and the elephantine rhythm is more akin to a polka band's than to the propulsive swing of a contemporary Southwestern stringband like the East Texas Serenaders (➤19). The Old World character of these tunes was evidently spotted by someone on the staff of the English label Parlophone, which issued it in the UK.

Despite the two-year contract, the Skileses did not record again, for Okeh or any other label. But there is more to most musicians' lives than record-making, and, what with broadcasts and personal appearances, the Skileses were kept fully employed in and around San Antonio until well into the '30s, and elsewhere for a further three decades. Afterward, their sons, having learned their trade in the family band, kept the Skiles name resonating in the entertainment business for another half-century.

★ ★ ★

Robert George Skiles was born in Sylvan Grove, in Lincoln County, Kansas, on September 23, 1888. By 1910, he was teaching the violin, and in 1917, when he registered for the draft, he declared himself a self-employed traveling musician. About 1912, he had married Nellie Casey (born in Norton County, Kansas, on June 15, 1894), whom he had met while traveling with his band in Nebraska. In 1960, a reporter talked to them about those early days.

> Bob Skiles, always a musician at heart, organized his own orchestra and toured the nation. Following the tour which included playing on a show boat that stopped at most of the towns along the banks of the Mississippi, he signed his show for a Nebraska theater. As time went on, Nellie, then a youngster in braids, became the band's permanent accompanist, and shortly, Bob's wife.
>
> Chautauqua, vaudeville and dance hall audiences throughout the country laughed and danced to the music and entertainment of these versatile artists. Radio audiences, too, knew them for over a period of years they were sponsored by many nationally known business firms. (Desert Hot Springs [California] *Desert Sentinel*, March 17, 1960)

In 1915, the Skileses were living in Joplin, Missouri, where their son Robert D. was born, but they were playing farther afield: ads in the *Emporia* (Kansas) *Gazette* reported several appearances there during 1915–16. By 1916, they had moved to Emporia and were attached to the Star Theatre. A *Gazette* ad from that year promised a "social dance at the Wigwam Friday night, March 24" with "Music by Skile's [*sic*] famous orchestra, featuring xylophone and Marondrouphone"—the latter doubtless one of the "novelty" instruments previously referred to, which, as we shall see, Bob Skiles had a gift for inventing.

The Skileses maintained their base in Emporia into 1917, when their second son, Jack V., was born, but within a few years they had moved again. Robert, Jr., recalled in a 1980 interview, speaking of his early youth:

> My folks were out of Kansas City at that time, and my daddy had the pit bands on a tent show. And they played the Southwest on weekend stands, really. They were just typical tent shows that played the circuit.
>
> They took the bands out every summer with three or four tents, and Daddy stayed with the main tent, which usually made Texas, all the Southwest area. . . . They got acquainted with San Antonio in those years, and in . . . I think it was '26, my Dad came down with a big band. It was a twelve-piece band that he had put together in Kansas City and called it The Kansas City Monarchs.

★ ★ ★

Returning to 1928: no doubt encouraged by their reception, the Skileses settled in San Antonio and secured a spot on KTSA, where their "old time fiddle music" attracted the attention of Henry Ford, who flew them to Detroit to play for him. But they could also satisfy other musical tastes, as noted in an article about KTSA's summer schedule: "Airport city hour, with Commander Bob Skiles and his co-pilots, who are regularly heard every Thursday night, will give a special recital between 10 and 11 p. m. to gratify the far cry that now has assumed the proportions of a tremendous howl for 'more' of the peppy jazz so characteristic of every presentation of Bob and his gang" (*San Antonio Light*, June 24, 1928).

By late 1929, and from then until 1933, the Skileses had a regular half-hour Sunday-morning program on KTSA, billed at first as "Bob Skiles and his Four Old Timers," later as "Bob Skiles and his Haywire Orchestra."

In the spring of 1932, as hard times were overtaking many of their fellow citizens, the Skileses plunged into good works. In the *Light*'s "Around the Plaza" column on April 18, Jeff Davis commented on "Bob Skiles and his one-man relief program."

> Mr. and Mrs. Skiles . . . alone and without any public appeal, are helping 800 needy families. Skiles started out a few months ago and now has a free restaurant at 433 South St. Mary's street, where he feeds around 200 people a day, and never takes in a nickel.
>
> He gets the groceries mainly through dances given by him and his Haywire orchestra. The city lets him have the auditorium when he wants it, and the Plaza and Gunter hotels give him a floor any time he wants to have a dance. Food, clothing or tobacco constitute the price of admittance, and money is refused at the door.
>
> Nearly 100 persons who wanted to pay their dollars and get in were refused admittance at a recent dance at the auditorium. One by one they all went away and came back with cigarettes, bread and fruit. One party came in late, and were admitted for two dozen drug store limes.
>
> Skiles frequently gets unusual contributions. One man brought a calf to the door one night for his admission price, and another brought a five-gallon jar of honey. Some times they show up with just a loaf of bread. The last time he had a dance at the auditorium he took in $2000 worth of groceries, all of which were distributed to needy families the following week. He has never asked for anything, and that goes for this little publicity.

By this time, the Skileses had enlisted their older children, sixteen-year-old Robert, or "Dude" as he was now known, on drums and fourteen-year-old Jack on banjo. "Daddy played all these homemade instruments," Dude would remember.

> He made a pitchfork fiddle, and we did a lot of schoolwork. We'd go all around the auditoriums of the local schools, and he would play cigar box fiddle and give out directions on how to make all these instruments to the kids. . . .

Haywirephonic

COWBOY ballads and Old West tunes are featured by the Haywire Orchestra of San Antonio at KTSA. From left: Bob Skiles, Mrs. Bob, Swede Braum, Kid Thompson, Joe Luther

37

From *Radio Digest*, March 1931. (Author's Collection)

> All during high school and all during junior [high] school, Jack and I were playing an average of three nights a week with my folks, dances. He would book 'em and, in those days, during the Depression, we would play on commission. I guess we played every little town that there was!

The Skileses spent most of 1934 away from home, broadcasting for the Crazy Water Crystals Co. of Mineral Wells, Texas, and in Salt Lake City. In December, they returned to San Antonio and resumed their morning show on KTSA.

In 1936, Dude and Jack went out looking for musical work on their own account. In June, Jeff Davis reported, "Two San Antonio boys . . . are traveling in some very fast swing company in the West. . . . The Brothers Skiles were heard last week with the famous Tommy Dorsey and others in the Los Angeles swing jam session." In December, the impresario Irving Mills recorded "Dude Skiles and His Vine Street Boys" for his new Variety label, Dude playing trumpet (his main instrument) and Jack guitar. Davis's column kept readers informed about these releases, and, in August 1937, told them that the brothers had landed jobs with Fred Waring's Pennsylvanians. Davis's tone made it clear that the heyday of the Haywire Orchestra was over. Plainly a jazz and swing fan, Davis lost no opportunity to point the difference between hip sons and square parents, dismissing Dude and Jack's forebears as "a rube radio band" and a "hill billy band."

Bob and Nellie had ceased to feature in the city's papers, and by 1938 they had moved to California. In 1949, the *Light* mentioned that they were "out on the west coast, playing for old-time dances four or five nights a week"; their drummer was their youngest son, Bill, born in 1931. In January 1963, Dude reported to the *Light* that his parents "now are in Palm Springs, where their six-piece group plays about four nights a week. [They] live in a mobile home . . . and play at the dances staged at the recreation halls in trailer parks." He added: "There are no youngsters in the band. I believe the ages of all members total 330 years."

Bob Skiles died on November 28, 1965. Nellie eventually moved back to San Antonio, where she died on August 8, 1979. Dude Skiles died in 1993 and Jack in 2004. Bill remained in show business, having developed a comedy routine with a bass-playing schoolfriend, Pete Henderson. They did well for a couple of seasons at Disneyland in the late '50s, and continued to work in Las Vegas, Lake Tahoe, Reno, and other resorts; they also made comedy albums, appeared on television's *Hollywood Squares*, and were active until shortly before Bill's death in 2011. Among their specialties was the playing of novelty instruments, many of which had been constructed for them by Bill's father.

26

"HALLELUJAH! I'M A BUM"/"THE BUM SONG"

"Mac" (Harry McClintock)
Victor 21343

Recorded in Oakland, CA, March 16, 1928 ["The Bum Song"] and March 31, 1928 ["Hallelujah! I'm a Bum"]
Released in April/May 1928

Reissued on *Poor Man's Heaven* (BMG/Bluebird 50958) ["Hallelujah! I'm a Bum"]

Online: Spotify ["Hallelujah! I'm a Bum"] • YT [both]

"The half century between 1880 and 1930 were [*sic*] the palmy days of the American tramp. He suffered often from hunger and exposure, but he escaped the priggishness and Babbitry of the period. Above all, he was free to travel where he liked: for him the whistle of a fast freight was an invitation to the unknown and to adventure. Thus, round the campfires in the hobo jungles, ballads were composed and passed on by word of mouth, which thumbed the nose at the lives of stable, hard-working folk." With these words, Alan Lomax introduced "Hallelujah! I'm a Bum" in *The Penguin Book of American Folk Songs*.

The song is probably best known in this, its first recording, by Harry McClintock, or "Mac," one of the outstanding characters of old-time music. (For a short biography, see *Country Music Originals*.) Since 1925, Mac had been a popular broadcaster in San Francisco, on the KFRC Blue Monday Jamboree. He told stories for kids, sang, and led a knockabout crew called the Haywire Orchestry. In the same month as the recording, *Radio Digest* noted that "MAC, Children's Hour Entertainer, a Favorite with 'Youngsters from 9 to 90', has probably wrecked the old '97' more times than anyone else."

The tune of "Hallelujah! I'm a Bum" is clearly taken from the Presbyterian hymn "Revive Us Again," but the origin of the words is uncertain. According to the hobo poetry researcher Bud L. McKillips, they were written by a member of the international labor union, the Industrial Workers of the World (IWW), or "Wobblies." It might have been McClintock himself, who sang it at the fourth IWW convention, in Chicago in 1908. In later years, he firmly claimed he did write it—a decade earlier, when he was fifteen. The text was printed by the IWW in 1908, and subsequently appeared in its *Little Red Songbook*.

The published version runs like this:

Why don't you work like other folks do?
How the hell can I work when there's no
work to do?
Hallelujah, I'm a bum,
Hallelujah, bum again,
Hallelujah, give us a handout
To revive us again . . .

Whenever I get all the money I earn,
The boss will be broke, and to work he must turn.

Oh, I like my boss, he's a good friend of mine,
That's why I am starving out on the bread line . . .

Other texts have been collected that differ considerably; the format of the song seems to have invited variation and addition. The version Mac recorded twenty years later is quite close to the text printed in 1927 by Carl Sandburg (who described it as an "old song heard at the water tanks of railroads in Kansas . . . picked up later by the I. W. W.'s") but scrubs all references to bosses; it is more concerned to paint a picture of a cheerful work-dodger enjoying the spring weather. The teeth of the 1908 text have not all been drawn, but the Victor record of "Hallelujah! I'm a Bum" is scarcely a prescription for working-class action.

★ ★ ★

In the text as published by the IWW, "bum" was more or less synonymous with "hobo," but later commentators made an important distinction: the hobo was an honest worker, itinerant

Harry "Mac" McClintock (center) with Frank Zirn (harmonica) and Virgil Ward (fiddle), members of his "Haywire Orchestry" on KFRC, 1928. (Author's Collection)

but industrious, whereas the bum was an idle vagrant: "The hobo works and wanders . . . the bum drinks and wanders."

The line between the two classes may have been fatally easy to cross. A traveling hobo was sometimes compelled to support himself by "bumming" (asking for handouts), and at any time a "legitimate" hobo need only be arrested as a vagrant to become a bum.

These shifting meanings were reflected in the piece that Victor chose to couple with "Hallelujah!," simply titled "The Bum Song," but better known as "The Great American Bum": "Come all you jolly jokers and listen while I hum; A story I'll relate to you of the great American bum . . ."

Over the back-and-forth rhythm of his guitar, the singer reads from his CV: "I've topped the spruce and worked the sluice and taken a turn at the plow, I've searched for gold in the rain and cold and worked on a river scow, I've dug the clam and built the dam and packed the elusive prune . . ." No slacker, this. But now he is on the road again and knocking at a door for a free meal. "Good morning, mum. I just got in." "Yes, but you can just get out again," retorts the lady of the house. For the rest of the song, the singer is a carefree work-shirker. Has rejection suddenly turned a deserving hobo into a worthless bum? Is there a moral or political point here, or is it all just a patched-pants vaudeville routine?

The fluidity of the terms "hobo" and "bum" is also present in "Who Said I Was a Bum?," written by Howard Johnson (not *that* Howard Johnson) in late summer 1928, possibly in response to "The Bum Song," and recorded soon afterward by Vernon Dalhart and Frank Luther:

Who said I was a bum? (x2)
I haven't worked in twenty years—
I guess I'm not so dumb.
And as I tramp along the road,
The people hear me hum:
"I know I'm a hobo,
But who said I was a bum?"

Ad in the *Oakland* [California] *Tribune*, April 25, 1928. (Author's Collection)

Johnson was a professional songwriter, not a Wobbly propagandist, but he did seem to be aware of a distinction between hobo and bum. For many songwriters, however, this was mere pedantry: hobohood (or bummery) was simply a new craze to be exploited, and indeed the next three years saw a flood of songs about it: Mac's own "Hobo's Spring Song," Bob Miller's "Free Wheeling Hobo," Fields and Hall's "Oh! For the Life of a Hobo," and dozens more, written or recorded by Gene Autry, Cliff Carlisle, Asa Martin, and many others. Goebel Reeves, "The Texas Drifter," the most assiduous documentarist of the hobo experience during the Depression, returned to the subject again and again in knowing, sometimes ironic pieces like "The Hobo's Last Letter," "Station H. O. B. O.," "The Hobo and the Cop," and "Hobo's Lullaby."

★ ★ ★

Abbe Niles plugged Mac's record in the September 1928 issue of *The Bookman*.

> The famous "Hallelujah, I'm a Bum" . . . has recently been withdrawn from the Communist and I. W. W. songbooks. Robert Wolf, protesting in *The New Masses* against this omission, alleges that "Hallelujah" is "more pointed, clever and *working-class* in thought and diction than many . . . that have replaced it." If you aren't acquainted with the song, and want to know what Mr. Wolf considers working-class thought, you can listen to it on a new Victor record, sung by Harry McClintock.

A month later, a more widely read columnist, Gilbert Swan, observed:

> A few years ago "Hallelujah, I'm a Bum" was frowned upon as the marching song of the "wobblies," or I. W. W. Today it's chanted on every corner and avenue of New York. A few years ago one might have flirted with those authorities who saw radicalism seizing the nation by its throat. Today they sell extra verses at 20 for five cents in Times Square. Phonograph shops in the Broadway belt grind out the "wobblie" anthem by the hour. Radios

The Australian issue not only put the bum in quotes but also added a note reassuring purchasers that no vulgarity was intended. (David Crisp Collection)

> broadcast it and every urchin chants it from his boot-black stand. (Cumberland [Maryland] *Evening Times*, October 19, 1928)

By then the song had been covered by Vernon Dalhart, the popular singer Ernest Hare in hillbilly guise as "Hobo Jack Turner," and Frank Luther under any number of pseudonyms. All these cover versions followed Mac's original in coupling "Hallelujah!" with "The Bum Song," and faithfully copied their guitar accompaniments, with what Mac described as their "rollicking, devil-may-care lilt." There was even a Swedish version of the record, "Halleluja, Ja' å Koling"/"Kolingens Visa" (Columbia, 1928) by singer Fred Carlsten, sung to a swaggering rhythm of accordion and banjo.

Mac had other hits, such as "The Big Rock Candy Mountains," which gained new popularity in a new century after its use in *O Brother, Where Art Thou?*, yet he lost his Victor recording contract in 1931, though he remained a fixture on San Francisco airwaves. But the melody of "Hallelujah! I'm a Bum" was heard across the nation again in Charlie Chaplin's 1936 movie *Modern Times*, first accompanying a march of protesting and placard-waving workers, then a couple of times later in more conventional scenes of down-and-outery.

Harry McClintock has, I believe, an unnoticed legatee. His dry and sometimes dark humor, his working-man's politics, the piled-up occupational checklist of "The Bum Song," lines like "I beat my way from Frisco Bay to the rockbound coast of Maine" . . . in 1928, these could have been richly suggestive things to the music-loving Oklahoma teenager Woody Guthrie.

27

"HOME AGAIN MEDLEY"

Red Mountain Trio
Columbia 15260-D

Recorded in Atlanta, GA, April 20, 1928
Released in late June 1928
Sold 13,121

As the pioneers of phonography proudly watched their inventions at work, the stylus making its steady circular passage in the groove of cylinder or disc, it must surely have occurred to someone that there was more than one way in which a recording could be a journey in time. What the phonographic medium dispensed in two, three, or four minutes need not just be songs, tunes, or recitations that took precisely that long to perform. It could also compress into that timespan longer events—such as a train or automobile ride, a trip of which the record would offer highlights.

Such phonotravelogs entered old-time music early (the first may have been Al Bernard's "On a Slow Train through Arkansas" in 1925) and remained a favorite device of storytellers. Automobile enthusiasts had several bards, preeminently Oscar Ford, promoter of "Henry Ford's Model A" and narrator of "Race Between a Ford and Chevrolet" (➤38). Cyclists are acknowledged in Uncle Eck Dunford's comically rueful monologue "My First Bicycle Ride" (Victor, 1927). Older forms of transportation, too, as in John Dilleshaw's "Walkin' Blues" (Vocalion, 1930): "Me and my girl went out for a buggy ride. I went round to the liver complaint stable. Hired myself a four-wheeled horse and a bobtailed buggy . . ."

But when it comes to stories about journeys, old-time musicians love to tell about trains. Grayson and Whitter opened their 1927 Victor record "Train Forty-Five" by announcing that it was "leavin' Terminal Station, Atlanta, Georgia"—which they knew because Atlanta was where they had gone to make the recording. Jimmie Davis took the same starting point for "The Davis Limited" (Victor, 1931): "This train leaves Atlanta all cocked and primed and headin' for points southwest. Go to bed, chillun, hush your cryin'—let's all take a ride on the old Peavine." And there were many instrumental evocations of train travel by fiddlers (➤60) and harmonica players.

Some musicians were more exact than just "leavin' Atlanta." Perhaps the first old-time recording that

Jimmy Yates's Boll Weevils, 1928, from a Victor catalog: possibly Al Treadway, Yates, possibly Alfred McCarty. (OTM Collection)

(Author's Collection)

could double as a route map was the Red Mountain Trio's "Home Again Medley." A bell rings. "All aboard! L&N north for Evergreen—Greenville—Montgomery—Wetumpka—Clanton—Calera—Birmingham. All aboard!" The departure station must be Mobile, Alabama. Then, while the musicians, on Hawaiian guitar, rhythm guitars, and harmonica, play a medley including "My Old Kentucky Home" and "Home Sweet Home," someone reads the script:

> Tickets, please . . . Magazines—*Snappy Stories, Whiz Bang, True Confessions* . . . candies, cigars, peanuts, Cracker Jack—a prize in every packet . . . sandwiches, coffee . . . All out for Birmingham!

The Red Mountain Trio was one of several recording aliases adopted by the steel guitarist Jimmy Yates and his colleagues during a productive two-year recording career. "Home Again Medley" is typical of the sides they cut under this billing, a carefully arranged playlet involving music, singing, talking, and sound effects. All the references are from real life: *Snappy Stories* and *True Confessions* were monthly 10-cent magazines devoted to slightly daring short stories and illustrations, while *Captain Billy's Whiz Bang* was a pocket-sized "men only" title that began at slightly daring and moved on up. Cracker Jack was, and is, a caramel-coated popcorn and peanut confection.

James F. Yates (1896–1975) was a longtime resident of Birmingham, Alabama, where he worked as a salesman for the Clark & Jones Piano Company—which, as a music store, probably gave him his contacts with record companies—and broadcast over WAPI, which moved from Auburn to Birmingham in 1928, and WBRC. One or both stations probably had transmitters high up on Red Mountain, a long ridge south of Birmingham. At other sessions, when he used band names like Jimmy Yates' Boll Weevils (Victor) or The Four Buzz Saws (Brunswick–Vocalion), he employed guitarists and Birmingham residents Alfred McCarty, Moses Sigler, and Chalmers Linthicum, and singer and ukulele player Al Treadway, and some of these may have participated in "Home Again Medley." Yates's groups extend the boundaries of recorded old-time music with their repertoire of popular songs ("Gypsy Love Song," "Sailing Down the Chesapeake Bay,"

(Author's Collection)

"Three O'Clock in the Morning"), waltzes, comic novelties ("Elevator Blues"), and blackface numbers ("Baptising Sister Lucy Lee").

A few months after the release of "Home Again Medley," another group recorded for Columbia that had surely been listening to it. The Rainey Old Time Band, a fiddle-led ensemble from southern Mississippi, opened "Engineer Frank Hawk" with a cry of "All aboard!," then listed the stops in a journey from (probably) Laurel, Mississippi, by way of Ellisville, Hattiesburg, Purvis, and Poplarville, to New Orleans. Since that was where they were making the recording, they may have been presenting their own itinerary.

Even more detailed route maps were provided in "Railroadin' Some," a 1929 Vocalion recording by the African American singer and guitarist Henry Thomas ("Ragtime Texas"), who enumerated the stops on the Texas & Pacific line from Fort Worth to Texarkana, and then on the "Katy" (the Missouri, Kansas and Texas Railway, or MKT) from Dallas to Chicago, punctuating the litanies of place-names with whistle and airbrake effects on the set of quills (panpipes) he carried on a rack round his neck.

The template was still operating more than a decade later, when Byron Parker and His Mountaineers' "Peanut Special" (Bluebird, 1940) charted the railroad journey from Columbia to Chester, South Carolina. The piece that lies behind "Peanut Special," the Rouse Brothers' "Orange Blossom Special" (Bluebird, 1939), offers no route map, but it does echo the Red Mountain Trio in its sales talk: "Popcorn, peanuts, and goobers! Yes, sir, buy 'em right here on this train, first train goin' south!"

★ ★ ★

"Home Again Medley" exemplifies an important fact about hillbilly records: how particular they are about *place*. By alluding to somewhere specific, a recording acquired authenticity, rootedness. It might not be a place the listener knew, more often than not it wasn't, but the people on the record knew it, and that made them hometown boys, proud of their raising, and thus admirable.

It was for this reason, or something akin to it, that Jimmie Rodgers so often namechecked places he knew, like Mississippi (in four different songs), Memphis, or New Orleans, as well as seven other states. Sometimes, in order to bond the music closer to the musicians who recorded it, a tune would be given a new name: when the Mississippi fiddler Hoyt Ming recorded a piece he knew as "Florida Blues," his producer Ralph Peer retitled it, closer to home, as "Tupelo Blues."

Band names, which were often invented by record producers rather than the musicians, also emphasized the authenticity of place, identifying the players' home state (Kentucky Thorobreds, Georgia Crackers, North Carolina Ramblers), or county (Leake County Revelers, Reaves White County Ramblers), or community (Proximity String Quartet, Scottdale String Band), or workplace (Avondale Mills Quartet, another group from Birmingham), or a topographical landmark (Lookout Mountain Revelers, White Mountain Orchestra). These locators conveyed an impression that *this* (and only this) was how a group from *here* (and only here) made music. You, the listener, might think you knew this music, but you would find instead that it was intriguingly not quite what you were used to. Calling a tune "Birmingham Rag," or a band the Red Mountain Trio, not only evoked pride in the music within that community but also had the power to excite curiosity about it, and create record sales, in the world beyond.

28

"A RED-HEADED WIDOW WAS THE CAUSE OF IT ALL"/"DON'T GET ONE WOMAN ON YOUR MIND"

Willard Hodgin (Banjo Joe)
Victor 21485

Recorded in New York, NY, May 7, 1928
Released c. July/August 1928

Reissued on *Turn Me Loose: Outsiders of Old-Time Music* (Tompkins Square TSQ2905) ["Don't Get One Woman on Your Mind"]

Online: Spotify ["Don't Get One Woman on Your Mind"]

I feel like calling Willard Hodgin the McGonagall of old-time music. William Topaz McGonagall of Dundee, Scotland (if you are not familiar with him), was one of the most prolific poets of the nineteenth century and is generally accounted as the worst. His verses were undisciplined in structure, tin-eared in rhythm, and full of plonking anticlimax. Hodgin was a match for him in every respect. But the Scotsman was at least a straightforward storyteller, whereas the American bard's tales were hectic journeys through a jungle of the imagination.

> Now there's a widow living not far from me,
> And she had a little banjo and she danced while
> she sung,
> Oh, she played the good old tune called "Go to It
> While You're Young" . . .
> Well, I was so happy I couldn't keep away,
> So I just up and married the little old gal one day.
> She had five children of her own, now we have
> ten in our home.
> There's a kid for top and bottom and all round
> my bed
> And every blamed one of them have to be fed . . .

"A Red-Headed Widow Was the Cause of It All," from which this passage comes, and "Don't Get One Woman on Your Mind" are stories of courtship and marriage, which are among Hodgin's favorite themes. "A Red-Headed Widow" begins by outlining the joys of single life, much like Chubby Parker in "I'm a Stern Old Bachelor" (➤10); but, as we just saw, conjugation awaits. Now a married man, he attempts to reclaim his former lay-about lifestyle, but his wife gets mad and declares, "You'll sleep with the kids and not with me." The song closes with the narrator ruefully recalling the joys of wooing:

> We met in the barnyard, and she says she cares,
> But while we made love, we smelled the pig tails
> and the ears.

Hodgin's performances are crazy quilts of storytelling, jokes, and patches of verse ripped from old minstrel songs. In "Don't Get One Woman on Your Mind," he alludes to "Climbin' up the Golden Stairs" and "When the Good Lord Sets You Free," stitches in phrases like "banjo on my knee" and "satisfied, tickled to death," and parodies the old bedtime prayer "Now I Lay Me Down to Sleep." In a minstrel commonplace, the red-headed widow kills a chicken and saves him a wing.

The instrumental setting for these hotchpotch narratives is a kind of stream-of-consciousness banjo playing, unstructured strumming with sudden slides to improbable chords. The instrument sounds like a tenor banjo, probably open-tuned. Hodgin plays as if he is self-taught and doesn't care who knows it. The musician and reissue producer Frank Fairfield has described him as an outsider artist. He merits that title more than anyone else in recorded old-time music.

★ ★ ★

Hodgin crammed almost all his record-making into seven months, November 1927–May 1928, when he made nine discs for five companies. A succession of producers were intrigued by him, but few for long. He didn't possess a wide range of subject matter: the songs that are not about courtship or marriage are chiefly about trains, generally ones that crash. Like McGonagall, again, whose most celebrated ode was on the collapse of the Tay Bridge, near Dundee, in 1879 while a train was crossing it, he was drawn to mechanical catastrophe.

(Author's Collection)

Now and then he may refer to an earlier composition: "I'm Just a Ramblin' Gambler"—which he recorded for Columbia as Banjo Joe, possibly his stage name—has a distant kinship to "Jack o' Diamonds" and other gambling songs, and "the train that never returned again" in "The Engineer's Hand Was on the Throttle" (Plaza, 1928) may have been prompted by "The Ship That Never Returned," a song of the Civil War era, still popular in 1925. But it's difficult to picture Hodgin singing received repertoire: his musical imagination was too peculiar. At an early trial session for Brunswick, he offered a couple of old minstrel favorites, possibly learned from recordings by Harry C. Browne, but they were rejected. When he next auditioned, for Okeh six months later, he had learned the lesson and came with his own compositions, and after that he sang almost exclusively from the Willard Hodgin folio: "Courtin' the Widow," "Don't Love a Smiling Sweetheart," "Quit Knockin' on the Jail House Door," "The Judge Done Me Wrong," "Love Is a Ticklish Thing," "An Ugly Gal's Got Something Hard to Beat" . . . they have a minstrel ring, and perhaps Hodgin performed some of them in blackface, but his professional career, such as it was, is cloaked in mystery.

He was born Willard Randolph Hodgin on July 8, 1897, in Roanoke, Virginia, where his father Jesse Franklin Hodgin worked in the liquor business. It seems probable that the family were Quakers. In 1918, Willard, his parents, and his three brothers moved to Greensboro, North Carolina, where J. F.'s family originated. A song that Willard later sang (but didn't claim to write), "The Girl That Lived on Polecat Creek," alludes to a waterway in southern Guilford County, below Greensboro, that flows southeast into Randolph County and enters Deep River. Another branch of the Hodgin family has owned a farm on Polecat Creek for almost two hundred years.

Willard studied at the University of North Carolina, then in New York. He may have gained some performing skills as a member of the University's Dialectic Literary Society, which held regular smokers. After his father's death in 1923, he lived at the family home, holding a variety of jobs or none. Following his spree around the record companies in 1927–28, he continued to write and publish songs, two of which, "Roll on, River" and "Yazoo Train on the Arkansaw Line," were broadcast and recorded by Vernon Dalhart during 1929. In the 1930 census, he gave his occupation as "composer [of] music." His last known published song was "Married Women Blues" in 1935.

There are hints that he continued to be musically active, or that he wished people to think so. In Greensboro city directories between 1946 and 1960, he was often listed as a musician, and when he died (at home, of heart disease, on February 26, 1964), the *Carolina Alumni Review* described him as "formerly a musical comedy actor."

In 1941, when he registered for the draft—living at the family home, "in business for [him]self"—he was five feet ten and a half inches tall, weighed 175, had blue eyes, brown hair, and a sallow complexion. These are the only personal details of Willard Hodgin to be gleaned from the dry soil of public records. No photograph has surfaced. I have found no one who remembers him. He never married. Perhaps the wild, unpredictable spirit of his music was mistress enough.

29

"STAY IN THE WAGON YARD"

"Peg" Moreland
Victor V-40008

Recorded in Chicago, IL, July 5, 1928
Released in January 1929
Sold 23,808

Online: YT

On January 4, 1929, Victor Records launched a new catalog, initially called "Native American Melodies," dedicated to new recordings of old-time music. The V-40000 list commenced with the Carter Family's "Wildwood Flower"/"Forsaken Love," which went on to sell over 120,000 copies. After that spirited start, the pace slackened considerably, and out of the next half-year's releases only one, other than a Jimmie Rodgers coupling, would top 20,000. It was not by one of the now revered stringband acts on the list, such as the Carolina Tar Heels or the Georgia Yellow Hammers, but by a radio singer from Dallas, "Peg" Moreland, singing a wry comic song.

"Stay in the Wagon Yard" has the venerable theme of the naif countryman who takes a trip to town and is outwitted by venal and streetwise urbanites. In eighteenth- and nineteenth-century broadsides, the simpleton is often a young army or navy recruit, let loose in a city for the first time, and the trickster a woman of the streets who drugs him and leaves him with empty pockets, if nothing worse. Whether in song, tale, or joke, such stories of guileless bumpkins amused several generations of more sophisticated listeners.

The setting of "Stay in the Wagon Yard" is carefully composed for a rural audience. A "jolly farmer" comes to the city to sell his cotton. He settles his horses in the wagon yard, buys some gin, and starts to take in the town. Accosted by a "dude," he buys several rounds of drinks, which leaves him broke. Sadder and wiser, he advises fellow farmers not to go sightseeing: "Just go get you a half a pint and stay in the wagon yard." But worse is to follow. At home "a deacon in a hardshell church," he fears "the sisters" will hear of his misdemeanors. He finds the men who bilked him, drunkenly carousing outside a "soul salvation hall," but they throw him out in a dry-goods box.

It has the ring of a song from the late nineteenth or early twentieth century. A similarly gullible rube strolls open-mouthed along the streets of New York in an 1895 composition by Walter P. Keen, "The Day the Farmer Came to See the Town," but research has not yet yielded a direct antecedent of Moreland's ditty.

So who was this bard of the yard?

Jackson Arnot Moreland (1892–1973) was from around Canyon, Texas, just south of Amarillo. As a young man he worked in the family grocery business and for the railroad as a brakeman or mail clerk, and studied law, which led him to be appointed a justice of the peace in Canyon in 1921, an office for which he campaigned by singing "witty ditties." A few years later, he tried that out on WFAA in Dallas, and mail from listeners quickly established him as a fixture at the station. Though there is no evidence that he had firsthand experience of the cattle range—which might have been difficult for a man with half his right leg missing—he was dubbed "Cowboy Bard," and a story printed in Southwestern papers in 1927 under the headline "BARNYARD TENOR SINGS OF RANGE" colorfully developed this theme:

> When the plaintive drone of "Bury Me Not on the Lone Prairie-e-e" is sailing over the ether and out of the speakers of thousand of sets in the Southwest it is a pretty safe bet that J. A. "Peg" Moreland is at the business end of the microphone at WFAA, the Dallas News–Sears Roebuck station. "Peg" . . . sings of the cowpuncher and the cow country with a sincerity that bespeaks long association with the business

"Peg" Moreland in *Rural Radio*, 1938. (OTM Collection)

> of which he sings. Moreland regards the microphone as the camp fire and the unseen radio audiences as his buddies circled around it after a hard day on the range, and sings and plays unconcerned with the knowledge that he is being heard and enjoyed in all parts of the country.

The story also gave what purported to be Moreland's own account of his injury.

> Waal, I got kinda tired punchin' cattle and thought I'd try herdin' box cars for a change. Got a job as a brakeman and locked horns with a fast rattler one day that threw me. If I'd stayed breakin' broncs instead of brakin' railroad trains I'd still have it [i.e., his leg]. But that's all right, I've got another one anyway. (*Eufaula* [Oklahoma] *Indian Journal*, August 18, 1927)

Moreland sometimes took radio jobs elsewhere: for part of 1928 he was on the WLS National Barn Dance, and he also had spells on stations in Oklahoma City and west Texas. But his association with WFAA spanned at least two decades. For much of the '30s he was part of a troupe called the Gladiola Gloom Chasers, broadcasting every weekday, sponsored by Gladiola, "The Washed-Wheat Flour You KNOW Is CLEAN."

He also made personal appearances all over the Southwest, at fiddlers' conventions, fairs, shows, and rodeos. In 1939, he and other WFAA acts were booked for the Southern Oklahoma Electrical & Industrial Show. "Songs from the range, from the section house, and from the hills are all included in the amazing list which 'Peg' Moreland has compiled during a long career" (*The Daily Ardmoreite*, September 10).

He claimed he knew over a thousand songs from memory. The WFAA librarian, who used him as a source for songs that weren't in the station's collection, said his recall of song lyrics was the most remarkable he had ever witnessed. Moreland seems to have been strictly a song-carrier rather than a composer. His own description of himself was "ditty editor"—if a song's lyrics didn't suit him, he rewrote them until they did.

"In addition to his radio work," remarked the writer of a profile in 1935, "he has recorded a number of phonograph records which are perennial best sellers" (*Waxahachie Daily Light*, September 25). Among the other ditties he recorded for Victor at four sessions between 1928 and 1930 were "He Never Came Back," "I'm Saving up Coupons" (another good seller), "When I Had but Fifty Cents," and "I Got Mine"—comic songs that were widely enjoyed and frequently recorded by other old-time acts. But, as the descriptions above hint, Moreland's repertoire was broader than this, and on his recordings he interspersed the rib-ticklers with sentimental pieces like "Over the Hills to the Poorhouse" (➤41) and Western songs, notably the touching "Make Me a Cowboy Again [for a Day]," which he was the only singer of his time to record.

But "Stay in the Wagon Yard" was his bestseller and was much copied: in guitar-accompanied treatments by the Shelton Brothers and Lew Childre, and fiddle-band versions by Lowe Stokes and Earl Johnson. Stokes's text, sung by banjoist Arthur Tanner, is very close to Moreland's, and I suspect it was learned from his recording. The urge among musicians not simply to take over other artists' material but to improve it, by devising more elaborate settings, would be a driving force for change in the young industry that was not yet called country music.

30

"ELEVEN CENT COTTON FORTY CENT MEAT"—PARTS 1 AND 2

Bob Ferguson [Bob Miller]
Columbia 15297-D

Recorded in New York, NY, August 17, 1928
Released in September or October 1928
Sold 23,831

Online: Spotify, YT

The American farmer was in bad shape in 1928. "For the most part," wrote the historian Elizabeth Stevenson, "the rural regions of the West and the South were excluded from the general prosperity as if they had been other countries." Cotton had been ravaged by the boll weevil and other crops by drought. Prices were going haywire. Sitting at a piano in a New York studio, Bob Miller took on the role of a reporter from the frontline of agricultural conflict.

> Eleven cent cotton, forty cent meat—how in the world can a poor man eat?
> Flour up high, cotton down low—how in the world can we raise the dough?
> Our clothes worn out, shoes run down, old slouch hat with a hole in the crown,
> Back nearly broken, fingers all worn, cotton goin' down to rise no more.
>
> Eleven cent cotton, ten dollar pants—who in the devil has got a chance?
> We can't buy clothes, we can't buy meat—got too much cotton, not enough to eat.
> Can't help each other, what shall we do? I can't solve the problem, so it's up to you.
> Eleven cent cotton, two dollar hose—guess we will have to go without any clothes.
>
> Eleven cent cotton, a carload of tax—the load's too heavy for our poor backs,
> Got a set of farmers we all know well—there's something wrong as sure as hell.
> We all work hard, we groan and sweat, we're plumb ruined and a blowed-up set.
> No use talkin', any man's beat, with eleven cent cotton and forty cent meat

. . . and so on for three more verses, and a further six on the other side of the record. Miller had published the song, "words & music by B. Miller & Emma Dermer," six months earlier, on February 25, 1928. The date is important.

Miller was from Memphis, where he was born in 1895. As a young man, he wrote jazz and blues numbers, publishing some of them through his own company Beale Street Music, played on WMC, and led the orchestra on the steamboat *Idlewild*. During the 1920s, he seems to have commuted between Memphis and New York, presumably intending to establish himself as a big-city songwriter. He had settled in New York by 1928 when he cut "Eleven Cent Cotton," his first vocal recording. Perhaps to create a persona distinct from Bob Miller the songwriter, he billed himself as "Bob Ferguson."

Emma Dermer was an older Memphian, of German parentage; her only other known connection with Miller is that they were both Jewish. On Vernon Dalhart's 1929 Victor record of "Eleven Cent Cotton," she is credited with composing the music and he the words. Miller's claim has never been questioned.

★ ★ ★

During the winter of 1926–27, a set of verses began appearing in Southwestern newspapers. The earliest examples I have traced were in the last week of December 1926 in papers in Lockhart and Robstown, Texas, where the verses were credited to Mrs. S. C. Ford of Frisco, Texas. They were reproduced in further Texas papers in January 1927, similarly credited; but the same verses had appeared in the *Shreveport Times* on January 2, now attributed to "Virginia Brown, Freshman, Hope Street." Two weeks later, the paper commented:

> Virginia Jones [*sic*] is only a school girl in the Hope street high school, but is showing splendid ability in writing verse. A poem that she wrote a few weeks ago on "Eleven-Cent Cotton and Forty-Cent Meat," and which was published on the school page of The Shreveport Times, is attracting more than local interest.

On January 28, far away in North Carolina, the *Gastonia Daily Gazette* reported: "A high school girl of Shreveport, La., has described the situation in the cotton belt so well that the lines have been published throughout the section." The paper then quoted two of the verses that had been published in the Southwestern press.

Over the next few weeks, Texas and Oklahoma papers continued to print the verses under Mrs. Ford's name, while the *Shreveport Times* and papers elsewhere insisted upon Ms. Brown's claim. The Opelousas [Louisiana] *Clarion-News* (February 18) reported that her text had been "posted in the cigar case of the Imperial Hotel at Minden, La.," where a traveling soap salesman had read it while waiting for his dinner and composed a reply, recommending farmers to switch from cotton to livestock.

Nor was this the first riposte to the verses. From the start, the Texas papers printing Mrs. Ford's text had often followed it with a response, "The Problem Solved," by Walter E. Lewis, a grocery store proprietor in his mid-fifties from Celeste, Texas:

> When cotton's low and eats are high,
> It appears to me to diversify
> Would be a sane and easy way
> To bring about a better day . . .

By March, some of the Texas press was being converted to Ms. Brown's cause, but as spring passed into summer, the story wilted and died.

The verses in question, whether credited to Mrs. Ford or Ms. Brown, appeared under the title "Eleven Cent Cotton and Forty Cent Meat." Except for one line, they are virtually identical to the first three stanzas of Miller's recording, made more than a year and a half later. His conclusion to the second verse, "Eleven cent cotton, two dollar hose—guess we will have to go without any clothes," replaces the earlier text's tougher "We've got no homes, we've got no wealth; losing our credit, ruining our health." That aside, Miller recites the Ford–Brown verses practically word for word. He might almost be reading them out of one of those newspapers.

We have no reason to think that Miller did not devise most of the remaining verses, in which he relentlessly catalogs the travails of the farming family: bugs, floods, extreme temperatures. But his climax, the final stanza of Part 2, a litany of deprivation—

> No corn in the crib, no chicks in the yard, no
> meat in the smokehouse, no tubs full of lard,
> No cream in the pitcher, no honey in the mug, no
> butter on the table and no 'lasses in the jug

—takes us straight back to those newspapers of a year or more ago. It is derived, word for word, from "The Problem Solved."

* * *

In 1935, the syndicated columnist James Aswell interviewed Miller at his "cubicle office on the eighth floor of the Brill Building," at 1619 Broadway, and reported: "Bob sang ['Eleven Cent Cotton'] himself

Cullman Democrat, October 20, 1938. (Author's Collection)

for the platter. He can't sing a note." Yet "Cotton" had sold "over 2,500,000 . . . more records than ever sold of a single song in the history of the world" (*Hammond* [Indiana] *Times*, November 2, 1935).

Horse feathers.

The song did get around. Vernon Dalhart covered it for Victor, selling 39,355, and Carson Robison for Champion, close behind with 37,280. Add Miller's original disc and sales rise to six figures. Besides, Miller remade it pseudonymously, and with different musical arrangements, for Grey Gull and Van Dyke; Dalhart did it again for Edison; Robison for four further labels; and "Hank Smith" (Al Bernard) for Vocalion—all in 1928–29. A substantial hit, for sure, but not a million seller, or anything like one.

In 1930, the Mississippi blues singer Son House in his "Dry Spell Blues—Part 1" offered slightly revised market prices: "Pork chops is forty-five cents a pound, cotton is only ten." In the same year, Miller redeployed the idea for a different farming constituency as "Four Cent Tobacco and Forty Cent Meat," and two years later he updated the original number as "Five Cent Cotton." In 1935, singer Buck Nation reconstructed it in a "things are getting better" spirit under the gently ironic title "Twelve Cent Cotton Rollin' in Wealth." Uncle Dave Macon was still singing "Eleven Cent Cotton" on the Grand Ole Opry in the late '30s.

A curious resonance from "Eleven Cent Cotton" sounds in Jimmie Rodgers's 1932 recording "No Hard Times." Buoyantly—or satirically?—dismissing Depression thinking, he tells the world how well he's doing, and, echoing three phrases from the verse last quoted, boasts that he's got corn in his crib, a bucket of lard, and chickens in his backyard.

★ ★ ★

Bob Miller stands tall in the history of country music, although he has been invisible to some of its historians. He claimed, or newspapers did for him,

Bob Miller (left) with his wife Charlotte, probably c. 1929/30. Either the banjoist or the guitarist is probably Barney Burnett. (Zach Sigall Collection)

that he had written thousands of songs. The true number is probably in the hundreds, but it included "Twenty-One Years," "Ninety-Nine Years," "The Little Red Caboose Behind the Train," "Seven Years with the Wrong Woman," and "Rockin' Alone (in an Old Rockin' Chair)," which for a while became hillbilly standards and, together with his extensive catalog as a music publisher, gave him an annual income that he said once reached $300,000.

He also had a recording career for most of a decade, cutting almost two hundred sides in a melée of formats, from sweet songs accompanied by studio musicians to somber duets with his first wife Charlotte, rustic playlets like "Jennie's Strawberry Festival" and "Practice Night at Chicken Bristle," gangland obituaries ("The Death of Jack 'Legs' Diamond"), and jailhouse elegies ("Walking the Last Mile").

If this makes him sound like a smooth, multiskilled operator, cast in the same mold as Carson Robison, it is only because the above resumé omits a key detail. Miller was a lifelong sympathizer with left-wing causes, in later years close to the American Communist Party. Above all, he was a songwriter not only for but also *about* the common man. Having made that known with his first record, he followed it with a series of topical numbers such as the "Farm Relief Blues" (originally titled "Those Campaign Lyin' Sugar Coated Ballot-Coaxin' Farm Relief Blues"), "Dry Votin' Wet Drinkers" (originally "The Dry Votin', Wet Drinkin' Better-Than-Thou Hypocritical Blues"), and "The Farmer's Letter to the President," all in 1929; "Five Cent Glass of Beer" and "Page Mr. Volstead" (1930); "1930 Drought" and "Bank Failures" (1931); and "The Rich Man and the Poor Man" (1932).

★ ★ ★

And what of those shadowy women who appear to have kick-started Miller into a recording career as a hillbilly documentarian? In Texas, Mrs. Ford still had her supporters. In January 1931, it was proposed that the verses ascribed to her—now price adjusted to "Eight-Cent Cotton and Forty-Cent Meat"—be printed in the *Journal of the Texas House of Representatives* "for the information of the House." The resolution was referred to the Committee on Agriculture.

Mrs. Ford eludes definite identification, but we know a little about Virginia Brown: she was born in 1908 in Arcadia, in Bienville Parish, Louisiana (where she might have been acquainted with the Griggs [➤47]), graduated from Hope Street High in 1926, and taught at various schools in Shreveport. Did either of these women ever know that the social commentary to which their names were once attached, and which one of them may actually have written, had been borrowed without acknowledgment and incorporated into a best-selling hillbilly record?

31

"LINDY"/"LOUISE"

Proximity String Quartet
Columbia 15533-D

Recorded in Johnson City, TN, October 16, 1928
Released in May 1930
Sold 1,984

Reissued on *"Can You Sing or Play Old-Time Music?": The Johnson City Sessions 1928–1929* (Bear Family BCD16083) [both] • *In the Pines: Tar Heel Folk Songs & Fiddle Tunes* (Old Hat CD-1006), *Protobilly: The Minstrel and Tin Pan Alley DNA of Country Music* (JSP JSP5202) ["Lindy"]

Online: YT

Some of the prettiest music captured on old-time records in the 1920s was by small bands playing late-nineteenth- and early-twentieth-century compositions on mandolins, banjos, and guitars. Many, like the Scottdale String Band (➤12), specialized in ragtime instrumentals, but around Greensboro, North Carolina, there was a group that remembered the parlor songs of yesteryear, fading but still aromatic blooms from a less hectic age.

On the one occasion they were asked to make records, the Proximity String Quartet gave delicate accounts of two sentimental songs from the first decade of the twentieth century, Thomas S. Allen's "By the Watermelon Vine (Lindy Lou)" and Charles K. Harris's "I've a Longing in My Heart for You, Louise." The musicians, or the record company, cut the lengthy titles back to single words. Perhaps they thought "Lindy" might ring a bell in the ears of people who had bought records about the aviator Charles Lindbergh, "Lucky Lindy," during his glory year of 1927. "Lindy" is further edited down to its chorus and a lone verse put together from bits of the published song's first two verses.

To the listener back in the day, the song's references to sugar cane, cotton, and melon patch would have clearly signaled where this train was heading, and phrases like "When the moon am shinin'" would have confirmed its arrival on the dark side of town. It was what was then known in the entertainment business as a "coon song," and just one of many, such as "Sweet Sunny South," "Lorena," "Kitty Wells," or "It's Moving Day," that were absorbed into the old-time repertoire. The band may have learned both tunes from sheet music or from earlier recordings, of which there were several in the first decade of the century. Their disc, however, holds the only recordings of either of these songs by a hillbilly stringband.

★ ★ ★

The Proximity String Quartet was essentially a family band, consisting of John Franklin Butler (1888–1940), the lead singer and guitarist, and his cousin Buchanan H. (Buck) Butler (1893–1982) and son-in-law Okel Moore (1905–93) on mandolins. The other guitarist was a friend, Jack Caudle. The band took its name from the Proximity mill complex and the mill village surrounding it, northeast of Greensboro. The Cone family of Baltimore had built the Proximity Cotton Mill in 1896, the nearby White Oak Cotton Mill in 1905, and the Proximity Print Works, said to be the first Southern factory devoted to fabric dying, in 1912.

The Cones, like some other mill owners, improved the quality of their workers' lives, building model homes and schools and providing recreational activities. (This philanthropy may not have been wholly disinterested: cared-for employees would be less likely to join labor unions, to which the Cones were implacably opposed.) Documents of the period frequently refer to mill-sponsored baseball teams and brass bands, and to music classes for workers' children. We don't know how far this patronage might have extended beyond "legitimate" music to vernacular idioms like old-time stringband music. The name of the band need not imply sponsorship by the Proximity Mill.

John F. Butler grew up in Caswell County but was living in Proximity by 1920. In 1930, he, Buck, and

Left to right: Buck Butler, Okel Moore Evans, J. F. Butler, Jack Caudle. (Courtesy of Kenneth Butler)

five of their children worked at the mill. Okel Moore was still in school at the time of the recordings, but by 1931 he was employed at Proximity Print Works. Shortly afterward, he married J. F.'s daughter Martha. Born Okel Evans, he was adopted by a couple named Moore and took their name until some time in the '30s, when he reverted to Evans. Jack Caudle is likely to have been Aubrey Brant Caudle (1884–1950), a loom fixer at the Proximity Print Works and long-time resident in the mill village.

Behind the small monument of the band's single 78rpm record lies a larger, if local, celebrity. During the late 1920s and early '30s, they are quite often mentioned in the Burlington paper's reports of fiddlers' contests and other musical events, for instance at Saxapahaw in Alamance County, where they were ranked "best band" at a fiddlers' convention at the school in March 1929; at Liberty and Franklinville in Randolph County; and at Siler City in Chatham County. They were not always a quartet: a May 1931 ad for a Saturday-afternoon sale at the Black Hawk Market in Burlington calls them the Proximity String Quintette. The identity of the

The Proximity String Quintette play for a store promotion. (*Burlington* [North Carolina] *Daily Times*, May 1, 1931.) (Author's Collection)

(Author's Collection)

extra member can perhaps be deduced from other reports: a February 1933 concert at the Altamahaw–Ossipee school auditorium featured "Fred Steele and his Proximity string quartet," while a March 1936 concert at the Elmira school auditorium boasted "the golden voice of Fred Steele with his Proximity string quartette." This fifth man was almost certainly Fred Byron Steele (1903–53), a weaver at the Proximity Cotton Mill who lived at 21 Maple—just down the street from the mill, which stood at 4th and Maple—from 1929 to 1940. The band must have carried on until at least 1936, when they are reported as playing on the Greensboro radio station WBIG.

J. F. Butler's granddaughter Joyce Blake recalled, "He was always singing. He used to come down the street in his bib overalls, singing, and it kinda used to scare me." Okel Evans became a Methodist preacher and had a church outside Greensboro. Joyce remembers that he had a large collection of old sheet music. Perhaps it harbored the originals of "Lindy" and "Louise."

The charm we find in the Proximity String Quartet's record did not make much impression on Columbia Records, which shelved the masters for a year and a half. When it was finally issued, it achieved only modest sales. Perhaps the company dickered over its decision because of what it might have considered a flaw in the recording: about forty-seven seconds into "Louise," you can hear in the background the whistle of a passing train. Johnson City was a major railroad hub, and the studio space Columbia was using there, part of the Marshall Brothers Lumber Company's premises on East Main Street, was only a couple of blocks from a railroad track. There's another train-whistle moment on a recording made at the same location on the previous day, the Roane County Ramblers' "Tennessee Waltz." Strict audiophiles may regret such disturbances, but for me these tiny eruptions of surrounding everyday life somehow contextualize and even humanize these recorded messages from the past.

32

"WHEN THE ROSES BLOOM FOR THE BOOTLEGGER"

Earl Shirkey and Roy Harper [Roy Harvey]

Columbia 15326-D

Recorded in Johnson City, TN, October 18, 1928
Released in February 1929
Sold 72,545

Reissued on *"Can You Sing or Play Old-Time Music?": The Johnson City Sessions 1928–1929* (Bear Family BCD16083)

Online: Spotify, YT

In the fall of 1928, Roy Harvey and Earl Shirkey journeyed from West Virginia to Johnson City, Tennessee, to cut a batch of yodeling songs for Columbia Records' location-recording unit. This had little, if anything, to do with the current success of Jimmie Rodgers. Exponents of yodeling had been a draw in the entertainment business for years, audiences responding to the exoticism of this notionally Swiss, or German, or Austrian, mountain music as delightedly as they did to the differently novel sound of the Hawaiian guitar. The pioneer recording artist Geo. P. Watson began waxing yodel songs fully thirty years before Rodgers, to be followed by other specialists like Frank Kamplain.

So Harvey and Shirkey brought not blue yodels but yodelized versions of "Poor Little Joe" and "We Parted at the Gate," pressed flowers from the Victorian–Edwardian garden of verses. Another was "When the Roses Bloom Again." Songs of lovers' partings were unfailingly popular in the late nineteenth and early twentieth centuries, but few were so eagerly seized upon by old-time record-makers as this 1908 composition by Will D. Cobb and Gus Edwards. Almost every label could boast a version, whether by Ernest Stoneman or Vernon Dalhart, Watts and Wilson, Burnett and Rutherford, or McFarland and Gardner.

But Harvey and Shirkey's version of "When the Roses Bloom Again" was not the familiar story of a soldier bidding farewell to his sweetheart. They rebuilt the old jalopy, using the melody and the general gist of the refrain but stripping out the pathos and relocating the story in the present. That much was clear from the first line: "I was going down the river to my little cottage home, The revenue men was waiting there for me . . ."

"When the Roses Bloom for the Bootlegger" opened with a spoken exchange about a friend, "old Slim," who "can't be here, just as usual." This dig about a fellow musician may have been aimed at Odell Smith, a tall, skinny fiddler who played with them sometimes and would record with them in Johnson City the following year. Then Roy took the part of a bootlegger, captured but unrepentant ("I am feelin' very frisky, but they've caught me with the whiskey"), and Earl threw in a cheerful yodeled refrain.

It made an entertaining three-minute topical playlet, but Columbia evidently saw no unusual potential in it and placed a fairly standard initial pressing order of 5,675. Advance orders more than tripled that number, and by the end of 1929 it had sold over 64,000 copies and given Columbia one of its biggest hits of the year in the "Old Familiar Tunes" catalog.

"Bootlegger"'s success not only single-handedly justified Columbia's decision to conduct location recording in Johnson City, where they returned in 1929, but also drew the attention of the competition. Asa Martin covered the song for Gennett, Frank Luther and Carson Robison for the Plaza–ARC group (reproducing Shirkey and Harvey's opening dialogue word for word), and Earl Johnson and His Dixie Entertainers for Okeh, adding three sprightly verses. The combined sales of the song on these

Earl Shirkey and Roy Harvey, alias Harper. (Kinney Rorrer Collection)

labels, more than a dozen in all, must have made it one of the more widely circulated old-time numbers of 1929–31. Shirkey and Harper themselves made another dozen recordings in 1929, returning, in "The Bootlegger's Dream of Home" and "We Have Moonshine in the West Virginia Hills," to the theme of their biggest hit.

★ ★ ★

Roy Harvey was an astute operator with extensive connections in the record business, and between 1926 and 1931 he appeared on almost two hundred sides. In an autobiographical political ad that he wrote for the *Raleigh* [West Virginia] *Register* in October 1936, when he was running for deputy sheriff of Beckley on the Republican ticket, he boasted: "The records [I] made during that time are prized possessions today of friends throughout the coal fields." (For more about his life and work, see "The Bluefield Murder" [➤23] and *Country Music Originals*.)

Earl Jennings Shirkey (1900–51) was born in Clay, in Wirt County, West Virginia. His father seems to have left the family circle during Earl's childhood, and he grew up first with his mother Laura's parents, then with her and her new husband. He sometimes worked as a chauffeur, though for the 1930 census he stated his occupation as "Swiss yodler [on] phonograph and radio." Charlie Poole, Jr., said Earl learned to yodel while at school in Switzerland, which seems improbable, and that he could yodel "forty-nine different ways."

"Earl Shirkey was a yodeler," Harvey's daughter Louise Yarbrough agreed, "but there's more to tell than his yodeling. He would go to South Carolina and Georgia with a truck and return to our house with a truckload of peaches, watermelon, cantaloupe and whatever seemed to be in season. He would then set up a stand beside our house and the Harvey children, mainly Nadine and I, would have to sell Earl's produce. I never knew what he did for a living except haul produce and yodel. He would always give us a quarter and all the fruit we wanted to eat."

The records of Shirkey and Harvey were last brave examples of the old-school Alpine yodel; for several years afterward, thanks to Jimmie Rodgers, the default shade of the yodel was blue. But in the mid-'30s a kind of composite style emerged, derived less from Swiss mountaineers or Rodgers's imitators, who at least had been real, than from the invented figures of the yodeling cowboy and cowgirl. We shall meet them later (➤70, 76).

33

"JUST OVER THE RIVER"/ "BEAUTIFUL"

Garland Brothers and Grinstead
Columbia 15679-D

Recorded in Johnson City, TN, October 18, 1928
Released in August 1931
Sold 737

Reissued on *"Can You Sing or Play Old-Time Music?": The Johnson City Sessions 1928–1929* (Bear Family BCD16083) [both] • *Times Ain't Like They Used to Be Vol. 5* (Yazoo 2063) ["Just Over the River"]

Online: Spotify, YT

These are hauntingly beautiful hymns, not quite like anything else in recorded old-time music, and we are fortunate to have them. The record containing them was one of the last two releases from Columbia's 1928 session in Johnson City, finally appearing almost three years later and selling not much more than its initial pressing of 625. It's likely that many records issued at that point in the Depression went to retailers who never succeeded in finding customers to buy them, so the discs languished for years in attics, basements, or outbuildings, unplayed and in their original paper sleeves, until someone offloaded them at a flea market or thrift store, whereupon a few survivors would take on a new commercial life as collectables.

"Just Over the River" and "Beautiful" were recorded by a group of musicians from Whitley and Knox Counties in southeastern Kentucky. Ashley Sidney Garland (1903–85) and his brother Hanford Garland (1906–88) lived in Gray, in Knox County, where they farmed and did carpentry work. Charley Grinstead (1876–1950) worked at various times as a farmer and a truck driver but was known in the Corbin–Gray–Barbourville area as a violinist and music teacher. It may have been he who recruited the fourth member of the group, unnamed on the record labels: Flora Sutton (1901–72), a young woman from Whitley County who worked at the L&N Railroad's YMCA in Corbin.

She sang the alto part on the recordings, Hanford Garland the tenor, and Ashley Garland the baritone. Grinstead played the violin—but not only that. Ashley Garland's daughter Ethel Slusher remembers Hanford telling her that Grinstead played both the violin, conventionally, and, *at the same time*, the bass fiddle—with his toes. Perhaps he gripped the bow with the toes of one foot and fretted the notes with the toes of the other? The bass part consists of short bow-strokes furnishing a kind of rhythmic grunt on beats 2 and 4, and it is possible—just barely possible—to imagine an extremely deft musician executing it pedally rather than digitally. The guitarist has not been identified. Perhaps Ms. Sutton played it, or maybe one of the other Corbin musicians at the Johnson City session helped out.

Both pieces were sung from *Lasting Hymns Revised with Greatest Hymns*, a collection edited by John A. Lee and published by him in Glencoe, Kentucky, in 1906. The Garland family possesses a copy of this hymnal with Flora Sutton's signature on the first page. According to Ethel Slusher, the participants received an outright payment of $50 each for the recordings. The Garlands were not sent copies of their record, but soon afterward Ashley found half a dozen of them in a Barbourville store, bought them all, kept one, and distributed the others among his brothers and sisters. Ethel Slusher grew up familiar with the record, and, she says, "Just Over the River" is still sometimes sung in her church.

Charley Grinstead died from injuries sustained in an automobile accident. Flora Sutton remained in Corbin, married, and continued to work at the YMCA. We don't know if she continued to sing. Ashley Garland certainly did: a lifelong singer and song leader, he taught shape-note singing and was active in Knox County singing conventions. In the '40s and '50s, he sang with the Heidrick Four and

The Garland brothers, Hanford (center) and Ashley (right) and their friend Sherman Burnett. (Courtesy of Ethel Garland Slusher)

Harmony Four, broadcasting from WCTT in Corbin on Sunday mornings.

Brother Hanford's chief claim to local fame was that he ran a sorghum mill and sold jars of the product from a little stand, staffed by family members, on US Highway 25E, part of what was then the Dixie Highway, a pioneering north–south route from Michigan to Florida, down which countless tourists drove to take their Southern vacation.

Since the Great Northern Railway's late-nineteenth-century campaign "See America First," homeland tourism, first by train, then by automobile, had become a national pastime. Marguerite S. Shaffer argues in *See America First: Tourism and National Identity, 1880–1940* that it was almost a national duty: "[It] mapped an idealized American history and tradition across the American landscape, defining an organic nationalism that linked national identity to a shared territory and history." According to the Automobile Club's Good Roads Committee, automobile tourism was a ritual of American citizenship; car travel was an extension of America's heroic pioneer past, and by touring, tourists could become better Americans. No longer restricted to railroad routes and their stops, they could visit off-grid America.

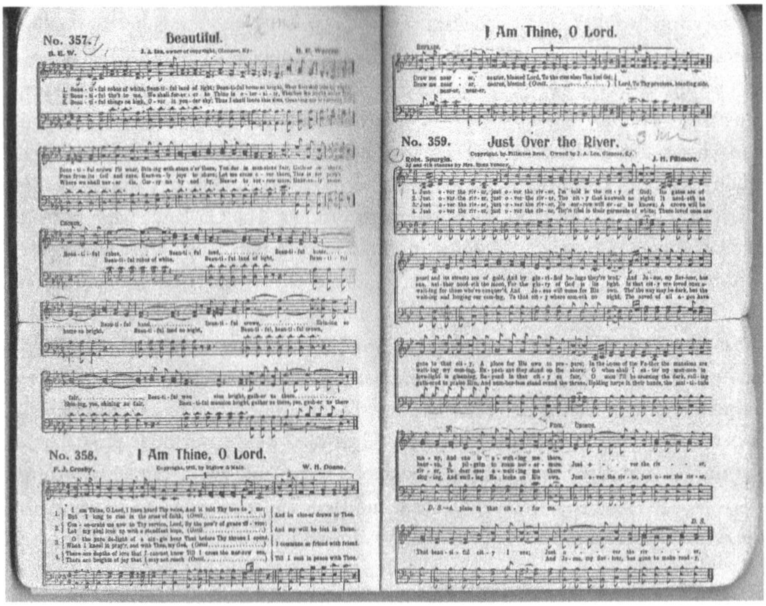

Pages from a Garland family copy of *Lasting Hymns Revised with Greatest Hymns.* (Courtesy of Ethel Garland Slusher)

And if they headed away from the Garland sorghum mill (which still stands, though no sorghum has been made or sold there for years), down Highway 25W into what is now North Corbin, they would come across Sanders Motor Court. The birthplace of Col. Harlan Sanders's Kentucky Fried Chicken enterprise was built on land bought in 1930 from garage owner and old-time musician Ancil McVay, who also recorded in Johnson City in

Dewey Golden's Music Store at 124 Depot, Corbin, Kentucky, ca. early 1930. (Courtesy of Victoria O'Connell)

1928. Eula Johnson, daughter of McVay's recording partner Roland Johnson, and herself a musician who recorded with the local Holiness minister Ernest Phipps, worked at Sanders Court and reputedly had a hand in devising KFC's "secret recipe."

Travelers visiting the sorghum mill and the motor court would probably have had no idea that they were skirting one of old-time music's most notable hotspots. Back in the day, Corbin was chiefly important as an L&N Railroad hub, vital to the movement of coal from the southeastern Kentucky coalfields. But it had another industry. Between the late 1920s and the mid-'30s, at least sixteen acts from around Corbin made records, involving over fifty musicians and more than 120 recordings. (Add groups from farther out in Whitley County, like the Bird family of Williamsburg or the Buffalo Ragged Five from Buffalo, and the number of recordings exceeds 170.) No other small city in the South can match these figures.

I like to imagine an inquisitive tourist, after stops at Hanford Garland's stand and Sanders Motor Court, driving to downtown Corbin, calling in at the record department of Sterchi's Furniture Store on East Main or Golden's Music Store on Depot Street, and taking home local artifacts that would last longer than a jar of sorghum or a fried chicken dinner.

34

"THE LOST CHILD"

Stripling Brothers
Vocalion 5321

Recorded in Birmingham, AL, November 15, 1928
Released in c. June 1929

Reissued on *Times Ain't Like They Used to Be Vol. 8* (Yazoo 2068), *Down in the Basement—Joe Bussard's Treasure Trove of Vintage 78s: 1926–1937* (Old Hat CD-1004), *Desperate Man Blues* (Dust-to-Digital DTD-05A)

Online: Spotify, YT

In spring 1928, J. D. Pope, who owned a music store in Searcy, Arkansas, got a recording deal for a local band, Reaves White County Ramblers, with Brunswick's Vocalion label. Tip McKinney, who had been in a Pope-created band that had recorded for Victor shortly before (➤22), but had since fallen out with its manager, dismissed the Reaves discs as "some kind of off-brand records." This was unjust. Vocalions were sold at the premium price of 75 cents, the same as rival product on Victor, Columbia, and Okeh, or in Brunswick's own old-time catalog. Yet many of the old-time records released on the ornate and handsome Vocalion label are much scarcer than those from the other companies, and the catalog—which, over about five years, amassed more than 500 releases—is replete with discs that seldom turn up, some of which collectors hold in enormous esteem.

The catalog was initiated in the fall of 1926, and its first hundred or so releases included a slew of reissues from an earlier, non-genre-specific Vocalion series by the Hill Billies, Uncle Dave Macon, George Reneau, Vernon Dalhart, Charlie Oaks, Uncle Am Stuart, and other acts of proved salesworthiness. Even when making new recordings for the new series, Vocalion persisted with this small core of talent, cautiously adding McFarland and Gardner and the McGee Brothers. The focus on Tennessee—where all these acts came from, except the Hill Billies and Dalhart—was not accidental, but a consequence of the close link between Brunswick–Vocalion and the Sterchi Brothers furniture store chain, based in Knoxville (➤3).

In 1928, however, there was a firm step into uncharted territory with new (to Vocalion) artists like the Reaves band, Emry Arthur from Kentucky, Welling and McGhee from West Virginia, and Otto Gray's Cowboy Band from Oklahoma.

It was then, too, that Brunswick began, years later than its competitors, to make forays into the South on location-recording trips, starting with a spring 1928 visit to Ashland, Kentucky (➤24), and Atlanta. In the December 1928 issue of *The Talking Machine World*, Brunswick's Chicago recording director Jack Kapp reported that, using portable equipment, he had "recorded and [would] have ready for dealers in the early part of 1929 a large number of very excellent recordings for the 'Hill-Billy' section of the Vocalion record catalog." He had just completed a trip of several weeks in which he had set up his traveling studio in Dallas, New Orleans, Birmingham, and Memphis. In Dallas, he had found The Red-Headed Fiddlers (fiddler "Red" Steeley and banjoist "Red" Graham), whose "Texas Quickstep," issued on Brunswick, gave the company its first record of Texas fiddling. Then, less than a month later, at the Bankhead Hotel in Birmingham, he came upon the Stripling Brothers.

★ ★ ★

The Striplings, Charles (1896–1966) and Ira (1898–1967), from Pickens County in west-central Alabama, had some reputation in fiddling contests, and occasionally played on WAPI in Birmingham, but Kapp was as cautious with them as he had been with the Texas duo, making just two recordings. One was a dashing reel in which Charlie Stripling skillfully alternated bowed and plucked passages at breakneck speed. "It won a lot of prizes," he remembered. He had learned it from a much older Pickens County fiddler, Pleasant "Plez" Carroll (1850–1930), as "The

Charles and Ira Stripling, 1930s. (Courtesy of Lee Stripling, Jeri Vaughn, W. B. Reid, and Joyce Cauthen.)

Lost Child." "He didn't do anything but just pick the strings with his fingers," Charlie Stripling told researcher Bob Pinson in 1963. "But I added that picking this-a-way and the other and bouncing the bow. Nobody would have paid much attention to it the way he played it. What I added to it made it more entertaining." The tune was known to other Alabama fiddlers (Carl Carmer included it in a list of tunes played by fiddlers he met while collecting material for his 1935 book *Stars Fell on Alabama*), but seemingly nowhere else.

There is nothing in the piece that immediately suggests either lostness or childhood, but the title may allude to "Lost Indian," a tune that can sound vaguely similar, as in the version by the Kentucky master fiddler Ed Haley. It would be possible to hear in Ira Stripling's galloping guitar chords an impression of Native American drumming. The alternation of *arco* and *pizzicato* passages also places "The Lost Child" amongst a group of tunes that includes, to take a couple of recorded examples from 1928–29, "Texas Farewell" by Victor's Fiddlin' Jim Pate from Nacogdoches County, Texas, and "Flying Engine" by the previously mentioned Reaves White County Ramblers, which I suspect the musicians actually called "Flying Indian," misheard ("injun"–"engine") by Vocalion's recording director.

In later years, the fiddler Leslie Keith, who was born in Virginia but a Birmingham resident at the time the Striplings were making their records, created another link by drawing on "The Lost Child," which he might have learned from Charlie Stripling, for part of his composition "Black Mountain Blues." Usually called "Black Mountain Rag," it became a country and bluegrass instrumental showpiece.

A further connection is the frequent use, in this scattered family of tunes, of the cross-tuning AEAC#. Uncle Dick Hutchinson of Disney, Oklahoma, when playing "Black Mountain Rag" for field recordists Chris and Kevin Delaney, referred to this tuning as "that stillhouse key," a good name but evidently one known only to him. Suggestively, the Cajun fiddler Dewey Balfa called it "the Indian tuning."

Following these clues leads us into the dark quantum world of the fiddle tune, where nothing is quite what it seems, different tunes share the same

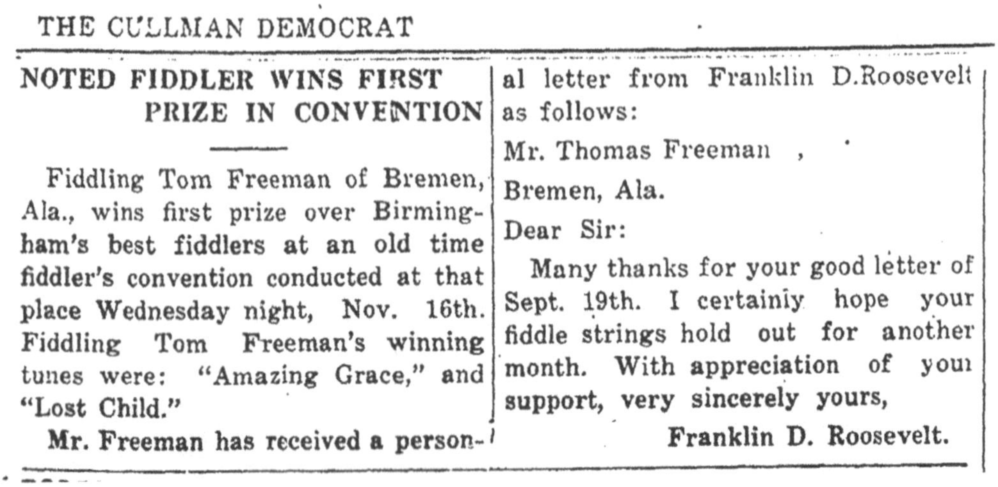

THE CULLMAN DEMOCRAT

NOTED FIDDLER WINS FIRST PRIZE IN CONVENTION

Fiddling Tom Freeman of Bremen, Ala., wins first prize over Birmingham's best fiddlers at an old time fiddler's convention conducted at that place Wednesday night, Nov. 16th. Fiddling Tom Freeman's winning tunes were: "Amazing Grace," and "Lost Child."

Mr. Freeman has received a personal letter from Franklin D.Roosevelt as follows:

Mr. Thomas Freeman ,

Bremen, Ala.

Dear Sir:

Many thanks for your good letter of Sept. 19th. I certainly hope your fiddle strings hold out for another month. With appreciation of your support, very sincerely yours,

Franklin D. Roosevelt.

Cullman Democrat, November 24, 1932. (Author's Collection)

name but similar tunes do not, and connections may stretch over extraordinary distances. The tune historian Gus Meade observed that a piece "remarkably resembling ['The Lost Child'] was played by a Norwegian Hardanger fiddler at the Smithsonian 1976 Folklife Festival under the title 'Devil's Tune.'" This is the widely known (in Norway) "Fanitullen," which does share both tuning and *arco/pizzicato* shape. But so too, at least in some renditions, does "Le Reel du Pendu" ("The Hanged Man's Reel"), a favorite tune of fiddlers in Québec.

"The Lost Child" poses another question, not about origins but about function. Was this a recording its purchasers would expect to dance to? Surely it's too fast for that. So was it, rather, a showpiece for listening to? Is this how we should regard all those other records of hell-for-leather reels by Clark Kessinger, Lowe Stokes, Clayton McMichen, and other virtuoso fiddlers?

Whatever the thinking behind this remarkable recording, it represents a huge leap forward from the playing of Fiddlin' John Carson or Gid Tanner just four or five years earlier. This is rural rhythm at a new tempo, with a foot hard down on the gas.

★ ★ ★

Almost eighty years later, musician and collector Ron Cole engaged fifteen other collectors in compiling a list, to be published in *The Old-Time Herald*, of a hundred "essential hillbilly recordings on 78s." The first name on the roll was the Stripling Brothers' "The Lost Child."

35

"WHO BROKE THE LOCK ON THE HEN-HOUSE DOOR?"/"SHE'LL BE COMIN' ROUND THE MOUNTAIN WHEN SHE COMES"

H. M. Barnes and His Blue Ridge Ramblers

Brunswick 310 [issued in the UK as Brunswick 1027]

Recorded in New York, NY, January 28, 1929
Released in c. May 1929

Online: YT

In the movie *Gold Diggers of 1933*, theatrical producer Barney Hopkins is sitting in his New York office wondering where his next show is coming from. His musings are interrupted by four young men who file in with their instrument cases and stand before him.

"Who are you?" the producer snarls.

"We are the Kentucky Hillbillies," reply the quartet in unison, and then, one by one: "Singing"—"Dancing"—"Music"—"Wisecracks."

The joke is that their accent belongs not to Kentucky but to Mittel-Europa. They are the latest arrivals on a hillbilly bandwagon that has been rattling into New York for several years, bringing to the theaters of Brooklyn and Broadway the banjos and barn dances of rural America.

Outfits like this—and by the '30s they were numerous: Italian hillbillies, Swedish hillbillies, Jewish hillbillies—would have been second-wave wagoneers. Never having been farther south than the Lower East Side, they needed predecessors to learn the hillbilly *schtick* from. We might imagine them kibitzing at a Fiddlin' John Carson recording session or bending attentively over a Victrola to decipher the downhome dialogue of the Skillet-Lickers. Or perhaps they just bought tickets for a show and witnessed the real thing.

In the spring of 1929, February through May, vaudeville houses of the Loew's chain in New York City and elsewhere on the East Coast were booking an act called the Blue Ridge Ramblers.

> Once every so often there comes to the stage an act of such unusual character that it stands out in a distinct class by itself and offers a refreshing change from the usual song and dance routine. Such an attraction is the Blue Ridge Ramblers.... The company consists of nine clever mountain boys from the famous Blue Ridge Mountains of Tennessee, Kentucky, Virginia and North Carolina, making no attempt at classical compositions nor modern jazz. The Hill boys bring only songs played and sung by their pioneer ancestors generations ago. Beloved folk songs, composed and sung in the early days of the American Republic, which have been handed down with each succeeding generation, these are the simple melodies which the mountain boys offer.
>
> While the primitive airs are featured on the program, there are also other pleasing specialties. There is plenty of comedy of a variety that gives insight unto the character of this interesting people.... (*Lebanon* [Pennsylvania] *Daily News*, March 2, 1929)

Although the tone is patronizing, this tells us exactly what the band was tasked with doing and what its audiences were expected to make of it. As in the fiddling contests that were a rage a few years earlier, in the wake of Henry Ford's attempts to revive old-time American dances, hillbilly music is presented as an alternative, if not an antidote, to jazz—an argument vigorously stated three years before in an article about the Hill Billies (➤2). The point is driven home by the reference to "pioneer ancestors generations ago": no sinuous strains from the shtetl here, but merry melodies from the mountains.

The Blue Ridge Ramblers, ca. 1929. Back row: Henry Roe, probably Jim Smith, Frank "Dad" Williams, Fred Roe, unknown; front row: Harry Brown, Jack Reedy, Russell Jones, unknown, possibly "Happy" Atkins. (Courtesy of the late Clarence H. Greene, Jr.)

But the description is short on detail. What did the Ramblers look and sound like? In the six years or thereabouts that they were active, they accrued hundreds of column inches of press copy, but much of it was previews, "coming next week," and hardly differed from newspaper to newspaper; it must have been derived from advance publicity. So it gave little impression of the specifics of a performance. Fortunately, when they played Loew's State in New York in late April 1929, the trade paper *Billboard* sent a reviewer.

> The rustic simplicity of these 10 West Virginia [*sic*] mountaineers combined in a string orchestra is the main factor upon which they rely for novelty. Clad in overalls and straw hats, the complement of the orchestra includes three fiddles, three guitars, two banjos, one mandolin and a piano. An eleventh man acts as a dude m. c. and introduces the artists in singing and instrumental groupings. Barn-dance music and some real old-fashioned country folk songs with well-blended crooning voices are dispensed.
>
> The single setting is a log and rough-hewn raftered barn with an antique piano in one corner, a string of packing boxes, used for seats, and a few dilapidated chairs, the ensemble being seated across the stage in a straight line. Old Dad, called the "youngest" member of the troupe, plays a mean fiddle with variations. He was encored to give his impression of an old reed organ. . . . One member sings a quaint number called *Who Broke the Lock on the Henhouse Door?*, with the rest of the company singing a soft harmony accompaniment.
>
> Several group selections by a Hawaiian quartet brought a fair hand at this performance. Another ensemble of violins played a few numbers, also to a fair reception. The act drags a bit in the middle, but manages to pick up toward the end again. A fast *Turkey-in-the-Straw* number . . . served to brighten the finale. Received a good reception at the finish. This is a good act for the family houses. (May 11, 1929)

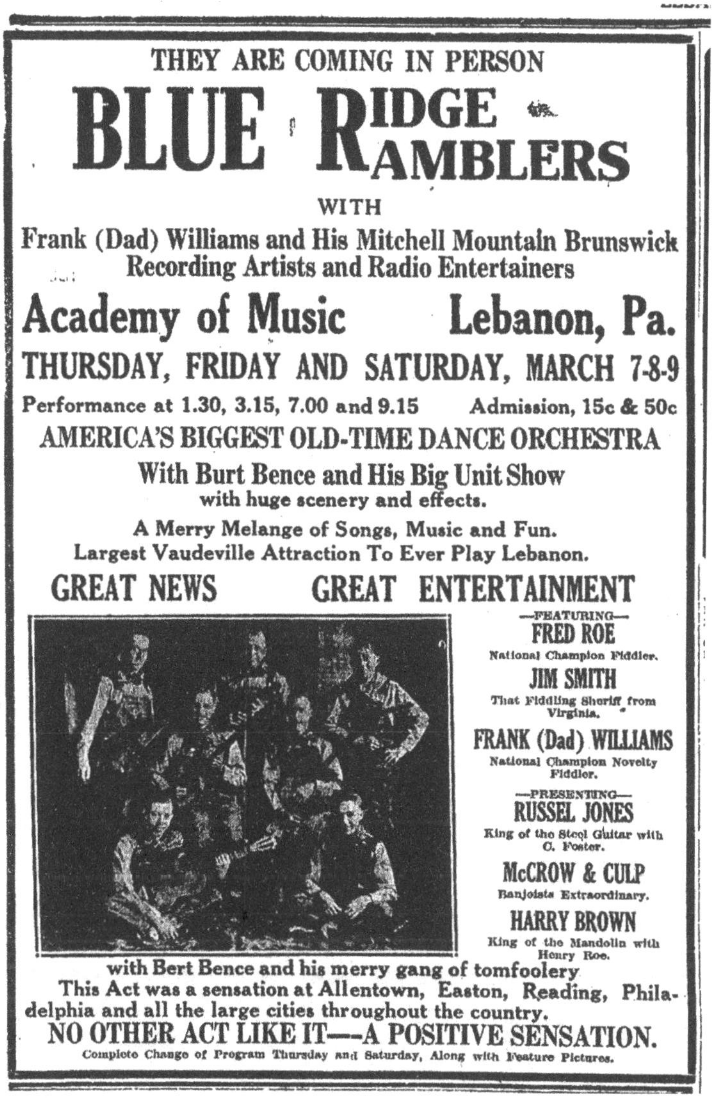

Ad in *Lebanon* [Pennsylvania] *Daily News*, March 6, 1929. (Author's Collection)

Numerous musicians wore the straw hat of a Blue Ridge Rambler. One we can confidently place in the band at a particular time is Lonnie Austin, whose diaries listed the venues they played in June–October 1928 and January–July 1929. Of their week at Loew's State in April '29, he noted: "This is Loew's biggest house and is on Broadway right amid the 'White Lights' of N. Y. City. Now the B–R–R–s are going some we are really playing in real theatres." The "Old Dad" mentioned by *Billboard*'s reviewer was Frank E. Williams. Other Ramblers named in newspaper articles include Jim Smith, fiddle, from Lima, Ohio, the band's road manager; the brothers Fred and Henry Roe, fiddle and guitar respectively; Jack Reedy, banjo; Russell Jones, steel guitar; Harry Brown, mandolin; and "Happy" Atkins, guitar; with Austin described as "the boy that plays 'em all," though he mainly doubled on fiddle and piano.

Old-time enthusiasts will recognize some of these names straightaway. In fact, the Blue Ridge Ramblers have a strong claim to be called country music's first supergroup. Austin, from Spray, North Carolina, played and recorded with Charlie Poole. The Roes, from Bristol, Tennessee, and Reedy, from Marion, Virginia, had passed through the ranks of the Hill Billies and recorded in their own names. Reedy's Walker Mountain String Band, which recorded for Brunswick in February 1928 and included the Roes, was closely associated with the early Blue Ridge Ramblers, perhaps even a prototype; ads for an early theater engagement in Beckley, West Virginia, couple them in the billing, "The Blue Ridge Ramblers with Jack Reedy and his Walker Mountain Entertainers" (*Beckley Post Herald*, June 21 and 23, 1928). "Dad" Williams, who is presented somewhat as a figurehead, and was probably a founding member of the Ramblers, was in his early sixties and from Iowa; the previous spring, he had been playing on WOC in Davenport.

But Henry Marshall Barnes, the Svengali behind the Ramblers, remains obscure. Though his name is on the band's records, it almost never shows up in their billings or previews. A rare exception is an item that appeared in the trade paper *The Vaudeville News* a week before the *Billboard* review.

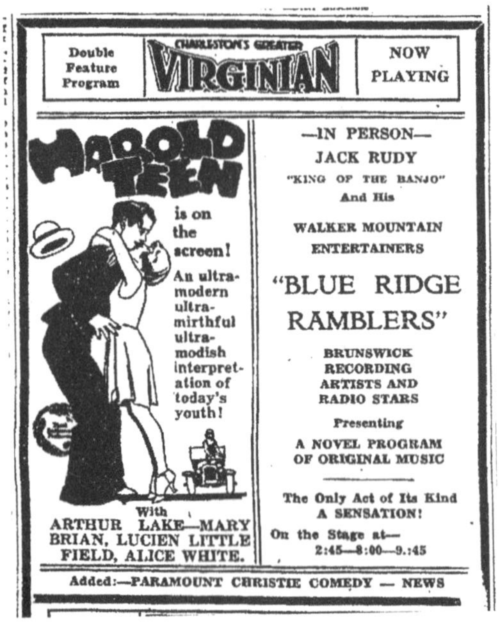

Ad in *Charleston* [West Virginia] *Gazette*, July 23, 1928. "Jack Rudy" is Jack Reedy, who had recorded with his Walker Mountain String Band some months earlier. Hence "Brunswick Recording Artists": the Blue Ridge Ramblers as such had not yet made records. (Author's Collection)

Henry M. Barnes presented "The Blue Ridge Ramblers" at Loew State Theatre, N. Y. C., last week. And as Rudyard Kipling might say, thereby hangs a tale. Mr. Barnes contends that all those in the act are genuine mountaineers, and are making their initial visit to New York. With the exception of Bert Bence, Master of Ceremonies, and Frank "Dad" Williams, the other members have had little stage experience prior to joining this unique troupe. For the past eighteen months, or since the inception of the aggregation, the offering has had steady employment. Appearances were confined exclusively to the South, in and around Virginia and the Carolinas and the country where the Blue Ridge chain runs. Striking Broadway for the first time was a revelation to the musicians, who since have taken advantage of their mornings in seeing the lights of the Metropolis. According to Mr. Barnes, his proteges cannot read a note. They are possessed of a splendid endowment with a natural tendency toward music, especially stringed instruments. Barnes himself is from North Carolina and was an actor up to nine years ago, when he conceived the idea of becoming a manager and going into business for himself. His specialty was minstrel tabs. (May 4, 1929)

Bert Bence, the "dude m. c." of the *Billboard* review, may have been Barnes's insurance policy. In his early fifties, he was a vaudeville veteran: "The South's Favorite Singing and Dancing Comedian," claimed

H. M. Barnes presents, 1931. (Bob Cox Collection)

an ad in the *High Point* [North Carolina] *Enterprise* (January 17, 1920), though he came from northern Michigan. As a theatrical manager he had toured and starred in song-and-dance shows like *Hello Girls* year after year since World War I. If inexperience or nerves should cause a hiccup in a Ramblers performance, Bence could be relied upon to cover it up with a joke or an eccentric dance.

★ ★ ★

When the *Billboard* reviewer singled out "Who Broke the Lock on the Hen-House Door?," he was probably unaware that he was promoting the Ramblers' recording of the song, which, coupled with "She'll Be Comin' Round the Mountain," was about to, or had just, become their first release. "Recorded for the Brunswick people," Lonnie Austin had noted in his diary in January 1929. "This was done only for publicity and it sure worked out nicely." One wonders if "done only for publicity" is a euphemism for "we didn't get paid for it."

As a debut release, it was well calculated. Brunswick selected the most familiar numbers in the band's repertoire, light-hearted singalongs that old Americans already knew and new Americans could easily pick up. Indeed, so could non-Americans: Brunswick promptly sent the masters to its Australian and English offices so they could be released in those territories too.

(OTM Collection)

Lonnie Austin, 1929. (Kinney Rorrer Collection)

The disc introduced listeners to a new sound on old-time records. "She'll Be Comin' Round the Mountain," delivered by a chorus of voices, presents a "hillbilly big band" sound that the Ramblers seem to have introduced into recorded music: two or three fiddles playing over a rhythm of guitars, banjo, mandolin, and piano. The arrangement is varied with passages where the fiddles give way to steel guitar, or one of the fiddlers duets with a banjoist. "Who Broke the Lock on the Hen-House Door?" is more stripped-down, the rustic singer backed by steel guitar, piano, and not much else, the unoccupied musicians no doubt forming the chorus that sings the refrain.

Oddly, in a music that was anything but jazz, "She'll Be Comin' Round the Mountain"'s alternation of ensemble and solo passages feels like a jazz device. Whatever their inspiration, these drop-outs and recombinations would be a trademark of the band. But they were something more.

Ever since the invention of the phonograph, artists and producers had been seeking ways to make a record more than just a demonstration of a performance; to create a context for it, perhaps one that resembled the original, "live" occasion, perhaps a dramatic reimagining. The minstrel show, the county fair, the fiddlers' contest (➤24); the train or car journey (➤27), the telephone conversation; all these were social settings that could readily be replicated in wax. But what could be done with the back-and-forth two-part fiddle tune, the uninflected repetitions of the country dance? How could these plain threads be woven into the brightly patterned fabric of a recording that would give pleasure not once or twice but over and over?

The Blue Ridge Ramblers' solution to this conundrum was to redesign basically familiar material in a textured and variegated form. Their recording of "Golden Slippers" includes passages of three fiddles playing alone, a chorus of guitar with rhythm mandolin, and another of raggy piano. "Old Joe Clark" has two piano choruses, first solo, then a duet with steel guitar. "Lineman's Serenade" seesaws between the fiddles and the steel guitar.

The ad (left) in the *Uniontown* [Pennsylvania] *Morning Herald*, February 18, 1931, used an out-of-date photograph for a twelve-person lineup that by then included the Bowman and DeForrest sisters, Kyle Roop, Bob Culp, and "Sparkplug" Hughes. Most of these new members are dimly visible in the ad (right) from the *Huntingdon* [Pennsylvania] *Daily News*, January 21, 1932. (Author's Collection)

One can hear the resonances of this innovation in later hillbilly recordings, for instance by the Highlanders (➤39) or the Walter Family (➤66). In time, it would become a template for the ensemble/solo figurations of bluegrass.

★ ★ ★

The Ramblers continued to tour the South and Midwest through spring and summer 1929 with most of the musicians who had played on the records. Lonnie Austin confided to his diary impressions of new sights like the Mississippi River ("It reminds me of the old tune 'Muddy Waters'"), Memphis ("wide open"), and New Orleans ("We went swimming with the lady of the house and I sure had a nice time"). But in the 1930–31 seasons, the management tinkered constantly with the lineup, adding and dropping musicians like "Sparkplug," alias Walter Hughes, a banjo player who had worked with the Hill Billies and Jack Reedy when he was sixteen, and was still being billed as a "sixteen-year-old boy wonder" two or three years later. Another former member of the Hill Billies to be enlisted was the east Tennessee fiddler Charlie Bowman, together with his singing daughters Pauline and Jennie. Also on the roster were banjoists Mac(k) Crow, Bob Culp, and Sam Phillips; guitarists Jack Douglass and Jack Donahue (or Donoghue); the De Forrest Sisters, "Champion Hill-Billie Clog Dancers"; Kyle Roop, "The Funniest Hill-Billie Comedian"; the red-headed sisters Florence and Madlin Grey; and doubtless others. It's impossible to keep an accurate log of the personnel changes because the theatrical bills often omitted the musicians' names and used photographs of out-of-date lineups.

The band's last traceable engagements were in Pennsylvania in March 1934. Barnes died in that year, and Frank Williams the year after, and after those losses the Blue Ridge Ramblers no doubt disbanded. (The name went on showing up in the press, but that's because it was a popular one, claimed also by a society orchestra in Ohio, an African American orchestra from Louisville, and dancebands in Virginia and Massachusetts.)

★ ★ ★

Opportunely, or opportunistically, the Blue Ridge Ramblers' place in the vaudeville business was grabbed by a group called the Blue Ridge Mountaineers, who had been gigging and broadcasting extensively, mainly in the Midwest, in 1933–34. (The Blue Ridge Mountaineers who made a pair of charming recordings of old-time stringband music for Gennett in 1929 were a different outfit.) The troupe, varying from ten to sixteen members, featured Chuck Peterson, a banjo instructor from Racine, Wisconsin, billed as "the 'Eddie Peabody' of the Mountains"; a quintet of dancing girls, the Blue Ridge Milk Maids; "that crazy mountainer 'Moonshine Bill'"; a group called the Novelty Aces; and Dale Rash, known as "the Second 'Jimmie Rogers [*sic*]'" or the "Silvertone Yodeling Mountaineer." The band was described in its publicity as being "from the hills of North Carolina," or sometimes "the hills of Tennessee," but it seems to have started out in unhilly Hardin County, Iowa, home to both Rash and another known member, Clarence Dooley.

The Blue Ridge Mountaineers offered "good old mountain tunes and oldtime square dance numbers, played by the largest hill-billy string band of either the stage or air." To a vaudeville booker, they would have seemed like a neat-fit substitute for the Blue Ridge Ramblers, whose bill matter their own sometimes strangely echoed, if not copied. But the Mountaineers had developed a brisker and more varied program—"two hours' worth of entertainment in forty minutes"—that was loaded with specialty acts: "Hezzy" and his "freak instruments," Ebenezer and His One String Fiddle, novelty dance teams, and the Boozophone, "an unusual instrument made entirely of bottles half filled with water," which sounded like a xylophone. How much of this they could enact in a radio studio we don't know, but their bill matter claimed they had been heard on more than 110 stations.

The Blue Ridge Mountaineers could come down from their factual or fictional hills and be welcomed on vaudeville stages and into radio stations because a path had been laid for them by a long line of predecessors in the hillbilly variety business. In March 1929, a trade-paper correspondent noted: "Hick harmonizers have a hot hold on vaudeville just now and the Hill Billies [not the Hopkins group—TR] do sap serenader stuff in sure satisfy style. [Producer] Freddie Ardath had two fives working last week and both the Providence Fay and Middletown Middlesex made much fuss over their delightful drolleries" (*Vaudeville News*, March 9, 1929). Also active at this time, as well as the Blue Ridge Ramblers, were the Pickard Family, the Crockett Family Mountaineers (➤44), and the Arkansas Travelers, a troupe from the Ozarks, led by Cicero and Abner Weaver and their sister Elviry, with their show "Home Folks":

> This year they have brought along rakes, forks, spoons, balloons, washboards and handsaws, from which they make music.
>
> Sister Elviry this season introduces a chorus of "hill belles," who with their backwoods wardrobe and antiquated ideas of dancing, is [*sic*] proving a riot of merriment. . . .
>
> Abner has assembled 10 "hill billies" with musical inclinations. Besides playing for Elviry's farmhouse charmers these plowhands and apple knockers play and sing several numbers which are novel and amusing. (*San Antonio Express*, March 11, 1929)

Perhaps most importantly for our theme, there were Otto Gray's Oklahoma Cowboys, who, under this and other names, had been broadcasting and playing the theater circuit since the mid-1920s, enchanting their audiences, who might know no more about cowboys than what they had read in Zane Grey novels, with instrumental virtuosity, Western weepies, and rope tricks. They were enormously popular for almost a decade, including the worst years of the Depression. (They are discussed in *Country Music Originals*.) And in their dust rode outfits like Doc Schneider and his Texas Yodeling Cowboys—"musicians, yodelers, singers, sharpshooters, a string band, and other novelties . . . a program for the whole family"—who also toured extensively, and in the early '30s were heard regularly over the Mexican border station XER.

By 1930, this down-from-the-mountain music had become a full-blown craze.

> Radio Fans Enjoy Rural Folk Humor—Stations Cater To Urban Desire For Farm life Fun—Chains Fall In Line.
> He-men from the mountains and backwoods, cowboys from the plains and "real folks" from the farms have come out of their seclusion and heeded the call of radio. So today we have on the air a wide variety of programs, all in popular favor,

Ad in *Mason City* [Iowa] *Globe-Gazette*, October 24, 1933. (Author's Collection)

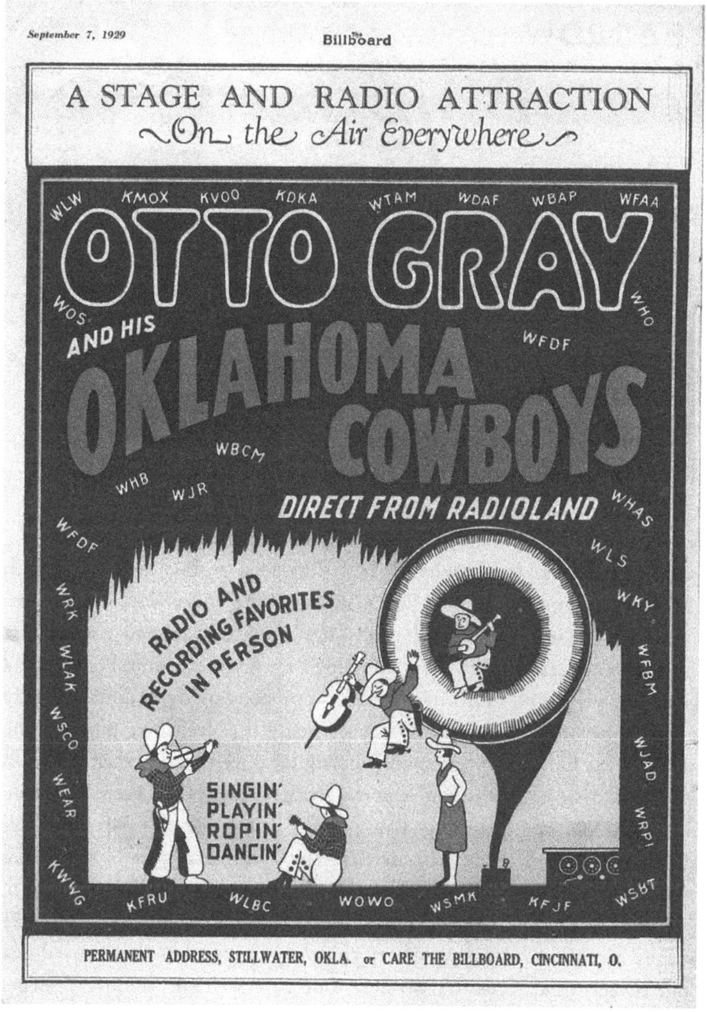

From the “Fall Special” issue of *Billboard*, September 7, 1929. (Author’s Collection)

> portraying the humor, tragedy and reality of rural American life. (*Syracuse Herald*, August 17, 1930)

The reporter namechecks the Crocketts, who had a Columbia chain program, the Pickards on NBC, Eddie Younger and His Mountaineers (aka the Colt Brothers [➤63]), also on NBC, Bradley Kincaid on WLS, and Otto Gray’s “cow-punchin’ radio entertainin’ aggregation,” then on WGY out of Schenectady, New York. Over the airwaves, as on the vaudeville theater circuit, hillbilly business was booming, and it would continue to do so for several years.

★ ★ ★

Collectors are romantics. We see phonograph records as winged messengers, carrying their small but potent dispatches to distant places, putting the music of Charlie Poole or Fiddlin’ John Carson on Victrolas in states neither man was ever likely to visit. I own a 78 by a band from Alabama, recorded in Tennessee, that turned up in Oregon. Any seasoned collector will have similar tales of the extraordinary diaspora of the shellac disc.

But there is only so much that records can do. Each sale of a Skillet-Lickers disc in Santa Fe or an Ernest Stoneman one in Albert Lea, Minnesota, might be a tiny conquest over distance and difference, a small candle lit in a faraway room, but to illumine the music of strangers on a larger scale, it is necessary to fill theater seats by the hundred, activate the valves of radio sets by the thousand. An averagely successful record, such as many in this book, sold maybe 5,000–10,000 copies. A rural revue might sell that many tickets in a couple of months. Place it before a radio microphone, and it reached that many listeners in seconds.

This is why they mattered, the touring and broadcasting hillbilly troupes: they took this music to an entire nation. Seated in Capitols, Colonials, Rialtos, and Tivolis, or amid radio’s invisible congregation, millions listened—perhaps for the first time—to another America.

36

"WIMBUSH RAG"/"BARROW COUNTY STOMP"

Theo. and Gus Clark

Okeh 45339

Recorded in Atlanta, GA, March 12, 1929
Released in June 1929

Reissued on *Georgia Stringbands—Vol. 1 (1927–1930)* (Document DOCD-8021)

Online: YT

These are *strange* tunes. "Wimbush Rag" alternates eight- and eleven-bar strains, while "Barrow County Stomp" is a sixteen-bar melody repeated over and over. Gus Clark's guitar, as upfront in the mix as his brother Theo's fiddle, is not content to keep time but goes on small journeys of rhythmic exploration. The effect of fiercely concentrated repetition, offset by puckishly unexpected accents, is uniquely hypnotic. Mississippi fiddlers and guitarists sometimes sound like this, and indeed the tune historian Gus Meade classed "Wimbush Rag" as a variant of "Sweet Milk and Peaches" as played by Narmour and Smith, but the Mississippi tune (recorded six months later) is more ordered in its structure, less venturesome, less willful.

"The opening phrases of both tunes are identical," observes fiddler Joe LaRose, "but 'Sweet Milk and Peaches' begins (and indeed continues) on the root chord. What makes 'Wimbush Rag' absolutely beautiful is that the guitar begins on the V chord (A), then quickly goes to the root chord of D. In fact it follows that V–I pattern throughout the A part, making a simple melody more intriguing. But it's the B part that fascinates me—beautiful and so off-kilter."

"Wimbush Rag," according to fiddler Craig Judelman, who recorded it as a member of the Dust Busters with John Cohen in 2012, "is not really a rag . . . but in the 1920s it was popular to call a modern sounding fiddle tune a rag, and this is definitely a bit modern, especially the guitar playing on the original record. . . . We [rearranged it] to bring out the psychedelic nature of this little gem."

Off-kilter, psychedelic . . . what did they make of music like this, the recording engineers, men from elsewhere? Did they feel, as the producer Frank Walker famously did of the Leake County Revelers, that such tunes "didn't have any sense to them at all"? Are we witnessing here another example of Okeh's unconventional approach to recording hillbilly talent? Whoever made the decisions, perhaps the A&R man Tommy Rockwell, had a daring streak. As you scan the further reaches of Okeh's old-time catalog, you gaze in wonder at the parade of exotic obscurities. The Three Stripped Gears! Mike Shaw's Alabama Entertainers! William Hanson, Albert Cain, Kyle Wooten, Webb Whipple! Of course, every company backed acts that proved not to be winners, but Rockwell (or whoever) seems to have been an irrepressible and unrepentant gambler.

Perhaps, buttressed by the regular income the company derived from acts like Fiddlin' John Carson, Earl Johnson, and the Scottdale String Band, he felt that anything from Georgia stood a chance in the market, even these two young men traipsing in from rural Barrow County with their odd music.

★ ★ ★

Theodore and Augustus Clark were the youngest sons of Hayden and Mamie Clark. Their mother was herself a fiddler and passed her instrument on to Theo. At the time of the recording, Theo was twenty-two and Gus nineteen. Gus was born in South Carolina, while the family was farming in Oconee County, but mostly they moved around north Georgia, living in Franklin, Barrow, Jackson, and Madison Counties. By 1929, they had settled in

Theo and Gus Clark. (Courtesy of Lorie Vaughn Skelton and Chris Williams)

the Pentecost district of Barrow County, not far from Dacula in Gwinnett County, home to Gid Tanner and his family, as well as to Robert Stanley (1858–1946), related to the Clarks by marriage, who made some of the earliest recordings of Georgia old-time music with his daughter Roba in 1924–25.

Theo worked as a truck farmer, growing squash, melons, corn, and turnip greens, which he sold to stores like the A&P and Kroger in Athens. Gus worked over toward Atlanta but made occasional visits to the family home. Evidently he had laid the guitar aside, for Theo's second daughter, Billie Clark Vaughn, never saw Gus and her father play together. She remembers that back in the day Theo played with a small band for socials and dances round Commerce in Jackson County. Later, probably in the '40s, he led an old-time stringband on an early-morning radio program in Athens called the Ted Clark Show, with the theme tune "Old Joe Clark." He also sang and played hymns in church, and on Sunday afternoons, Billie Vaughn remembers, liked to get out his violin and play worldly tunes like "Down Yonder," "Orange Blossom Special," or "Wildwood Flower."

Neither brother ever talked about having made a record, and Billie Vaughn had no notion they had done so until many years later, when her cousin Chris Williams, a folklorist, brought home a CD of Georgia stringband music containing the Clarks' tunes. The recording, she explained, was done before she was born, before the Depression, when times were better. Afterward, the brothers had no money for trips to Atlanta to further their music, and besides, Theo had a new wife, Mary. They raised three daughters and spent their lives in Madison County, where Theo died in 1969; Mary survived him by almost thirty years. Gus died on the last day of 1983.

★ ★ ★

"Barrow County Stomp" explains itself as a title, but where, or who, or what, was Wimbush? There is no Wimbush, Georgia, and apparently never has been. The Clarks' descendants do not remember anyone of that name, which is a scarce one in Georgia, usually found in the south and west of the state, more often as Wimbish. Etymologically, it's an Anglo-Saxon word meaning a reedy meadow (OE *winn*, meadow, pasture + *beos*, reeds). This may be one conundrum of old-time music history that will remain unsolved.

Rare name, rare record. There may be fewer than ten copies in collectors' hands. It seems not to have sold out its first pressing. For Okeh, it was another unsuccessful roll of the hillbilly dice, a venture to file alongside acts like the blind yodeler Ralph Richardson or the farmyard impressionist Barnyard Steve. For Theo and Gus Clark, it meant a rare, perhaps first-time, trip to Atlanta, a chance to see the big city before responsibility fenced them in. And to make a record that, nearly a century later, still intrigues and captivates.

37

"BIRMINGHAM JAIL"/"SIX MONTHS AIN'T LONG"

Ezra Hill and Henry Johnson [Robinette and Moore]/Marlow and Young [Rutherford and Foster]

Champion 15750

Recorded in Richmond, IN, April 10, 1929 ["Birmingham Jail"] and January 14, 1929 ["Six Months Ain't Long"]
Released in June 1929
Sold 30,034

Reissued on *Grayson & Whitter Vol. 2 (1928–29)/ Robinette & Moore (1929)* (Document DOCD-8055) ["Birmingham Jail"] • *Old-Time Mountain Ballads* (County CD-3504), *Kentucky Mountain Music* (Yazoo 2200) ["Six Months Ain't Long"]

Online: Spotify ["Birmingham Jail"] • YT

In some ways, Gennett Records was the most ingenious company in the old-time record business. It may not have invented, but it certainly exploited, practices like reissuing recordings on subsidiary or licensed labels with bogus artist credits or cross-coupling—putting different artists on each side of the record—so that the purchaser could sample two Gennett acts for the price of one. But its primary tactic was the cover version. Let another company have a hit, and, within months, Gennett would have produced its own recording of the song. All three strategies are at work on this record.

Melvin Robinette (1905–99) was born in Coeburn, in Wise County, Virginia, and took up the fiddle in his late teens after hearing Fiddlin' Cowan Powers. In spring 1929, he was contacted by the singer-guitarist Byrd Moore (1899?–1949) (➤48), who may have been living in Wise County and had already worked for Gennett, as well as other labels. Through the talent agent Dennis W. Taylor (➤14), Moore had an engagement to record at the Gennett studio. Robinette and Moore met at Taylor's house near Richmond, Kentucky, and remained as his guests. Also staying in the house were the fiddler Leonard Rutherford, originally from Somerset, Kentucky, and until recently the partner of the blind singer Richard Burnett on a series of popular Columbia discs; and singer-guitarist John Foster from Scott County, Tennessee. Taylor had been promoting Rutherford and Foster to Gennett as, in effect, Burnett and Rutherford without the ornery blind man. The two duos spent a week practicing, in different rooms, with Taylor listening and making comments. Preparation over, they got aboard Taylor's car and rode to Richmond, Indiana.

★ ★ ★

April 10, 1929, proved to be one of Gennett's most profitable days of record-making. Byrd Moore's vocal number "When the Snowflakes Fall Again," coupled with Rutherford and Foster's duet on "My Carolina Home," sold over 19,000 copies on Champion 15732, while the Robinette–Foster duet "Birmingham Jail," coupled on Champion 15750 with a Rutherford–Foster duet from an earlier 1929 session, "Six Months Ain't Long," passed 30,000, making it one of Gennett's best-sellers in the old-time field. Both releases were name changed, Robinette and Moore becoming Ezra Hill and Henry Johnson, Rutherford and Foster reborn as Marlow and Young. (There was a further set of fake names when the recordings were issued on the Sears label Supertone.) Years later, Robinette remembered how impressed the recording supervisor had been by his ability to fiddle and sing tenor harmony at the same time. (Not so impressed

Melvin Robinette. (OTM Collection)

The intent was not to deceive record-buyers but rather to offer them the thing they most wanted—the song—at a cheaper price than the original recording. (Columbias and Victors cost 75 cents, Champions only 35.) People who didn't care for Hawaiian-style guitar may actually have preferred Robinette and Moore's "Birmingham Jail" to Darby and Tarlton's.

★ ★ ★

The brisk sales of records like this must have seemed to validate Gennett's predatory approach to catalog acquisition. Specially attentive to the success of Jimmie Rodgers, the company assembled a team of singer-guitarists capable of covering his records, such as Hoke Rice from Georgia and Howard Keesee from Bristol, Virginia, both of whom racked up respectable sales on Champion in 1929–30. Another was Jess Hillard, from Union County, Indiana, who moved to nearby Richmond to be on hand whenever Gennett needed a quick cover version of Rodgers's latest blue yodel, sometimes aided by his teenaged

Guitarist Byrd Moore with one of his recording partners, the fiddler, guitarist, and pianist Jess Johnston of McDowell County, West Virginia. (Kinney Rorrer Collection)

that he ever invited Robinette back to the studio, though.)

Three of these four sides were cover versions. "When the Snowflakes Fall Again" was an arrant copy, right down to the opening dialogue, of Roy Harvey and Earl Shirkey's "When the Roses Bloom for the Bootlegger" (➤32), recorded six months earlier and issued in February 1929. "My Carolina Home" had been a huge hit in 1926 for Bob Nichols (Clayton McMichen) and Riley Puckett, and "Birmingham Jail" a substantial one in 1928 for Tom Darby and Jimmie Tarlton. The only recording that didn't have recent forerunners was "Six Months Ain't Long"—at least under that title, but many listeners would have known theme and melody already, under titles like "Poor Boy," "Ninety-Nine Years in Jail," or "Cold Penitentiary Blues."

I called these cover versions, but they were not soundalikes. The Gennett recordings were all made with fiddle and guitar, whereas the originals of "Snowflakes" and "Birmingham Jail" had only guitars.

Fiddler Leonard Rutherford (right) with a friend, Jim Gregory. (OTM Collection, from the late Dick Burnett)

son Nelson. Jess's younger brother Harry joined in too, all five of his issued recordings being Rodgers covers. Given his skill with Rodgers's songs, Jess Hillard was also the natural choice to cover Jimmie Davis, and he reproduced at least half a dozen of his songs, often in similar guitar-based settings.

Yet one wonders why anyone bothered. Jess Hillard did all his recording in 1931–33. In those economic wasteland years, Victor was having trouble pushing the sales even of Rodgers's or Davis's discs into four figures, while Gennett's cover versions were logging monthly sales in dozens, and by 1933, not even that. Looking back from here, it all seems hopelessly quixotic. But within a year or so, the arrival of vigorously promoted cut-price labels like Bluebird and Decca would reenergize the hillbilly record business. Could Gennett have reconstructed itself as a player in that market? Only, I think, if it had broken with its previous practice and engaged, as the new labels did, in location recording: going looking for talent, rather than waiting for it to turn up at its door.

38

"HENRY FORD'S MODEL A"/ "MARRIED LIFE BLUES"

Oscar Ford
Columbia 15437-D

Recorded in Atlanta, GA, April 11, 1929
Released in October 1929
Sold 5,217

Reissued on *Georgia Songsters (1926–1930)* (Document DOCD-8024)

Online: Spotify ["Married Life Blues"] • YT

There's not much product placement on old-time records: just a few staple goods of rural and small-town life. This would change, as businessmen and country musicians signed contracts to promote or be promoted by Martha White and Playboy flour, Jewel oil and shortening, JFG coffee, Prince Albert tobacco, or Crazy Water Crystals laxative. But in the 1920s, this was not big-brand music.

With one exception.

All you folks listen to what I say
About a new Ford called the Model A:
Old John Henry knew his biz,
When he said, "I'm a-gonna make a lady out of Liz."

Few events of 1927 were so breathlessly awaited as the emergence, after months of secret planning, of Henry Ford's new car. Compared with the reliable but slow Model T, or "Tin Lizzie," introduced in 1908, the Model A ($385 for the roadster, $395 the phaeton, $495 the coupe and sedan) promised new vistas of comfort and speed.

Now if you go to heaven I will give you all a tip:
Drive an old Ford because it's bound to make
the trip.
But if you go to torment, drive a Model A,
'Cause it'll outrun the devil and you're bound to
get away.

This uncommissioned advertising copy was delivered by a crackly voiced Georgian neatly named Oscar Ford, who had somewhere acquired the skills of an old-school vaudevillian or minstrel-show man. He was not the first old-time singer to wave the Ford flag. Uncle Dave Macon had greeted "that Henry Ford of mine" in 1926 and announced "The New Ford Car" in 1928, while Red Henderson, the guitarist with Earl Johnson's Clodhoppers, took an "Automobile Ride Through Alabama," also in 1928, in a "brand-new Ford"—surely a Model A—on a tall tale of a journey, involving bears, wasps, snakes, and a vehicle that reconfigures itself like a Transformer toy. A Stamps quartet from Texas, the Owen Brothers and Ellis, sang "If You Don't Like My Ford Coupe, Don't You Cadillac Me." Various popular artists had recorded Walter O'Keefe's jaunty 1928 composition "Henry's Made a Lady out of Lizzie," to which Oscar Ford refers. In March 1929, soon after sales of the Model A passed a million, Fiddlin' John Carson had sung about "My Ford Sedan," and three days later, in the same Atlanta studio, the African American blues singer Cleo Gibson had boasted, "I've Got Ford Movements in My Hips" ("ten thousand miles guarantee").

But none of these singers was as keen on the brand as Oscar Ford. He was born Robert Oscar Ford on October 2, 1890, in or near Macon in Bibb County. As a young man he followed his father into blacksmithing, but he transferred that skill into automobilism and spent the second half of the 1920s working at, and for a time managing, the Montpelier Garage in Macon. Working there too, as a mechanic, was a fellow Maconite, Admiral Dewey Grace (1893–1947). The two men began making music together, Ford singing and fiddling, Grace playing guitar. They secured a date with Okeh in Atlanta in October 1927, two months before the Model A came on the market, and made some boisterous recordings, Oscar dropping a Ford namecheck into the first, "Down in the Old Home Town."

His next chance to record came in April 1929. Now with Columbia, and no longer partnered with Grace, though they were still workmates, he was accompanied on guitar by Riley Puckett, and these are the men we hear on "Henry Ford's Model A," Oscar jauntily fiddling a variant of the tune "Eighth of January," one that would reappear in country music thirty years later as Jimmy Driftwood's "The Battle of New Orleans."

Perhaps encouraged by the moderate success of "Henry Ford's Model A," Oscar plugged the marque again on his December 1930 recording "Race Between a Ford and Chevrolet," in which "old man Johnson" pits his Model A against "old man Jones" and his Chevrolet, up to the top of the hill and back into town. In a postmodernist touch, the singer inserts himself and his friends into the narrative:

> Oscar Ford give the signal for the start,
> McMichen was the judge on the stand,
> Old Riley Puckett was to hold the jug of gin
> And turn it over to the lucky man.

Puckett was right there on the recording, and although Clayton McMichen wasn't—the fiddling is by Ford himself—he was probably in the studio, having just recorded with his Melody Men. The two men had worked with each other before: earlier in 1930, Ford had participated alongside Mac and other Skillet-Lickers in the sketch recordings "Taking the Census" and "Jeremiah Hopkins' Store at Sand Mountain." In the former, he delivered some lines of dialogue and sang a few phrases of "Cotton Eyed Joe." In the store sketch, he mentioned the new-model Chevrolet and warned Gid Tanner that a boll weevil was trying to crawl into his fiddle.

The result of the race? The cars cross the finish line at the same time, McMichen declares it a tie, and the musicians make off with the gin.

Oscar Ford and his wife, Mamie Lee Davis Ford. (Courtesy of Terry Ford)

* * *

On the other side of "Henry Ford's Model A," Oscar Ford tells us a very different story. He finds a sweetheart, marries her, and they honeymoon in Arkansas. Back home, he drinks, loses his job, and can't pay the grocery bill. His wife and mother-in-law gang up on him, and in the tagline to that verse he complains, "I had those henpecked husband blues." He takes to staying

Oscar Ford, about 1929. (Courtesy of Terry Ford)

out late, but when he comes home, his wife is waiting with a rolling pin, and "I had those Jiggs and Maggie blues." Jiggs and Maggie were the squabbling nouveau riche husband and wife in George McManus's syndicated cartoon strip *Bringing Up Father*. Next, Oscar's wife sues him for divorce and alimony, and "I had those separation blues." Unrepentant, he moves on:

> Soon I found me another little girl,
> Her name was Julia Ann.
> The second time I took her out
> I met the Ku Klux Klan—
> I had the blue-ooh-hoo—oh, Lord!

They take him for a ride and tie him up, but only to dust his pants. Luckier than some.

At the beginning of the 1920s, the Ku Klux Klan had been relatively small and localized, numbering a few thousands and concentrated in north Georgia, where it had been reborn in 1915, not long after the Mary Phagan affair (➤4), in a ceremony on Stone Mountain. By mid-decade, its membership had risen to perhaps four or five million (some historians put it a good deal higher), and it exercised real political power in at least half a dozen states. During the 1920s, as described earlier (➤14), it disseminated dozens of Klan-themed songs through sheet music, songbooks, and records. Little of that had anything to do with old-time music, but the Klan did interest itself in events like fiddlers' conventions, such as a gathering in Mountain City, Tennessee, in May 1925. In a well-known photograph of some of the participants, a flyer declaring the Klan's sponsorship is visible in the window of the bank building behind them. But in the same year the organization was rocked by scandal, "betrayed," as the historian T. H. Watkins says, "by the uncertain morals and sordid financial shenanigans of its own leadership," and its membership plummeted. The one Southern city in which it hung on was Atlanta, where Oscar Ford recorded his mild joke about it—the only explicit reference to the Klan in recorded old-time music.

This merry troubadour died of a stroke, just a few months after recording "Race Between a Ford and Chevrolet," on April 20, 1931. The Model A ceased production in the same year.

39

"FLOP EARED MULE"/ "LYNCHBURG TOWN"

The Highlanders

Paramount 3171

Recorded in New York, NY, May 9, 1929
Released in July 1929

Reissued on *Charlie Poole with the Highlanders: The Complete Paramount & Brunswick Recordings, 1929* (Tompkins Square TSQ2875)

Online: Spotify, YT

This is a story of hillbilly opportunism. The choice of the tunes on this record, the way they were played, the name of the band that played them, all tell us something about the workings of the old-time record market and the strategies employed by musicians and record companies alike to negotiate them.

In the first week of May 1929, Charlie Poole and some of his associates were in New York to record for Columbia, the label with which Poole had been associated since 1925. Until then, his recordings had been in a trio format of fiddle, banjo, and guitar, and very successful they had been too, but for this date he wanted to add a second fiddler and a pianist. Some writers have interpreted this as evidence of Poole's aspiration to become more of an uptown musician, the leader of a small dance orchestra rather than a stringband. Perhaps so—but he may have been prompted by something more specific.

One of the New York party was the young Lonnie Austin, who had been touring with a showband, the Blue Ridge Ramblers (➤35), and in January had played piano at their three-day recording session for Brunswick. The Ramblers' records provided a model for what might be called old-time big-band music, and it is hardly possible that Poole had not heard them, or about them, and seen them pointing in a direction he himself wanted to take.

What he proposed to Columbia's recording director Frank Walker, then, was a breakaway from the trio music of previous recordings, toward a fuller sound. Walker, who saw no role for a piano in old-time stringband music, would have none of it, and the session of May 6–7 followed the existing model. So, having fulfilled his duty to Columbia, Poole took his musicians to Paramount to see if he could sell the idea of a larger band there. His guitarist Roy Harvey had already recorded for Paramount, and had a further link to the company through his brother-in-law E. D. Terry, who ran the music store in Beckley, West Virginia—at which Harvey worked for much of the 1920s—and was a Paramount dealer.

Accordingly, on May 9, Poole, Harvey, fiddlers Lonnie Austin and Odell Smith, and pianist Lucy Harvey Terry gathered at Paramount's studio to record some high-octane dance music. The first four tunes they cut, including "Flop Eared Mule" and "Lynchburg Town," had all been recorded for Columbia three years earlier by a band well known to Poole and his circle, fiddler Charlie La Prade and his Blue Ridge Highballers from Danville, Virginia (➤7). It would be natural to think that the musicians, and Paramount, hoped to match La Prade's sales.

Since Poole and the North Carolina Ramblers were under contract to Columbia, their identity had to be masked. Most of the Paramount sides came out as by the Highlanders. Similarly, when the same quintet called, two days later, at the New York office of Brunswick and made further recordings, it was under the name Allegheny Highlanders. It would be interesting to know whether Walker became aware of this contract jumping; if he heard the third and last of the Paramount releases, the only coupling to

The Allegheny Highlanders, 1929. Left to right, standing: Roy Harvey, Odell Smith, Lonnie Austin, E. D. Terry, Lucy Harvey Terry; seated: Hamon Newman, Earl Shirkey. (Kinney Rorrer Collection)

feature vocals, he could hardly miss Poole's utterly characteristic singing voice. We do know that Poole never strayed again, recording solely for Columbia until his death in 1931.

Part of the reason for that fidelity may have been the commercial failure of the Paramount experiment. In 1929, Poole's Columbia releases were selling around 5,000–7,000, but, according to a royalty statement preserved by Lucy Terry, in the final quarter of the year, "Flop Eared Mule," though a relatively new release, sold a mere 100 copies. This would not have surprised record producers like Walker, Ralph Peer, or Bill Brown. They believed that the record-buying public had tired of purely instrumental old-time dance music and now insisted on vocals, or at least banter (➤20). The Highlanders' flop with "Flop Eared Mule" would simply have proved their point.

40

"LEVEE BREAKING BLUES"—PARTS I AND II

Happy Bud Harrison
Vocalion 5332

Recorded in Chicago, IL, May 29, 1929
Released in September 1929

Listen while I tell you 'bout the levee blues," the singer begins. "If the water should break"—as the Mississippi River so disastrously had, less than two years earlier—"this is what I sure got to lose." And he begins an inventory, listing the livestock, the furniture, even the wildlife of his imaginary property:

> Got a little log cabin and my old dog Nig,
> Three old sows and one boar pig . . .
>
> Flock of chickens and the old cat Tommy,
> A rattly board and my lovin' mammy . . .
>
> It's mud from the barn, from the house to the road,
> There's a lot of singin' crickets and plenty hop-toads . . .

This is the "before" picture. By the time he begins "Part II"—"I'm back again to tell you 'bout the levee blues"—the floods have done their work:

> The grass is dyin', the flowers are dead,
> The barn's a-floatin', wind's blowed away the shed . . .
>
> The lights are out, there's a candle in the jug,
> If you want more light, you get the lightnin' bugs . . .

But amidst the chaos, his woman keeps her head. "Still, my mama, she's long and tall, If the water should break, it wouldn't worry her at all." And the song ends with a verse of carefree yodeling against the descending, darkening, dying cadences of the horns. Yes, horns—we'll come back to that.

It is strangely beautiful.

★ ★ ★

We don't know much about Happy Bud Harrison, but on record, at least, he specialized in blue yodels, and in 1929, he could reasonably expect to grab a seat on that particular bandwagon as it rolled through the country. But posterity, though it embraces the original Blue Yodeler, is more standoffish about the others, and Harrison has been relegated by researchers and most collectors to the lowly class of Jimmie Rodgers imitators. None of his recordings has been reissued, and he doesn't make it into even the footnotes of country music history.

The only person I've met who remembered him was the amateur songwriter and singer Bernard "Slim" Smith, author of the Depression anthem "Bread Line Blues," who ran into him in Memphis in the late 1920s, when Harrison was singing over WREC: "We opened the Peabody Hotel Roof Garden together." (If Smith's memory was reliable, this would have been in May 1928.) Smith, who was from Mississippi, thought Harrison might have been, too, and there are clues that support this. Harrison's song "The Wreck of G. & S. I." is about the Gulf and Ship Island Railroad, which operated only in Mississippi, running from Gulfport to Jackson. One of the stops on the line was Hattiesburg, and it's here that we find Harrison in January 1929.

> J. Bud (Happy) Harrison, the boy who picks a mean banjo and broadcasts from WRBJ, Woodruff Furniture Store, is filling a good many request numbers during his stay in Hattiesburg.

"HAPPY BUD" HARRISON, recording artist, known as the "Yodeling Fool From Dixie," who played several selections over Station WDAE this morning. He was featured during the broadcast of Red Gay's band, and will appear with the band frequently during his stay in Tampa.

Tampa Times, September 27, 1930. (Author's Collection)

> A great many local radios were tuned in on his program last night. (*Hattiesburg American*, January 17, 1929)

The following day, the paper reported on the entertainer at more length, describing him now as an "expert guitarist" (journalists often confused guitars and banjos, though perhaps Harrison played both) who had "entertained the employes [*sic*] in the Illinois Central shops here yesterday afternoon." (The I. C. had absorbed the G. & S. I. in 1924.) The article continued:

> Since "Happy" started making his melodies over the local station, he has received more than 400 requests for special numbers, some of the telegrams coming from points in New York state, while most of them are from places in Alabama, Louisiana and Tennessee. Tonight Harrison will broadcast a series of guitar selections, accompanied by Charlie "Hoot" Gibson, who will be heard as a "human saxophone."

(This "Hoot" Gibson was not the Western movie star, but the former first baseman of the Hattiesburg Pinetoppers baseball team.) The paper also revealed that, within a couple of days, Harrison would be leaving for Nashville to fill an engagement at WSM, but this may have been premature: a week later, he was still in town, playing at a house party. Wherever he went next, by October he was on KPRC in Houston, where he had a fifteen-minute mid-morning slot. In January 1930, he appeared, billed as a "Famous Recording Artist," at the Durham Chevrolet Co. showroom in Reno, Nevada, evidently to give a live broadcast. In September 1930, he was in Tampa, Florida, where he joined fiddler Red Gay on WDAE (*Tampa Times*, September 27). In June 1931, he stopped by the office of the *Longview* [Texas] *Journal*, a "tall clownish gentleman . . . wearing a miniature comical straw hat . . . [who] twangs guitar" (June 23, 1931).

In these random sightings, we glimpse one of a class of practitioners who played a large role in early country music: radio-friendly performers constantly shifting from station to station, itinerant hands like Steinbeck's George and Lennie, coming with the dust, going with the wind. Hattiesburg—Nashville—Houston—Reno—Tampa—Longview—Anytown.

★ ★ ★

Wedged into Harrison's schedule during 1929 were three trips to Chicago, in February, May, and August, to record for Vocalion. Mostly he sang blue yodels, but even when he didn't, he came up with song titles Rodgers might have chosen, like "The Wreck of G. & S. I." or "I'm Glad I'm Free."

Like Rodgers too, he varied his accompaniment, making some recordings with just his guitar, a couple with steel guitar, and at one session with a trumpeter and a clarinetist, a setting that may have been suggested to artist or producer by the arrangement of Rodgers's "Waiting for a Train" for a small danceband. This is the soundscape of "Levee Breaking Blues." Trumpet and clarinet play hide-and-seek with the vocal, popping up to mimic a phrase or to echo the downward steps of the yodel. The effect is not uptown at all but pastoral, the trumpet murmuring one- and two-note phrases, the clarinet evoking a shepherd's pipe. And rightly so, for the song is all about the countryside.

It is perhaps the most vivid rural scene any old-time singer ever depicted on a record, a subject

NEW RELEASES OF

OLD-TIME-TUNES

ON VOCALION RECORDS

ALL VOCALION RECORDS SEVENTY-FIVE CENTS EACH

HAPPY BUD HARRISON

The Dixie Entertainer

Levee Breaking Blues—Part I . 5332
Levee Breaking Blues—Part II
Vocal with Yodeling, Guitar, Clarinet and Trumpet
Happy Bud Harrison

Prairie County Waltz—Waltz . 5329
Arkansas Waltz—Waltz
Fiddle, Guitar and Piano
Bob Larkan and Family

Hilarious Zeb (Traditional) . 5330
Raisin' 'Ell (Traditional)
McLaughlin's Old-Time Melody Makers

Red Wing 5331
Snow Deer With Emry Arthur
Floyd Thompson and His Home Towners

I Slept Beautifully 5309
Gonzales Two Step
Accordion Solos
Frank King (Black Frank)

The White Rose Vocal Duet with Two Guitars and Banjo 5335
The Wanderer Vocal Duet with Guitar and Mouth Organ
Emry Arthur, William Rexroat

I Can't Change It 5337
Midnight Special
Vocal with Cowboy Band
Otto Gray and His Cowboy Band

Miss Iola Instrumental with Fiddle, Guitar and Piano 5336
Lime Rock Instrumental with Fiddle and Guitar
Smith's Garage Fiddle Band

From the *Vocalion Record Almanac of Old Time Tunes* for September 1929. (OTM Collection)

Thomas Hart Benton might have painted, or Walker Evans photographed: not a landscape, like those stretching and symbolic cottonfields, or Appalachia's shadowing pines, but a particular place, busy with chickens and crickets, hop-toads and lightning bugs. A home.

"OVER THE HILLS TO THE POORHOUSE"

W. C. Childers
Champion 45166

Recorded in Richmond, IN, July 9, 1929
Released in December 1935

No sales figures are available for Champion 45166, but the 1929 issue on Champion 15791 sold 5,631

One of the most striking divergences between country music and blues is in their treatment of old age. For the blues singer, the elderly, when they appear in songs at all, are objects of condescension, either mocked for their inability to do like they used to or patted on the back if they can still cut up a little. Country music is kinder, not to say mushier. The full complement of gray-haired mothers in the country and bluegrass songbook would pack the Grand Ole Opry, assuming they could totter there.

But age, for the old-time singer, was not all silver threads among the gold, or cabins with roses round the door. One of the abiding terrors of nineteenth-century working-class life was the possibility of sinking, through age, poverty, or incapacity, below the waterline of family and community and ending up in the steerage class of society, institutionalized and unremembered. This is the prospect held up in songs like "Don't Forget the Old Folks," "Old and Only in the Way," and, most pitifully, George L. Catlin and David Braham's 1874 composition "Over the Hill to the Poor-House," in which an old widower laments the perfidy of his children, who have turned him away from the door of the home that was once his. Most people who know it today probably heard it from Lester Flatt and Earl Scruggs, but it was recorded several times in the 1920s and '30s, notably by the blind singer and guitarist William C. Childers.

His name means little now, but between 1928 and 1931 Childers made more than thirty issuable recordings for four companies, traveling to sessions in Texas, Indiana, Wisconsin, and Georgia. Some found their way onto labels in Canada, Australia, and the United Kingdom. Many of his Gennett sides appeared on several of the company's labels and must have sold well, in particular "Over the Hills to the Poorhouse," which evidently had enough selling power to be reissued six and a half years after it was made. From this and other repertoire choices like "Your Mother's Always Waiting" and "Crepe on the Little Cabin Door," we may guess that Childers deliberately chose late-nineteenth- and early-twentieth-century compositions about mothers, childhood, and death, believing that listeners would be particularly well disposed to hearing such songs from a blind man.

Record-collectors and students of old-time music have been less soft-hearted: Childers's recordings have received little attention, and his life still less. He was that moderately unusual, but by no means unique, figure in recorded old-time music, a Native American: a Cherokee, born on March 29, 1890, in the Indian Territory of Oklahoma. By the age of twenty, he was farming in the small community of Gans, in Sequoyah County, where he spent at least the next ten years. During this time, he taught singing school and was regularly heard at singing conventions. In 1917, when considered for war service, he was registered as having defective sight in both eyes and was unable to sign his name, though neither disadvantage appears to have prevented him working as a loan agent or, in the previous year, seeking nomination as a County Commissioner.

In his submission for that office, he wrote: "My educational efficiency is far above the average. I am not handicapped in the way of correspondence, as I use a typewriter for all writing." The *Sallisaw* [Oklahoma] *Star Gazette* described him, though "nearly blind," as "one of the most energetic young

(Author's Collection)

men of the county. . . . [H]e is forging ahead and is destined to be one of the factors to be reckoned with in the affairs of the county." His candidacy, however, was unsuccessful.

During the 1920s, he had periods of residence in Ada—during which he broadcast over KFJF in Oklahoma City and made his first recordings, for Okeh—and in Oklahoma City itself, but he probably moved around a good deal as he pursued the career of an itinerant musician, traveling with his wife Lena and two daughters. In 1930, when a census taker encountered the family at a tourist camp in Lincoln, Kansas, W. C. stated that he was singing on radio. Lena sang with him on some of his records, and another singer from Ada, Clyde G. White, on others.

His longest association with a record company was with Gennett, for whom he recorded on four occasions. The banjoist Haskell Harkleroad from Richmond, Indiana, who accompanied the blind singer at a 1929 Gennett session in that city, told the historian Gus Meade that when Childers discovered that the company had issued some of his numbers with made-up artist credits, such as "Enos Wanner" on Champion or "Andy Hopkins" on Supertone, "he sued them for changing his name on records." Perhaps as a riposte, Childers used the name Wanner when making his final recordings, for Columbia, in 1931.

By the mid-'30s, he appears to have moved with his wife and children to Chicago. The family was enumerated there in 1940, but W. C. was absent; possibly he was traveling for musical work. A couple of years later he was back in Gans, visiting, or perhaps now living with, his younger sister Eliza, who had never left. He evidently returned to Chicago, where he died on March 15, 1968.

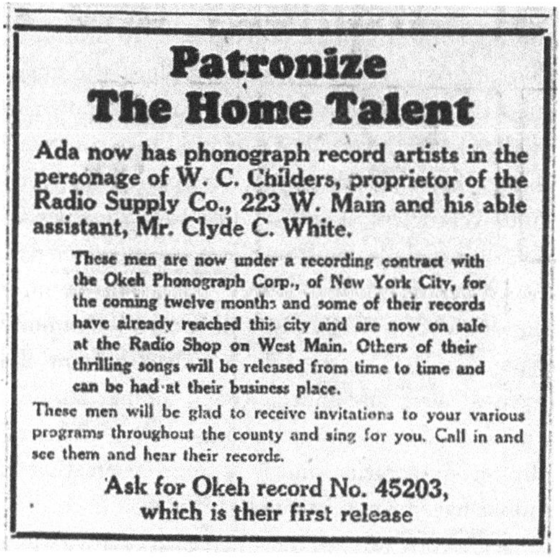
Patronize
The Home Talent

Ada now has phonograph record artists in the personage of W. C. Childers, proprietor of the Radio Supply Co., 223 W. Main and his able assistant, Mr. Clyde C. White.

These men are now under a recording contract with the Okeh Phonograph Corp., of New York City, for the coming twelve months and some of their records have already reached this city and are now on sale at the Radio Shop on West Main. Others of their thrilling songs will be released from time to time and can be had at their business place.

These men will be glad to receive invitations to your various programs throughout the county and sing for you. Call in and see them and hear their records.

Ask for Okeh record No. 45203,
which is their first release

Another New Phonograph
Record---*by two Ada Boys*

"The Red River Valley"
"Your Mother Always Cares for You"

Okeh Record No. 45208 Sung By

W. C. Childers and Clyde White

Both of the Radio Supply Co.
223 W. Main, Ada, Oklahoma

This record will be one of the most sensational ever put on the market in Ada. Hear it! Also have a large supply of the Edward Hickman and Marion Parker records.

PHONE 219 WE WILL DELIVER THEM TO YOUR HOME

The *Ada Evening News* announced Childers's first record on April 15, 1928, and his second on April 27. (Author's Collection)

42

"HAUNTED HUNTER"

Billie Maxwell (The Cowgirl Singer)
Victor V-40241

Recorded in El Paso, TX, July 11, 1929
Released on May 16, 1930
Sold 1,134

Reissued on *When I Was a Cowboy Vol. 1* (Yazoo 2022)

Online: Spotify, YT

Speed on, speed on, brave comrade, our camp lies far away;
We must reach that haunted valley before the close of day.
How I became snow-blinded I will tell you as I go:
By the blight of the haunted hunter as he walks the midnight snow.

The story is in every sense a chilling one. As the speaker trudges through woods and over hills, she is joined by a gray-cloaked stranger who silently accompanies her, leaving no footprints in the snow. She falls into a drift and is found at dawn next day, "with my dark hair bleached as white as the snow on which I lay . . . I had seen that haunted hunter and withered in its blight." It might be a tale out of Algernon Blackwood, whose Wendigo also stalked the frozen prairies and forests of the North, except that the Wendigo subsisted on human flesh.

It is actually a poem, "The Walker of the Snow," by Charles Dawson Shanly (1811–75). A Dubliner who emigrated to Canada in the 1830s to work as a civil servant, he moved in the late 1850s to New York and became a journalist, contributing to, and doing editorial work for, *Vanity Fair*, *The Atlantic Monthly*, and other publications. As well as essays and other prose pieces, he wrote many poems and ballads. "The Walker of the Snow" first appeared in the May 1859 issue of *The Atlantic Monthly*. It has been anthologized and is held in some regard as an example of Canadian Gothic. In 1888, it inspired *The Phantom Hunter*, one of the best-known works of the Canadian painter William Blair Bruce. (So well known that in 2014 it was reproduced on a grande coffee mug.)

We owe the appearance of Shanly's poem on a phonograph disc to Billie Maxwell, "The Cowgirl Singer" (1906–54). Now the supernatural does not figure much in recorded old-time music. In Clarence Ashley's "Haunted Road Blues" the singer takes that route to a graveyard to "look down in [his] good girl's face," but this is a blues commonplace. Ghosts mostly appear for comic effect. The Tune Wranglers' "Look out for the Ghost, Red" (1937) is melodrama from the midway, singer Red Brown serenading Mr. Bones like a San Antonio tent-show Cab Calloway. Bill Cox, in "Alimony Woman" (1931), sees his ex-wife rise from the grave to wail, and indeed yodel, for her support payments. So, as a serious ghost story, "Haunted Hunter" is a rarity, and it is appropriate that it should have been presented as if it were a cowboy song. Cowboy verse in the nineteenth century was a distinct literary genre, but its makers were attuned to other strains in the writing of the period, not least the supernatural. More than twenty years before Shanly wrote "The Walker of the Snow," Charles Dickens found an enormous American readership, through both legitimate and pirated editions, with *The Pickwick Papers*, which contains five long ghost stories.

★ ★ ★

Billie Maxwell showed up at a Victor session in El Paso, Texas, in July 1929. Ralph Peer, who would supervise the recordings, had arrived in the city at the end of June, intending, as he told a local paper, to make test recordings of local talent.

NEW ORTHOPHONIC VICTOR RECORDS

Title	Artist	Number	Size	List prc.
Man on the Flying Trapeze	"Mac" (Harry McClintock)	21567	10	.75
Circus Days	*"Mac" (Harry McClintock)*			
Many, Many Years Ago	Vernon Dalhart	19681	10	.75
Boy's Best Friend is His Mother	*Vernon Dalhart*			
Many Years Ago	Vernon Dalhart	V-40094	10	.75
I Long to See the One I Left Behind	*Vernon Dalhart*			
Maple in the Lane	"Peg" Moreland	21724	10	.75
Clover Blossoms with Guitar	*"Peg" Moreland*			
Maria, Mari—Waltz	Walter Kolomoku's Honoluluans	21263	10	.75
Girl of My Dreams—Waltz Medley	*Walter Kolomoku's Honoluluans*			
Married Man in Trouble	Vaughan Happy Two	V-40001	10	.75
Chicken with Piano	*Vaughan Happy Two*			
Marthie Campbell *Violin with Guitar*	Jilson Setters (J. W. Day)	21353	10	.75
Wild Wagoner	*Jilson Setters (J. W. Day)*			

MARVIN, FRANKIE—with Guitar

- Girl I Left Behind V-40233
- Mother's Song of Love V-40233
- Oklahoma, Land of Sunny West V-40159
- Old Family Album V-40159

MARVIN, JOHNNY—with Guitar

- Watermelon Smilin' on the Vine 21653

Title	Artist	Number	Size	List prc.
Mary, Don't You Weep	Georgia Yellow Hammers	20928	10	.75
Going to Raise a Ruckus Tonight	*Georgia Yellow Hammers*			
Mary Malone	McGettigan with the Killarney Trio	21380	10	.75
Fitzmaurice, the Dublin Flier	*McGettigan with the Killarney Trio*			
Master of the Storm *with Piano*	Vaughan Quartet	21756	10	.75
What a Morning That Will Be	*Vaughan Quartet*			
Matrimonial Intentions	Buddy Baker	V-40017	10	.75
Alimony Blues with Guitar	*Buddy Baker*			

Billie Maxwell

MAXWELL, BILLIE (The Cowgirl Singer)—with Guitar

- Arizona Girl V-40188
- Billy Venero V-40148
- Cowboy's Wife V-40188
- Haunted Hunter V-40241
- Where Your Sweetheart Waits V-40241

McABEE, PALMER—Harmonica

- Lost Boy Blues 21352
- McAbee's Railroad Piece 21352

Title	Artist	Number	Size	List prc.
McAbee's Railroad Piece *Harmonica Solo*	Palmer McAbee	21352	10	.75
Lost Boy Blues	*Palmer McAbee*			

McCLINTOCK, HARRY, "RADIO MAC"

- Ain't We Crazy? V-40101
- Big Rock Candy Mountains 21704
- Billy Venero 21487
- Bum Song 21343
- Bum Song No. 2 21704
- Circus Days 21567
- Fireman Save My Child V-40234
- Get Along, Little Doggies V-40016
- Hallelujah! I'm a Bum 21343
- Hobo's Spring Song V-40112
- If I Had My Druthers V-40112
- Jerry, Go Ile That Car 21521
- Jesse James 21420
- Man on the Flying Trapeze 21567
- My Dad's Dinner Pail 21521
- Sam Bass 21420
- Texas Rangers 21487
- Trusty Lariat V-40234

33

From a Victor catalog, 1930. (OTM Collection)

> Untrained talent and old-time music—remnants of a vanishing west—are what Mr. Peer is looking for.
>
> "We want persons who have learned their songs years ago from old-timers, songs that are almost ballads," he said.
>
> In an effort to round up talent with western color that is authentic, Mr. Peer sent out 30 telegrams to people living near El Paso asking them to try out, according to F. Luyster of the Tri-State Music company.
>
> "Not all of these will make test records, but enough of them will to advertise the west and El Paso," he said. (*El Paso Herald*, June 28, 1929)

Among the untrained, colorful figures who would make satisfactory test recordings were the brothers Dempson and Denmon Lewis, ranchmen from nearby Otero County, New Mexico, who played fiddle and guitar and are revered by collectors for their muscular performances of "Bull at the Wagon" and "Sally Johnson."

Billie Maxwell came to El Paso to play banjo in the family stringband led by her fiddling father E. Curtis Maxwell, with her uncle F. L. and teenage brother Marion on guitars. The Maxwells were then living in Grant County, New Mexico, the state of Billie's birth, but they had moved around in the past, and most of her eight siblings were born in Arizona.

The band auditioned; then, according to Billie's husband, Alvin Chester Warner, who drove them to El Paso, Peer asked Billie if she sang. Yes, she said, a little, and gave him a few verses of the old bad-man ballad "Billy Venero." Peer liked what he heard and promised to record her. The day before the scheduled session,

> Mrs. Warner sat in a tourist camp just outside of El Paso and practiced her songs. Her voice is absolutely untrained but it has a note of pathos and a note of sweetness that is sometimes lacking in a more brilliant performer. "Billy Venero," the Arizona version of "The Girl I Left Behind Me," and other airs, typically western, she sings gently as if she loved to sing them.
>
> She is pretty, of a gentle rather than vivid prettiness with light brown hair that reaches her shoulders and a shy expression in her face that seems to say, "Please like me a little." (*El Paso Herald*, July 2, 1929)

Peer recorded four tunes by the band, to which he had given the name of the White Mountain Orchestra, after the range in eastern Arizona, close to the New Mexico border. Then Billie sang her two-part story of "Billy Venero." Peer already had this song in the Victor catalog, having recorded it the previous year from "Mac" McClintock, but evidently he heard something different in Billie's slightly hesitant manner, and he asked her to work up some more material and come back the following week.

When she next stood before the microphone, between a couple of heart songs, "The Arizona Girl I Left Behind Me" and "Your Sweetheart Waits for You, Jack," she sang a piece titled "The Cowboy's Wife," written by a friend, in which she conscientiously logged the chores of a woman at home on the prairie, her day ending as she serves her husband supper and "swallows [her] own disappointment, for I know that's the way to his heart." The melody is a tricky one and she does not negotiate it without a few slips and slides, but it's a fascinating song.

Then, as a last shot, she offered "Haunted Hunter," an imperfectly remembered but broadly faithful text of "The Walker of the Snow." Victor issued it last of her three 78s, and it sold very poorly, the lowest seller in the "Old Familiar Tunes & Novelties" series up to that point, the sort of total that would not be matched until the dark days of 1931. But it was the first (and, for a long time, the only one) of her recordings to be reissued, and rightly so, for her performance is as haunting as the tale itself.

43

"LONELY COWBOY"—PARTS 1 AND 2

Arthur Miles
Victor V-40156

Recorded in Dallas, TX, August 8, 1929
Released on December 6, 1929
Sold 3,867

Reissued on *When I Was a Cowboy Vol. 1* (Yazoo 2022), *Texas Hillbillies* (JSP JSPCD77213)

Online: Spotify, YT

The Victor recording team were coming to the end of a Texas trip. They had spent part of July in El Paso, where they picked up Billie Maxwell's "Haunted Hunter" (➤42), and in San Antonio; then they moved on to Dallas, to record new songs by Jimmie Rodgers and restock their old-time, "race," and Mexican catalogs. For the old-time list, they would have been keen to collect cowboy songs. Ever since the success of Carl T. Sprague's "When the Work's All Done This Fall" (➤5) and "O Bury Me Not on the Lone Prairie" in 1925–26, Victor had been alert to the appeal and salesworthiness of cowboy material, and with further strong sales for Jules V. Allen, "The Singing Cowboy," and Harry "Mac" McClintock (➤26), the company now dominated that sector of the market. Before the slump of 1932, Victor amassed a cowboy catalog of around eighty discs, while all the other labels together could barely stack up fifty.

The company's persistent interest in cowboy songs was probably inspired by recording director Ralph Peer, who, as he would prove several times in his career, had an acute weather eye for the changeable climate of popular taste and could have spotted the dawning potential of Western music, both in movies, where Western themes were already a staple of the industry, and on records, where Western songs could be reinterpreted by pop singers. Although recording trips to centers like El Paso, San Antonio, and Dallas did elicit tolerably good sellers from local radio cowboys like Allen or "Peg" Moreland (➤29), Peer may also have hoped to return to New York with songs copyrighted to his publishing company Southern Music that would earn him money in a mainstream pop market.

So, during their week in Dallas, the Victor crew recorded Moreland, and Jack Cartwright of the Cartwright Brothers singing, very affectingly, the stories of "The Dying Ranger" and the "Texas Ranger." But first they called to the microphone Arthur Miles, from the small town of Loraine, Texas. He was almost twenty-five, a commercial traveler in candy products, a singer, and a guitarist. He had never made a record before and, as far as we know, never would again. But the record he did make ensured that he would never be forgotten.

The story opens with cowboys gathered round a campfire, smoking, singing, and telling stories. The scene is clearly set, to anyone who knows their cowboy songs, for a moment of high pathos—but Miles has something else to show us first. The first verse completed, he emits an extraordinary vocal effect. It sounds as if he is humming and whistling *at the same time*. This remarkable talent revealed, he goes back to his story. The talk turns to "distant friends so dear." A boy raises his head from his saddle and brushes away a tear. "This boy was tall and handsome, and his face showed a lack of good care; His eyes were of a heavenly blue and he had light wavy hair." "Boys," said this Adonis, "I'll tell you the reason why I stay at home no more." That ends Part 1. The listener eagerly turns the disc over and discovers that the young cowboy has fallen in love with a girl—but so has his best friend, Tommy Smith. They quarrel and he stabs Tommy, only to fall on his knees and try vainly to stop the bleeding. As his friend dies, he warns his slayer: "Bob, old boy, you'll remember me when I am under the ground." The tale is punctuated

(OTM Collection)

with further displays of humwhistling, and, for good measure, some yodeling refrains.

I use the cautious term "humwhistling" because a good deal of disputative heat has been generated over the question, What is Miles *doing?* There is wide agreement that it's a form of overtone singing, in which the singer emits, simultaneously, both fundamental and harmonic tones. This happens to be a technique found in Mongolian, Tuvan, and Siberian throat singing, which deploys a midrange fundamental and whistling-like harmonics. Is it conceivable that Miles, in Mitchell County, Texas, almost as far from Mongolia as it's possible to get, had gained access to this obscure art? Or might he have discovered it for, or in, himself?

However he learned it, he was the only American singer of his era to have been recorded doing it.

★ ★ ★

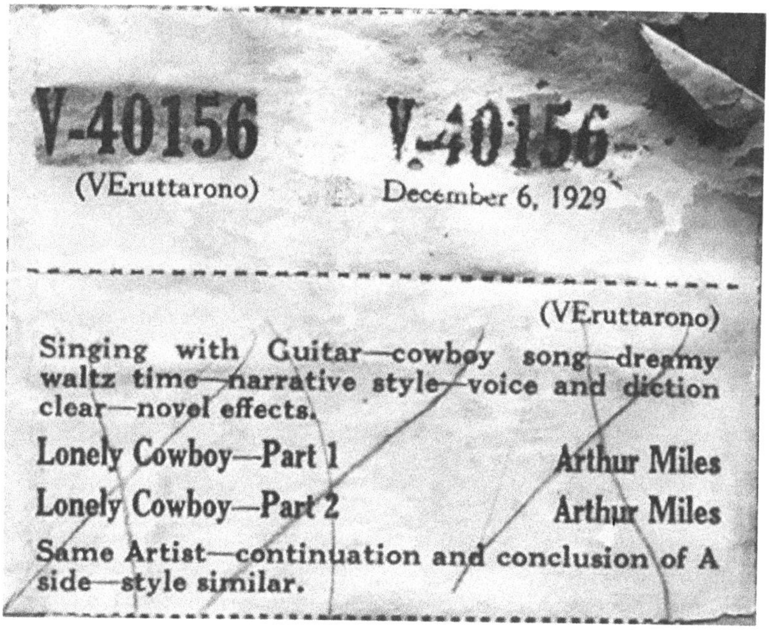
V-40156 V-40156
(VEruttarono) December 6, 1929
(VEruttarono)
Singing with Guitar—cowboy song—dreamy waltz time—narrative style—voice and diction clear—novel effects.
Lonely Cowboy—Part 1 Arthur Miles
Lonely Cowboy—Part 2 Arthur Miles
Same Artist—continuation and conclusion of A side—style similar.

Dealer stock label. The codeword VEruttarono was provided for reordering this release. (Author's Collection)

Although the opening allusion to "a group of jolly cowboys," and the setting of a cowboy telling his coworkers an evening story, recalls "When the Work's All Done This Fall," "Lonely Cowboy" is a distinct composition, also recorded, in variant forms, as "Cowboy's Home Sweet Home" by Jimmie Davis in 1930 and by Edward L. Crain in 1931. Miles's text is longer and more detailed than either, which may justify his claiming the song as his own when it was registered for copyright in December 1929.

Despite the record's fairly good sales, Peer did not call the artist back. It wasn't because Miles had quit music for commerce. In September 1931, a newspaper in Big Spring noted him playing a "novelty guitar number" at an Odd Fellows lodge meeting. In August 1936, the *Abilene Daily Reporter* announced that "[t]housands of Mitchell countians who thronged the Ruddick park band shell at Colorado [City] for the fifth weekly 'amateur hour' program of the Colorado chamber of commerce gave their loudest applause to 'Mocking Bird' Miles, who lives south of Loraine, for his bird imitations to guitar accompaniment."

"'Mocking Bird' Miles of Loraine Is First In Sweetwater Amateur Unit; Will Be Heard In Program Over krbc" ran an October 19 headline in the *Reporter*, which owned the station. When the program was transmitted on November 5, Miles and Mrs. Jack Yarbrough of Sweetwater, soprano, were declared the best performers and awarded trips to Dallas to broadcast over WFAA. Miles, the *Reporter* wrote the next day, "has established quite a reputation as a whistler, animal imitator and composer. 'Down On the Farm,' his own composition, was his number last night, and into it were woven imitations of a variety of barnyard fowls. Previously, he has broadcast over a number of stations and at the Texas Centennial, in Dallas."

In 1938, on the other side of the country, a band had almost certainly been listening to "Lonely Cowboy." The Four Pickled Peppers, a hillbilly swing band whose chief singer, Norman Woodlieff, had played with Charlie Poole, completed their first Bluebird session with "Jolly Group of Cowboys," a condensed version of the story with many of Miles's turns of phrase.

Arthur Miles was still playing in the mid-'40s. In 1946, the *Abilene Reporter News* announced that "[w]hen Loraine presented the program at the amateur hour in Colorado City" the previous day, "Mockingbird Miles was awarded first prize for singing and playing his own composition" (September 3). And while he may not still have been performing a decade later, he was at least composing. A news column from Loraine reported: "A. R. (Mockingbird) Miles, cattle buyer and seller living near here, is somewhat of a popular song writer. In recent years he has composed songs that became popular over the area, and one or two were recorded. He plans to go soon to Fort Worth to collaborate with a former Loraine youth who is a 'songsmith,' he said" (*Abilene Reporter News*, March 25, 1957).

Whether he made that trip, and if so, whether anything came of it, we don't know. If he ever left Loraine, it probably wasn't for long. He died there in 1984, aged seventy-nine. His grave marker preserves his nickname, "Mockingbird."

44

"SUGAR HILL"/ "FRESNO BLUES"

"Dad" Crockett/Johnny and Albert Crockett

Brunswick 372

Recorded in Chicago, IL, August 9, 1929
Released ca. January 1930

Reissued on *Kentucky Mountain Music* (Yazoo 2200) ["Sugar Hill"] • *Old-Time Mountain Guitar* (County CO-CD-3512) ["Fresno Blues"]

Online: Spotify, YT

No disc of its era epitomizes so concisely where country music had come from and where it might be going. Think of it as a split-screen genre painting. On the left side of the canvas, "Dad" Crockett, paterfamilias, accompanied by his eldest son George on banjo, sings "Sugar Hill," a rowdy old number in the spirit of the minstrel show: "Possum up a 'simmon tree, raccoon on the ground, possum up a 'simmon tree, shakin' 'simmons down." On the right of the picture, there are no banjos, no old men, just a couple of youngsters—Johnny was nineteen, Albert twenty-one—with expensive Gibson guitars, Johnny's a six-string, Albert's a four-string tenor, playing the blues.

Johnny wrote "Fresno Blues" while on tour and missing his girlfriend. Guitar instrumentals had not been particularly common in recorded old-time music, but then Johnny was not a commonplace player: he claimed he made it into a list of the leading guitarists of the day, up there in the top five with the jazz virtuoso Eddie Lang. We may wonder, listening to "Fresno Blues," if Johnny was aware of Lang's guitar duets with Lonnie Johnson, such as "Have to Change Keys to Play These Blues" (1928) or, in particular, "Bullfrog Moan," recorded in May 1929, which "Fresno Blues" distantly echoes in its measured tempo and deep, resonant bass notes. Annotating the County LP *Old-Time Mountain Guitar*, Rob Fleder suggested that "Fresno Blues" "displays more influences than a geographically stable rural family would have felt. The lead plays some standard blues and jazz riffs, with the rhythm and melody smoothed out and squared off, resulting in a kind of folk–vaudeville–jazz mixture."

So in coupling "Sugar Hill" and "Fresno Blues," Brunswick created a record that was all contrasts. The sound of the mountains: the sound of the city. The sound of tradition: the sound of innovation. The sound of age: the sound of youth.

★ ★ ★

In 1919, John Crockett, Sr., his wife Admonia, and their five sons left their home near Sharpsburg, Kentucky, and headed west—far west. In the town of Fowler, California, some ten miles south of Fresno, they stopped at a garage so that Dad could fix a problem with their automobile. He borrowed some tools, made the repair, paid for the use of the tools, and drove off. A couple of miles down the road, he remembered that he hadn't paid for the oil he'd used, and drove back. He was promptly offered a job at the garage, and the family settled in Fowler.

All the young Crocketts played an instrument, or several, but John, Jr.—Johnny—was the keenest. By the time he was fourteen he had been spotted by an announcer from KMJ in Fresno and awarded a spot on the station, singing and picking banjo or guitar. After a while, he was joined by his brother Albert, playing tenor guitar. Then the boys persuaded their more reticent father, who played fiddle and banjo, and brothers George (fiddle, banjo), Clarence (guitar), and Alan (fiddle and bones) to bring their instruments down to KMJ and create a family stringband. They began to appear on theater programs and in minstrel shows, making a name that in 1927 or '28 won them a slot on a larger radio station, KNX in Los Angeles, and in November 1928 the attention of Brunswick Records.

Crockett's Kentucky Mountaineers. Left to right, Clarence, Alan, Albert, George, Johnnie, John, Sr. ("Dad"). (Courtesy of Dottie Blankenship)

The company would have found them an attractive proposition. Their first sides were a pair of sparkling medleys of old-time dance tunes, but as well as stringband ensemble music they could offer vocal solos, duets, and trios, banjo songs, and guitar pieces, all executed with skill and polish. Moreover, the Crockett Family Mountaineers were about to go national. In October 1928, they signed a fifteen-month contract with the Keith–Orpheum vaudeville circuit, which took them to theaters across the country. A San Francisco reviewer (quoted in the Fresno *Bee*, October 28, 1928) asked: "Are the Crockett family real? Who has protected them from this standardized world?" They whipped up enough publicity that the CBS radio chain decided to give them a primetime radio slot, 7–7:15 p.m. every night on WABC out of New York City.

Primetime, and then some. This quarter-hour was known in the business as "the toughest spot in the air." It was occupied, on NBC's Blue and Orange Networks, by the Amos 'n' Andy Show, sponsored by Pepsodent toothpaste. As the 1920s turned into the '30s, this blackface sitcom was the most popular show on American radio.

The syndicated columnist Gilbert Swan was amused by the notion of this "family group from the hills" unwittingly playing a part in "a major engagement of the entertainment war upon the air."

> They were, quite suddenly, moved into the very hour when Amos and Andy were up to their pranks and there the Crockett Mountaineers have remained—for better or for worse—singing old tunes . . . fiddling the hill songs and doing their backwoods stunts. What they had to offer was the trade-mark of Americana; it was definitely native and a contrast from the vogue of sophistication which had been spreading over the nation. . . . Such talents as they possess grew out of the social requirements and needs of their little hill communities. They had played and sung for themselves and their neighbors; they had led the square dances of their settlement; unspoiled and untutored, knowing as little about

The Crockett Mountaineers play the California Theatre in Ontario, California, September 1928. (Courtesy of Dottie Blankenship)

> metropolitan life as the city folk know of their hill lives.
>
> Rather odd, then, that of all the obtainable attractions they should have held out against one of the most amazingly popular attractions of the generations. ("Air 'Battles' Of The Radio Celebrities," *Charleston* [West Virginia] *Gazette*, September 21, 1930)

We have met this condescension before, in urban journalists' observations on the Hill Billies (➤2), "The Death of Floyd Collins" (➤4), and the Blue Ridge Ramblers (➤35). We meet it again two months later:

> The Crocketts represent simplicity, a refreshing contrast to sophisticism [*sic*]. They come from . . . the Kentucky mountains. How they ever ventured to leave the confines of that remote district for the worldiness [*sic*] of New York, no one knows. . . .
>
> The Crocketts are not comfortable in New York. They miss their hominy and home-baked ham. They miss certain beverages and yellow corn meal and sorgham [*sic*] molasses. (*Charleston* [West Virginia] *Daily Mail*, December 21, 1930)

No one countered these patronizing narratives by pointing out that Dad Crockett, who had driven his entire family across the country in a Model T, was an adept mechanic who, when he got to California, bought an early carbide projector and went round showing movies on it. Or that Johnny Crockett had not lived in a "little hill community" since he was nine or ten and had been performing on radio since his early teens. The Crocketts might present themselves in check shirts and galluses for a publicity picture or a songbook cover, but they were far from being "untutored" in the ways of "metropolitan life."

Professionally, they achieved a balancing act, poised between old times and new: they offered "quaint tunes of the Kentucky hills" (though most of the family were born in West Virginia, and they had made their home in Kentucky for only about four years), but they presented them in carefully fashioned arrangements that would please theatergoer and radio listener. The boundaries of this repertoire that they dispensed so dexterously are marked by their record of "Sugar Hill" and "Fresno Blues." The sound of the past: the sound of the present.

45

"TIM BROOK"

Carver Boys
Paramount 3199

Recorded in Richmond, IN, September 6, 1929
Released in January 1930

Reissued on *The Return of the Stuff That Dreams Are Made of* (Yazoo 2203)

Online: Spotify, YT

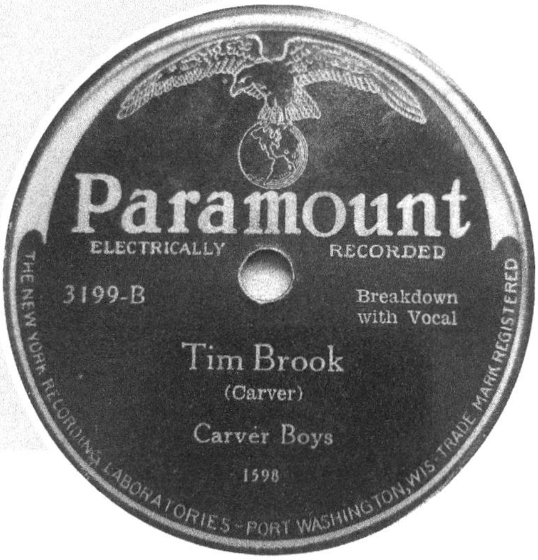

In the late '40s, Bill Monroe introduced into the bluegrass repertoire the song "Molly and Tenbrooks," about a race held in Louisville, Kentucky, between the local horse Ten Broeck, a six-year-old bay, and his California rival Mollie McCarthy, a five-year-old brown mare. It would become a bluegrass standard, but the tale had first been told on a record almost twenty years earlier, by a group called the Carver Boys—Kentuckians themselves, as was Monroe. Oral transmission twisted Ten Broeck into various shapes: for the Carvers he was Tim Brook.

> People of Louisville goin' to the fair,
> Go out to the racetrack, old Tim Brook was there.
>
> Road was so dusty, the wind blowed so high,
> Just could see little Mollie as old Tim Brook went by.
>
> Tim Brook's skippin' and gone away,
> Tim Brook's skippin' and flyin'.

When the Carvers recorded their commentary, the event was more than fifty years old, and when Monroe, and subsequently the Stanley Brothers, retold it, seventy. Ten Broeck and Mollie McCarthy fought their epic duel on July 4, 1878.

But how epic was it? Newspaper accounts tell oddly different stories.

The *Indianapolis Journal* devoted two and a half columns of small type to "The Event Witnessed by Twenty Thousand People."

> LOUISVILLE, July 4.—A steaming, sweating, yelling crowd . . . assembled to-day under a red-hot, blistering, boiling sun to witness the "big race" between Ten Broeck and Mollie McCarthy for a purse of $10,000. The great event attracted visitors from every quarter of the United States, and vast throngs of strangers have been filling up the city for two or three days. . . . [T]o-day opened bright, and oh! so hot. . . . Starched linen melted like snow before a blow-pipe, and everybody looked wilted even before starting for the grounds . . . nothing but a heroic determination to be pleased could have induced the suffering thousands to endure the discomfort and positive misery of the occasion.

After three lesser events, the two horses (the only entrants) came out onto the track. A tap on a drum, and they were off, Mollie promptly taking the lead. At the end of the first mile, she was two lengths ahead, and she still led at the end of the second. Ten Broeck seemed to be having some difficulty. Then, a little after the two-and-a-quarter-miles mark, Mollie faltered. Ten Broeck seized the lead, and at the end of the third mile was five lengths ahead. Soon after passing the three-and-a-half-miles post, Mollie stopped, her jockey dismounted, and Ten Broeck galloped slowly in to win, amid what the *Journal* described as intense excitement.

The same day's report in the *New York World*, however, headlined "THE LOUISVILLE FIZZLE," declared that "a greater disappointment was never known on any race track." Mollie had been described by the *Journal* as in "perfect form," but according to the *World*, a majority of the "large and excited crowds . . . loudly expressed their opinion that the mare was in no condition for such a race."

Next day, it was suggested that Ten Broeck had been drugged with morphine. According to the *Louisville Commercial*, "After a remarkably slow run . . . he could hardly stand on his feet, and it is probable that there was something more than the fatigue of the race working upon him." The writer believed that, had Mollie not faltered during the third mile, she would have won.

The differences in the reporting of the race no doubt reflect a time before wire services, when sporting events were written up in the press by unreliable coalitions of eye-witnesses and imaginative subs, but, whether the result was a "fizzle" or not, there could be no arguing with the fact of a Kentucky victory, or with the *Journal*'s assertion that "no turf event for the past thirty years has brought such numbers of celebrated sportsmen from all over the land." Those elements of the story dictated the triumphal tone of the songs that would be sung about Mollie and Ten Broeck.

> Tim Brook said to Mollie, "Ain't you ashamed
> To come from California to scandalize my name?"
>
> Tim Brook's skippin' and gone away,
> Tim Brook's skippin' and flyin'.

The impetuous drive of banjo and two guitars (the label calls it a "breakdown with vocal") creates a vivid picture in sound of the horses' drumming hooves and the onlookers' anxiously drumming hearts.

★ ★ ★

The Carvers' song is not a detailed account of the race but a sequence of novelistic highlights, imagined details like the dust and the high wind or the horses talking to each other, pieces of a forming mosaic of myth. Folklorists classify the "Tim Brook"/"Molly and Tenbrooks" song nexus as a blues ballad, probably originating in verses composed and sung by African American Kentuckians and gradually diffused throughout the state and beyond. The first African American singer we know to have recorded a song on the subject, the blues ballad "Old Timbrook Blues" (Paramount, 1930), was John Byrd, probably from Huntington, West Virginia, less than 200 miles east of Louisville. (The Texas songster Henry Thomas's "Run, Mollie, Run" [Vocalion, 1927], often cited as a related piece, is essentially a gambler's brag. The phrase "run, Molly, run" is documented as early as 1886 as an expression used by African Americans playing craps. If there is an allusion to the race, it is vestigial.)

Since blues ballads emerge in different places at different times, sharing some details, differing in others, there is no point in trying to plot a line between the Carver Boys' "Tim Brook" and Monroe's "Molly and Tenbrooks." The two versions share melodic and textual elements, but there is much more in Monroe's text than in the Carvers', so he must have drawn upon other, probably oral, sources.

There is also an assonance between the "Tim Brook"/"Molly and Tenbrooks" songs and older compositions about horse races, such as the Irish songs "The Plains of Kildare" and "The Noble Skewball," as well as the American folksong "Stewball," which is plainly based on Irish antecedents but has been known in the United States since the early nineteenth century. There is a not inconsiderable scholarly literature about all this, and the possible connections are provocative, but necessarily uncertain. About the Carver Boys themselves, however, we have some solid facts.

★ ★ ★

They were two brothers, Warner (1891–1940) and Noble (1896–1978), and their cousin Robert (1893–1970), all born in Barren County in southwestern Kentucky. They had a rich musical background, for Robert's father Lorenzo Dow Carver and his brothers and sisters had a band that played around southern Kentucky and northern Tennessee in the first decade of the twentieth century. As boys, Noble and Warner played for community events such as bean hullings, candy breakings, peach suppers, and ice-cream socials, Warner doing the fiddling (though he also played banjo, and does so on "Tim Brook"), and Noble picking the guitar. They graduated to putting on shows and became well known throughout Barren, Monroe, and Cumberland Counties. In the 1920s, Noble also traveled with Dr. Kelso's Medicine Show out of Indianapolis.

The Carver Boys had a single recording session, in the summer of 1929. Remarkably, we have Noble's own description of it, in an autobiographical account of his life in music, *52 Years of Uncle Bozo*. ("Uncle Bozo" was a nickname he acquired in the '30s, possibly borrowed from a Rube Goldberg cartoon character.)

> Uncle Bozo and Warner were living at home with their parents at Etoile in Barren Co., Ky. The boys bought their fiddle, banjo and guitar strings from M. L. Drain and Rich and A. L. Sisco at Glasgow, who had music stores. About mid-July, that year, two men from New York, representing the Paramount Recording Co., came to Glasgow,

looking for musicians. They sent a cab to the Carver farm to bring the boys into Glasgow, a distance of about 18 miles. They asked the boys if they "would come to New York and make records and play if you were paid for it?" Both agreed that they would accept the offer, providing it would cover their expenses. Their father told them: "That's all you'll probably ever hear of them."

But, on Aug. 2, the men returned, coming out to the Carver farm, and telling them to get ready—and to go to Richmond, Ind., where they would make the recordings. And so it was on Aug. 14, 1929, that Bozo, Warner, and Robert, their cousin, made the recordings—eight of them. Songs that they recorded included "Wreck of the Old 97," "No One To Welcome Me Home," "Anchored in Love Divine," "Log Cabin in the Lane," "Wreck of the No. 9," "Whang Whang Blues," and "Timbrook and Molly"—the song about the famous English [*sic*] race horse that was brought to America to race against Timbrook "to the hole in the wall."

At the conclusion of the recording session, it was found that one of the records needed another number for the "flip side," so Warner was prevailed upon to play one that he had "made up" on the harmonica. They named the record the "Sisco Harmonica Blues," after their friend back in Glasgow, who had helped them. . . .

After finishing the records, they conferred with the Paramount men. Typical of the day and times, they completed the work, then talked about the pay. They had never discussed how much they were to receive, and all three of the boys thought that they would be lucky if they were able to collect $75 for the day. First, they were offered a royalty, if they so desired. But, they said that they would just as soon forget about anything like that, and take a lump settlement. They were elated to receive a large sum for playing and their expenses back home. It was the most money they had ever made in a month's time.

The records were soon manufactured, and a great many shipped to Glasgow, where a few weeks later, at the Co. Fair, Mr. Sisco sold 1400 records in one week. Uncle Bozo says that he has no idea how many of the records were produced. He did run into some funny experiences about the recordings, however.

When he was in Wheeling, West Va., in 1937, he recalls that he went into a music store to buy some records. The girl waiting on him said: "Here's a real nice hillbilly record"—and lo, and behold, it was one of their records, under a new label, by "the Cramer Brothers."

Later, when Uncle Bozo was in Atlanta, in 1940, he was browsing in a record shop and hearing a familiar recording, investigated and found it was another of their records, under another label, and by the "Carson Family."

In the 1932 the Par[a]mount people again wrote Bozo and Warner, saying that they planned to record in Louisville. Warner wrote them back—and the next thing they heard was that the Paramount Recording Co. had gone out of business.

That was all of the recording that the Carver's [*sic*] done. One day in August, 1929.

★ ★ ★

"All of the recording," perhaps, but not all of the playing and operating. In the early '30s, the Carver brothers worked in the Midwest with Smilie Burnette and Slim Miller, sponsored by Georgie Porgie Breakfast Foods. Their paths often crossed that of their cousin Cynthia May Carver, a young singer and banjo player making her name as Cousin Emmy. Noble also served as an advance man for the WLS National Barn Dance touring shows, working for the talent booker J. L. Frank, and later in a similar role for Grand Ole Opry traveling units. In the '50s, he appeared regularly on radio in Glasgow, and in the '60s he would "spend the summer as booking agent for Cherokee Ranch Wild West Rodeo, driving his yellow and red Chrysler with its loud speaker on it, and ballyhooing the appearance of the Rodeo. Each year he would tour the states of Tennessee, Georgia, North Carolina, Virginia, West Virginia, Ohio, Kentucky and Indiana."

Over the years, "Uncle Bozo" greased the wheels of many a country music career that moved faster and farther than his own. "These people will know," wrote Ernie Lawson, the newspaper-editor friend who helped him with his book, "that Uncle Bozo is the fellow who was handy to have around. Maybe he put out advance window cards, sold tickets or candy for the show, or was their booking agent—but he was the man in the background that helped to further their ambitions."

Noble Carver offers a striking example of how some musicians found a bridge leading out of old-time music, determinedly put their foot down, and drove across it into new worlds.

46

"TENNESSEE COON HUNT"/ "HEN CACKLIN' PIECE"

Whit Gaydon
Victor V-40315

Recorded in Memphis, TN, September 17, 1929
Released on November 7, 1930
Sold 1,446

Reissued on *Work Hard, Play Hard, Pray Hard: Hard Time, Good Time, and End Time Music, 1923–1936* (Tompkins Square TSQ2783) ["Tennessee Coon Hunt"]

Online: Spotify ["Tennessee Coon Hunt"]

The roots of instrumental impressionism lie deep in American vernacular music. Put a fiddle or harmonica in a musician's hands and he or she may use it not to play a tune but to conjure up everyday sounds: hounds crying on the trail of a fox or raccoon, or wheels rattling along railroad tracks (➤60). One of the first hillbilly records offered both, harmonica player Henry Whitter's 1923 Okeh disc of "The Old Time Fox Chase" and "Lost Train Blues."

Some impressionists worked without instruments, evoking rural life in purely vocal tours de force, like Freeman Stowers, a Texas-born African American who recorded "Texas Wild Cat Chase" and "Sunrise on the Farm," or Stephen E. Austin, known in Texas and Arkansas in the 1920s and '30s as the entertainer "Barnyard Steve," who advertised that he could imitate fifteen animals and fowls and a fire siren. A sampling of his talents, "Out on the Farm," coupled with a jew's harp solo, made one of Okeh's more bizarre releases of 1929.

Recorded sound was still enough of a novelty that people really would sit, captive for three minutes, while a man imitated dogs or chickens. Hard to imagine, but no odder than that staple of the early phonographic industry, the laughing record, which presented the consumer with nothing more than a man laughing.

In the extraordinary sonic drama of Whit Gaydon's "Tennessee Coon Hunt," the chase segues from fiddling to a barking dog, a howling dog, and then a dogfight—a melée of effects achieved with voice or fiddle or both, and a few phrases of decipherable speech. "Hen Cacklin' Piece" is the fiddle tune "Old Hen Cackle," with a little singing and a lot of chicken noises.

A singular record. Fittingly so, for it was made by a singular man.

* * *

Whitmore Anderson Gaydon was born in Auraria in Lumpkin County, Georgia, on September 26, 1869. He may have inherited not only his forenames but the fiddling gene from his uncle G. Whitmore Anderson, a fiddler of local repute who placed second at the 1870 Georgia State Fair, playing "The Arkansas Traveler." Auraria had earned its name during the Georgia Gold Rush of the 1830s, but after 1848, many of the prospectors it had attracted were drawn to the richer promise of the California goldfields; Auraria today is a ghost town. In the year Gaydon was born, the first transcontinental railroad was completed, and in the month of his birth, its first passengers disembarked near San Francisco Bay.

By 1900, three of his four brothers and their sister, Susan, were prospecting around Georgetown in El Dorado County, California, where they came to own a mine known as the Golden Egg. By 1920, Whit had followed them west and was working as a goldminer in Hammonton in Yuba County, the address he gave Ralph Peer when they met in Memphis in 1929.

But we are moving too fast through Whit's story, and it is time to call upon a witness to his musical doings. In an article written in 1934 for the *Gainesville* [Georgia] *News*, the author (of whom more later) described the twenty-year-old Whit visiting Gainesville (in Hall County, which adjoins Lumpkin), being enchanted by the streetlights, and taking his first train ride. The reporter then sped through the years to "the Georgia–Alabama fiddlers convention at East Lake, Alabama[,] where upon the final night he won second place, beaten only by the great A. A. [*sic*] Stokes." This was in June 1924, when Whit was living in Selma, Alabama, and working as

Ad from *Miami News*, October 13, 1926. (Author's Collection)

a night yard clerk for the Southern Railroad (*Selma Times-Journal*, June 20).

"Stumbling onto the State Fiddler convention in Birmingham," our reporter continued, "the managers laughingly took him on 'to break a hoo-doo.' Whit then played hillbilly style and won the State Championship. [He] was featured as a world champ in a challenge broadcast over WMBF located on the roof garden of the Fleetwood hotel, Miami Beach." This too we can date, for in Miami papers during summer and fall 1926, "Whitmore Gaydon, Champion Fiddler of the State of Alabama," appeared in theaters and "challenged the fiddlers of the world to meet him in an international fiddling contest . . . next February." Our source also noted Whit's "brilliancy as guest artist on 'Smilin' Ed McConnell's program over WJAX Jacksonville followed by his amazingly successful tour with Stokes[,] McMichin [*sic*][,] and others described as 'fixed stars of the fiddlin' firmament.'"

By 1928, Whit had reached Nashville, where he appeared on the Grand Ole Opry (*Tennessean*, July 1). "His fan mail," our writer noted, "began pouring in when he began 'barking' over this station [WSM]. . . . People flocked to the studio to get proof that one man could accomplish this amazing feat. The quick changes from the yelp of the first dog to the deep bays of a pack of hounds is [*sic*] done in his 'Tennessee Coon Hunt.' His 'Hen Cacklin Piece' is [a] work of fiddling art."

Whit also reportedly broadcast over WCOC in Meridian, Mississippi, WREC in Memphis, and KTHS in Hot Springs, Arkansas; was present at the Scopes trial in Dayton, Tennessee, in 1925 (➤16); and played his fiddle when the English motorist Sir Malcolm Campbell broke the land speed record at Daytona Beach, Florida, in 1932 or '33.

All these nuggets of biography were heaped up by a man named Ernest B. Mincey, a shoe salesman living in Long Beach, California, who had grown up in Gainesville, a generation younger than Gaydon. It would be fair to say that Mr. Mincey liked to put pencil to paper. In 1932, he wrote a cousin in Gainesville a letter 30,000 words long, an achievement blazoned five years later in Robert L. Ripley's syndicated column "Believe It or Not." When the wordsmith drafted his piece for his old hometown newspaper, he emphasized the local angle:

The policy of the Gainesville News in encouraging by frequent recognition the talents of many who have gone from the city and vicinity . . . is in itself a highly commendable community enterprise. Gainesville became the gate of a new world to an obscure hillbilly fiddler whose talents not only flashed like a meteor thru radio and stage circles and culminated in Victor recordings but secured for him a place as a columnist and philosopher of note.

Fiddling was only one of the ways Whit Gaydon used his hands. He was also adept with pen and probably typewriter, and an indefatigable writer of letters to newspapers and magazines. He wrote to the *Nashville Tennessean* in 1928 about the McNary–Haugen Farm Relief Act (a stratagem to subsidize farmers by raising the prices of their produce) and again the following year about usages like "you-uns" and "hit" (for "it") in Southern Appalachian speech, remarking that he had "spent twenty years as a mountaineer in the Blue Ridge and afterward as a traveling man throughout that region. . . . I was not only raised in a log cabin but I also plowed a steer. So I think I may be pardoned for claiming to be an authority on mountain dialect" (September 18, 1929). In 1935, he addressed the *Literary Digest* on the correct use of the word "tote."

He was also drawn to the fantastic. In February 1924, he wrote to the magazine *Weird Tales*: "I enjoyed 'The Phantom Violinist' [published in November 1923] more than any of the stories, probably from the fact that I knew how to appreciate it. As most of my prizes that I have won as a fiddler has been while seemingly under a mysterious outside Power. Playing by inspiration, as it were." Perhaps inspired by *Weird Tales* writers like H. P. Lovecraft, he produced a novel, *The White Lily of the Gates of Glohm*, reportedly serialized in a Florida paper, though I have found no trace of it there or anywhere else.

At the time of Mincey's article, Gaydon was contributing a column called "Whit'lings" to the *Stanley News and Press* in Albemarle, North Carolina, where he and other family members had lived for a while around 1900. We may be able to sample its tone in a letter he wrote as "Whit'lings Columnist" to the *Clarion* [Pennsylvania] *Democrat* (June 2, 1938), where he mused on the names of Clarion County post offices:

I like the name of Clarion because that's the kind of sound I make when I play the fiddle. . . . Blairs Corners. The hero of the first full-length novel I ever wrote was named Dalton Blair. . . . Fairmount City. I once had a funny experience at Fairmount, Georgia, which I was chuckling over just a few days ago. But I cannot tell it here. Foxburg. I used to play the Fox and Hounds over the radio. . . .

Whit Gaydon, Dobbins, California, 1945. (Courtesy of Beth Preddy)

He was living in Miami again in 1940, with his eldest daughter Brooks Elizabeth and her family, but he returned to California, perhaps to be close to his surviving siblings, and spent his last years in Yuba County, where he died on April 15, 1947.

His great-granddaughter Beth Preddy recalls some of the stories she was told about him.

He was somewhat itinerant and left my great-grandmother and their children frequently for his cross-country jaunts. I remember my grandmother [Brooks Elizabeth] telling me he was a mummer in the New Orleans Mardi Gras parade. He also wrote a poem for each state in the union. I saw them when I was young, but now they are lost. He could take a piano apart and put it back together and taught all his children to play. He had immense talent and intellect.

47

"WHERE THE SWEET MAGNOLIAS BLOOM"

Taylor–Griggs Louisiana Melody Makers
Victor V-40184

Recorded in Memphis, TN, September 24, 1929
Released on January 17, 1930
Sold 4,483

Reissued on *How Low Can You Go?: Anthology of the String Bass (1925–1941)* (Dust-to-Digital DTD04)

In the early days of record-collecting, lovers of jazz and hot dance music, alert to even a four-bar eruption of improvisation in an otherwise sedate foxtrot, considered waltzes to be three-minute tracts of irredeemable dullness. When they listed records for sale or auction, they would often not even bother to give a waltz its title but abbreviate it to a mere "wz." Something of this uninterest was inherited by the first collectors of hillbilly music, so that a common record of a couple of reels or breakdowns would be more highly esteemed, and fetch a higher price, than a rare one of two waltzes. Many of the current generation of record collectors, however, are justly appreciative of an attractive or well-executed waltz.

So was the original audience, to judge by the number of waltzes that were put on record by old-time fiddlers and stringbands. Conducting a headcount of songs and tunes in 3/4 time is not straightforward, because many are not titular waltzes and can be identified as such only by a seasoned listener who has heard and remembered them all. But from a preliminary survey of the old-time catalogs of Brunswick, Columbia, Okeh, Victor, and Vocalion, a library of around 6,000 recordings, I calculate that between 8 and 12 percent—roughly, between 500 and 750 titles—are waltzes.

The proportion seems to rise a little in the Depression years, and to tilt slightly toward the Deep South and Southwest, with untypically high waltz scores for bands like the East Texas Serenaders (thirteen out of twenty-four recordings) or the Leake County Revelers from Mississippi (seventeen out of forty), compared to lower scores by bands from Georgia or Alabama. The Leake County Revelers achieved the highest known sales of a hillbilly waltz record with their 1927 Columbia disc "Wednesday Night Waltz"/"Good Night Waltz," which sold almost 200,000 copies.

★ ★ ★

Some of the most exquisite waltz music on old-time records was made by the Louisiana Melody Makers, a group of men and women who lived around Arcadia, a town of about 1,500 people in Bienville Parish, Louisiana. They played at neighbors' houses, then graduated to school plays, Lions Club banquets, and other community occasions, enjoying a reputation as excellent providers of music that a local journalist described as "restful and sweet and throbbing with old-time favorites" (Ruston [Louisiana] *Daily Leader*, December 18, 1929).

Ed Conger, who ran the furniture store founded by his father, S. A. Conger, in Arcadia, and sold Victor records, took note and reported on them to Ralph Peer, who came to town, auditioned them at the store, and signed them.

On the first occasion they made records, in Memphis in September 1928, the Melody Makers were as large a family band as any that gathered in a recording studio in that era: a father, fiddler Robert Crowder Grigg (c. 1870–1943); two sons, Crockett, who sang, and Ausie, who played the stand-up bass; and two daughters, Lorene on mandolin and Ione on guitar. A third daughter, Johnnie Maud, went to the session but did not perform on the records. The Grigg clan was assisted by another father and son, the Arcadia attorney Foster R. Taylor (1877–1959) and his boy Clavie. The group's first and most successful

The Grigg family band, Bear Creek, Louisiana, ca. 1928. Left to right: R. C., Ione, Crockett, Lorean, Johnnie Maud, Ausie B. (OTM Collection)

recording was a waltz, "Sweet Rose of Heaven," featuring Mr. Taylor on fiddle and Clavie as vocalist.

A year later, Peer summoned the band back to Memphis, but now, Ausie Grigg told me, he expressly didn't want breakdowns. So the senior Grigg stayed at home, leaving the fiddling role to Mr. Taylor, who, as Ausie said, "wasn't one of these old breakdown fiddlers." The supporting cast was Ausie on bass, with Arcadians Byron Hiser (mandolin) and Henry Galloway (guitar), and singer Oscar Logan from Heflin. Peer had requested singing on every record, even if it was brief, so Logan, according to Ausie, "was the fill-in for this refrain that we needed." The group made six recordings, all waltzes: the only substantial hillbilly recording session of the period conducted exclusively in waltz time.

Meade and Spottswood identified "Where the Sweet Magnolias Bloom" as the song written by Andrew Sterling and Harry von Tilzer, published in 1899 and recorded both in the early 1900s and subsequently by old-time singers like Buell Kazee or Mac and Bob. But von Tilzer's tune is not a waltz, and Sterling's mother-directed text doesn't include the single verse of the Taylor–Griggs recording, a sugary confection from the Victorian musical bakery: "The sun-kissed flowers speak to my heart, Of the love in the faraway home. Say, my dear, we'll never more part, Where the sweet magnolias bloom." This cozy lyric makes a stark contrast to some of the other songs recorded at this session, like "On the Bridge at Midnight" and "It's All Over Now," lyrics draped in depression and darkness, as if penned by Ella Wheeler Wilcox on a particularly bad day.

★ ★ ★

Around this time, a local newspaper reported that the Melody Makers,

> which made such a hit with the radio fans of the nation two weeks ago Saturday night when they broadcast a program from KWKH, the station of the W. K. Henderson Iron Works of Shreveport, will put another program on the air from the Henderson station this coming Saturday night. . . . The Melody Makers have just returned home from a trip to Memphis where for several days they were engaged in making phonograph records for the Victor Talking Machine Company. Last night these popular entertainers gave a program at the Brownie Theatre, and it was vigorously applauded by an appreciative audience.

This was not the first time the Melody Makers had broadcast from KWKH. Back in 1928, Ausie said, "We did something that was very unusual."

The Louisiana Melody Makers when they recorded for Victor in 1928. Standing: R. C. Grigg, Johnnie Maud Grigg, Crockett Grigg, Ausie B. Grigg; seated: F. R. Taylor, Ione Grigg, Lorean Grigg. The photograph was taken on the tenth floor of the Peabody Hotel in Memphis. Clavie Taylor was absent because he had a pressing business (literally) at home in Arcadia. (OTM Collection)

> It was the time that the presidential campaign was on, and Herbert Hoover was running against Al Smith of New York. . . . So he [Henderson] asked us to come over and play and he'd make a campaign speech for Al Smith. . . . And I know we came on with "Sidewalks of New York," that was Al's theme song. . . . And so that program went over real good, and they began to get telegrams all out of the Midwest, over on the East Coast, up in the Northeast, and we went back on the Saturday night following that and there was a stack of telegrams there, I imagine five or six inches thick, that come from all over the United States, telling about how the program come in. And I think we made four trips back there on that presidential campaign.

Remarkably, three of the band's 1929 recordings were pressed in England for the South African market. (Author's Collection)

The Melody Makers' fame was spread by radio in another way. In March 1930, Lawson Caskey of Bienville Parish, serving in the Signal Corps in Hawaii, wrote to the *Bienville Democrat*:

> Last week K. G. M. B. (Honolulu's newest broadcasting station with studios in the Royal Hawaiian Hotel) opened with an assortment of musical selections. . . . One of the selections [records] was "Sweet Rose of Heaven" . . . by the Taylor–Griggs Melody Makers. Since then K. G. M. B. has dozens of requests for that number each day and I can truthfully say that this selection has taken Honolulu by storm.

Ausie Grigg did his last recording in February 1932, when he accompanied Jimmie Davis, a Bienville Parish boy whom he knew from their childhood in the community of Bear Creek, on some sides for Victor, and had the chance to sit in the studio and watch Jimmie Rodgers. But after that—

> We were farmers, you know, and this music business started out just as a matter of likin' to play, you know . . . likin' to entertain. [Then] we had a little depression in there about that time, you know, and the sale of records kind of dropped off, and people began to buy the radios. So that kindly cooled the thing down. . . . And we just kind of disbanded. . . . But the fact that we did get to play in this presidential campaign and we were heard all over the United States, that was the high point of our playing.

48

"THREE MEN WENT A HUNTING"

Byrd Moore and His Hot Shots
Columbia 15496-D

Recorded in Johnson City, TN, October 23, 1929
Released in February 1930
Sold 3,748

Reissued on *"Can You Sing or Play Old-Time Music?": The Johnson City Sessions 1928–1929* (Bear Family BCD16083), *My Bonnie Lies Over the Ocean: British Songs in the USA* (Nehi NEH3X1)

Online: Spotify, YT

Old World ballads aside, this may be the most ancient song to have been translated into hillbilly music. Versions of "Three Jolly Welshmen" have been traced back to the seventeenth century. It is surely the only song to have made the 4,000-mile journey to a recording session in Tennessee from a theater in London and the text of a play by Shakespeare.

In *The Two Noble Kinsmen*, written in collaboration with John Fletcher, published in 1634 but evidently first performed some twenty years earlier, the Jailer's Daughter—who is something of an old-time singer herself, with a repertoire of more than twenty songs—announces, "There was three fools, fell out about an owlet." Then she sings:

> The one said it was an owl,
> The other he said nay,
> The third he said it was a hawk,
> And her bells were cut away.

Three hundred years on, the Hot Shots exactly preserve the "one said"/"the other said"/"the third said" form of the jest, while the unbelled hawk becomes "a jaybird with the feathers blowed away." Lightly reshaping the song as an Irishman–Scotsman–Frenchman joke, they deliver it with enormous brio, throwing in a humorously uncomplimentary reference to the town of Norton, Virginia: "The Irishman said, 'It's Norton,' the Scotsman he said, 'Nay,' the Frenchman said, 'It's the end of the world—let's go back the other way.'"

According to the headnote above the transcription of "Three Men Went a Hunting" in *The New Lost City Ramblers Songbook*, "The Hot Shots used this song as a show tune, changing the name of the town in the last verse to match the town they were playing. [This detail came from Clarence Ashley.] . . . The tune is similar to 'The Preacher And The Bear.'" True, but it's even closer, in fact remarkably so, to "Wish I Had Stayed in the Wagon Yard" as recorded by Lowe Stokes and His North Georgians—also for Columbia but in Atlanta, just nine days later.

★ ★ ★

The leader of the Hot Shots, guitarist Byrd Moore (1899–1949), had been busy as a recordist since early 1927, when he joined the fiery Georgia fiddler Earl Johnson and His Clodhoppers to make a dozen sides for Okeh. During 1928–30, he cut more than fifty sides for Gennett (➤37), but he evidently had no contractual restraints on recording elsewhere and was able to put his name on the band that showed up in Johnson City to record for Columbia.

The other Hot Shots were fiddler Clarence Greene (1894–1961) from Cranberry in what is now Avery County, North Carolina, and guitarist and lead vocalist Clarence Ashley (1895–1967), who grew up in Johnson County, Tennessee. Greene's insistent fiddling and Moore's sturdy bass-string runs give the four sides cut in Johnson City tremendous drive, and "Three Men Went a Hunting" is considered a classic of old-time stringband music.

The lives of the two Clarences are fairly well documented, but Byrd Moore is one of the great enigmas of old-time music. In less than four years, he attended ten recording sessions, sometimes singing with his guitar, more often playing a muscular backup to a fiddler such as Leonard Rutherford, Melvin Robinette, or Jess Johnston. With a résumé like his, he must have spent time in Georgia, Kentucky, Tennessee, North Carolina, and West Virginia, yet he left remarkably few traces.

Byrd Moore (left) and His Hot Shots: Clarence Greene (center), Clarence "Tom" Ashley (right). (Marshall Wyatt Collection)

The Norton namecheck on the record was not random. Musicians whose paths Byrd Moore crossed have recalled that for a time he ran a barbershop there. Barbering was a common trade among old-time musicians; among the men who recorded for Columbia in Johnson City were four other barber-pickers. Possibly the slack times of the day offered opportunities for practice, but perhaps too it's because the barbershop was a place where men met to socialize, tell jokes, shoot the breeze, and maybe pick up the guitar standing in a corner or the fiddle hanging on a wall. In such a setting, an ambitious musician could build a repertoire and hone his skills.

Byrd Moore may be the Bird Moore who in 1920 was working as a coal miner in Gladeville, Virginia, close to Norton; and he is probably the Bird Moore who had a barbershop in 1930 in Elizabethton, in Carter County, Tennessee. At some point in the late 1920s, he must have been in Russell County, Virginia, where he taught guitar to Carrie Powers, one of the daughters of Fiddlin' Cowan Powers. It was in Virginia that Dick Burnett ran into him in 1928. "He run a barbershop up there. We got in with him, got to talking with him, found out he was a guitar picker. And we went to inquiring about him and we found that he took the prize of being the best guitar picker in Indiana, so we just got him to go with us over there [Richmond, Indiana] and make records [for Gennett in October 1928]."

Moore's last recordings were in 1932. The music historian Kip Lornell learned that in later life he remarried, his new wife was a bootlegger, and they lived in Esserville in Wise County. He became an alcoholic, lost everything he owned, and died in a Wise County poorhouse.

★ ★ ★

"Three Men Went a Hunting" owns not only a curious history but also a resonant legacy. It was brought to the notice of stringband music fans first by the New Lost City Ramblers, on a 1961 album and subsequently in their *Songbook*, then by the reissue of the original recording on a 1965 LP, *Old-Time Southern Dance Music: The String Bands Vol. 2* (Old Timey 101) (which also contained the Scottdale String Band's "Carbolic Rag" [➤12]). This and other albums on Old Timey, a subsidiary label of Arhoolie Records, played an important role in the '60s by rebroadcasting one of the messages of Harry Smith's *Anthology of American Folk Music* (1952): there were extraordinary riches lying unplundered in the old hillbilly catalogs of the 1920s and early '30s.

Yet Smith's work had been curiously slow to inspire others. It took a decade or more before LP compilations on County, Old Timey, and a few other labels, drawn from those long-deleted lists, dramatically expanded the available repertoire of Southern song and dance music for the generation of young musicians who would create the stringband revival of the '60s and '70s. As John Cohen of the New Lost City Ramblers once said, "Sometimes the most radical thing you can do to move ahead is to go backwards." But seldom can going backwards have led curious listeners so far into the past as with the extraordinary time-capsule from Jacobean England that is "Three Men Went a Hunting."

49

"DOWN ON PENNY'S FARM"

The Bentley Boys
Columbia 15565-D

Recorded in Johnson City, TN, October 23, 1929
Released in August 1930
Sold 1,583

Reissued on *"Can You Sing or Play Old-Time Music?": The Johnson City Sessions 1928–1929* (Bear Family BCD16083), *Hard Times in the Country* (County CD-CD-3527), *Hard Times Come Again No More Vol. 1* (Yazoo 2036), *Anthology of American Folk Music* (Smithsonian Folkways SFW40090), *American Epic* (Sony 88875099692)

Online: Spotify, YT

Come, you ladies and gentlemen, listen to my song,
Sing it to you right but you might think it's wrong,
May make you mad but I mean no harm,
It's just about the renters on Penny's farm.
It's a hard times in the country
Out on Penny's farm . . .

Hadn't George Penny got a flattering mouth?
Move you to the country in a little log house.
Got no windows but the cracks in the wall.
He'll work you all summer and he'll rob you in the fall . . .

George Penny's renters, they'll come into town
With their hands in their pockets, and their head a-hangin' down.
Go in the store and the merchant will say,
"Your mortgage is due and I'm lookin' for my pay."

Down in his pocket with a tremblin' hand,
"Can't pay you all but I'll pay you what I can."
Then to the telephone the merchant makes a call.
They'll put you on the chain gang [if] you don't pay it all.
It's a hard times in the country
Out on Penny's farm.

"Down on Penny's Farm" is a vivid picture of rural hard times, and, given its recording date, six days before the Wall Street Crash, it's tempting to see it as a preview of the Great Depression. Folksong scholarship suggests that its roots are deeper and older than that. I believe it should be interpreted as a sardonic commentary on the life of a tenant farmer or sharecropper, subject to the whims and extortions of a landowner—a condition that existed for decades before October 29, 1929.

Whenever it may have originated, "Down on Penny's Farm" was first documented on this recording, made at Columbia's second location session in Johnson City, Tennessee, later on the same day as "Three Men Went a Hunting" (➤48). On this number we hear, I think, just two Bentley boys: the singer, who is probably also the guitarist, and a banjo player. The other side, "Henhouse Blues," a partial version of Paul J. Knox's blackface composition of 1899, "I Don't Care If I Never Wake Up," adds a fiddler.

★ ★ ★

"How about the Bentley Boys?" Mike Seeger asked Frank Walker, who supervised the Johnson City session, when he interviewed him in 1962. "Do you remember anything about them?"

"Not very much," Walker replied. "No great shakes."

"Do you remember where they came from?" Seeger persisted.

"No, I'm going to pass up on that," Walker admitted. "I don't remember, I really don't."

In the almost sixty years since that interview, we have yet to fully solve the mystery of The Bentley Boys.

But we can locate them. The Bentley Boys were active in and around Burlington and Greensboro, North Carolina, as we know from reports of their performances in the local press. Possibly the earliest of these references (*Burlington Daily Times*, July 29, 1930) finds "The Bentley boys, of Greensboro" holding "headline positions on the program" at an old-time fiddlers' convention at the E. M. Holt School, near the Standard mill village in Alamance County. On November 22, 1930, they performed at a fiddlers' convention at Liberty in Randolph County, one of more than a dozen groups; the Proximity String Quartet (➤31) were another (*Daily Times*, November 20). Misidentified as "Bentley brothers," they appeared at another fiddlers' convention in Liberty on February 21, 1931, again with the Proximity group (*Daily Times*, February 18).

Only one Bentley living in Greensboro in the late 1920s and early '30s appears to fit the bill. Clement Lester Bentley was born in north Georgia on August 26, 1904, grew up in Walton and Barrow Counties, and in 1926 moved to Greensboro, where he worked as a machinist in an overall factory and rented rooms at 341 West Lee Street. At 343 lived a young woman named Ethel Lockamy. In December 1928, the two were married, and for several years they continued to live at 343 W. Lee. Clement subsequently worked at a hosiery mill, the El Moro Cigar Company, and Talley Laundry Machinery. He retired because of knee trouble and died September 10, 1977; Ethel survived him by more than twenty years, dying in 1999.

Clement and Ethel Bentley, probably in the 1950s. (Courtesy of Tom Lockamy)

Tom Lockamy, Clement's nephew, born in 1943, lived with him and Ethel for much of his youth and remembers him singing and playing guitar, two of his favorite songs being "Won't You Ride in My Little Red Wagon?" and Eddy Arnold's "Bouquet of Roses." He also recalls Clement telling him he had performed on radio. He never heard Clement sing "Down on Penny's Farm" and does not recognize the voice on the record as his, though he points out that his earliest memories of his uncle date from more than twenty years after the record was made. The late Kathleen Wheeler, Ethel's younger sister, also failed to recognize her brother-in-law as the singer when "Down on Penny's Farm" was played to her (she was then in her late nineties), but she did recall some of its lyrics and associate the song with him.

It may be significant, given Clement's origins in north Georgia, that the only other recording of the period that can be connected with "Down on Penny's Farm" is by Gid Tanner, born in Gwinnett County, which adjoins Walton and Barrow. Were both The Bentley Boys and Tanner drawing on the same source song, perhaps composed about a real George Penny? It's possible, but "On Tanner's Farm," which Gid recorded with Riley Puckett in 1934, is so close to the text of the Bentley recording that I assume it was copied from it.

★ ★ ★

Thanks to being selected by Harry Smith for the *Anthology*, "Down on Penny's Farm" has resonated long and loud in the American folk-singing community, where it has acquired the status of an authentic, and unusually explicit, document of hillbilly serfdom. Pete Seeger took it up, and The Holy Modal Rounders, and Jim Kweskin and Geoff Muldaur, and Happy and Artie Traum, and more recently Natalie Merchant, and the actor Katherine Heigl in the 2014 movie *Jackie & Ryan*. And so, most notably, did Bob Dylan. During September–November 1961, preparing material for his first album, Dylan immersed himself in the *Anthology*, and although he didn't record "Hard Times in New York" in the studio, he did tape it at an informal session in a friend's apartment in December, and the following year sang it on a radio show. Both the melody and the opening couplet are based on "Down on Penny's Farm."

50

"THE FATE OF RHODA SWEETIN"

Charles Freshour and The Lonely Eagles
Paramount 3247

Recorded in New York, NY, October 28, 29, or 30, 1929
Released in September/October 1930

Reissued on *People Take Warning!* (Tompkins Square TSQ1875)

A story of a maiden I'll tell you,
Whose name to you I can't breath[e],
For why should I now disgrace her,
When she is now sleeping in death?

Songs about the untimely death of a young woman are not uncommon in old-time music. We have already witnessed the murders of Little Mary Phagan (➤4) and Ethel Sullivan (➤23), and the casebook could be swelled by many more. But in "The Fate of Rhoda Sweetin" we have a song that may be unique in the old-time record catalog, for it was composed and sung by the victim's brother.

Rhoda Sweeten (as her name should be spelled) was born in Cocke County, Tennessee, about August 1909, to James and Sallie Sweeten. Among her older siblings was a brother, Charles Hubert (or Herbert). By 1920, the family had moved to Cross Anchor, in Spartanburg County, South Carolina, where James and Sallie took jobs in a cotton mill. Probably in the later 1920s, Rhoda married a man named Cooper in Gaffney, South Carolina (where the Sweetens may have moved; they were living there in 1930), but, as the song relates, "after a few weeks' experience, the tragedy then changed her mind."

Her husband had stolen a car in Union, South Carolina, and had been caught, arrested, and brought back to Gaffney. While he was serving jail time, Rhoda seems to have gone a little wild: she deserted her husband, "forgot she was some mother's child," spurned her parents' entreaties to come home, and "wandered around through the country to pass her troubles away." In May 1927, now going by the name of Rosa Lee Medlin, she was jailed in Gaffney for disorderly conduct (*Gaffney Ledger*, May 26) but released on promising to leave the state and was escorted by police officers as far as Spartanburg. Perhaps she stayed there, for in April of the following year she was picked up on East Main Street "heavily under the influence of liquor" (*Ledger*, April 12, 1928) and sentenced to sixty days in jail.

Evidently, during her months of erratic behavior, she had acquired a boyfriend, for she now fell into "despondency [because of] the failure of either her mother or lover to visit her while in jail" (*Ledger*, May 19). On May 10, she took four tablets of bichloride of mercury, in those days a treatment for syphilis and generally available at drug stores. Local Salvation Army officers traced Sallie Sweeten and enabled her to visit her daughter, but the young woman died in the hospital in the early hours of May 16. Later that day, her brother Charles, then living in Lincolnton, North Carolina, north of Gastonia, provided the information for her death certificate. It was afterward reported that "she had attempted suicide by taking tablets once before in the city jail of Asheville, N. C. She also threatened to make another attempt at self destruction if she was taken back to the [Spartanburg] city jail" (*Spartanburg Herald*, May 17).

A year and a half on, Charles commemorated her in this recording. For a few years, he had been using the surname Freshour, which he retained for the rest of his life. Freshour was a common name in Cocke County in the early twentieth century, and it's likely that there was a family connection with the Sweetens.

"The Fate of Rhoda Sweetin" was recorded during a session by Wilmer Watts and His Lonely Eagles, a name that resonates among collectors, since the recordings from this session are generally held to be exceptional. This 1929 session in New York was part of a lengthy series of recordings made under the supervision of talent scout Harry Charles, the man who had introduced Watts to Paramount in 1927 (➤13). Commissioned by Paramount to enliven its then somewhat comatose old-time catalog, Charles summoned dozens of musicians, several of whom he had worked with before, from Georgia, West Virginia, Kentucky, and North Carolina and produced around 180 recordings, most of which were issued. The timing, however, was unfortunate: Wall Street crashed while the sessions were going on. What with that and Paramount's poor distribution of hillbilly records, all these fall 1929 recordings are rare, some almost mythically so. Of "The Fate of Rhoda Sweetin," maybe half a dozen copies survive in collectors' hands.

The band's name was borrowed from the aviator Charles Lindbergh, whom the American press had dubbed "the lone eagle" during his 1927 solo flight across the Atlantic, perhaps the only historical event commemorated by both Tin Pan Alley songwriters and Bertolt Brecht. Sometimes a trio, on this recording The Lonely Eagles consisted of just Watts, on banjo, and Freshour, playing guitar and, for the only time at this session, singing solo. Did he feel that, in commemorating his sister on a record, he could salvage something morally or socially worthwhile from her fate? A lesson, perhaps, for other troubled young women?

So listen, young girls, to this story,
I pray you will heed to this song.
You may think your parents are cruel,
But remember there's no place like home.

51

"COTTON MILL GIRL"

Earl McCoy and Jessie Brock
Columbia 15499-D

Recorded in Atlanta, GA, November 5, 1929
Released in February 1930
Sold 4,562

Reissued on *"Wait for Me": Songs of Love, Lust and Discontent from the 1920s and 1930s* (East River 1007)

Online: Spotify, YT

The threads that were woven in Southern textile mills were also part of the fabric of old-time music. Recordings of cotton-mill songs, from Wilmer Watts's "Cotton Mill Blues" to David McCarn's "Cotton Mill Colic" and the Dixon Brothers' "Weave Room Blues," tend to focus on the work itself and only occasionally expand into the life of the mill village. But not all of that life. Where are the songs of sweethearts in the spinning-room, of love among the lintheads?

Prompted by that thought, perhaps, in 1929 someone wrote one.

Beneath the heading "THE COTTON MILL GIRL—J. Byrum Lawson, Correspondent," this story first appeared in the *Union* [South Carolina] *Times* and was reprinted shortly afterward by the Rock Hill [South Carolina] *Herald*.

> We have heard songs of Mother, sweethearts, wrecks, home, and everything imaginable . . . but we are soon to hear a song that is different from any of these. Although it brings in the sweetheart and love stuff, it also gives us a touch of real life that really exists among most of us in this Southland of ours. This song will bring you right into the mill among the spinning frames where the pretty girls are spinning the yarn that goes to the loom to clothe the world. You see a courtship that commences and ends right at the spinning frame. The little spinner girl is courted, we presume, by a doffer or section man. He is madly in love with this little lassie; they have their lover quarrels, but always make up as is the case with not only the cotton mill girl, but with the fair ones of all walks of life. This song pictures to you, too, the largest industry in the Southland, as well as the little girl that makes the spinning frame hum, and the lover who helped turn these wheels of industry. . . .
>
> This song will soon be heard over the country from coast to coast on Columbia phonograph records. This song being composed by a cotton mill girl and also sung by a cotton mill girl and boy on this record. . . . Mrs. Jessie Smith Brock and Earl McCoy of Union, South Carolina, have recently recorded this song for the Columbia Phonograph Company of New York, and it will be released at an early date. This song is coupled with another real old time love song, "Are You Tired Of Me Darling?" . . . Mrs. Brock has an unusual alto voice, and is backed up by the baritone voice of Mr. McCoy. Both of these selections are very pretty, to all that love real old Southern tunes. (December 23, 1929)

This is a most unusual document. First, it's that rare thing, a press release for a hillbilly record that was not written in the press office of a record company. Secondly, although it employs tropes often used in promoting hillbilly records, such as "songs of Mother" and "sweetheart and love stuff," it emphasizes that *this* song is different. It is designed to take listeners by the hand and lead them "right into the mill," into "the largest industry in the Southland." The song appears to have an agenda. Of that, more later, but first, let's meet the "cotton mill girl and boy" whom this record presents to us.

Logan Earl McCoy (1906–76) came originally from Rock Hill in York County, South Carolina. His main trade was barbering. "That's how he met my grandmother in 1927," remembers their granddaughter Vonda Yeary. Earl was working at a barbershop in Union where the teenaged Alma Garner went "to get her hair cut (in the '20s flapper style) and he asked her out." They married in February 1928 and lived in Rock Hill for a while, but by 1929 they had settled in Union. In the early years of their marriage they both worked in a local cotton mill, probably the Monarch or the Ottaray, before Earl took a job at Shipman's Barber Shop, across from the courthouse on Main Street. He would work there for the rest of his life.

"He loved to sing and play the guitar," says Vonda Yeary, "as well as other instruments." She remembers that he was the state banjo champion three years in a row at the Clemson fiddlers' convention. He also played in bands and in the '30s led a group of Union musicians who used the name of the Shamrock String Band.

Jessie Smith Brock (1909–90) may have been living in Goldville, in Laurens County, at the time of the recordings; she was certainly doing so a few months later, when she was enumerated as a spinner, probably at the Joanna Mill. She subsequently moved with her husband William Brock to Union, his hometown, and in 1940 was living in the Ottaray-Monarch mill village. Vonda Yeary remembers meeting her once: "She came to see my grandmother (after my grandfather died) when I was young."

Earl McCoy and Jessie Smith Brock may have met as co-workers, say at the Monarch or Ottaray mill, and discovered their compatibility as singers; or they may have been brought together by the third figure in our press story. J. Byrum Lawson (1897–1971) worked at the Cooper Furniture Co. in Union, where he was responsible for the music and phonograph record department, and, like other men in that position, such as Phil Reeve in Calhoun, Georgia (➤15), acted as a scout for local talent. During several years' collaboration with Columbia Records, he would deliver numerous Union County artists to their seasonal recording sessions in Atlanta: in 1928, the Shamrock String Band (probably before McCoy was a member) and the Stapleton Brothers, Mitchell and Mason, from the Buffalo mill; in 1929, McCoy and Brock; and in 1930, McCoy again, but with Alfred Meng and Clem Garner (➤57), possibly Jessie Brock again as half of the duo Brock and Dudley, and the Murphy Brothers Harp Band (➤64) from Cross Keys, where Lawson himself had been born.

He also sent to Columbia the African American singer-guitarists Lil McClintock, who lived near Lawson in Union, and Gussie Nesbitt, from Cross Keys. Later, with Columbia reducing their location recording, Lawson may have supplied some talent to Victor: I suspect he had a hand in the recordings, made on the same day in Charlotte, North Carolina, in May 1931, of the Stapleton Brothers and the African American singer-guitarist Jack Gowdlock or Goudelock, who lived in Union or Spartanburg County and was acquainted with Gussie Nesbitt.

The Shamrock String Band, probably ca. 1926. John M. O'Shields (bass), possibly Winston W. Windsor and Dewey Fowler (guitars), possibly Herman Sprouse (fiddle), possibly Julius Hendrix, Noah Hendrix, D. U. Allman (mandolins), Willie H. Blackwood (piano), with their manager J. Byrum Lawson (rear). (Courtesy of David Sloan)

(Author's Collection)

Lawson would reminisce to his grandson David Sloan about driving musicians to Atlanta to record. It was on these journeys that he was attracted by the town of Sandy Springs, in Anderson County, where he moved in about 1933 and built a house for himself and his family. "A real entrepreneur," as his grandson says, he opened stores in Anderson and in Union, dealing in furniture, antiques, and children's toys. He entered politics, and in the '40s and '50s served in both the state house of representatives and the state senate. In the words of his obituary, he was "an outstanding figure in Anderson County political, commercial, and civic affairs for the better part of a generation . . . and was father of much progressive legislation that remains as permanent memorial to his service to the people of the county and state" (*The State* [Columbia, South Carolina], August 27, 1971).

★ ★ ★

In his piece for the Union paper, Lawson noted that the composer of "Cotton Mill Girl" was one herself. Perhaps he was referring to Jessie Brock; or perhaps he was just lending the song some color of authenticity since it's in a familiar vein of rueful-comic courtship verse, with occasional allusions to the detail of mill life. McCoy sings lead and plays slide guitar, and Brock adds a tough, stringy harmony to a tale of squabbling but appreciative lovers.

> My girl is a cotton mill girl,
> One of the finest in town.
> She's a spinner, a dadgum winner,
> Eyes [of] a lovely brown . . .

The man gets a little fresh, they have a falling out, and he announces nonchalantly, "If the girls in this town don't like me, I'll bid them a long farewell." But this is mere bluster, and, returning to the refrain, he confesses, "I'll tell you this minute, there's no other in it, Than the girl that works at the mill."

I said earlier that this song had an agenda. I believe it was composed to pay respect to those hitherto almost hidden figures in the American musical landscape, the workforce of the Southern textile mills. If a cotton-mill girl was good enough to write a song about—a song, moreover, that was put on a record "to be heard over the country from coast to coast"—she must be a person of some consequence, worthy of anthems, fit to join the company of working-class heroes: Frank Hutchison's miner, John Carson's honest farmer, or his daughter Rosa Lee's jolly railroad man.

This honoring of working men and women, which lies at the heart of Byrum Lawson's promotional article, also explains the interest of the record company. By producing a record of life amidst shuttle and loom, Columbia could pique the interest of both workers and consumers in the textile heartland of the Southeast, a huge constituency that the record industry was only just beginning to acknowledge.

"Cotton Mill Girl" was not the first cotton-mill record. It was not even the first "Cotton Mill Girl." A year earlier, Lester Smallwood, a singer and banjoist from Hall County, Georgia, had recorded a song with that title for Victor, though it was actually a version of a well-known song with the refrain "Hard times in this old mill, hard times everywhere." Wilmer Watts's "Cotton Mill Blues" (➤13) also preceded McCoy and Brock's recording, though by only a month or so. But in 1930, in the wake of McCoy and Brock's disc, came releases such as David McCarn's "Cotton Mill Colic"; "Little Cotton Mill Girl," written by Andrew Jenkins and recorded by Bob Miller; and another reading of the "Hard times in this old mill" song, "Cotton Mill Blues" by the Lee Brothers Trio, actually the Chumbler brothers, also from Hall County, Georgia. A spotlight had been switched on that illuminated the world of the textile mill, and it continued to do so in the ensuing decade, in records by the Dixon Brothers, Daddy John Love, and Lester "Pete" Bivins (➤75).

52

"THE ROAMIN' MUSICIAN"

Bill Tuttle

Columbia 15697-D

Recorded in New Orleans, LA, December 10, 1929
Released in December 1931
Sold 624

Jimmie Rodgers, in his 1929 recording "Jimmie's Texas Blues," declares, "I'm not singin' the blues, I'm tellin' you the hard luck I've had." This seems a puzzling distinction. Isn't "tellin' you the hard luck I've had" one of the things, maybe the most important thing, the blues is *for?* Does Rodgers mean that here he is telling a true story, unvarnished, whereas "singin' the blues" is, for him, a different kind of presentation, not factual but dramatic?

Scores of recordings by Rodgers and his imitators and followers—Gene Autry, Jimmie Davis, Cliff and Bill Carlisle, Daddy John Love, and so forth—are first-person blues using familiar blues tropes of desire, loss, determination, resignation, showing off, moving on, fun times, and, yes, hard times. They are often vivid and plausible, but it would be naïve to suppose that they are all factually true, that the narrator's "I" is autobiographical. Singing the blues *is* a theatrical act: professional, not confessional. Historically, it has often been a comedy routine. As noted earlier (➤18), to at least some of Rodgers's contemporaries, his blue yodels were strings of jokes, wry grins at life's ups and downs.

But to acknowledge the artfulness in hillbilly blues is not to deny that it can often be emotionally stirring, as in Frank Hutchison's "Worried Blues," Dock Boggs's "Down South Blues," Darby and Tarlton's "Slow Wicked Blues" and "Heavy Hearted Blues," Bill Shepherd's "Bound Steel Blues". . . . Readers will have their own shortlists. Performances like these compel our attention because they seem *imaginatively* true. Listening, we feel a shiver of recognition. And for me, a little-known record issued in the depth of the Depression also has that effect: "The Roamin' Musician" by Bill Tuttle.

> I'm just a roaming musician, I've roamed around all my life,
> I've roamed around from state to state and never satisfied.
>
> I have no education, for I never went to school,
> I thought I was a sensation, but I was just a fool.
>
> I've rode on tops of boxcars, I've slept out in the rain,
> But the hardest night I ever spent was one night in Maine.
>
> While standing in the railroad yard, wasn't meaning any harm,
> An officer of the law came up to me and took me by my arm.
>
> He said, "You are a crim'nal, that's plain enough to see."
> So he took me to the courthouse and it was three long years for me.

The rambler's narrative, the deployment of African American blues commonplaces (hanging around in a railroad yard, being arrested and brought to trial), and the yodel all suggest Rodgers, and the old-time music historian Gus Meade chose to catalog this recording as a variant of Rodgers's "Waiting for a Train," which also has a hobo sleeping in the rain. But this is the only verbal connection, and Tuttle's performance leaves a strong impression of personal testimony. He accompanies himself on slide guitar, playing as if he wants to sound like Jimmie Tarlton but hasn't quite achieved the other man's facility or his honeyed tone.

Columbia waited two years before issuing the record. Its sales may seem paltry, but at that date they were about average for releases in the "Old Familiar Tunes" series. By then, such records were issued with little or no advertisement, and without the expense of a promotional photograph. So we know nothing about Bill Tuttle beyond what we can guess from his one record. He may have hailed, like other artists at this New Orleans session, from southern Mississippi; he recorded immediately after the Bush Brothers, a sacred group from Jones County. As it happens, a William Tuttle, aged about thirty, was then running an automobile sales outlet in Laurel, Jones County's largest town. He was originally from Georgia, and he doesn't seem to have stayed around. Maybe he really was a roamin' musician.

Why should we care? After all, Bill Tuttle was a one-record one-off, the briefest of footnotes to the grand narrative of country music. But I am moved by that one record, by the desperate directness with which he addresses us, and I want to place this tiny marker for the man who made it, and for that unforgettable, nakedly confessional line: "I thought I was a sensation, but I was just a fool."

53

"THAT'S THE BLUE HEAVEN FOR ME"/"SINCE I'VE GROWN SO USED TO YOU"

George E. Harris
Columbia 15543-D

Recorded in Los Angeles, CA, February 12, 1930
Released in June 1930
Sold 1,571

This may not be, in the words of Ford Madox Ford, the saddest story ever told. But parts of it may break your heart.

George E. Harris was a singer, guitarist, harmonica player, and amateur songwriter who decided, sometime in 1928, that he had four numbers worth pitching to a record company. He registered them for copyright in July, and in October took them to Richmond, Indiana, where Gennett recorded them, listened to them, and rejected the lot.

A week later he was in Chicago, offering the same four numbers to Brunswick–Vocalion, which recorded them, listened to them, and rejected the lot.

Either Harris was a stubborn man or these were the best songs he had because when, sixteen months later, he secured an audition at Columbia Records' studios in Los Angeles, he offered the recording team the same four pieces. They recorded them, listened to them, and—

—and finally, a shaft of sunlight pierces the fog of frustration and failure that has enveloped George E. Harris. Columbia does not reject his songs. At least, it takes two of them. His stock-in-trade had been a pair of sentimental pieces and a pair of blues, "Dear Old Texas Blues" and "Black Bottle Blues." Rather uncharacteristically for the period, Columbia didn't pick the blues but issued the others. The record staggered to somewhat over 1,500 sales, the second-lowest total yet seen in the "Old Familiar Tunes" series. Harris was paid $10 apiece for his four numbers and offered a royalty deal—1 cent per side on 90 percent of those sold—that could eventually have earned him a further $28 and change. One can imagine him, like the beggar in Monty Python's *Life of Brian*, murmuring, "Sixty-eight dollars for my life story?"—or at least his life's work, or what we know of it, up to that point.

Except that it wasn't really his work at all.

★ ★ ★

In "That's the Blue Heaven for Me," Harris offers his blueprint for a perfect life:

> A cottage with sunshine and roses,
> Where happiness and love reposes . . .
> Where someone is singing a love song,
> Where smiles are as sweet as can be;
> A baby to love and to cherish—
> That's the blue heaven for me.

It's a concoction of elements of "My Blue Heaven," written by Walter Donaldson and George Whiting and a huge hit in 1928 on Gene Austin's Victor recording, and "What Is a Home Without Love," written by Charles K. Harris and published in 1900. The song on the other side also evokes an ideal life, that of two people growing old together: "For us to part, it would break my heart, since I've grown so used to you." Again, the sentiment is not Harris's invention: the song was composed in 1901 by Thurland Chattaway and had been recorded eight months earlier by McFarland and Gardner.

Harris was in his early forties when he made this record, but his voice sounds older, almost frail, and his delivery is artless, with awkwardly long breaks in the middle of words:

(Author's Collection)

One night alone in a cot . . . tage,
I saw a picture so sweet;
Stopped and looked in at the win . . . dow . . .

The harmonica choruses, played in first position, simply sketch the melody.

Given its low sales, this must be a scarce disc, but its combination of greeting-card verses and functional accompaniment has consigned it to oblivion, ignored by most collectors and, so far, all reissuers. The point of hauling it into the light is that, whatever present-day appraisers may think of it, experienced men in 1930 considered it worth recording—and, more to the point, worth releasing—and we should ask ourselves why.

We may judge the subjects banal and the musicianship unspectacular, but in the old-time field these were not necessarily drawbacks; many recorded performances were on about the same modest level. If the song was judged to have potential, its setting might be a secondary matter. Perhaps, coming just a few months after the Wall Street Crash, songs celebrating the joys of a secure home seemed like the sort of tonic the nation might need. As the entertainer Wendell Hall (or his ghostwriter) observed in February 1931, in his column "Ramblin' 'Roun' Radioland" in the radio magazine *What's on the Air*: "After a financial crash such as we've just gone through, people react two ways: They either want the real giddy [i.e., humor] . . . or folks want the sobby, sentimental, tear-wipin' stuff such as the Hokum Ballads that are now ridin' so high."

★ ★ ★

As recording careers go, this is an almost invisible one, and yet we know something about George Emanuel Harris. He was born in Illinois in 1887. By 1927, he had found his way to Oklahoma City, where he and his new wife, Lauretta, ran a restaurant. In his busy year of 1928, when he published all his known compositions, he was listed in the city directory as a musician. In 1930, two months after his Columbia recording date, he was living with Lauretta and her seventeen-year-old son in a rooming house in Long Beach, California, where he gave his occupation to a census taker, with touching confidence, as "making records."

By 1933, however, the couple was back in Oklahoma City, working for the charity Volunteers of America. They divorced soon afterward, and for the next quarter of a century George E. Harris seems to have lived below the public-records radar. He reappeared suddenly in the 1959 Oklahoma City directory, living at 815 N. Hudson—an appropriate address for an old record-maker, since Decca had a distributor in the same block, and there were a couple more distributors only two blocks down the street.

Then, on July 6, 1960, the *Daily Oklahoman* reported: "The badly decomposed body of a man was found Tuesday afternoon [July 5] by police in a small frame home at 815 N. Hudson. Police identified the dead man as George E. Harris, about 79, who operated the 'George the Oklahoma Troubador Sheet Music and Marvel Record Salon' at that address."

54

"STREAK O' LEAN—STREAK O' FAT"

A. A. Gray and Seven Foot Dilly Vocalion 5430

Recorded in Atlanta, GA, March 20, 1930
Released in July 1930

Reissued on *Times Ain't Like They Used to Be Vol. 1* (Yazoo 2028)

Online: Spotify, YT

Like most old-time fiddle tunes, this goes by several names. Earl Johnson recorded it as "Birmingham Rag," Lowe Stokes as "Possum up a Gum Stump," the Skillet-Lickers as "Hell's Broke Loose in Georgia." There were other fiddlers and other titles, but the best name for this exhilarating breakdown has to be "Streak o' Lean—Streak o' Fat," and maybe A. A. Gray was the best man to play it. His guitar accompanist John Dilleshaw, in one of his trademark stream-of-consciousness raps, certainly cracks him up to be:

> Yee-hoo! Listen! I hear music. Why, that's that old tune "Streak o' Lean, Streak o' Fat." Boy, I've danced for many a night to that . . . Listen to that man play that "Tennessee Chicken." Watch him, he pats both feet at the same time . . . Boy, he likes his "Cincinnati Chicken" . . . Go crazy! Ain't gon' live long now! . . . Reminds me of when I used to carry that Johnson gal around to those dances . . . Such fiddlin'! Never heard nothin' like it before . . . Boys, I'll take a streak o' lean, streak o' fat on that.

Ahaz Augustus Gray (1881–1939) spent most of his life farming around Tallapoosa, in Haralson County, Georgia; Dilleshaw (1897–1941) grew up in neighboring Paulding County, though by the time they made this record he had been living in Atlanta for a decade or so, working for the fire department and occasionally playing on WSB. (Dilleshaw's life and music are examined in *Country Music Originals*.) During the 1920s, Gray headed a stringband that played for dances, and, as a woman who knew him told Georgia music historian Wayne Daniel, "The young people in the community kept an eye on where [he] went and followed him, because they knew wherever he went there'd be fun, music, and dancing." He also won numerous fiddlers' contests. "I find that the tune you play has a lot to do with winning prizes," he told a newspaper reporter in 1934.

> A fellow just ahead of me used "Bully of the Town," and that's a mighty good piece. He won four prizes in a row. Finally, I happened to think of "Bucking Mule." It's a hard piece, but it's snappy, and you do a lot of fancy work behind the bridge that makes the fiddle bray like a mule. I won so many prizes [with that] that the other fellows got to calling me "Mule" Gray.

Apart from a disc of unaccompanied fiddling made for Okeh in 1924, Gray's playing is preserved on records that all have a connection with Dilleshaw: two fiddle-and-guitar pieces, two duet songs, and a pair of two-part sketch recordings, "A Fiddler's Tryout in Georgia" and "A Georgia Barbecue at Stone Mountain." "Tryout" stages a fiddling contest between Gray, who demonstrates his famous "Bucking Mule," and "Fiddlin' Joe Brown from Burnt Hickory," who, improbable as it may seem, was a real person from a real place, near Dallas, Georgia, the Paulding County seat. Dilleshaw acts as m. c., and other musicians, among them Archer Lee Chumbler and Hoke Rice, as onlookers. The barbecue sketch goes into cookbook detail about the preparation of a hog for the pit (the squeamish may want to skip this extract):

A. A. Gray. (Wayne Daniel Collection)

A. A. Gray and Riley Puckett. (Wayne Daniel Collection)

> Now, boys, I want all them hogs' heads turned one way, feet cut off, ears burred, shoulders and hams unjointed from backbone, and crack the ribs all the way down. That's right, turn him right up on his back. Now take this ax and don't hit him too hard, now—you'll cut him plumb through . . . Now you take this rod and stick it right in his ham, run it all the way up through his line and right out at his neck . . .

Meanwhile Gray and Dilly's band, the Dill Pickles, furnish musical interludes. Toward the end of Part 1, Dilly calls for a tune and they play half a minute of "Streak o' Lean" without identifying it. The following day, Gray and Dilly returned to the studio to play the piece in full, each negotiating the curves of the tune like a skilled driver on a twisting mountain road. Coupled with another vivacious breakdown, "Tallapoosa Bound," in which Dilly rhapsodizes about the tall pines, red hills, and yellow-legged chickens of north Georgia, it's a disc of almost cinematic color and atmosphere.

★ ★ ★

"Streak o' Lean—Streak o' Fat" has had a curious afterlife, or resurrection. In 2008 (seventy-eight years after the original recording: a nice touch), the old-time band Uncle Earl, with fiddler Rayna Gellert, made a video in which they played the tune for a clog-dancing team, with banjoist Abigail Washburn doing the calling—but the cloggers were dressed like kickboxers, the calls were in Mandarin, and the staging was like a martial-arts movie. This was not as random as it might seem. According to Washburn, fat with a streak of lean meat in it, *hong shao rou* in Mandarin, was a favorite dish of Mao Zedong. Even Dilly, genial blabbermouth that he was, might not have known what to say about *that*.

55

"SALVATION IS FOR ALL"

Rev. Edward Boone
Gennett 7248

Recorded in Richmond, IN, March 28, 1930
Released in 1930

The minister stands at the recording microphone, the words of his song before him. "I have a gospel message," he begins, "that I want to bring to you—"

> It is about salvation for the Gentile and the Jew,
> It is for every nation, yes, for all and not a few—
> Salvation is for all.

And lest we doubt him, he begins to enumerate the destined recipients of his gospel message.

> Salvation for the Chinese, who must walk on little feet,
> Salvation for the Danish, who make butter hard to beat,
> And there's a rich Italian selling fruit upon the street—
> Salvation is for all.

Next, he offers salvation for "the Scotchman, though some call him very tight" and "the folks in Switzerland that polish watches bright." The list runs on, verse after verse, as the man of God cheerfully identifies each nation by a stock characteristic: Japan—little; Germany—short and fat; Ireland—witty; Spain—tattooed; Holland—wearers of wooden shoes. (But what of England? Where is "Salvation for the Englishman, who likes his cup of tea"?) This *omnium gatherum* of stereotypes—not forgetting "the Gypsy people who would steal a hen or two"—is set to the tune, buoyantly played on tiple and guitar, of "The Battle Hymn of the Republic."

This remarkable piece is from the small cache of mostly original gospel songs recorded during 1929–30 by Reverend Edward Boone (1892–1984), pastor of the West Side Mission Pilgrim Holiness church in Grand Rapids, Michigan, with the assistance of his wife Rose and teenaged daughter Olive. They were a musically adept family: the paterfamilias played tiple (as here), mandolin, and harmonica, his wife piano, and Olive guitar (as here), autoharp, and probably banjo and ukulele.

"I remember the night that the gift of songwriting fell upon him," Olive told me. "He was sitting by an open coal fire, playing his tiple. Wrote his first song as fast as it came to him: 'When Jesus Took Me In.'"

In the late 1920s, Rev. Boone had a radio program on WOOD in Grand Rapids, and he conceived the plan of making records to sell to his listeners. Sensibly, he approached Gennett, who, as we know (➤14), were in that line of business. He borrowed money to pay for his first pair of recordings in June 1929, but evidently Gennett saw a wider audience for his music, for they not only gave the record the company label and listed it in their catalog but also had the Boones return to Richmond to make more records three times during the following year. Altogether they made seven discs, all issued on Gennett, and several also on the subsidiary labels Champion and Superior. They earned a recommendation in the Gibson guitar company's house magazine *Mastertone*, and Rev. Boone assiduously plugged them on the many song sheets he published.

★ ★ ★

In August 1937, Rev. Boone was asked by the Elders of the Pilgrim Holiness church to go on radio in Des Moines, Iowa, and solicit contributions to build a church there. The family followed him from Michigan

Song sheets from 1929–30. (Author's Collection)

soon afterward, and in January 1938, he became pastor of the First Pilgrim Church in Des Moines. The Boones soon became known in their new home for their radio programs, first The Boone Family on KRNT, then from February 1939 on WHO, a powerful station that took the message of their Pilgrim Program to forty-three states (*Williamsburg* [Iowa] *Journal-Tribune*, October 24, 1940). When, as often, Rev. Boone was away on missionary work, Olive's husband Leland Roesink would take his place, giving a short sermon and sometimes joining the singing, though, according to Olive, he "couldn't carry a tune in a bushel basket." The family troupe now included Olive's teenaged sisters Beatrice and Beulah, who sang with her in a trio, and Beulah added to the family's armory of instruments an accordion given to her by one of their listeners.

Two nights of the week, the Boones would travel from Des Moines and hold services in other towns. On one occasion, Olive recalled, in Oskaloosa, they drew 2,000 people, and the doors of the church were locked. It was an old building, and they were afraid to let any more in.

Rev. Boone maintained both his Des Moines pastorship and his missionary work, at home and overseas, far into old age. He had always kept his ties with Michigan, returning frequently to the Grand Rapids–Holland–Zeeland area, in which his Dutch forefathers had settled in the mid-nineteenth century. At the age of eighty, he gave a series of special services in the Church of the Nazarene in Cass City, where he was advertised in the *Chronicle* (October 19, 1972) as author, "student of Prophecy," and "an evangelist that has ministered to the people of the Caribbean Islands, British West Indies, and South America."

* * *

While Rev. Boone's church meetings are remembered by a decreasing throng, and his recordings by only a handful of collectors, his name has considerable cachet among the readers of religious literature, particularly as the author of *Ruth's Romance of Redemption*, a dense exegesis of the Book of Ruth, first published in 1936 and still in print. Olive remembered taking it down in shorthand from her father's dictation, at 200 words a minute. He also wrote *The Second Coming in the Parables* and numerous other books and edited hymn collections like *Pearls of Praise and Promise* (1936) and *Rubies of Rapture and Redemption* (1939). Attuned to alliteration, he gave the title *Sunshine Sacred Specials*

(1935) to a collection of his own compositions and continued to offer the recorded ones at 75 cents a disc plus 15 cents postage. "Salvation Is for All" is the last song in this folio. The book's title may have been suggested by one of the Boones' records, which Gennett had issued on Champion with the credit "Sunshine Sacred Trio."

Today, "Salvation Is for All" is unlikely to elicit any response but amusement, and perhaps it would be unsubtle of us not to wonder if Rev. Boone intended it to be received with a smile. Or maybe not: the congregations he addressed in Iowa, in communities like Columbia and Moravia, Pella and Sioux Center, and elsewhere in the Midwest and Northwest, though they might not come across Chinamen every day of the week, would have been familiar with many of the other groups he named. "When my dad was young," recalls the Iowan (and Desmoinesian) writer Bill Bryson, referring to the 1920s and early '30s, "if you drove across Iowa you would regularly come across towns or villages where all the inhabitants spoke German or Dutch or Czech or Danish or almost any other tongue from northern and central Europe." So Rev. Boone's recourse to stock representations could have been a useful shortcut to the point that salvation was a possible goal for everyone, wherever they might have started out.

This is a longish recording, edging close to the industry's desired maximum playing time of 200 seconds, and Rev. Boone needed to edit his text. Perhaps reckoning that these were the ethnic groups rural Midwesterners were least accustomed to, he omitted verses about "the Hebrew man" ("much laughter does he bring"), "the colored man, who makes the banjo ring," and—coupled with "the Russian, under Communistic rule"—"the Mexicans, who love to drink 'white mule.'" But they are all there in the full text of the song in *Sunshine Sacred Specials*, equal members, in Rev. Boone's neat phrase, of "the whosoever throng."

56

"THE BALD HEADED END OF THE BROOM"/"THE NICK NACK SONG"

Ridgel's Fountain Citians
Vocalion 5455

Recorded in Knoxville, TN, April 3, 1930
Released in October 1930

Reissued on *The Knoxville Sessions, 1929–1930: Knox County Stomp* (Bear Family BCD16097) • *The Story That the Crow Told Me Vol. 1* (Yazoo 2051) ["The Nick Nack Song"]

Online: Spotify ["The Nick Nack Song"] • YT [both]

Scores of old-time recordings are humorous songs with stringband accompaniment, and so are these, a pair of husbands' laments about unsatisfactory spouses. Yet they represent something new in the marketing of this music. The verses are not simply dealt out, like cards from a pack of Unhappy Families, but interspersed with wry comments from bystanders, played by "Heavy Martin"—singer Hugh Cross, the pseudonym presumably referring to his guitar—and fiddler Lowe Stokes, both in Knoxville to make recordings themselves.

Contemplating the broom-wielding wife, Stokes muses: "Glad it ain't a rollin' pin, ain't you, Heavy?"

"Yeah, if it was I'd want it to be a glass one," Cross replies, " so it'd break the first time she hit me."

On the other side of the disc, the two listen as the singer describes his wife's faults: she milks the old sow, makes butter in Dad's old boot, and sweeps the floor once a year—with a chair. "Thought this was a nick nack party," grumbles Stokes. "Sounds like a marriage . . . to me. Somethin' like that 'Fatal Weddin.'"

In another song from the session, "Baby Call Your Dog Off," an old bachelor woos a younger woman but is deterred by her father's dogs, whose barks and growls someone in the studio performs with gusto. The final number, "Gittin' Upstairs," is based on the fiddle tune "Shoot the Turkey Buzzard" (encountered earlier as Fiddlin' Sam Long's "Seneca Square Dance" [➤6]). Two of the band bellow a selection of rustic verses out of "Little Liza Jane," with the enigmatic chorus line "Gittin' upstairs, the monkey-o, and see th' old lady there." Stokes and Cross again throw conversational pebbles into the path of the music.

"Has old Liza got down here yet?" asks Cross.

"She wants to dance, it seems like," Stokes replies, and when the music ends, he growls, "Get up them stairs, will you, Liza?"

There were a lot of these interpolations at this Knoxville session, further scattered through recordings by the Smoky Mountain Ramblers, the Southern Moonlight Entertainers, and Alex Hood and His Railroad Boys. They were probably suggested by the deputy recording manager Bill Brown, who contributed some of them himself. During the time Brown was working for the Brunswick–Vocalion old-time catalogs, around 1929–30, they suddenly proliferate with recordings of tunes decorated with humorous comments, as well as full-blown comedy sketches. Perhaps it was Brown who prompted John Dilleshaw, "Seven Foot Dilly," to develop his talent for hillbilly standup (➤54).

The aim of Brown's strategy was to pique the interest of jaded record-buyers by injecting into familiar old-time songs and tunes some of the rustic vaudeville flavor of the "Corn Licker Still in Georgia" and other rural skits in which he had earlier been involved (➤17). Even a listener acquainted with "The Bald Headed End of the Broom" and "The Nick Nack Song" would find in these versions, with their jokes and sardonic commentary, a piquantly different aural experience: not just playing, but a playlet.

★ ★ ★

Leroy Ridgel (fiddle), and (seated, left to right) Ancil Ridgel (mandolin), Millard Whited (guitar), Earnest Ridgel (guitar). (Courtesy of the JEMF Memorial Collection/Southern Folklife Center)

Earnest, Leroy, and Ancil Ridgel. (Courtesy of Betty Tudor)

Ridgel's Fountain Citians, who came to the session from the community of Fountain City, a few miles from downtown Knoxville, were essentially a family band, consisting of Leroy R. Ridgel (1887–1965) and his sons Charles Ancil (1908–76) and Carthel Earnest (1912–2003). Leroy played fiddle, and each of the sons played both guitar and mandolin. Surviving photographs show Ancil playing the mandolin and Earnest the guitar, but family members say they swapped instruments back and forth when making their records. The trio was joined, for the recordings, by the Tennessee-born twelve-string guitarist and singer Millard Whited (1905–69), who lived nearby.

The material the band produced at their two sessions in 1929–30 came from a very mixed songbag. According to researcher Don Nelson, who interviewed members of the family in 1972, Leroy Ridgel "steered his band towards a religious path, and twice a week gave sacred concerts in the area." This was reflected in the first two numbers the group waxed in 1929, "Hallelujah to the Lamb" and "Be Ready." They were followed by two well-known old-time songs, "Free Little Bird" and "Little Bonnie," sung by Ancil Ridgel and Whited.

In 1930, however, the Ridgels responded to Brunswick Records' second invitation to the improvised studio in the St. James Hotel by concentrating on old-time comic songs. "The Bald Headed End of the Broom," first published in the 1870s, had been recorded by several other old-time artists, including a 1924 version for Vocalion by Knoxville resident George Reneau (➤3); perhaps the Ridgels' take on it attracted recording director Dick Voynow as a replacement for an ageing item in the company's catalog. "The Nick Nack Song" was a nonsensical number launched into the old-time record domain a few years earlier by the singer and banjoist Chubby Parker (➤10) as "Nickety Nackety Now Now Now."

★ ★ ★

Patrons of fiddlers' contests and other old-time musical events will be familiar with the "Who Came the Furthest?" prize. (Attending them as a visitor from England, I discovered, confers an almost impregnable chance of winning.) Had such an award been offered during the Knoxville recording sessions, one could argue that it should rightfully have gone to Ridgel's Fountain Citians. The family had lived in the area for only three or four years; their roots lay more than 600 miles west.

Leroy Ridgel was born in Columbus, Illinois, but by 1910 he and his wife Mary were farming in Oklahoma. Nelson reported that Leroy was drawn to the fiddle as a young man and became proficient enough "to be in demand for many dances in social gatherings in the area." The couple moved around eastern Oklahoma as Leroy took jobs in the rapidly growing zinc-smelting industry. Ancil, Earnest, and a third son, Orrin Wesley, grew up in Collinsville in Tulsa County. But around 1925–26, they pulled up stakes and moved east, to Fountain City, where Mary had originally come from, and Leroy took work at the Gray Knox Marble Mill.

According to Nelson, "They played for dances and socials, often receiving supper as their only remuneration. . . . In late 1927 or early 1928 the group began to appear over WNOX, and became acquainted with Hugh Cross of nearby Oliver Springs. . . . The Ridgels received a small stipend for their radio work and broadcast over the radio station nearly every Saturday night until 1931."

But playing music seriously—forming a band, building a repertoire, holding down regular gigs, maybe traveling, making records when the opportunity presents itself—tends to be young men's work. Once they marry, start families, and settle into steady jobs, the time for music diminishes, and perhaps, for some, the appetite fades. And then, of course, there was the Depression. In the early '30s, the Ridgels scattered. Ancil returned to Oklahoma and zinc smelting, and in 1937, Earnest and his family followed them there. During World War II, Ancil and his family moved to California, then to Colorado, where Ancil worked as a logger. Earnest returned to Fountain City and spent the rest of his life there, raising with his wife, Alma, two sons and two daughters.

Leroy had remained in Fountain City, still working at the marble mill. According to Nelson, he "had always been a devout man, but a more urgent sense of religion engulfed him," and he became a minister: "He later refused to fiddle at dances or any place other than church affairs." This was confirmed by Betty Tudor, Earnest's elder daughter, who only ever knew of Leroy playing fiddle in church. She was somewhat nonplussed when she heard the worldly, not to say raunchy, music he and his sons, and their wisecracking sidekicks, had committed to wax all those years before.

57

"FORTY PER CENT"

Earl McCoy, Alfred Meng and Clem Garner

Columbia 15622-D

Recorded in Atlanta, GA, April 23, 1930
Released in January 1931
Sold 1,157

Online: YT

> Listen now, people, while I'll tell to you,
> This is the story about that big kangaroo.
> Old Uncle Bimbo's a jolly old soul,
> Never has been busted and he has lots of gold.
>
> Andy, oh, Andy, why do you grin?
> It is a shame for Chester and Min.
> When old Andy gets busy at home,
> Old Tildy hollers, "The soup is on."

For a long time, I thought this must be the oddest, most puzzling record in the whole catalog of recorded old-time music. Who is Uncle Bimbo and why might he be a big kangaroo? Who is Andy, and why, indeed, does he grin? And what's this about soup?

The following three verses extend this knockabout gang with characters called Austin, Mary Gold, Tommy, and Henrietta, who is described as being "after Uncle Bim's roll." Bim, a fool in love, buys her "a four-million stone," but in the final couplet ends up "badly bent—when Old Scooge gets that forty per cent."

Because the allusions are so specific, my first guess was that the song might be a local satire, a series of jokes at the expense of folks in the musicians' community. Then, pondering names like Uncle Bimbo and Old Tildy, I wondered if they might be characters from the world of cartoons and comics. So, at the 2017 Asheville Shellac Bash, a gathering of collectors of 78s, my friend Hunter Holmes played his copy of the record, and I dangled that suggestion before the audience. Some weeks later, one of the Bashers, the English researcher Chris Smith, gave me a thumbs-up. Uncle Bimbo, he'd discovered, was a character in *The Gumps*.

To those who are not vintage comic buffs, this may not mean much, but in the 1920s and '30s, following this syndicated comic strip was a national pastime; sometimes, a national mania. In spring 1929, when the strip's creator Sidney Smith abruptly killed off the character Mary Gold, just as she was about to marry her sweetheart Tom Carr, he was pelted with outraged editorials. "Beauty shops, barber shops, restaurants, offices, business houses, parties—wherever people congregate—have become the centers of comment on the tragic climax to a beautiful story," wrote Joe Shuman in the *Charleston* [West Virginia] *Gazette* on May 5. "Reporters on their beats have difficulty in going about their duties for the barrage of questions." The *Gazette* wired Smith, asking what he could do to bring Mary Gold back, but "it has brought no answer to date."

The centerpiece of the strip was the Gump family: the chinless paterfamilias Andy, his wife Min (Minerva), sons Chester and Goliath, and their formidable servant Tilda. As the comic historian Win Wiacek describes them, "Andy was a regular blowhard with lots of schemes to make his fortune, Min was shrewish and nagging, the boys were troublesome and Tilda was a nosy tartar. The domestic scene occasional drifted into thrilling adventure and flights of fancy whenever eccentric, two-fisted globetrotting millionaire Uncle Bim paid a visit. . . ."

The incidents described in "Forty Per Cent"—Uncle Bim's courtship of the scheming widow Henrietta, whom he calls "Heaven's Eyes," the phone call from the loan shark Scooge, who has advanced Henrietta money at 40 percent to cover her spendthriftiness, Tildy's message about soup—all featured in strips published in the first half of March 1930, just a few weeks before the song was recorded. I suspect one of the musicians wrote it, or perhaps a friend. Did the trio figure that this topical composition would seize recording director Frank Walker's attention when they turned up in Atlanta in April? Or did they have more faith in the other number they would pitch him, a Hawaiianized version of "John Henry," and just offer "Forty Per Cent" as something to go on the other side?

★ ★ ★

We have met Earl McCoy singing "Cotton Mill Girl" (➤51). On "Forty Per Cent," he sings and plays rhythm guitar, accompanied by two fellow citizens of Union County, South Carolina, his brother-in-law Clem Garner, singing tenor harmony, and Hawaiian guitarist Alfred Meng.

Alfred A. Meng (1902–87) was a devotee of Hawaiian music and would always go to hear Hawaiian troupes when they came into that section. He must have seen Irene West's Royal Hawaiians, or heard the records they made in the mid-1910s, because he was so impressed by their steel guitarist Pale K. Lua that he named his younger son after him. "My father could play about any stringed instrument except the violin," Kaliure Meng told me. He never played professionally, but he played every day. At the

The songwriter, whoever (s)he was, could have followed *The Gumps* in a local paper, the *Greenville* [South Carolina] *News*, where these strips were published in early March 1930. (© Chicago Tribune)

time of the recordings, he was working as a weaver in the Lockhart Mill, but later he moved to Greenville, working first in a mill, then in the insurance and mobile home businesses. He was distantly related to the Mississippi fiddler Hoyt Ming.

Clem Thompson Garner (1911–85) "worked at Union Mill from the age of nine," says his daughter Sybil Crow, "until he retired—and then some, until they made him stop coming in." At first a weaver, he moved on to making machine rollers and later worked as a gatekeeper. "Mother told me that Daddy didn't continue [making music] because he was too shy," Sybil Crow recalls. "He wouldn't let anyone take his picture.... He always wore a Stetson hat and a dress shirt, and he had that ever-lovin' rag sticking out his back pocket.... He sang all the time. He could read shapenotes." In later years, he overcame his shyness enough to sing in a local sacred quartet.

★ ★ ★

So: "the oddest, most puzzling record in ... recorded old-time music"? The puzzle may have been solved, but some of the oddity remains. Compositions like this are rare in country music. Dolly Parton has not written about *Doonesbury*, nor Brad Paisley about the characters in *Peanuts*. (Though they have pastiched *him*.) But the real question is: why do we call this old-time music? How does a newly written song about the cast of a nationally read comic strip fit into a body of vocal music substantially made up of nineteenth-century sentimental verse, minstrelsy, and refashioned Tin Pan Alley songs?

The answer, I believe, is that, at the time, there was no other marketing drawer in which a record company could file it. In its subject matter, "Forty Per Cent" was a novelty number not unlike "Felix Kept on Walking," inspired by the strip *Felix the Cat*, or "Barney Google," and had it been recorded (as they were) by recognized popular artists like Paul Whiteman, or Billy Jones and Ernest Hare, in a kind of musical setting people were accustomed to hearing on mainstream popular records, Columbia, or any other record company, would have categorized it as a popular release. But since it featured a Hawaiian-hillbilly guitarist and was sung in a Southern regional accent, Columbia could only file it under "Old Familiar Tunes," even though it was neither old nor familiar. Like Raney Van Vink's piano accordion tunes (➤11), "Forty Per Cent" was defined as old-time music because the record industry's self-imposed rules made it impossible for it to be anything else.

Alfred Meng, c. 1937, with his sons Kaliure (left) and Arthur and his 1929 Ford Model A convertible. (Donna Meng Collection)

58

"I'VE GOT THE CHAIN STORE BLUES"

Allen Brothers
Victor V-40276

Recorded in Memphis, TN, May 5, 1930
Released on August 8, 1930
Sold 4,115

Reissued on *Allen Brothers Volume 1 (1927–1930)* (Document DOCD-8033), *Work Hard, Play Hard, Pray Hard: Hard Time, Good Time, and End Time Music, 1923-1936* (Tompkins Square TSQ2783)

Online: Spotify, YT

If you want your money to stay in your own
homeland,
Don't trade with the chain-store man, but trade
with a home-store man.

As the Allen Brothers see it, "the chain-store man" takes their cash but cheats them: "Mister chain-store man, your scales don't weigh just right." He refuses them credit, so who can they trade with but "a home-store man"?

"Play it, brother, while I get this old chain-store man told," says the singer and banjoist, Austin Allen, to the guitar-playing, kazoo-tooting Lee, before urging: "Buy from the home-store man and run the chain store from your town."

By 1930, the chain store was a familiar feature of the American retail landscape. The twenty leading chains had over 37,000 stores. Heading that list was A&P (originally the Atlantic & Pacific Tea Company), the oldest and by far the largest of the grocery chains, followed by names like Kroger, American, Safeway, First National, Woolworth's, and J. C. Penney. All had expanded rapidly in the preceding decade, rousing the animosity of small, independent storekeepers and their representatives. According to the chain-store historian Godfrey Lebhar, an Indiana politician wrote to some of his constituents: "The chain stores . . . [are] sapping the life-blood of prosperous communities and leaving about as much in return as a travelling band of gypsies." One wonders if he knew how apt his figure of speech was: among the decade's most popular radio features was a concert orchestra sponsored by a grocery chain, The A&P Gypsies.

It was widely felt that the chains put local stores out of business. The service was impersonal; the workers had no commitment to the store because they did not own it. The chain store was an expression of corporatism that was at odds with the independent spirit of small-town America. In many states, there were attempts to enact anti-chain laws or impose anti-chain taxes, but the vast majority were judged unconstitutional. Meanwhile, the chain-store lobby insisted that they offered fresher and more varied goods, better-looking stores in superior locations, and lower prices.

One of the chain stores' most voluble opponents was W. K. Henderson, businessman and owner of the powerful station KWKH in Shreveport, Louisiana. "Things were getting rather dull last autumn with KWKH," drily commented a journalist in January 1930, in a profile of "Old Man" Henderson. "He decided to start a fight on the chain stores. He opened with an attack on the chain groceries. He soon had many independent grocers' organizations backing him and money began to pour in for an organization of 'minute men' to aid the station in its fight" (*Ogden* [Utah] *Standard-Examiner*, January 12, 1930). A few weeks

ALLEN BROTHERS

(OTM Collection)

The Chain Store Menace

Too much cannot be said against certain chain stores and their methods. Their local managers are "mechanical operators" controlled entirely by a set formula. These local managers cannot participate in any action, cause, or activity, for the good of all Springfield. It is so written in their instructions. They are not permitted to "give until it hurts" either of their time or their company's money. Their duties, boiled down, are to "get Springfield's money," and to send it to the Home Office.

Cities are not built on this basis

Your loyalty to the Home Owned Stores—your patronage and friendliness to these stores—and your recognition of the Chain Store, in its true light—that of a parasite upon legitimate business, and a menace to our city's prosperity, will result in a CONTINUATION of that prosperity which has made Springfield so outstanding.

Chamber of Commerce

This is the fifth of a series of statements sponsored by the Community Building Bureau of the Chamber of Commerce. Watch for the next one.

By Community Building Bureau

Springfield Leader, May 13, 1929 (Author's Collection)

later, another reporter listened in to Henderson's 8pm KWKH broadcast:

> "Hello you common people—you 80 per cent of the population—are you listenin' to me? . . . Why don't ya buy from the man who's been helping build up your community and keep these pusillanimous parasites from coming in and taking your money to New York, not paying any taxes in your community. . . ." (*Gastonia* [North Carolina] *Daily Gazette*, February 5, 1930)

Henderson was used to public dispute. For some time, he had been lambasting the Federal Radio Commission, which regulated broadcasting in the United States, because, he claimed, his wavelength of 850kc was too close to that of a large rival station, KVOO in Tulsa, whose signal was obscuring his. In February 1930, he even paid Okeh to make a record for him, on one side of which he replicated one of his broadcasts, identifying other intruding stations, such as WABC in New York and WLS in Chicago, owned by Sears, Roebuck but scornfully dismissed as "the Sears Ratback station." The recording was issued on a vanity label, Hello World Doggone, named after two of Henderson's trademark phrases. On the other side, the Atlanta minister-turned-recording-professional Andrew Jenkins, "Blind Andy," wrote and

Hello, World!

Station KWKH

Is working to get the People to buy from their Local Merchant instead of the Chain Store.

We Are With You

MR. HENDERSON

And shall continue to give 16 ounces to the pound. Our Groceries are always Staple and Priced Right. Besides we help build your churches and streets. We also deliver your Groceries to your home and extend Credit to Reputable Citizens. KEEP ABBEVILLE MONEY AT HOME.

L. A. MORELAND

Abbeville [Louisiana] *Meridional*, March 1, 1930. (Author's Collection)

(Author's Collection)

"PIPES DOWN"

HELLO, WORLD.—This is W. K. Henderson, whose radio arugments against chain stores have been spiced with words some folks call "cussing." With a radio inquiry threatened and the U. S. senate all stirred up, "W. K. H." has promised not to get rough any more.

(Kinney Rorrer Collection)

sang a "Hello World Song," subtitled "Don't You Go 'Way"—another of Henderson's catchphrases—and fervently supporting the "Old Man"'s fight against the FRC, Wall Street, chain stations, and chain stores.

KWKH was regarded by some in radio as the Peck's Bad Boy of the medium, because, instead of providing informative or improving programs, it devoted most of its airtime to playing records. To its critics' annoyance, the radio audience did not share their disdain but regularly placed it high in listeners' polls. *Radio Digest* announced in May 1930 that its readers had voted KWKH the most popular station in the South. (The national winner was a station owned by another colorful personality, the rejuvenation therapist Dr John R. Brinkley, who advertised his goat-gland procedures to cure impotence, against a background of live old-time music, on KFKB in Milford, Kansas.) In a letter in the same issue of *Radio Digest*, "a boy, 19 years old, just out of high school," said, "There is no future as long as these Wall Street chains run this country. Here's to KWKH!" An editorial in the *Shreveport Times* (February 4, 1930) declared that the station had put the city on the map: "KWKH . . . has become a great civic attraction. From all quarters of the country and beyond travelers come to Shreveport, . . . some with the express purpose of seeing what is to them the city's best known asset."

★ ★ ★

The Allens' was the only old-time song about chain stores to be released. Bob Miller waxed a two-part "Chain Store Blues" for Brunswick in July 1930, and the Louisiana fiddler and singer Leo Soileau a "Chain Store Blues" for Decca in 1936. Given Miller's politics (➤30) and Soileau's provenance, it would be reasonable to suppose that both compositions supported the Henderson–Allen ticket, but the recordings were suppressed, or judged uncommercial. . . . We may never know.

It was no accident that all these pieces were titled "Blues." Along with the other factors that made hillbilly musicians take so enthusiastically to it (➤18, 52), the blues offered a structure—loose, conversational, with openings for humor and sarcasm—ideally suited to topical reportage and social comment. Singing the blues could also be singing the news. The Allens did it again in "Jake Walk Blues" (➤61) and "Price of Cotton Blues," and Dan Hornsby in Lowe Stokes and His North Georgians' Prohibition song "Bone Dry Blues." Often, simply the *word* "Blues" was enough to imply a kind of skeptical scrutiny, regardless of the song it was attached to. Lester Bivins's "Cotton Mill Blues" (➤75), the Dixon Brothers' "Weave Room Blues" and "Spinning Room Blues," Slim Smith's "Bread Line Blues," Bob Miller's "Farm Relief Blues," Uncle Dave Macon's "All In Down and Out Blues"—none of them was a blues as a musicologist would define it, but calling them so gave their listeners a clue to what they were really about.

59

"MY FATHER DOESN'T LOVE ME"

Louis McDaniel—Gid Smith [actually Lewis McDaniel solo] Timely Tunes C-1560

Recorded in New York, NY, May 12, 1930
Released on July 1, 1931

Reissued on *Walter Smith & Friends Vol. 2 (1930–1931)* (Document DOCD-8063)

Online: Spotify

I first encountered this song when Lewis McDaniel, who recorded it, told me something of its story. It was composed, he said, by a girl from Virginia who went to Draper, North Carolina. "That was a true song about her father.... Yeah, that is really true, every bit of that." A few years later, I came across a copy of the record, which gives us the composer's name.

Like an old broadside ballad, the song opens with a come-all-ye—"Now, girls, you all must listen, while these few words I tell"—and then a warning: "Just stay at home with mother, the one who loves you well." The listener, it seems, is being offered a secular sermonette on home and family. But then the picture snaps into sharper focus: "I was born in old Virginia, two miles from Cockeram's Store." This is not going to be a commonplace homily on living right. This is someone's own story. The story of Virgie Bowling.

* * *

It is early in 1930, and twenty-one-year-old Virgie Mae is looking back on her life so far, perhaps trying to make sense of it, and in the process making a song. Every detail is authentic. "Two miles from Cockeram's Store" would be between Vesta and Stuart in Patrick County, Virginia, where she did indeed grow up. The store is gone, but Cockram's Mill (the spelling has changed over the years), owned by the same family, still stands, in nearby Meadows of Dan. "My brother and my sister have gone on before": she had lost her brother Willie in 1928, her oldest sister Osee in December 1929. And there is worse to tell. "I have an old, old father, who's still living there, But oh, he doesn't love me or neither does he care." For reasons we can only guess at, Nathaniel Abram Bowling has rejected Susan, his wife of more than forty years and mother of ten children, together with his youngest daughter. They have been forced to leave the homeplace, come down from the mountains, and move to Draper, where Virgie works as a cloth inspector in one of the town's cotton mills.

> I'm lonely, oh, so lonely as anyone can be,
> For I'm not among my schoolmates who used to play with me;
> I'm living in a little town, just my mother and me,
> And how I long to go back home, though it seems it'll never be.

Virgie Mae Bowling. (Courtesy of Daniel Bowling)

It is not only her father that she has lost, but family, home, community, *place*: "How I love the Blue Ridge, if I never go home any more." Amid the slamming shuttles of a Draper mill, the peace of rural Patrick County must seem very far away.

★ ★ ★

Virgie wrote her story, but she needed someone else to tell it. Lewis McDaniel was from Alleghany County, North Carolina, and about nine months older than Virgie. By his early twenties, he was living in Schoolfield, Virginia, the mill village near Danville (➤7), and working for the Dan River Cotton Mill. He fell in with old-time singers and pickers from that section of the Virginia–North Carolina border area: fiddler Posey Rorer, banjoist Buster Carter, singer and songwriter Walter Smith. In March 1930, the four men made their way to New York. (Forty years later, McDaniel remembered the car, a '29 Pontiac Roadster, and the address of the apartment building where they stayed.) They made some excellent recordings for Columbia under the billing "Carolina Buddies," then, unwilling to return home without making the most of their opportunity, dropped in on ARC and did a couple more days' recording, gladly sacrificing their identities for the fee: as a group they were the "Dixie Ramblers," individually they were "Kid Williams" (Smith), "Bill Morgan" (Carter), and "Roy Martin" (McDaniel). When McDaniel stood, or sat, at the microphone to record some solo pieces, he began with "My Father Doesn't Love Me."

About six weeks later, Smith and McDaniel returned to New York, this time to record for Victor. Probably not knowing whether ARC intended to issue his earlier recording, McDaniel again submitted "My Father Doesn't Love Me." This time, he gave it a more obvious flavor of Jimmie Rodgers, borrowing the guitar intro Rodgers used on "You and My Old Guitar" and "My Little Old Home Down in New Orleans," and adding a few bars of yodeling.

★ ★ ★

In 1971, when Lewis McDaniel told Janet Kerr and Kinney Rorrer, and later me, about "My Father Doesn't Love Me," what none of us thought to ask was how he came by the song. Did he know Virgie Bowling? Did she seek him out? Did she intend her story to be publicly told?

I believe these details are worth pursuing, because "My Father Doesn't Love Me," despite its obscurity, appears to be something singular in the history of country music: the first specifically autobiographical composition to appear on a record.

There had been "I" songs before, of course. Some were comic narratives, such as "I'm A Stern Old Bachelor" (➤10) and "I Had But Fifteen Cents," or the picaresque adventures of Jimmie Davis ("I'm a pea-pickin' papa from Peanut Prairie"), or the wry blues of Jimmie Rodgers ("I'm goin' to California, where they sleep out every night"). In all of these, the narrator is a fiction, a stage "I," a voice from behind a mask. Or they were pieces like "I Am a Man of Constant Sorrow" or "I Never Will Marry:" existential laments by a generic, symbolic "I," typical rather than specific—not pages torn from someone's diary. Perhaps they had once been personal stories, but that was long before they showed up on discs; the people who recorded the stories were not the people who owned them. The voices on the records were delivering messages from another place and time, another history.

It isn't simply a matter of truth. There had been true stories aplenty in old-time music, tales of deaths and disasters (➤4), and there would continue to be. In one of their border radio programs in the late '30s, the Carter Family sing about the "Cyclone of Rye Cove" that swept away a Virginia school. "Yes, sir, a true story set to song," comments Brother Bill Rinehart, their announcer. But a cyclone afflicts a community, not an individual, and the song represents a community's collective response.

Virgie Bowling's song is something quite different. This is my own story, she tells us, not Everywoman's; *my* lot, *my* life. She makes no generalizations, reaches no conclusions. Unlike the writers of topical tragedy songs, she draws no moral. She acknowledges religion, but without enthusiasm. Her father "says he's Christ's apostle," but, she asks, "D'you reckon it can be? Do you think, if he was a Christian, that he'd hate mother and me?"

★ ★ ★

Victor was scrupulous in crediting Virgie Bowling, and there is no reason to think that their accounting would have been any less careful, but she can have earned little from her song. The Timely Tunes record, released in Depression-stricken 1931, remained in catalog for less than a year, and may have sold a thousand or so; it is scarce today, and its licensed Canadian issue on the Aurora label is probably even rarer. McDaniel's other recording of the song, for

Lewis McDaniels, ca. 1930. (Kinney Rorrer Collection)

(Author's Collection)

which Virgie received no composer credit, is hardly common.

So far as we know, it was the only song Virgie Bowling ever wrote, though she can never have been short of subject matter. In June 1931, she had a son, and some weeks later she married his father, but by January 1934 she was a widow. In June that year, her mother Susan formally divorced Abe Bowling on grounds of desertion. She and Virgie were now living in Danville, where Virgie continued in mill work. In 1935, Abe Bowling died in a state asylum in Marion, and Susan returned to the family house on Buffalo Ridge in Patrick County.

Virgie endured two more marriages, and two divorces, before she found the right man. Edward Duld was a truck driver from Philadelphia, and she moved there to live with him. She had finally found happiness, and when he died in 1959, family members say, she was devastated. She moved back to Buffalo Ridge to live with her mother. Her great-nephew Daniel Bowling, who visited the house in his childhood, remembers her as a quiet, self-effacing figure. Susan Bowling died in 1962, and Virgie passed her remaining years in a trailer home in Stuart, where she died in 1986. Lewis McDaniel lived until 1998, the last survivor of the group of musicians from around Draper, Spray, and Leaksville (now amalgamated as Eden, North Carolina) who had inscribed so much fine old-time music on phonograph records.

60

"FLAT WHEEL TRAIN BLUES"—NOS. 1 AND 2

Red Gay and Jack Wellman
Brunswick 523

Recorded in Atlanta, November 13, 1930
Released in July 1931

Reissued on *Work Hard, Play Hard, Pray Hard: Hard Time, Good Time, and End Time Music, 1923–1936* (Tompkins Square TSQ2783)

Online: Spotify, YT

Many hillbilly records evoke movement, whether it's natural—horse races (➤45), fox chases, coon hunts (➤46)—or machine assisted, as in journeys by automobile (➤38) or locomotive. "Home Again Medley" (➤27) visualizes a train's passage through southern Alabama, but it's a sedate affair compared with the elaborate evocation of railroading in "Flat Wheel Train Blues," a two-part dialogue with fiddle and guitar, now accelerating, now slowing, dramatizing a trip over crossings and hills.

The picture it paints is only one of the reasons for examining this singular record. Another is that it appears to be the only hillbilly disc of its period made by musicians who were from, and based in, Florida. (The Rouse Brothers, originators of the "Orange Blossom Special"—which has a slight melodic similarity to "Flat Wheel Train Blues"—came along a few years later.) Fiddler Reiman E. Duval Gay (1898–1950), "Red" by his initials but also red-haired, was from Slaughter (now Clay Sink) in Pasco County, and his guitar accompanist Conrad "Jack" Wellman (1896–1969), a railroad mail clerk, was born in Fort Pierce in St. Lucie County. In the 1920s and '30s, both men were residents of Tampa.

But the "Flat Wheel Train" can deliver us to yet another destination. The career of Red Gay reveals an unusually detailed picture of how an old-time musician might, through native wit and commercial support, make a living *as* an old-time musician.

★ ★ ★

WDAE in Tampa was one of the state's first licensed radio stations, launched in 1922 and based in the Florida Citrus Exchange Building. Its programming was vigorously publicized by its owner, the *Tampa Times*, and from the late 1920s until well into the '30s, if Red Gay's name was not known to most Tampans, it was not the newspaper's fault. (Though actually he first made it into the paper in March 1927, when, shotgun by his side, he followed his wife, Bertha, and a gentleman friend as they drove out for a roadside meal and shot and wounded them both.)

In 1928, WDAE got into the hillbilly radio business.

> Times Radio To Broadcast Old Fiddlers
>
> WDAE has gone into the old-time "fiddlin'" racket!
>
> Georgia opry! Hill-billies! Quadrilles and square sets!
>
> The object of the old-time fiddlin' programs is to prove to the rest of the world beyond a shadow of a doubt that all the good radio fiddlers aren't up in Tennessee; and that good old cracker fiddlers can fiddle more fiddle any time than other fiddlers anywhere.
>
> If you don't think so listen in on WDAE Saturday night between 9 and 10 o'clock and find out....
>
> Red Gay, one of the younger well-known cracker fiddlers, from Dade County [*sic*], is to be in charge of the contest and each old timer who comes to WDAE Saturday night for the contest will play two numbers of his own choice, a square set and a waltz. The old timers will be chosen by the radio audience whose letters and telephone calls will be counted as votes. (*Tampa Times*, December 7)

Fiddlin' Band Awards Flowers to Beauty Winners

Red Gay, head of the Brown Jug Fiddlin' band of WDAE, presents flowers to the winners of a radio beauty contest held recently. At the wheel of the car is Miss Florence Bishop, 5702 Seminole avenue, who won the title of Miss Tampa. by her side is Miss Virginia Stone, of Inverness, Miss Florida.

Both young women will speak to the radio audience next Saturday night, when the Fiddlin' band makes its next appearance over WDAE. The Saturday night programs, begun last Saturday, are sponsored by local business men.

And WDAE listeners like fiddlin'.

Tampa Times, September 24, 1929. (Author's Collection)

Ten days later, the paper reported that "hundreds of radio listeners stormed WDAE's phone Saturday night . . . [when the] final count on the old time fiddlers' contest of the week previous was made and the decisions rendered by the judges." Red Gay, "bossman of the Little Brown Jug Fiddlin' band of Dade City," was narrowly defeated by Fiddlin' John Rawls. The "two friendly rivals" ended the program with "a dialogue presentation of the famous old 'Arkinsaw Traviller.'"

A few days afterward, Gay led the Piggly Wiggly hour program, featuring band tunes and fiddling solos and duets by himself and Rawls (*Tampa Times*, December 22). He then spent time "up-country . . . consulting with some of the oldest of the old time Cracker fiddlers regarding a proposed inter-state contest between Florida and Tennessee" (*Tampa Times*, December 27), and two days later the paper commented: "Tonight's program will probably work up this Florida-Tennessee fiddlin' feud to such white heat that we may have a band of mountain fiddlers in town for a big set-to some time soon." It's interesting that Tennessee fiddlers are regarded as the ones to beat, when there were so many distinguished bowmen closer at hand in Georgia. Probably WDAE was thumbing its nose at WSM and the Grand Ole Opry.

Nothing more seems to have been heard of an interstate fiddling contest, but Red Gay did organize a Florida championship at St. Petersburg in May 1929. Henry Ford asked "to be advised of the time and station, so that he may hear the most varied program of early American tunes ever broadcast in one entertainment" (*Tampa Times*, May 11). Ford already had an interest in Florida fiddlers, having recently invited sixty-three-year-old Capt. Conrad Menge of Fort Myers, whom he reportedly considered "the best old-time fiddler he ever heard," to join his orchestra in Detroit.

That summer, Gay stepped into another world of competition: from the fiddling contest to the beauty contest. His band was now broadcasting over another Tampa Bay station, WSUN in St. Petersburg, which solicited photographs of "the many beauties who have been listening to the Red Gay band broadcast. Gay and his fellows in bucolic harmony are going over each photograph carefully as it arrives and classifying it for the final judging" (*Tampa Bay Times*, July 7). A couple of weeks later, during their program, they announced the winner, a Miss Florence Bishop. They pursued this line of work through the summer of '29, playing at Egypt Lake with a "Special Added Attraction—Florida Radio Beauties" (*Tampa Times*, August 8). Their heightened reputation drew WDAE to re-enlist them to "conduct the Saturday evening feature as a radio fiddlin' club for requests and novelties" (*Tampa Times*, September 19), and in November, the station and Gay sponsored a Second Annual Statewide Old Fiddlers Contest, supported by many Tampa businesses, and won by Gay on a postal vote (*Tampa Times*, December 7).

The ever-ingenious fiddler next made the *Tampa Times* headlines when he married Loca Ruth Seagle in a "mystery wedding" on WDAE.

> Not until the ceremony was read . . . did the radio audience know the identity of the couple whose marriage they were "witnessing" through the help of the microphone. . . . [G]ifts presented by various merchants in town were opened and "shown" to the "wedding guests", after which Red Gay led his band in a program of old time music. (February 24, 1930)

Gay's Brown Jug Fiddlin' Band had originally consisted of himself and John Rawls on fiddles, and men named Roe and Anderson on banjo and guitar respectively, though reports of their

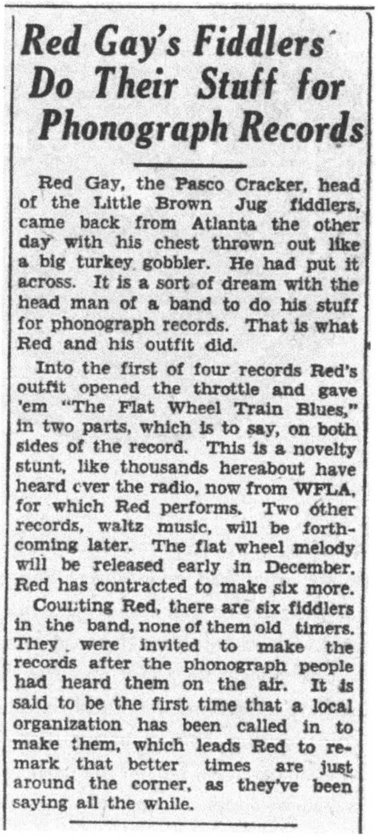

Red Gay's Fiddlers Do Their Stuff for Phonograph Records

Red Gay, the Pasco Cracker, head of the Little Brown Jug fiddlers, came back from Atlanta the other day with his chest thrown out like a big turkey gobbler. He had put it across. It is a sort of dream with the head man of a band to do his stuff for phonograph records. That is what Red and his outfit did.

Into the first of four records Red's outfit opened the throttle and gave 'em "The Flat Wheel Train Blues," in two parts, which is to say, on both sides of the record. This is a novelty stunt, like thousands hereabout have heard over the radio, now from WFLA, for which Red performs. Two other records, waltz music, will be forthcoming later. The flat wheel melody will be released early in December. Red has contracted to make six more.

Counting Red, there are six fiddlers in the band, none of them old timers. They were invited to make the records after the phonograph people had heard them on the air. It is said to be the first time that a local organization has been called in to make them, which leads Red to remark that better times are just around the corner, as they've been saying all the while.

Red Gay reports on his Brunswick recording date, ten days earlier. "Flat Wheel Train Blues" would not be released until eight months later. *Tampa Tribune*, November 23, 1930. (Author's Collection)

Tampa Tribune, November 7, 1930. (Author's Collection)

engagements imply that the lineup was sometimes fluid; a band picture of July 1929 shows a seven piece. By the fall of 1929, Roe and Anderson had been replaced by Molten Christie, banjo, and Curtis "Smitty" Smith, guitar; and in April 1930, Smith was succeeded by Jack Wellman, who played guitar, banjo, and harmonica. Seven months later, a contingent of six Brown Jug Fiddlers were called to Atlanta to make records. As well as the duet record by Gay and Wellman, Brunswick had the full Brown Jug crew play two waltzes, but they were never issued.

Appearing as it did in 1931, "Flat Wheel Train Blues" was unlikely to make anyone's fortune, and today it is a scarce record. But Gay was proud of his brush with the phonograph industry: he listed himself in the 1931 Tampa city directory as "recording artist," and as late as 1938 the *Tampa Times* was still calling the Brown Jug Fiddlers "radio and recording entertainers." By then, however, Gay had left WDAE and had various business interests. During the '40s, he owned a restaurant, the Gayville Lodge, but this was no great career change: in the 1920s and early '30s, he had managed entertainment venues such as the Trilcoochee dancehall near Dade City, and "an all-American Boozeless dance hall, the B. B. B. Club" in Tampa. It was boozeless, of course, because of Prohibition; Red Gay was no enemy of alcohol, and after Repeal, his fiddlin' days behind him, he went into the liquor business, working for the Southern Brewing Co. and later forming his own distributorship.

When men die who were musicians in their youth but have gone on to become civic personalities, their obituaries often concentrate, sometimes exclusively, on their later and more respectable lives. Not so with Red Gay. He, or his family, was evidently comfortable with his past, and his death notices truly reported that he had been "popular as a 'cracker' fiddler."

61

"GOT THE JAKE LEG TOO"

Ray Brothers
Victor 23508

Recorded in Memphis, TN, November 21, 1930
Released on January 16, 1931
Sold 2,229

Reissued on *My Rough and Rowdy Ways Vol. 1* (Yazoo 2039), *Mississippi String Bands Vol. 2* (Document DOCD-8028), *Rough Guide to the Roots of Country Music* (Rough Guide RGNET1391DD), *Mississippi Hillbillies* (JSP JSP77215)

Online: Spotify, YT

In the early months of 1930, physicians in many parts of the United States found themselves dealing with a mysterious new disease. Men—it was almost always men—reported that they had lost feeling and muscle control in their feet or sometimes their arms. The phenomenon was widespread in the South, Southwest, and Midwest, with odd areas of concentration such as Cincinnati; Oklahoma City; Wichita; and Johnson City, Tennessee.

(Author's Collection)

It was quickly learned that these scattered cases had something in common: those afflicted had been consumers of a patent medicine, Jamaica ginger extract, popularly known as "jake." It was supposed to relieve abdominal cramps and such, and it was widely available in stores, in two-ounce bottles that sold for around 35 cents. More to the point in Prohibition America, it typically contained 70 to 80 percent alcohol. For committed drinkers, jake was a legal high.

But it had been around for years without causing these symptoms. Analysts hastened to work out what had gone wrong and discovered that a batch, or batches, of jake had been adulterated with an industrial chemical compound, triorthocresyl phosphate (TOCP). The additive proved to have a toxic and irreversible effect on the spinal cord, causing what clinicians described as "sudden flaccid paralysis." Unable to flex their ankles, sufferers had to adopt an ungainly high-stepping gait, with their drooping feet slapping the ground, toe-heel, tap-click. People called it the "jake leg" or "jake walk."

From his desk at the *Emporia* [Kansas] *Weekly Gazette*, Walt Mason, author of the syndicated poetic column "Rippling Rhymes," described the plight of the paralyzed in his trademark run-on manner:

> Stalwart men, in strength exulting, each could whip a python snake; but they sent, a-catapulting, down their throats a drink of "Jake;" now their legs are dead and useless and their flesh is shrunk and juiceless, and their agony is truceless, and their lives are but an ache. Who compounds such noxious bitters, who's behind such frightful crimes, making wrecks of human critters, just to make some tainted dimes?

Who indeed? Investigators determined that the contaminated shipments, distributed by a network of sometimes shadowy entities, originated with a wholesaler in Boston, the Hub Product Company, Inc. Its directors, Harry Gross and Max Reisman (who also operated as bootleggers), were given derisory penalties: a $1,000 fine, two years in jail for Gross, and for Reisman no time at all.

No doubt the hastily created support organizations for jake leg sufferers were outraged, but the response of the general public was ambivalent. The condition of the men was pitiful, to be sure, but if they were the kind of folks who got their jollies by swigging drugstore tinctures, they were perhaps not persons deserving much sympathy. As William Shepherd observed in a long article for *Collier's* magazine in July 1930, "Jake paralysis is a poor folks' disease. . . . [A] man with a ten-dollar bill can buy a whole bottle or even a whole gallon of safe liquor, but a man with fifty cents or a dollar has to take his chances with what he can get." Ministers preached that the paralysis was divine judgement on sinners. "God is hanging out a red flag," said Dr. Roper of Johnson City, "as a danger signal to those who violate his laws."

Journalists discovered in the outbreak a vein of black humor. "In Oklahoma City, where there are more than 100 cases, the victims are staging jake-leg races," reported the *Atchison* [Kansas] *Daily Globe* on May 12. The *Johnson City Staff-News* ran what purported to be a press release about a "Jakeleg Convention," with hurdle races, jumping matches, and a "Jakeleg Band." A widely circulated story attributed jake leg to eating too many ginger biscuits. An enterprising auto services company in Hutchinson, Kansas, ran an ad saying: "If Your Car Has 'Jake Leg' Bring it to us—we have a POSITIVE CURE for this AILMENT. The Prescription Number is '86'"—the garage's phone number (*Hutchinson News*, May 5).

Among these dark comedians were a considerable number of musicians. The first jake-related recording seems to be "Jake Bottle Blues" (Victor, 1928) by Lemuel Turner: an instrumental solo, played on steel guitar with a Jamaica ginger bottle used as a slide. Turner was then living in Louisiana, but a year earlier he was claimed as a McComb, Mississippi, boy in a writeup in the *Hattiesburg American* (April 15, 1927), which said: "He is among the first to invent what is known as 'jake bottle guitaring,' using an empty 'jake' bottle and getting tones unheard of before out of a guitar or any other instrument." After his Victor session, several Mississippi papers ran stories about this "vagabond musician."

The first *songs* about jake were by African American blues singers from the Mississippi Delta. Tommy Johnson's "Alcohol and Jake Blues" and Ishman Bracey's "Jake Liquor Blues" were recorded only days apart in about April 1930. According to the *Collier's* article, jake leg had "ruined the lives of over 8,000 persons" in Mississippi. If this figure was accurate, it accounted for half the cases in the entire country.

Over the next four and a half years, at least ten other jake-related songs and tunes were recorded,

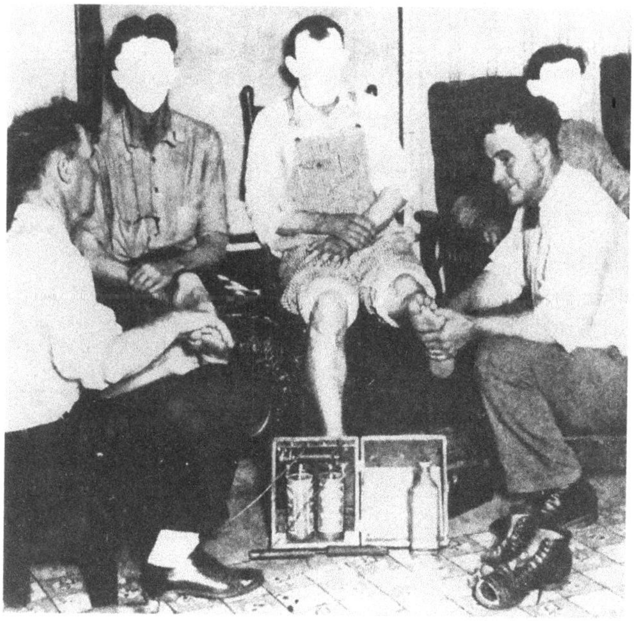

John S. Lehr, veterinarian and tree surgeon, and his assistant, a jockey, give jake leg sufferers "electrical battery treatments and liniment rubs." Wichita, Kansas, 1930. (OTM Collection)

The Ray family band. (Big Boy Woods Collection)

by both black and white musicians. There was an ironic appropriateness about this: one of the industrial uses of TOCP was in the manufacture of shellac, from which phonograph records were made. Curious to think that a jake leg song might have been pressed on material partly composed of the substance that had caused jake leg in the first place.

★ ★ ★

For recording men on the alert for topical songs, here was a perfect fit between subject and subculture: the hobbling company of jake leg victims belonged to the economic class that constituted much of the audience for hillbilly and blues records. In a more blatant age like our own, there would probably be a search for a musician who *had* jake leg . . . *The Jake Factor? America's Got Jake?*

As we shall see, one may have been found.

The most successful of the jake songs was the Allen Brothers' "Jake Walk Blues," recorded in May 1930 and issued in October, which shifted more

Clayton Tyler. (OTM Collection)

"JAKE LEG" BREAKS OUT IN KENTUCKY

Louisville, April 7.—The popularity of prohibition, never a one-sided issue in Kentucky, is decidedly on the wan, according to those who advocate modification or repeal of the existing dry laws. The latest manifestation of this attitude has shown itself in remarks in the press, in clubs, on street cars, trains, buses and the streets, following the outbreak of a form of partial paralysis, commonly referred to as "jake leg," in the eastern and central sections of the state.

No less than 350 cases of this ailment have been reported to the state board of health, with new ones coming in almost hourly from widely separated cities. So far, the trouble seems to be confined principally to the smaller cities and towns, Louisville being free of it, and the rural districts not having many instances of the disorder. The malady apparently is caused by the drinking of an intoxicating decoction known as "jake" the basis of which is Jamaica ginger, but which has been reinforced, evidently, by the admixture of reprocessed industrial alcohol.

Malady Developed Quickly

About 100 cases developed very quickly in Corbin, a city of some 11,000 inhabitants, located in the three mountain counties of Whitley, Laurel and Knox. One of the physicians of that place, when the first few cases were reported, drank some of the suspected liquor, to see if that was the cause, and he soon developed the ailment, which manifests itself as an almost complete paralysis of the legs below the knees, although in some cases the hands and arms are also affected.

Jake leg comes to Corbin, Kentucky. (*Moorhead* [Minnesota] *Daily News*, April 7, 1930). (Author's Collection)

than 20,000 copies on Victor, an unknown but probably considerable number on Bluebird, and a further 6,000-plus on Montgomery Ward. This small black comedy, jauntily arranged for banjo, guitar, and kazoo, is framed as a dialogue between a "jake walk papa" and his "red hot mama," who tells him, "You can't drink jake and get along with me," possibly implying that jake paralysis caused sexual incapacity. According to Dr. John P. Morgan and Thomas C. Tulloss, authors of an authoritative toxico-musicological study of the jake leg phenomenon, "None of the medical reports of the '30s mentions male impotence . . . [but] an informant with the jake leg in eastern Tennessee [where the Allens came from] told [us] that he had heard of men who had this trouble associated with the jake leg."

In an aside to his brother Lee, Austin Allen remarks: "Be wearin' jake socks after a while—you know, they call them iron socks." This was not a joke. Soon after the Allens' record, newspapers ran a story about jake victims being "equipped with improvised iron shoes."

Perhaps the deftest jake song was done by the Ray Brothers, Will and Vardaman, a fiddle-guitar duo from Choctaw County, Mississippi. At the same Victor session in Memphis as the Allen Brothers' recording, they had cut a descriptive instrumental, the "Jake Leg Wobble," so named by the talent scout who brought them to Victor, the Winona, Mississippi, veterinarian Dr. A. M. Bailey. (Their Mississippi contemporaries Narmour and Smith, whom Bailey also helped steer toward a recording deal, promptly replied by recording for Okeh, in June, a "Jake Leg Rag.") When the Rays returned to Memphis six months later, they brought a song called "Got the Jake Leg Too."

> I went to bed last night, feeling mighty fine;
> Two o'clock this morning, the jake leg went down
>   my spine—
>   I had the jake leg too,
>   I had the jake leg too.
> A preacher drank some ginger, he said he did it
>   for flu;
> That was his excuse for havin' the jake leg too.
>
> Boys, Jamaica ginger sure will do its part;
> Boys, Jamaica ginger will kill your honest
>   heart . . .
>
> Now you've heard my story, but I haven't told
>   half;
> This on your tomb will be your epitaph:
>   I had the jake leg too,
>   Had the jake leg too.

On the label the song is credited to Vardaman Ray, but it was actually written by Clayton Tyler, a fellow Choctaw Countian. "The way it came about," Tyler wrote me in 1977,

> my brother and I were plowing on one of the Montgomery hills of our farm and we came up

> with the idea of composing this song. He would think up a verse and sing it at the top of his voice while I listened and thought. Then I would do likewise. This continued until we had the song complete. I remember our daddy scolded us for making such a loud noise. However, we thought it real funny.

Dr. Bailey bought the piece from Tyler for the Rays to record. By chance, "Got the Jake Leg Too" was waxed on Tyler's twenty-first birthday.

★ ★ ★

By the mid-1930s, the end of Prohibition had made substitutes like Jamaica ginger irrelevant. Nevertheless, TOCP would return to ravage the unsuspecting several times over the next half-century, usually as an illicit additive to cooking oil or flour. But by 1934, when the last commercial recording was released on the subject, "Jake Leg Blues" by Willie Lofton, an African American blues singer from Jackson, Mississippi, the jake leg epidemic was on the way to being forgotten—except by those whose lives had been twisted by it.

In 1937, however, Alan Lomax, on the road with his recording machine on behalf of the Archive of Folk Song at the Library of Congress, collected a couple of jake songs from singer-guitarist Maynard Britton of Big Creek in Clay County, Kentucky. They were covers, of the Allens' "Jake Walk Blues" and Byrd Moore's "Jake Leg Blues," but Lomax was unaware of this and assumed that Britton had written them. The folklorist noted that his informant had a severe limp. Britton confirmed (though his family would later deny) that he had been a jake leg victim.

★ ★ ★

Clayton Tyler maintained a small local celebrity as a singer, guitarist, and songwriter, even making an album in the early '70s. I met him in Kilmichael, Mississippi, in 1977, when he generously gave an afternoon to playing guitar with a musician I was recording, fiddler Homer Grice. During a break in the fiddle tunes, I asked Tyler if he remembered his jake song. He did, in pieces, and so did I, in different pieces, and between us we came up with enough of the lyrics to make a recording: probably the first time "Got the Jake Leg Too" had been sung in almost half a century. At that date, a good many jake leg survivors would still have been around.

62

"THE NIGHT HERDING SONG"

Marc Williams
Panachord 25510

Recorded in Dallas, TX, November 26, 1930
Released c. 1933. [Originally released on Brunswick 497 in c. February 1931.]

Reissued on *The Forgotten Singing Cowboy* (Jasmine JASMCD3534)

Online: Spotify, YT

Late in the year 1909, as he was preparing the manuscript of *Cowboy Songs and Other Frontier Ballads*, John A. Lomax received a letter from Harry Stephens, a former student of his at Texas A&M. No, not a letter, exactly, but a piece of a shoebox, on which Stephens had written the words of a song he composed, a cowboy's lullaby to his restless cattle. Lomax thought well enough of "Night-Herding Song" to hurry it into the book, where it stands (in the 1910 first edition) as the last of 112 texts, and the only one in a collection of more or less traditional songs to bear a composer credit.

Half a lifetime later, in 1946, Lomax and Stephens sat at a recording machine, and Stephens told his old professor the story of the song.

> Night herd years ago . . . was the biggest job of the cowboy. . . . [W]e always had so many different squalls and yells and hollers a-trying to keep the cattle quiet, I thought I might as well have a kind of a song to it. So I drifted on up into Yellowstone Park, and got a job a-herding stage horses for Wylie Permanent Camping Company. . . . Well, I had all night to myself, and black gnats eating me up, and those horses didn't have sense enough to stay together . . . so I went ahead and put this song together after several nights' trying.
>
> "Oh, slow up, dogies, quit your roving around . . ."

By then, as both men probably knew, Stephens's song had become a cowboy standard, frequently published in songbooks—generally as "traditional," despite Lomax's clear statement that it wasn't—and on records. During 1927, Vernon Dalhart had cut it three times, as "Lay Down Dogies" or "Cowboy's Night Song," using a motley text only partly derived from Stephens's. The first recording to take Lomax's *Cowboy Songs* text as the authorized version was made in 1930 by a twenty-seven-year-old Texas radio singer named Marc Williams.

Two years earlier, Williams's celebrity on KRLD in Dallas had won him a recording contract with Brunswick, and in 1928–30 he cut twenty sides. Many were cowboy songs, among them the first recording of the bad-man ballad "Cole Younger" and several pieces already waxed by Carl T. Sprague, including "When the Work's All Done This Fall" (➤5). Williams's texts of these, too, were close to those in *Cowboy Songs*. But his delivery was not the jogalong narrative style of older cowboy singers such as Sprague, Jules Verne Allen, or Powder River Jack Lee. Williams was billed "The Cowboy Crooner," and, as well as excellent diction and a microphone-friendly voice, he brought a touch of radio drama to his presentation of these Western tales. In "The Night Herding Song," following the contours of a graceful melody, he skillfully paints the scene: the night, the open ground, the uneasy herd, "forever a-shiftin' around," and the lone rider calming their jitters: "Bunch up . . . lay down . . . lay still."

Such sound-pictures may have charmed radio audiences, but men who had actually been cowboys could be skeptical. In his book *Lone Cowboy: My Life Story*, published three months before Williams's recording, Will James recalled:

> I . . . remember once when I started to sing while on nightguard [i.e., nightwatch]. I'd started sudden and on a pretty high note and come daggone near causing a good stampede. There's writers who say that cowboys sort of sing cattle to sleep and sing on nightherd only for that reason. That strikes me funny, specially when I think of how I near caused a stampede by doing just that. If a cowboy sings on nightherd it's only because he wants to, and not at all to sing any cattle to sleep. Sometimes, on real dark and spooky nights, a rider will hum or sing or whistle while going around the herd, but that's only so they'll know of his coming and won't scare as they might if they didn't see him till he got near.

But Ramon F. Adams, author of *The Old-Time Cowhand*, disagreed:

> If a storm blowed up and the weather got wholesale, the cattle were mighty apt to be so restless you'd have to ride a mile to spit. . . . That was when you had to do some real singin'—maybe till you was plumb tired of it. You might be cussin' the very steers you was ridin' herd on, but as long as you did it to a tune that had that soft accompaniment of squeakin' saddle leather and the tinkle of bridle chains, it was mighty soothin' to a spooky longhorn.

He is supported by the Texas folklorist J. Frank Dobie: "[At night] the cattle seemed to sense that their guards were protectors. Singing to them in the darkness not only kept them aware of their guardians but dimmed out other noises. . . . Some men had an indefinably soothing effect on the longhorns."

★ ★ ★

Released first on Brunswick in 1931, "The Night Herding Song" was reissued a couple of years later on labels in the United Kingdom. These overseas issues have a story of their own.

Since the early days of the business, American record companies had provided foreign subsidiaries or licensees with recordings by popular American singers, instrumentalists, and orchestras. When they developed old-time catalogs, they followed the same policy. The primary overseas market proved to be Australia, where old-time music perhaps appealed to rural homesteading communities who found a kinship between their own lives and attitudes and those of similarly placed folk in the American heartlands. Australia responded with particular warmth to Jimmie Rodgers, licensing the majority of his records, and there arose an indigenous Australian country music cast in much the same mold of singing, yodeling, and guitar-picking, a distant but cousinly echo of the American brand.

The second-largest foreign market for hillbilly music was the UK. Records of American hillbilly music had been released there, very sporadically, since 1924, but the market was galvanized by Carson Robison, whose long stay in England during 1932, making personal appearances, broadcasts, movie shorts, and more than fifty issued recordings, exposed an enormous curiosity about hillbilly music. From London's music publishers and record companies came a stream of hillbilly song folios and discs by other American artists, the records mostly released on cut-price labels in second-tier catalogs, where they were listed alongside accordion bands, brass bands, all-girl pipe bands, comedians, theater organists, minor radio personalities, and veterans of the music hall. One of these labels was Panachord.

Marc Williams and His Cowboys, "each morning (except Sunday) from 7:00 to 7:30 over Radio Station KFJZ. Good Entertainment. Interesting Announcements." The Cowboys are (left to right) "Bill" Stockard, "Pete" Scarborough, and "Bob" Arwine. (Kevin Coffey Collection)

Initially a subsidiary of Warner Brothers–Brunswick, whose blue-and-silver Melotone label provided the model for the English marque, Panachord had access to the riches of the American ARC–Brunswick catalog. In 1932, it was acquired by British Decca, and after 1934 it could also draw on that label's American holdings. Of the 1,047 discs released on Panachord between 1931 and 1939, a remarkable 169 were American hillbilly music: about 16 percent, or almost one release in six—a commitment to this kind of music unequaled by any other British company.

Whoever sat in the selector's chair at Panachord's London offices had the opportunity to sift multifarious monthly stacks of new American releases; to open a window wide on the astonishing diversity of Southern and Western music-making. Lucky him, or her. But not so lucky the curious English record-buyer. The fiddlers, banjo players, and stringbands, the singers of Old and New World ballads and old Tin Pan Alley songs, that predominated in the American catalogs were almost all ignored. Whether it was a rip-roaring stringband like Seven Foot Dilly and His Dill Pickles, or the old-time harmony of the Carter Family, Panachord, though they owned the rights to recordings by both, would have none of them. In all those 169 discs, performances with old-time fiddling or five-string banjo playing amount to no more than a handful.

Exercising this near-total embargo on both instrumental dance music and a large part of the old-time song folio, Panachord focused tightly on three kinds of artist. One was the guitar-playing, yodeling singer in the mold of Jimmie Rodgers, who had built a considerable following in the UK, as in Australia, through local issues of his Victor recordings. Panachord covered this base with Gene Autry, Cliff Carlisle, and an obscure Memphis-based radio singer, "Ramblin' Red" Lowery. Then there were the citybillies like Robison, Frank Luther, Frank Marvin, and Fields and Hall, alias the Colt Brothers (➤63). Above all, the company promoted singers of cowboy or Western songs. The Panachord catalog held a dozen discs each by Goebel Reeves ("The Texas Drifter") and the Ranch Boys, ten by Tex Ritter, seven by the Sons of the Pioneers, five by the Beverly Hill Billies—and eight by Marc Williams. "The Night Herding Song" still shows up, commoner on Panachord than on its original Brunswick pressing.

Hillbilly songs, it appears, were valued by British appraisers not for the regional or stylistic idiosyncrasies of their performers, nor for the particular musical devices they embodied, but for what they seemed to reveal of a storied American West.

One consequence of this bias toward what was thought to be Western music—identified accurately enough in the work of the cowboy artists, but mistakenly in that of Rodgers or Autry—was an enduring British misconception of how country music developed. It was considered the music not of Appalachian farmers or textile-mill workers but of cowboys. So, in the UK, "country and western" remained the standard term for country music long after it had been mothballed in Nashville, resulting, as late as the '60s, in such anomalies as bluegrass albums by the Stanley Brothers being given cover designs of Western gunfighters.

★ ★ ★

When "The Night Herding Song" was issued in the UK, Marcus Dumont "Marc" Williams was working on radio in Texas. He was born on October 21, 1903, in Ellis County, south of Dallas, grew up around the town of Midlothian, and attended the University of Texas. After his spell on KRLD in the late 1920s, he worked briefly on WACO in—well, Waco—then moved to Fort Worth's KSAT, owned by the airline Southern Air Transport, where he shared time with Bob Wills and other acts on a show called Flying the Sunrise Trail: "The entertainers are flying an imaginary airplane, and when a request comes in, they direct the airplane to the home of the fan requesting the number, and sing or play the selection en route" (*Lubbock Avalanche Journal*, July 20, 1930). The article claimed: "Marc gathered his songs first hand on a ranch near Midlothian."

Soon, however, Williams embarked on a voyage over the airwaves: like the dogies he addressed in his song, "forever a-shiftin' around." In 1931, he was on KSTP in St. Paul, Minnesota. He recalled playing at the Hennepin Orpheum in Minneapolis, the posters outside declaring, "Marc Williams in Person," and below, in smaller type, "Also Presenting Bob Hope." A year or two later, he returned to the Dallas–Fort Worth area, and this may be when he worked on KFJZ Fort Worth with a cowboy trio.

Then there was a spell on WLW in Cincinnati: the only job, he would say, that he was ever fired from. "I was doing a show and time came for a commercial. The announcer said to me, 'Could I borrow a

HAPPY HANK OF WHO

Shown here with Squeakie and Popcorn and their magic telescope. They are heard over WHO and the Corn Belt Wireless each weekday morning at 7:45 A. M.

Rural Radio, February 1939. (Courtesy of Dave Sichak)

(Author's Collection)

minute of your time?' and I said, 'Sure, let's sell some of these Frigidaires.'" Unfortunately the show was sponsored by Crosley, Frigidaire's rival in the refrigerator business—and the owner of WLW.

In the mid- to late '30s, Williams made further recordings, for Decca in New York, worked on WTIC in Hartford, Connecticut, and WGY in Schenectady, New York, and published a songbook, *Marc Williams Collection of Favorite Cowboy Songs*. Then, under the moniker "Happy Hank," he wrote, acted in, and produced a children's radio show, which he introduced in 1939 on WHO in Des Moines, Iowa. The program, every weekday morning at 7:45, promoted Coco-Wheats breakfast cereal, and for a while packets of the product contained a "Happy Hank" pitch-pipe. "The folks at WHO," wrote Woody Woods in a feature in *Rural Radio* in 1939,

> know Happy Hank as Marc Williams, a native Texan who was a real cowboy on ranches from the state of his birth to Montana and back again before he was persuaded that the voice [that] had carried melodies across Western ranges while he stood lonely watch over beef on the hoof would please the folks who listened to radio programs.... Into a busy life he has found time to crowd many activities—phonograph recordings, dramatic acting, a series of lectures at Union College [in Lincoln, Nebraska] on "Southwestern Music and Folk Lore" during the summer of 1938—and, of course, selling Coco-Wheats.

In 1941 or '42, Williams's sponsor moved the show to WJR in Detroit. There, for more than a decade, on radio and later television, he was a well-loved figure for a generation of children, who sent him fan letters by the thousands. When he quit the entertainment business is uncertain, but by the mid-'50s he was studying for a law degree. He graduated from Wayne State University in 1960 and practiced as an attorney in Detroit until 1971, when he returned to Fort Worth. "Happy Hank is alive and well and living on Eighth Avenue," proclaimed the *Star-Telegram* in a long article in January 1974. "I can still sing," Williams assured the reporter. "I could still do a radio show. . . . I'm not going to get old if I can help it." He didn't: on June 18 of that year, he suffered a heart attack and was found dead at his office.

63

"ELEVEN MORE MONTHS AND TEN MORE DAYS"—PARTS 1 AND 2

Colt Brothers Accompanied by Rex Cole Mountaineers

Panachord 25029

Recorded in New York, NY, February 5, 1931

Released c. summer 1931. [Originally released on Melotone 12106 and other US issues in spring 1931.]

Online: YT

H. L. Mencken regarded the South as a cultural desert and relished saying so. When he declared Arkansas to be "the most shiftless and backward State in the whole galaxy," the Arkansas House of Representatives responded, on February 6, 1931, with an angry condemnation, one Representative suggesting that the House "have a few minutes of prayer" for the erring journalist. Mencken tersely replied: "My only defense is that I didn't make Arkansas the butt of ridicule—God did it."

Mencken (an almost exact contemporary of Blind Alfred Reed) never, as far as I know, wrote about Southern vernacular music. The nearest he came was to remark that the arts in the South were held in suspicion, "save in the lower reaches of the gospel hymn, the phonograph and the chautauqua harangue." So, even at what we think of as its best, hillbilly music would probably not have charmed him. But encountering it at what might have been somewhere near its *worst* . . . what a jeremiad he might have composed!

He would soon have had the opportunity. The day before that mighty decision by the solons of Arkansas, a gang of radio and recording-studio hired hands in New York had gathered to put on wax a number called "Eleven More Months and Ten More Days." For the next year or so, it would be one of the most irritatingly memorable sounds to rise above the babel of Tin Pan Alley.

The song is the sardonic reflection of a convict who has been "in the hoosegow twenty days . . . all on account of a gallon of corn that I thought I could drink." He recounts the old joke about the jailbird who asks what time it is, only to be told: "What do you care? You ain't goin' any place." In Part 2, the narrator is back in jail again, similarly sentenced, because "I didn't like the wife's blue hat, so I socked her in the eye." Threaded through this decrepit vaudeville routine is the refrain

> In eleven more months and ten more days,
> I'll be out of the calaboose;
> In eleven more months and ten more days,
> They're going to turn me loose.

Cornball clarinet, accordion, and banjo accompany the vocal duettists, billed as the "Colt Brothers." They were actually a pair of experienced recording-studio professionals, singer Arthur Fields, born Abraham Finkelstein (1888–1953), a veteran of the minstrel and vaudeville stage and a seasoned freelance recordist, and pianist/singer Fred Hall (1898–1964), who led a busy recording orchestra known as Fred "Sugar" Hall's Sugar Babies. The two men were also a prolific songwriting team.

Early in 1930, Hall had decided to redeploy some of his studio associates, including clarinetist Ed Grosso, accordionist Charles Magnante, and guitarist and banjoist Al Russo, in hillbilly lineups, for which he and Fields unreeled a string of songs with titles like "Down at the Bottom of the Mountain," "Down by the Old Cabin Door," "In Dear Old Tennessee," "After the Old Barn Dance," and "On the Old Hay Ride in the Morning." These recording

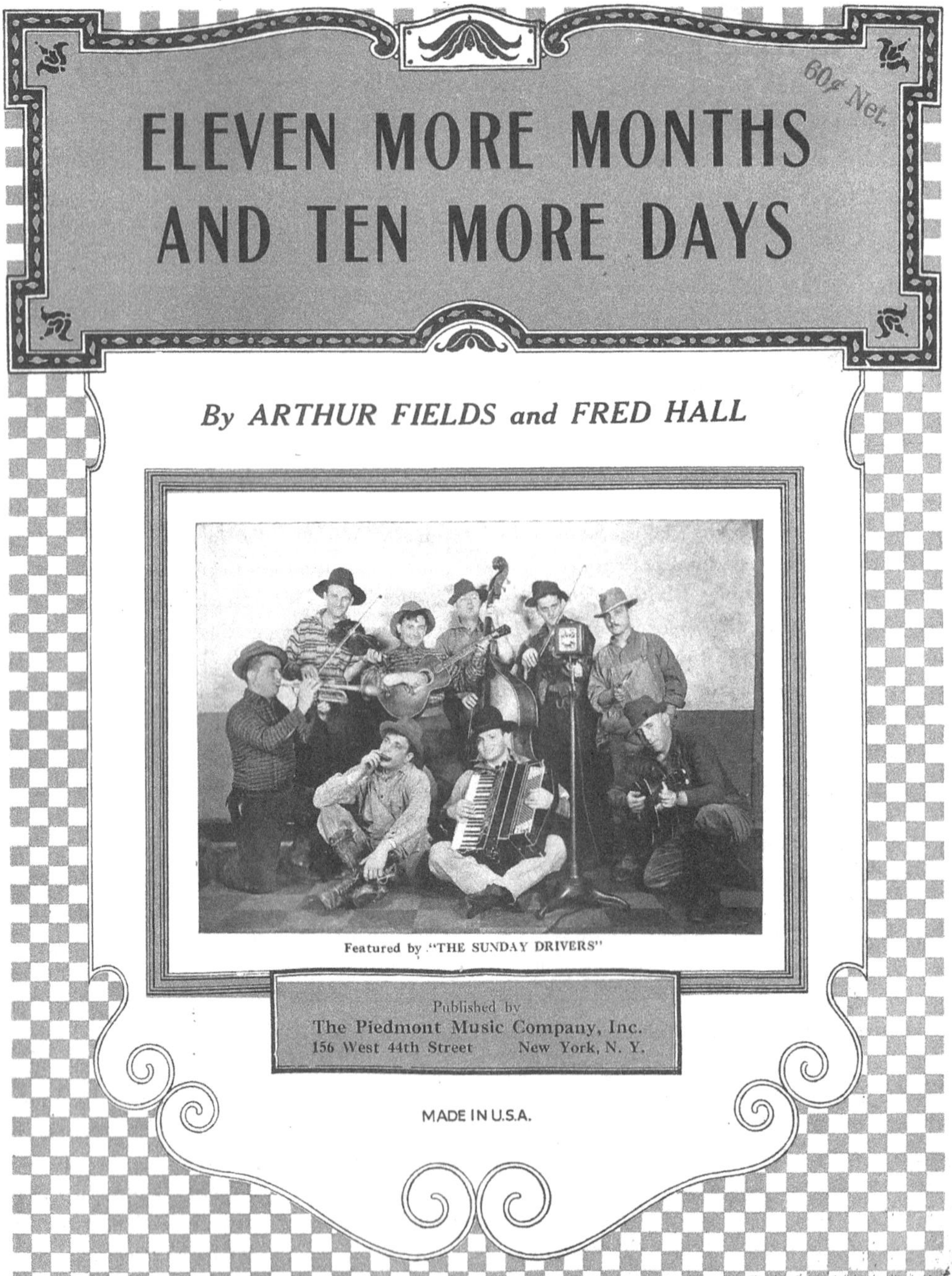

(Author's Collection)

entities were variously named "Eddie Younger and His Mountaineers," "Buck Wilson and His Rangers," "Sam Cole and His Cornhuskers," and the "Rex Cole Mountaineers." The only one of these titular bandleaders who was real was Rex Cole, a Michigander who had made his name in New York as an inventive lighting company salesman, was now in charge of promoting General Electric's new electric refrigerator, and had the notion of doing so through hillbilly radio programs.

The music historian Allan Sutton tentatively dates Hall's first move "from pseudo-jazz to pseudo-country" to spring 1929, when Fields recorded a couple of rustic numbers composed by himself and Hall, and credits the two men with devising "one of the first acts to develop and exploit the unfortunate 'hillbilly' stereotype that later found expression in the like of the 'Lil' Abner' comic strip and the long-running TV series *The Beverly Hillbillies*." As described earlier (➤35), several other ensembles had already contributed to the creation of the hillbilly as an archetype of all-American entertainment, from Al Hopkins's Hill Billies (➤2) and Otto Gray's Oklahoma Cowboys to the Arkansas Travelers and the Pickard and Crockett families. Indeed, they were perhaps doing so more effectively, since they were stage as well as broadcasting and recording acts, whereas the Fields–Hall musicians operated mostly in the studio.

Sutton argues that, unlike the (original) Beverly Hill Billies, a contemporary radio hillbilly band based in Los Angeles, "which made some attempt to honor the musical traditions they were scavenging so successfully, Fields and Hall often lampooned those traditions and pandered to their audience with the most blatant stereotypes. For their film short, various band members donned bib overalls and false beards, passed around a jug, and waved a shotgun. . . ." This gives the Fields–Hall crew too much historical (dis) credit: the Hill Billies were bearding-up years earlier, bib overalls had long been staples of the stage-hillbilly wardrobe, and the description of the movie short could probably be reapplied without many changes (possibly losing the shotgun) to the Blue Ridge Ramblers (➤35).

Some New York reviewers were unenthusiastic: "Caught the Rex Cole Mountaineers at WEAF. Fifteen minutes of nasal noises" . . . "The longest five minutes I ever sat through: when one of the Rex Cole mountaineers did 'Just Break the News to Mother' as a vocal solo." Nevertheless, the group appealed to Northeastern radio listeners and in spring 1931, NBC signed them up to a new contract worth $175,000, more than even Amos 'n' Andy were earning. One of the columnists reporting the deal sourly commented, "The Rex Cole Mountaineers . . . are just a bunch of city slickers who think the Mason–Dixon line is a jerk-water railroad in Kentucky" (Madison [Wisconsin] *Capital Times*, March 15, 1931). But the syndicated columnist A. T. S., "The Man in the Street," greeted it with a whoop:

> Their fan mail indicates that millions of listeners prefer the sentimental ballads and melodies of the nasal hillbillies to the frenzied jazz pieces and the tiresome blues songs which have been worn to a frazzle by constant and apparently never-ending repetition. . . .
>
> The Rex Cole Mountaineers are: Long Tom of Tennessee [i.e., Arthur Fields], singer of ballads; Tom Emerson, who plays the bull fiddle; Eddie Young [i.e., probably, Fred Hall], director; Al McCoy [i.e., Al Russo], who plays the guitar; Eddie Stokes, player of the violin, jewsharp, harmonica and sweet potato; his brother, Gus Stokes, who plays the bass jug; Leo Hartman [i.e., Leo McConville], cornetist; and Charley Briggs [i.e., Charles Magnante], accordionist.
>
> They are real hillbillies and through Cole they are receiving more money than they believed ever existed.
>
> Well brother, all of us differ in our tastes when it comes to doughnuts, likker and music but personally we prefer to hear the Rex Cole Mountaineers play "The Waltz of the Hills" or "The Train That Never Arrived" to the crooning of Rudy Vallee, the lisping of the "Boopdeboop" gal, Helen Kane[,] or the throaty "Surrender" of Helen Morgan. (Port Huron [Michigan] *Times Herald*, February 21, 1931)

But what would a Southern or Midwestern audience have made of the Mountaineers? They might not have cared about the accuracy of the New Yorkers' self-presentation, but wouldn't they at least have been puzzled by the inaccuracy of their *music*, the caricature of hillbilly playing proffered by those squawking clarinets, chug-a-lug accordions, jew's harps, and ocarinas?

Another UK issue, pseudonymized. (Author's Collection)

Probably not. All those instruments had already featured on records by Carson Robison and Frank Luther, Vernon Dalhart, and Bob Miller. Such supposedly uncanonical sounds may discomfit some present-day enthusiasts, but the people who originally bought the records were evidently untroubled, or they would have stopped buying them.

★ ★ ★

All that said, perhaps no special pleading can save "Eleven More Months and Ten More Days" from scorn and derision. But there is a reason for taking it at least half-seriously: its extraordinary popularity, not merely in the United States, but across the English-speaking world.

It was first recorded by Dalhart, for Victor in November 1929, and twice for other labels the following January, when Arthur Fields also did it, for Okeh, under the name of Lem Greene. John I. White, "The Lone Star Ranger," was commissioned to record it on February 5, 1930, a year to the day before the Colt Brothers. A specialist in cowboy songs, White didn't care for such Northern novelties, but they earned him $75 a selection, so he held his peace and made the record, which eventually appeared on more than a dozen labels. Perhaps prompted by this activity with their composition, in April, Fields and Hall registered it for copyright. In September, Dalhart introduced it, "a jail epic which has never before been publicly presented," on the coast-to-coast Maxwell House Ensemble radio program, as announced in the *Atlanta Constitution* (September 25) and other papers. At the end of the year, the Hal Roach movie comedy *High C's* featured "Eleven More Months" as its closing number.

When Fields and Hall finally waxed it themselves in February 1931, the recording was promptly issued in the United States, Canada, where a reviewer in the *Winnipeg Evening Tribune* greeted it as "a comedy negro duet . . . very funny as to words, and sprightly as to air," the United Kingdom (twice), and Australia, where the reviewer for the *Sydney Morning Herald*, having praised the first recordings of pianist Vladimir Horowitz, even-handedly commended the Colt Brothers' record for its "good amusement."

Later that month, Fields and Hall recorded it again, for Crown, under yet another billing, Gunboat Billy and The Sparrow. Almost a year later, the Colt Brothers were reconstituted for Parts 3 and 4 of the hoosegow saga. The song was retained in the public memory long enough for Gene Autry to sing it with Smiley Burnette in the 1940 Western movie *Ride, Tenderfoot, Ride.*

But this was nothing compared to its success in the UK. Though American renditions were readily available by the Colt Brothers and John I. White, English recording directors feverishly commissioned versions by leading dance orchestras such as those of Jack Hylton, Debroy Somers, Billy Cotton, and Bert Ambrose, who turned it into a comedy-foxtrot farrago of the original text with added verses, an opening in a courtroom, and interpolations of popular songs from "Sonny Boy" to "I'm Happy When I'm Hiking." It was done by studio groups and by popular vocalists, even, improbably, the romantic crooner Al Bowlly. One of the more eccentrically billed covers was by The Borstal Collegians—supposed alumni of the British correctional institution, actually studio musicians including the prolific singer Fred Douglas. Seventy years later, the song turned up on an album of pub singalongs by the Cockney duo Chas and Dave.

Why did the British take so warmly to "Eleven More Months?" Because it was so hilarious? Because it seemed like an authentic vignette of hard-boiled American low life—Damon Runyon set to music? Neither explanation seems to fit. Maybe it was just a craze, irrational and ephemeral, like flagpole sitting, marathon dancing, or mahjong. If so, it was the only one to implicate hillbilly music, for better or worse.

64

"WHEN KATIE COMES DOWN TO THE GATE"/ "A LITTLE WHITE ROSE"

Murphy Bros.
Superior 2716

Recorded in Richmond, IN, June 11, 1931
Released in September 1931
Sold 352

William Judson Murphy, farmer, of Cross Keys, South Carolina, had the habit of noting his expenses in a small pocketbook. In May 1931, he bought brown sugar (10 cents), matches (20 cents), beans (25 cents), "record needles" (10 cents), a bucket of lard (95 cents), and other everyday goods. June's accounts were similar at first, but then, on the 6th, he paid a dime to his nieces "Cecil & Evelin for song ballards [*sic*]." A week later, he logged the purchase, for a dollar, of five gallons of gas for a "trip to Richmond Ind."

Later, he wrote alongside this entry, "557 miles"—no easy journey on 1931 roads, and that was only one way. The whole venture must have taken several days. Judson noted expenses of $6.55, presumably for more gas and maybe lodging, and a disbursement of $10 to his son Ralph, perhaps for doing the driving.

And the point of this round trip of over 1,100 miles? The clue is "Richmond Ind." Judson Murphy was heading for Gennett Records.

On June 11, there gathered in the company's studio, under the billing "Murphy Bros.," probably four men, two playing harmonicas, two guitars, three of them singing. For their first number they selected "When Katie Comes Down to the Gate," a playful, teasing song in which a girl, off to meet her sweetheart, assures her mother that she won't go astray: "Only as far as the gate, dear Ma." They followed it with a heart-piercing ode of betrayed love, "A Little White Rose."

These are archetypal old-time songs, published pieces of the late nineteenth century that held their appeal for later generations and through them took on a new life, breaking out of the chrysalis of sheet music and alighting on the whirling surface of a phonograph record. Such translated compositions were the bedrock of old-time music, the reason why it was *called* old-time music. And here, eight years on—almost to the day—from Fiddlin' John Carson's log cabin song (➤1), we find artists and record companies still engaged in the double collaboration of presenting these old songs anew on phonograph records, and busily searching for more to keep the whole operation going.

★ ★ ★

On a manuscript of "When Katie Comes Down to the Gate" that the Murphys took with them to

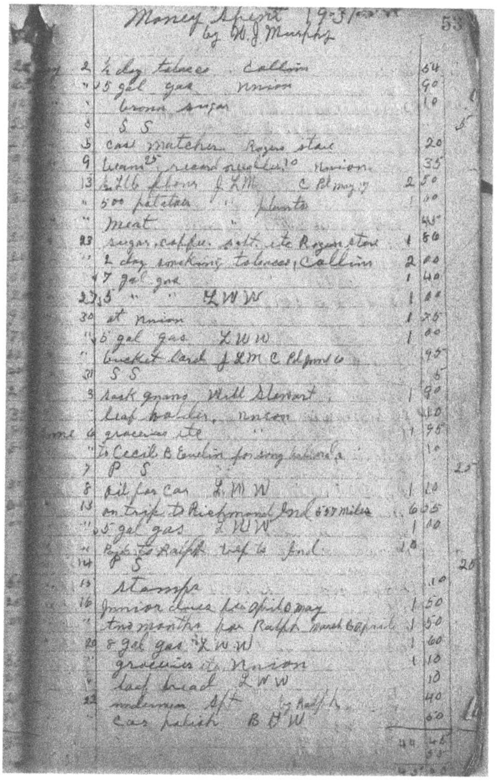
Money Spent 1931
by W. J. Murphy

Judson Murphy's expenses, May–June 1931. (Dale Murphy Collection)

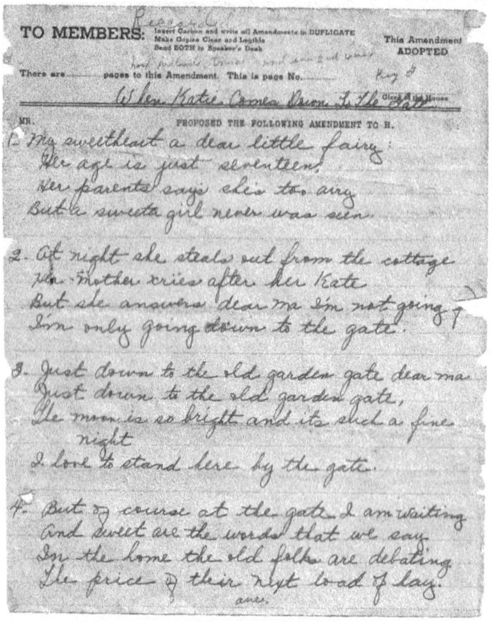

TO MEMBERS: Insert Carbon and write all Amendments in DUPLICATE
Make Copies Clear and Legible
Send BOTH to Speaker's Desk

This Amendment
ADOPTED

There are ——— pages to this Amendment. This is page No. ———

When Katie Comes Down To The Gate — Clerk of the House

MR. ——— PROPOSED THE FOLLOWING AMENDMENT TO H.

1. My sweetheart a dear little fairy:
Her age is just seventeen;
Her parents says she's too airy
But a sweeta girl never was seen.

2. At night she steals out from the cottage
Her mother cries after her Kate
But she answers dear ma I'm not going
I'm only going down to the gate.

3. Just down to the old garden gate dear ma
Just down to the old garden gate,
The moon is so bright and its such a fine night
I love to stand here by the gate.

4. But of course at the gate I am waiting
And sweet are the words that we say
In the home the old folks are debating
The price of their next load of hay.

(Dale Murphy Collection)

Richmond, Judson noted: "Written by Jason Brown, Boaz, Ala." Brown was originally from Beech Springs in Spartanburg County, South Carolina, while the Murphys lived just a few miles south in Union County. Presumably, they had the song from Brown, but it was not his. It had been published in 1882, when Judson Murphy was two years old and Brown not even born, under the title "I'm Just Going Down to the Gate," written, and introduced to the stage, by Gus Williams, a comedian and singer who made his name in the 1870s with Tony Pastor's vaudeville company. Another of his compositions was taken up in the recording era, "See That My Grave Is Kept Green," which was recorded by the Virginian banjo player and singer Bela Lam, and by the Carter Family.

When the Murphys brought their version of "I'm Just Going Down to the Gate" to Richmond, it had already been recorded by Uncle Dave Macon as "Only As Far As the Gate, Dear Ma" (Vocalion, 1926) and by Red Patterson's Piedmont Log Rollers as "My Sweetheart's a Shy Little Fairy" (Victor, 1927). The Log Rollers had also recorded the Murphys' "white rose" number, as had the Kentucky Ramblers. We know Judson Murphy listened to records—remember that dime he spent on Victrola needles—but none of these recordings is particularly like the Murphys' texts, which are more likely to have been derived from the "ballards" Judson had bought from his nieces.

However they came by "When Katie Comes Down to the Gate," why did the Murphys choose to record it? Because others had given it status by doing so? Because it had been a favorite piece of their parents? What did this gently amusing, half-a-century-old tale of youthful courtship *mean* to long-married men in their forties or fifties? Perhaps it was simply a pretty tune that they enjoyed playing. But we may wonder if a song like this gave musicians and listeners alike an access to, or a release of, sentimental feeling that might otherwise be regarded as unmanly.

★ ★ ★

The Cross Keys Murphys trace their ancestry back to an Irishman, Richard Murphy, who was kidnaped in 1670 to be a cabin boy and work for a Byrd family in Virginia. There had been Murphys in Cross Keys since the late eighteenth century, when Simon Murphy II received a land grant in Union County. Judson's grandfather Jason Wiley Murphy, born in 1811, was a well-to-do farmer who in 1860 owned land worth $5,000. He and several later generations of Murphys lie in the graveyard of Padgetts Creek Baptist Church, among them most of the men we shall meet here. Cross Keys was once an extensive plantation, but by 1931 it was a small community, and it remains so today.

According to R. D. Murphy of Cross Keys, the Murphy Brothers we hear on the record are Judson and his cousin David (R. D.'s grandfather) on harmonicas, together with R. D.'s father Dewey and cousin Merrill on guitars. The only problem about this lineup is that no two of those men were brothers.

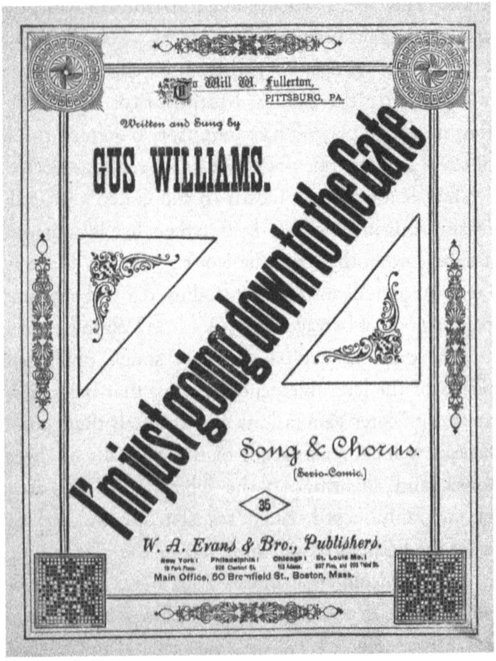

(Author's Collection)

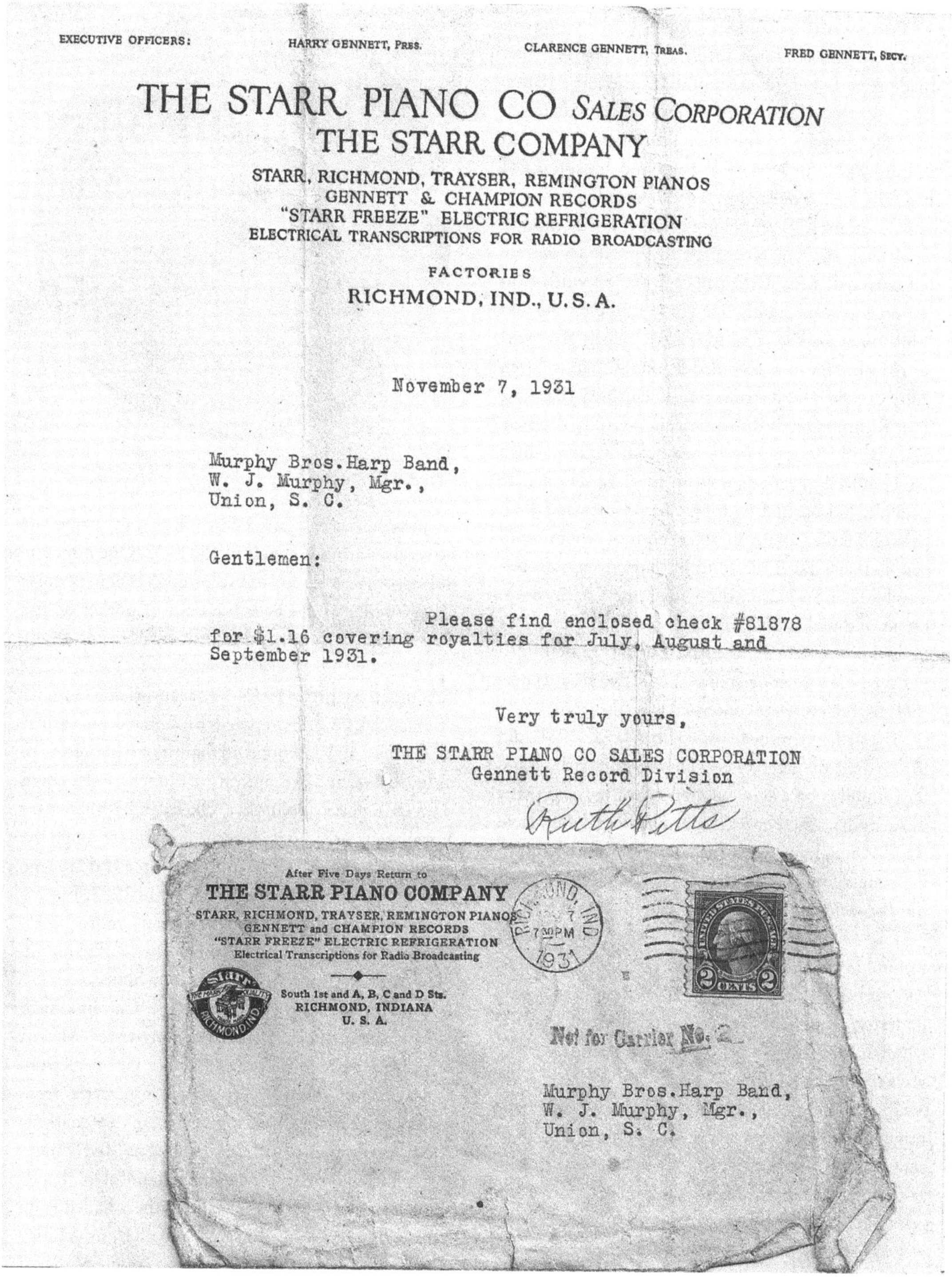

EXECUTIVE OFFICERS: HARRY GENNETT, PRES. CLARENCE GENNETT, TREAS. FRED GENNETT, SECY.

THE STARR PIANO CO SALES CORPORATION
THE STARR COMPANY
STARR, RICHMOND, TRAYSER, REMINGTON PIANOS
GENNETT & CHAMPION RECORDS
"STARR FREEZE" ELECTRIC REFRIGERATION
ELECTRICAL TRANSCRIPTIONS FOR RADIO BROADCASTING
FACTORIES
RICHMOND, IND., U. S. A.

November 7, 1931

Murphy Bros.Harp Band,
W. J. Murphy, Mgr.,
Union, S. C.

Gentlemen:

Please find enclosed check #81878 for $1.16 covering royalties for July, August and September 1931.

Very truly yours,
THE STARR PIANO CO SALES CORPORATION
Gennett Record Division
Ruth Pitts

(Dale Murphy Collection)

Perhaps the Richmond crew were relying on name recognition, for Murphy family members had made records before: six months earlier, in Atlanta, for Columbia. They were very likely put in touch with the company by the talent scout Byrum Lawson in nearby Union (➤51, 57). Then, too, Judson noted his outgoings: a dollar for gas, 20 cents for bananas, and, in Atlanta, 50 cents for a Hohner harmonica.

Among the four recordings they made (two were left unissued) were "Downfall of Paris," in which twin harmonicas exuberantly fox-chase through the old fiddle tune, and the vocal trio "Little Bunch of Roses," an old-time favorite, recorded by more than a dozen other artists. The instrumental lineup was the same as at Richmond, billed this time as "Murphy Brothers Harp Band." So again we have a brother claim, which can be solved in various ways in this large family: for example, Judson had twin brothers, James and John (Merrill's father), born in 1883, both of whom could play and sing. For Dale Murphy, Judson's grandson, a possible lineup is Judson, his twin brothers, their cousin David, and perhaps Merrill. R. D. Murphy believes it's his dad Dewey singing the bass part on "Little Bunch of Roses." The exact personnel on the two records may elude us, but everyone concerned was a Murphy.

The Atlanta record, issued in March 1931, did better than the later one, selling almost a thousand for Columbia on the home market but twice as many in Australia, where it was issued on Regal and, later, Regal-Zonophone. Since the Murphys were unknown in that territory, and the term "Harp Band" ambiguous, the disc was simply credited to "Mouth Organ Band."

★ ★ ★

Columbia paid respectable fees, typically $50 a side, and perhaps Judson Murphy, as the band's manager, undertook the Richmond trip in the hope of a similar windfall. In 1931, there would have been few other ways to earn that kind of money.

If he knew much about the record business, though, he might have been disappointed that their songs were first issued on a Gennett subsidiary. Superior had an extensive catalog of nearly 350 releases, including blues, jazz, and popular songs, as well as old-time music, but it operated in the economically straitened period of 1930–32, and although the sales of "When Katie Comes Down to the Gate"/"A Little White Rose" would prove to be meager, they were by no means the label's lowest. Surprisingly, when the record was reissued a year later on Gennett's more widely distributed Champion label, it did even worse: in the nine months it was on the market, it sold just 193 copies.

(Chris King Collection)

Judson Murphy jotted down the royalty payments he received from Gennett in 1931–32. One hopes he did negotiate a fee for the recording session, because otherwise he would have been out of pocket on the deal. Fifteen months' royalties amounted to just $4.40.

★ ★ ★

Around that time, 1931–33, a surprising number of musicians were prepared to embark on similar expeditions to Richmond, in a spirit of what seems to us like brave, or naïve, optimism. But where else could they have gone? Columbia, Okeh, and Brunswick–Vocalion had ceased their recording trips through the South in 1930 or '31; Victor hung on a little longer, making trips to Atlanta and Dallas in 1932. But for many would-be recordists, Gennett, more accessible in eastern Indiana than the other companies in New York or Chicago, was their only hope.

A few more came up from South Carolina, such as the shoemaker, singer, and songwriter Merritt Smith from Greenville; singer Arthur Cornwall from Chester; and the Palmetto Male Quartette from Glendale. Probably from somewhere in the Ozarks, a trio of fiddle, piano, and guitar, billed as "Ted" Sharp, Hinman, and Sharp, brought a handful of handsome tunes such as "Pike's Peak." Others hailed from West Virginia, Ohio, or Missouri. And from Whitley County in southeastern Kentucky, a couple of sacred groups, the Buffalo Ragged Five and the S. E. Mullis Blue Diamond Sextette, drove to Richmond to dispense the good word in a bad season.

Like the Murphys' disc, few if any of these records sold more than a few hundred. There was nothing wrong with the music, which was strong and fine. It was the times that were out of joint.

65

"PROSPERITY IS JUST AROUND WHICH CORNER?"/ "WHAT ARE YOU SQUAWKIN' ABOUT?"

Carson Robison Trio
Conqueror 7935

Recorded in New York, January 7, 1932
Released in 1932

Online: YT ["Prosperity Is Just Around Which Corner?"]

"Prosperity is just around the corner" was a phrase much bandied about in the aftermath of the Wall Street Crash. "How many times have we heard that expression used in the last two years?" asked an ad in the Opelousas [Louisiana] *Clarion-News* on June 25, 1931. "How many times have we said[,] 'It means nothing, they are empty words'? Still we have used them, we have listened to them, we have laughed at them and sneered at them, still through all of this depression they have been the one thing that has kept us hopeful; that has kept us in the fight. . . ." All this was a preamble to an advertisement for farm equipment and supplies: calcium arsenate, dusting guns, poultry mash.

Roaming through the newspaper archives of the early '30s, one stumbles repeatedly on this optimistic phrase: in editorials, in letters, in cartoon strips; spoken in hope, in jest, in disgust. It is supposed to have been said by Herbert Hoover, but historians have searched in vain for a documented instance of him uttering those words in that order. Possibly he used similar expressions, such as "good times are around the corner," in his broadcasts at any time from 1929 to 1932. More likely, "prosperity is just around the corner" was (as *The American Heritage Dictionary of American Quotations* suggests) "a popular distillation of various statements of assurance made by Hoover and others following the 1929 stock market crash. . . . Eventually the phrase became an ironic joke, used mockingly as a political attack phrase by the Democrats."

Whatever the origin of the phrase, Carson Robison brilliantly deployed it to evoke the skeptical mood of the time in his song "Prosperity Is Just Around Which Corner?"

> Everywhere you go, everyone you meet,
> All they talk about is this Depression.
> They blame it on the war, they blame it on Wall Street,
> On politics and this administration.
> For two years now we've been assured, good times are on the way.
> I wonder how much longer we must hear them talk this way—
>
> *Prosperity is just around the corner!*
> What we'd like to know is, which corner?
> We've turned so many corners now, we're dizzy.
> *But still I'm positive we'll soon be busy!*
> *Why, I read in Monday's paper how ten thousand men were hired!*
> Yes, but Tuesday they forgot to say twelve thousand more were fired.
> *But I insist this land of ours is stable!*
> Stable? Sound like horses' to me.

Robison is the primary vocalist, but someone else, probably his regular duet partner Frank Luther, takes on the Hooveresque role of the perpetual optimist (speaking the italicized lines), sounding like a typically orotund politician, while Robison replies in the pinched, snarky voice of the eternal doubter.

"*Why, can't you understand why I'm so cheery?*

"Yes, just like I understand the Einstein theory."

It is an excellent song, one of Robison's best: clever, funny, and relevant. Nearly ninety years on, its point is still sharp.

On the reverse of the record (actually selected as the A-side), "What Are You Squawkin' About?" is put over

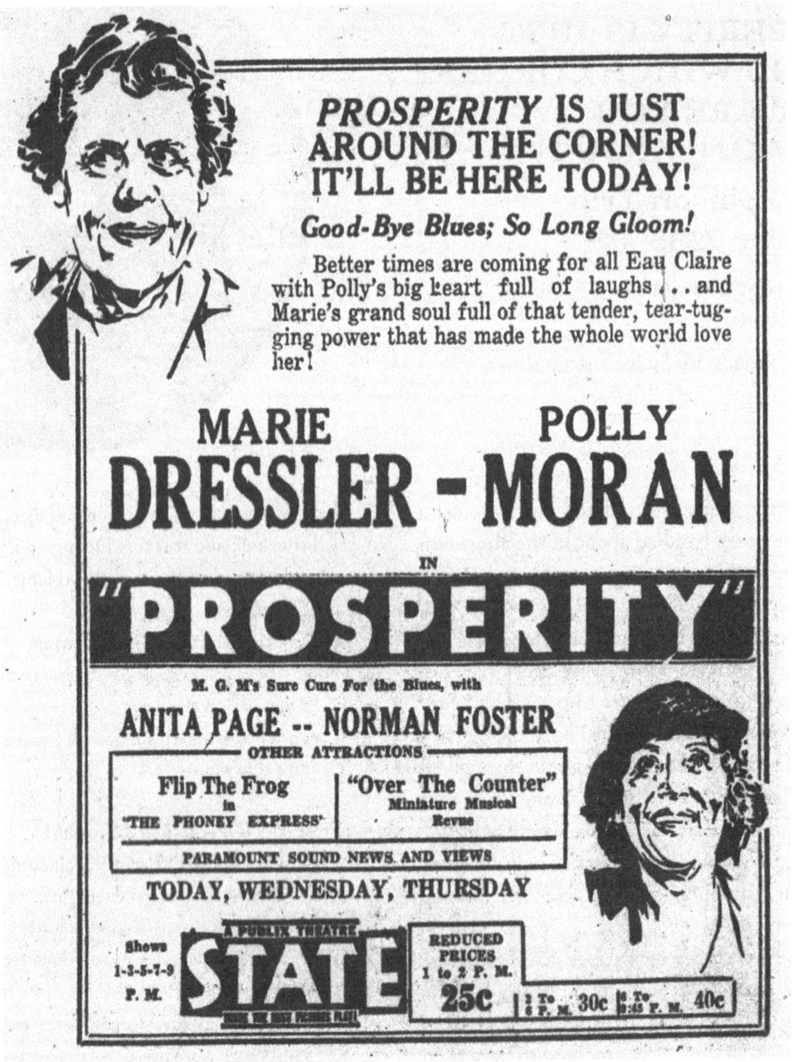

Movie ad in the Eau Claire [Wisconsin] *Leader-Telegraph*, December 13, 1932. (Author's Collection)

in the swaggering style of Robison's earlier hit "Barnacle Bill the Sailor," with a clumping accompaniment of mandolin, guitar, and brass bass. Robison's attitude is brusque and challenging: you think you've got troubles? Get over yourself. What about the farmers? He then directs his scorn toward the New Woman—smoke and drink all you please, but don't complain if no one gives you his seat—and finally at Prohibitionists, who have created a world where "good honest people are hungry and bare, And the bootlegger making a million a year."

★ ★ ★

Carson Robison had experience with topical songs. He and Luther had collaborated on recordings of "When the Roses Bloom for the Bootlegger" (➤32), "Farm Relief Song," and Robison's sansculottic fantasy "Poor Man's Heaven," in which the hobos take over the banks and feast on strawberry pie. The two men had also covered Bob Miller's "Eleven Cent Cotton" (➤30) for several labels and since late 1931 had been working closely with Miller, recording his compositions like "Twenty-One Years." Miller probably plays the piano on "Prosperity," but the session may owe more to him than that. Until then, Robison, though expert at concocting many of the kinds of material required by the hillbilly disc industry, had never written an explicit, state-of-the-nation

(OTM Collection)

political song. Perhaps Miller, who had, inspired him to try.

So Robison produced these two topical pieces—only to return, at his next session, to the American-pastoral songs he had made his name with, like "When It's Springtime in the Blue Ridge Mountains." If he was so skillful at writing political songs that accurately, amusingly, and even angrily caught the popular mood of the moment, why did he stop?

The answer may lie in the state of the hillbilly music industry. Most of the energy of the previous decade's recording impulse had drained away. Jimmie Rodgers, the Carter Family, and Gene Autry were still making records, as were Miller (the most prolific of all of them, with sixty-some sides to Rodgers's twenty), Welling and McGhee, the Allen Brothers, Cliff Carlisle, and a few other acts; but the majority of the money-making recordists of 1920s hillbilly music were no longer on a record-company payroll. During 1932, there would be no recordings at all by Fiddlin' John Carson, Ernest V. Stoneman, Henry Whitter, Riley Puckett, Gid Tanner, Uncle Dave Macon, Smith's Sacred Singers, the McCravy Brothers, Frankie Marvin. . . . The list could be prolonged. If prosperity in the record business was just around the corner, it was well hidden.

NOTES AND COMMENTS.

By the Editor.

CARSON ROBISON'S AMERICAN PIONEERS.

SEVERAL days ago, at the invitation of Alvin D. Keech, I went over to the Savoy Hotel and there met Carson Robison's American Pioneers. This well-known quartet of American fretted-instrumentalists and vocalists are on a visit to this country for the purpose of fulfilling radio, recording, cabaret and concert recitals.

A special feature of their entertainment is the singing of Hill-Billies to the quiet accompaniment of guitars and banjos. A Hill-Billy is a sort of folk-song and, like the Negro spiritual, its whole appeal is in the way it is sung—with sincerity and emotion.

On this page is reproduced a photograph showing the players as they appear in their stage costumes. Carson Robison, the leader, is the third from the left holding the guitar. He it is who orchestrates for the quartet and who is the prime mover in the exploitation of the Hill-Billy songs. On the right and left of the photo are the brothers Mitchell, Bill and John, natives of Tennessee, and players of both banjo and guitar. They played me several excellent banjo duets, with good musical taste and extraordinary technical ability. The other member of the troupe is Pearl Pickens, contralto vocalist.

Since their arrival in this country two or three weeks ago, Carson Robison's American Pioneers have recorded many of their best numbers for H.M.V., Columbia, Decca and other companies. I advise readers to look out for these in the new gramophone lists.

CARSON ROBISON'S AMERICAN PIONEERS.

* * *

COMPETITION FOR BANJO QUARTETS, FINGER STYLE.

The Southern Section of the British Federation of Banjoists, Mandolinists and Guitarists has decided to run a

Soon after his arrival in London, Robison was visited by Emile Grimshaw, banjoist and editor of *B. M. G.*, a British magazine for banjo, mandolin, and guitar players. This article appeared in the June 1932 issue. (Author's Collection)

So record companies' doors—if they were not already swinging in the wind because the offices had closed down—were opening less readily than they used to, even to proven money-makers like Robison. For the rest of the '30s, he would log only a couple of dozen recordings on American soil. He was now working mostly on radio, where nervous program-makers and sponsors would look dubiously at songs satirizing politicians and bankers. Then, in April 1932, he and his Pioneers, the guitar- and banjo-playing Mitchell brothers and singer Pearl Pickens, sailed to London, where they would be based for the next five months, and where songs about the American political scene would only have confused British audiences that looked to Robison and his gang for campfire cowboy singsongs.

★ ★ ★

Robison returned home in time to witness November's presidential election, in which Franklin D. Roosevelt trounced Hoover in both the electoral college and the popular vote and initiated one of the most remarkable periods in twentieth-century American history: the era not only of immense New Deal public works projects—the

Two decades after Robison's trips to the UK, his legacy was still visible in publications like this, given away with copies of the British comic *The Hotspur* in the late 1950s. The contents range from songs Robison claimed as his own, such as "Hand Me Down My Walking Cane" and "Red River Valley," and "She'll Be Comin' Round the Mountain" (➤35), to English songs associated with World War II and the Boy Scouts. (Author's Collection)

Civilian Conservation Corps, the National Recovery Administration, the Public Works Administration, the Works Progress Administration—but also of cultural expansion, through the Federal Writers Project, the Federal Theater Project, the photographers working for the Resettlement Administration and subsequently the Farm Security Administration, the ethnomusicologists collecting for the Archive of Folk Song at the Library of Congress, the series of *American Guides* to each of the forty-eight states in the Union, the post-office muralists. . . .

If the topical hillbilly recordings the industry chose to release during the Roosevelt years are representative, such as Gid Tanner's "Prosperity and Politics" (1934) (➤17) and Bill Cox's "Franklin Roosevelt's Back Again"/"The Democratic Donkey (Is in His Stall Again)" (1936), then old-time musicians were solidly behind FDR. Maybe Robison was too, or perhaps he just sensed that political satire was out of favor. At any rate, for almost a decade, the writer of "Prosperity Is Just Around Which Corner?" and "What Are You Squawkin' About?" checked his topical guns at the studio door. He left them there until he needed them again: in December 1941, when he recorded a quartet of anti-Japanese songs in response to the attack on Pearl Harbor eleven days earlier. Soon afterward, he expanded his patriotic portfolio with pieces like "Mussolini's Letter to Hitler" and "1942 Turkey in the Straw," reputedly that year's best-selling country record.

Robison's remarkable career as singer and songwriter culminated not with a cinematic evocation of mountain, prairie, or trail, but with a dry-as-dust narration put in the mouth of a dejected countryman, "Life Gets Tee-Jus, Don't It?" (1948). "The tin roof leaks and the chimney leans. . . . The cow's gone dry and the hens won't lay. . . . Debts and taxes, and so it goes . . ." If prosperity had indeed been waiting round the corner for rural America, it had passed this luckless farmer by; but, with an irony that Carson Robison might have greeted with a wry grin, this weary catalog of agricultural woe became the most valuable property of his thirty-some years in music.

66

"THAT'S MY RABBIT—MY DOG CAUGHT IT"

Walter Family
Champion S-16653

Recorded in Richmond, IN, March 29, 1933
Released in c. October 1933
Sold 108

Reissued on *Kentucky Mountain Music* (Yazoo 2200), *Ruckus Juice & Chittlins, Vol. 1* (Yazoo 2032)

Online: Spotify, YT

In a magisterial television history of modern art, the critic Robert Hughes argued that the twentieth-century art market had made it impossible to look at a famous painting and simply absorb it as art: our contemplation was now irredeemably tainted by the thought of how much it was worth.

Records have not attained the saleroom value of Leonardos or Légers, partly for the obvious reason that they are not singular but were manufactured in quantity. But they are no longer available in quantity, and in some cases only one or two copies are known to exist. These few survivors from the shipwreck of history are on their way up the price ladder. Numerous blues 78s command five figures. In 2013, a Tommy Johnson Paramount, one of two known copies, fetched $37,100, still an eBay record for a 78. In May 2020, a fine copy of a Charlie Patton Vocalion fetched $23,855.55. Old-time 78s have been slower to rise into that stratosphere, but in 2005, one of two known copies of Brunswick 595, the Georgia Pot Lickers' "Up Jumped the Rabbit"/"Chicken Don't Roost Too High," featuring fiddlers Lowe Stokes and A. A. Gray, was sold for $10,126.05. In 2017, a probably unique Paramount test-pressing of "Whoa Mule"/"Some Mother's Boy" by the Kentucky Ramblers (the Bird family from Williamsburg, Kentucky) reached $9,350 at auction. Such precise figures are usually hard to come by, because when records of this value change hands, the negotiations are often private. But seasoned collectors know what these rarities are.

One such record is "That's My Rabbit—My Dog Caught It" by the Walter Family. Paterfamilias and fiddler Draper Eades Walter (1870–1955) was born in Jessamine County, Kentucky, in or near the largely African American community of Camp Nelson. This was also home to a close contemporary, the African American fiddler Jim Booker, and the two men knew and played music with each other. Booker came to the attention of the talent agent Dennis W. Taylor in adjoining Madison County, and twice in 1927 he and other Taylor talent were dispatched to the Gennett studios in Richmond, Indiana (➤14). Possibly, when he did so, he paid a visit to the Walters, for Draper, his wife Mary, and most of their children had moved to that city a decade earlier, Draper working as a carpenter. It took years for Draper to follow Booker's example and put his music on record, and by then it was 1933, perhaps as inauspicious a year for getting into the business as he could possibly have chosen.

The family members of the band were Draper, Mary, who played piano, their son Welbern on washboard, and son-in-law Ray Agee on banjo. Fellow Richmond residents Charlie Estes (guitar) and Charles Burdette (jug) completed the sextet. They recorded eight tunes, all of them issued on Champion during 1933. One disc, a pair of waltzes, exists in a single worn copy. The coupling of "That's My Rabbit" and "Shaker Ben," which, as the last of the four releases, you might expect to be the rarest, survives in two copies, one damaged. But it was a close thing: in its eight months' availability, it only just scraped past a hundred sales. Draper Walter received a royalty of 96 cents.

Today, the better copy of "That's My Rabbit"/ "Shaker Ben" is likely to be worth at least $10,000. The waltz record would command a lower price; waltzes always do (➤47). The other two couplings have never been found, so any valuation must be

LARGE CROWD ENTERTAINED IN AMPHITHEATRE

The Old Time entertainers who have been playing on Friday nights in Glen Miller park since Decoration day moved onto the amphitheatre stage last night to present their program before the amplification system. A large crowd was on the hillside for the stage entertainment and soft ball games of the city league.

The Old Timers were organized into acts by Joe Phillips and they presented a varied program of instrumental numbers, singing, dancing and novelty acts.

The entertainment was opened with selections by the Junior Cowboys. Succeeding acts included the Waltz Serenaders, Helen Jean Wilson, tap dancer; Walter Family, old time orchestra; Ted Lunsford, yodeling southerner; Harold Ruhl, accordionist; Richmond Aces; Benny Moore, harmonica; Walter Hahn and Russell Phenis, human dogs; Lawrence Hilliard, guitar and vocalist and several others.

In the months after their recording session, the Walter Family made several appearances in Richmond's Glen Miller Park, such as this concert in July. Singer-guitarist Ted Lunsford had also recorded for Gennett, while Lawrence Hillard was a younger brother of Jess, a frequent visitor to Gennett's Richmond studio (➤37) (*Richmond* [Indiana] *Palladium & Sun-Telegram*, July 22, 1933). (Author's Collection)

hypothetical, but if a playable copy came on to the market of "Tennessee Wagner"/"Too Young to Get Married" (which we know sold more than twice as many as "That's My Rabbit") or "Patty on the Turnpike"/"Granny, Will Your Dog Bite," it would probably draw offers in five figures.

The inaccessibility of these discs would be less regrettable if the surviving recordings were merely ordinary, but they are not. Hughes feared that the monetary value of an artwork might render its quality irrelevant, or at least secondary, but, in this case at least, that isn't a concern: we may marvel at the price-tag, but we are equally impressed by the music. For one thing, the Walter Family was not just a stringband but a jugband, which is rare in recorded old-time music; more than that, it was a washboard band too, which gives it a unique historical interest. The waltzes are sprightly, and "Shaker Ben," a reel, is played at a furious pace, as if the musicians had taken a bet on how many circuits round the tune they could complete in three-and-a-half minutes. The tune's name may allude to the Shaker community established in the early nineteenth century in Pleasant Hill, a few miles from Camp Nelson.

And then there is "That's My Rabbit." Like "Shaker Ben," it's a tune we know only from this recording, an intensely rhythmic reel, but it's also a performance without parallel in recorded old-time music, developing by incrementation from a single voice into an ensemble. First we hear Draper Walter's fiddle, alone, issuing a call to the floor, then Mary joins him on piano, then the guitar, then the jug and washboard. Thus for a little over a minute; then everyone but Draper Walter drops out and the sequence repeats itself, from solo fiddle to full band. Was this a device the Walters dreamed up themselves? An idea contributed by someone from the record company? Some ancient practice revived?

Or was it an accident? Gus Meade, annotating the first reissue of the recording in 1980, recounted that Draper Walter started playing before the "go" light came on, so the rest of the band hung back, then, one by one, decided to join in. After a while, the engineers switched on another light to signal a false start and the musicians fell silent—except for the fiddler, who either didn't see the light or didn't care, and soldiered on, so once again the others severally picked up the tune and carried on to the end.

As Rich Nevins remarked in his notes to the CD box-set *Kentucky Mountain Music*, it's a story so improbable that you would laugh it off, were it not that the account came from one of the musicians who was there, Ray Agee. According to Gennett paperwork, Agee wasn't actually playing on these two tunes, but no doubt he was on the sidelines, watching.

I'm still not entirely convinced; the way the instruments are added and subtracted seems too orderly, and besides, in a situation like that, surely the engineers would have asked for another take?

Perhaps not. Perhaps they liked this unplanned effect and decided to freeze the moment for posterity—unaware of the long odds against posterity ever hearing it.

67

"CHINATOWN, MY CHINATOWN"

Milton Brown and His Brownies
Decca 5166

Recorded in Chicago, IL January 27, 1935
Released on December 9, 1935

Reissued on *Milton Brown & The Musical Brownies: The Complete Recordings of the Father of Western Swing 1932–1937* (Texas Rose TXRCD1–5), *Western Swing: Hot Hillbilly Jazz & Blues 1935–1947* (ASV Living Era CD AJA5214), *Daddy of Western Swing* (Proper PROPERBOX59)

Online: Spotify, YT

Western Swing was a wind of change blowing through hillbilly music in the 1930s. It was young men's music, much of it made by teenagers and twentysomethings who had grown up in the era of radio and the phonograph, and knew, as their parents generally did not, about jazz and hot dance music. And they were determined to *play* that music, in whatever context was offered—even a hillbilly band.

"Chinatown, My Chinatown" embodies what a Western Swing band did best: it took a popular dance tune polished by thirty years of use, and jubilantly splintered it into hot jazz.

The song had been written by William Jerome and Jean Schwartz in 1906. It didn't catch on at the time but had some success in 1915 when it was recorded by the singer Billy Murray with the American Quartet. The arrangement was typical of the period, played by a military-style band, with faux-Oriental splash cymbal effects. The verses were long and forgettable, but the chorus . . . ah, that chorus.

In August 1923, the journalist Ruth Cameron, in her syndicated column "Side Talks," conducted "a symposium on popular songs . . . and their sometimes engaging and sometimes disgusting idiocies. . . . We could not agree on the most idiotic lyric. [Someone] wanted to give it to 'Chinatown, my Chinatown, when the lights are low/Hearts that know no other land, drifting to and fro' . . .'"

Ms. Cameron forbore quoting the rest of the chorus, but it is hardly more fathomable: "Dreamy, dreamy Chinatown, hair and eyes of brown; Skies are bright and hearts are light, in dreamy Chinatown." This is all that Milton Brown and His Brownies give us of the song, one chorus, twice over, because what they're chiefly concerned with is getting this Oriental stir-fry onto the stove, gas on high.

First, fiddler Cecil Brower plays the melody over the crisp syncopation of Fred Calhoun, piano, Ocie Stockard, tenor banjo, Derwood Brown, guitar, and Wanna Coffman, string bass, the tightest rhythm section in '30s Western Swing. Milton Brown takes a vocal chorus, sounding like Jack Teagarden on a coffee bender. "Papa" Calhoun romps awhile on piano, then hands over to Bob Dunn for a solo characteristic of this most inventive of early amplified steel guitarists, breaking the melody down into long notes and stuttering staccatos.

"The staccato notes are a first-generation Hawaiian device, learned by Dunn from Frank Ferera and others," comments the steel-guitar historian Guy Cundell,

> but his swing interpretation is very modern, derived from jazzers generally but also modern steelers like Pana'ole [Robert Panole of the '30s Hawaiian guitar act Jim and Bob] and [Sol] Ho'opi'i. . . . "Chinatown" needs to be viewed in the context of a performance on the first day of recording with his new band on newly acquired technology. Technically he was up against it. The faster the tempo, the more difficult it is to phrase. He deals with the demanding tempo by ghosting

The Brownies, ca. 1935. Left to right: Ocie Stockard, Fred Calhoun, Wanna Coffman, Milton Brown, Cecil Brower, Bob Dunn, Derwood Brown. (From the collection of the late Bob Pinson)

> notes on one hand and using extended durations to catch his breath and mentally regroup on the other. [Altogether,] it is a synthesis of personal style that he develops over his career.

Brower returns for a hot chorus, à la Joe Venuti, before Milton takes another go at the lyrics, Dunn's steel guitar poking him from behind like a farmer prodding a slow-moving cow, and with the last "dreamy Chinatown" the band snaps to a halt. It has taken them less than three minutes.

★ ★ ★

Over two days in Chicago, January 27 and 28, 1935, the Brownies made thirty-five recordings under their new contract. Decca didn't rush to issue "Chinatown," and when they did, it was on the B-side of a mostly instrumental tune titled "Cheesy Breeze." "Oh, bree–eeze, cheesy breeze, blowin' through the trees," Brown croons. "Just my gal and me, sittin' in that cheesy breeze."

When the Brownies grouped in Chicago, they had already recorded for Bluebird, so by the end of the Decca session they had logged fifty-three sides. Bob Wills's Texas Playboys were still eight months away from entering a recording studio for the first time. Yet they are generally regarded as the founders of Western Swing.

If the Brownies' recordings had sounded dated or had the rawness of work in progress, the precedence accorded to Wills might be understandable, but they emphatically did not. Many seasoned judges consider the 1935 Brownies—and, even more, the 1936 Brownies, augmented by the young hot fiddler Cliff Bruner—a stronger band than the contemporary Texas Playboys in almost every department. Certainly, in Milton Brown they had a singer almost perfectly suited to his chosen idiom, his voice warm, virile, mellow, his style by turns rhythmic and lyrical, his range expansive, from the vaudeville blues of "A Good Man Is Hard to Find"

(Author's Collection)

and the Cab Calloway barnstorming of "Stay on the Right Side Sister" to the hearth-and-home sentimentality of "My Mary."

Wills's vocalist Tommy Duncan had similar gifts, and a few others: his way with Jimmie Rodgers songs, his rapport with the blues, his ability to strike a serious note. But, unlike Brown, he was the front man only when he was singing; actually, not always even then, because Wills constantly broke in with remarks and cries of encouragement. And once Duncan's vocals were over, the leader's personality ballooned to fill the stage. Wills not only gave the audience a show—music, movement, mirth, moxie—but also dynamized the musicians' on-stage creativity. The Playboys might lag behind the Brownies in 1935, but a shrewd observer, seeing the effect of Wills's magnetism upon players and public alike, might have put down a long-term bet on the second-runners.

But they were not really running in the same race. The two leaders' ambitions seem to have been quite different. Wills saw himself leading a hillbilly *swing* band, Benny Goodman with a straw in his mouth, Tommy Dorsey in overalls, a thirteen-to- fifteen-piece orchestra with horn sections. As far as we know, Milton Brown had no such goal. The Brownies were a fine swing band, but they were at bottom a *string* band, seven or eight pieces, foregrounding fiddles and steel guitar, not trumpets and saxophones. Thus equipped, they could be no rivals of Goodman or Dorsey; they had more in common with the small bands headed by Venuti and Eddie Lang, or Stéphane Grappelly and Django Reinhardt—a kind of Hot Club de Fort Worth.

In its early days, what Brown and Wills played was known in the business as "hot dance" or "hot string band music." So my opening sentence was strictly an anachronism, because the term "Western Swing" properly belongs not to the '30s but to the '40s, and not to the Southwest but to the West Coast, when Wills, and contemporary bandleaders from elsewhere, like Spade Cooley and Hank Penny, defined the idiom with the sound colors and the muscularity of brass and reeds. In *that* sense, a pedant might mutter, the Brownies were not a Western Swing band at all; but country music historians cannot agree on a better term.

We can play with "what if"s, imagine alternative histories, but what actually happened next was definitive. In the early hours of Monday, April 13, 1936, returning from a dance at Crystal Springs, Milton Brown drove into a telephone pole. A few days later, he died in the hospital of pneumonia. His younger brother Derwood led the Brownies for another year or so, then they broke up and the players re-formed as other groups: Cliff Bruner's Texas Wanderers, Ocie Stockard's Wanderers, Bob Dunn's Vagabonds—still small, still stringbands. By then, Bob Wills's Texas Playboys were invincible, and the founding myth of Western Swing was set in stone.

68

"BANKHEAD BLUES"

Nations Brothers (Shelton and Marshall)

Vocalion 03118, Banner/Melotone/Perfect 6-11-54

Recorded in Jackson, Mississippi, October 13, 1935
Released in c. November/December 1935 (Vocalion) and November 1936 (Banner/Melotone/Perfect)

Reissued on *Mississippi String Bands Volume Two* (County CO-CD-3514), *Hillbilly Blues* (ASV Living Era CD AJA5361), *Mississippi Hillbillies* (JSP JSP77215)

Online: Spotify, YT

By the mid-'30s, the hillbilly record business was in the hands of just three companies: Vocalion (owned by Brunswick), Bluebird (owned by Victor), and Decca. Throughout the second half of the decade, they sourced much of their talent from location sessions in the South and Southwest. All three spent a great deal of time in Texas, where the pickings were rich and varied, from hillbilly swing and barrelhouse blues to the *corridos* of the TexMex border and the polka music of the state's German, Czech, and Polish communities. Between 1935 and 1939, Brunswick sent producers and engineers to ten Southern and Southwestern cities and made almost 3,000 recordings, but three-quarters of them were cut in San Antonio, Dallas, and Fort Worth, where the company regularly satisfied the demands of the hillbilly jukebox trade with exclusive Vocalion signings like Bob Wills's Texas Playboys, the Light Crust Doughboys, the Hi-Flyers, and Roy Newman and His Boys.

The other seven cities visited by the Brunswick recording men ranged from Columbia, South Carolina, to Hot Springs, Arkansas, taking in Augusta, Georgia; Birmingham, Alabama; Hattiesburg and Jackson, Mississippi; and Memphis, Tennessee. Here their strategy is more puzzling. Four of these locations had never seen a recording crew before; Jackson had been used once and Birmingham twice; only Memphis had been a frequent recording center. What was *in* these places? Did Brunswick choose them simply because they were ignored by its rivals? Or did the company's Southern talent expert, Art Satherley, know something that Bluebird's Eli Oberstein or Decca's Dave Kapp didn't? It was a considerable undertaking to make these trips: in all, Brunswick employees spent about three and a half months in these seven cities and cut more than 700 recordings. There must surely have been a game plan.

If it was to discover new and durable talent, it was a conspicuous failure. Of the nearly hundred acts they did business with, about 80 percent were making records for the first time, and almost all of those for the last time. A third of all the recordings Brunswick made at these locations were never issued.

★ ★ ★

Brunswick–Vocalion's first location session outside Texas was in Jackson, Mississippi, in October 1935. Over thirteen days, the crew achieved a modest workload of 116 recordings, about 40 percent of which were judged issuable. The session was set up with the help of H. C. Speir, a Jackson music-store proprietor, talent scout, and lover of fiddling, who probably recommended a fiddle–guitar duet from Brookhaven, Mississippi, Sheldon Nations (misspelled Shelton on the record labels), who was twenty-five, and his brother Marshall, who was twenty-three.

The first two of the ten tunes they played for the microphone were "Bankhead Blues" and "Magnolia One Step." "Bankhead Blues" is an angular blues in the spirit of fellow Mississippians Narmour and Smith, one of those tunes that feel as if they can go on forever, back and forth, with minute variations of rhythm and phrasing. Admittedly, this is true of many fiddle tunes except the most elaborate, but you feel it particularly acutely in these Mississippi blues melodies, as they go round and round like perpetual-motion carousels.

The Nations Brothers, 1935. (Courtesy of Mary Nations Smith)

"Magnolia One Step" may allude to a campaign held in Mississippi that year to choose a state tree, which the magnolia won by a wide margin. "Bankhead Blues" is a puzzle. There seems never to have been a community of that name in the state. The transcontinental Bankhead Highway passed through Mississippi, but much farther north.

"We were influenced in our music by our father, Luther C. Nations, who played a violin," Marshall wrote to me.

> We never had any formal musical training, but all played by ear. The [family] band consisted of two violins, two guitars, an autoharp and bass fiddle. We played at school gatherings, picnics, musical and community affairs. We played only dance music with no vocal tunes. As the family grew up and departed the band was finally left to my older brother Sheldon, who played the fiddle, and myself with a guitar. We were still living at home and farming for our living. Music was just part time for us. . . . We played at several hundred fiddlers' conventions and were always lucky enough to win first place. These conventions were all over South Mississippi. We were usually playing every Friday and Saturday nights. We played on radio stations and finally Brunswick Recording Co. from New Jersey came to Jackson, Miss. and invited us up for an audition.

"Bankhead Blues" is a spellbinding record, but it was a surprising one for Brunswick to have made, for the fiddle–guitar format—on discs, at least—was on its way out. It had once been a staple of the old-time business, creating stars out of acts like the Kessinger Brothers and the Stripling Brothers (➤34), Narmour and Smith, Asa Martin and Doc Roberts, Clayton McMichen and Riley Puckett, and a good many others. By the mid-'30s, though, such acts had either transformed themselves into stringbands playing a wider range of material than fiddle-tunes, like Martin, Roberts, and McMichen, or lost their contracts. Narmour and Smith had a final session in 1934, but they merely recycled their best-known numbers from five or six years earlier.

The few new acts of this kind were younger men like Arthur Smith, made famous by the Grand Ole Opry, or Curly Fox, another Tennessean, who moved to Texas to play with the Shelton Brothers and claimed a few minutes of their recording sessions for fiddling showpieces. Clifford Gross, a Kentuckian who had also gone to Texas, to play with the Light Crust Doughboys, made ten estimable sides in 1937–38, a set of reels, waltzes, and schottisches that may have been designed for dancers as much as seated listeners.

The one fiddle–guitar act that had made an impact before the Depression and returned to be (moderately) successful again afterward was the Striplings, who made two dozen sides for Decca in 1934 and 1936. Possibly the Nations Brothers were picked by Brunswick to give the Alabamians some competition. Or maybe they seemed to evoke the odd, errant spirit of Narmour and Smith but with a sharper blues edge.

★ ★ ★

Though "Bankhead Blues"/"Magnolia One Step" was given reasonable circulation—it was issued first on Vocalion and then, about a year later, on Banner, Melotone, and Perfect—it's now an uncommon record. But at least one other band heard it and liked "Bankhead Blues" enough to incorporate it in their repertoire. Years ago, I came upon an acetate disc of the tune, cut on a home-recording machine, probably in the late '30s or '40s, by a group featuring fiddle and Hawaiian guitar. The title was handwritten on the label, but the band did not identify itself. Why should it? The musicians who made it knew who they were, and the disc was a private memento. But at some point it was discarded and ended up where I found it, in an antique store in Clinton, Tennessee. Which happens to be the hometown of a band that boasted both fiddlers and Hawaiian guitarists, the Tennessee Ramblers (➤24).

I don't know if this battered acetate really is by the Sievers family, a decade or more after their last commercial recordings. Musically, both "Bankhead Blues" and the other side, "Royal Hawaiian Hotel," are compatible with what we know of their abilities and interests. But the question is unanswerable and likely to remain so. It doesn't matter. The existence of this disc, whoever made it, reminds us that records, even modest-selling records, were ramblers too, and might go anywhere. Messages from other places, dispatches of difference—unfamiliar tunes, known tunes in unfamiliar guises—they had the power to intrigue and inspire other musicians for years afterward.

69

"FEELS GOOD"/"LET ME PLAY WITH IT"

Hartman's Heart Breakers
Bluebird B-6481

Recorded in Charlotte, North Carolina, June 22, 1936
Released in c. Fall 1936

Reissued on *She's Selling What She Used to Give Away* (Bear Family BCD17550) [both] • *Baby, How Can It Be?: Songs of Love, Lust and Contempt from the 1920s and 1930s* (Dust-to-Digital DTD-16) ["Let Me Play with It"]

Online: Spotify, YT

In the summer of 1936, Dick Hartman's Tennessee Ramblers were riding high. They had recently been featured on the Crazy Barn Dance at WBT in Charlotte, North Carolina, and were still broadcasting on the station with other sponsors. They had also become prolific contributors to Bluebird Records' hillbilly catalog, making more than three dozen sides in 1935. And now they were booked at Charlotte's Southern Radio Building for another recording session. To be exact, they were booked for three.

Most of the band also constituted a studio group called the Washboard Wonders. Designed to cash in on the popularity of the Hoosier Hot Shots, the combo borrowed the Indiana group's car-horn effects, swanee whistle, and even, on "You've Got to Eat Your Spinach, Baby," their trademark introduction, "Are you ready, Hezzie?," which they recast as "Are you ready, Pappy?" for bandmember and effects-merchant Kenneth "Pappy" Wolfe.

But now they were going to introduce a third band persona. Hartman's Heart Breakers consisted of most of the usual personnel, playing fiddle, banjo, guitars, string bass, swanee whistle, and trap drumkit, plus guest singer Betty Lou. Bluebird may have designed the Washboard Wonders to clean up in the novelty-band market, but with the Heart Breakers, the label was getting its hands dirty.

> Some like 'em fat, some like 'em lean,
> But I like a daddy who uses Vaseline . . .
>
> Some like it slick, some like it rough,
> But I like a daddy who'll give me enough . . .
>
> Now you've got the wiener, and I've got the bun,
> Let's put them together, boy, we'll have some fun.

There was nothing new about this. In 1896, the pioneering record-maker Russell Hunting had been jailed for three months for making cylinder recordings of "bad songs." A decade before the recording of "Feels Good"/"Let Me Play with It" (the former is the source of the first two couplets above, the latter the third), an AP wire story had described "a numerous fraternity which bootlegs 'off color' talking machine records . . . wild jazz coupled with risque versification." An investigator traced these items to "a dingy second-hand shop" in Kansas City, where

> a door to a back room was thrown open. Thousands of phonograph records were stacked around the walls. . . . Many of them were made by negro singers. . . . [C]ustomers were from many walks of life, from mischievous high school boys to proprietors of exclusive establishments on Kansas City's "Gold Coast." ("RISQUE MUSIC IS BEING BOOTLEGGED IN MANY STATES," *Charleston* [West Virginia] *Gazette*, June 18, 1926)

A few weeks later, this pestilence had reached Charleston, West Virginia.

> Yes, it is true. Some specialty shops in the city are making a feature of records which are taboo in the music stores . . . with the vulgar suggestive titles that have become so popular in the past few months. In the bootleg record there is nothing left to the imagination, all vulgarities are set out in full. . . . An investigation determined that the purchasers of these records are boys growing into manhood and toothless old men with one foot

in the grave and the other on a banana peeling. (*Charleston Gazette*, July 24, 1926)

It isn't clear whether these were bootlegs in the strict sense of pirated recordings or merely normal records of a kind the journalists hadn't come across before. I suspect the latter. Given descriptions like "wild jazz coupled with risque versification," no one would have been expecting Paul Whiteman—or any kind of white man. "Off color records . . . by negro singers" had been around practically since African American jazz and blues artists were first recorded, both on reputable brands like Victor and Columbia for 75 cents and on humbler labels for a quarter.

But there was a deeper level of phonopornography. "Party records" were songs or comedy routines, somewhere between risqué and explicit; unbroadcastable and, as far as companies like Victor and Columbia were concerned, unrecordable, so issued instead on labels with giveaway names like Bang or Gaiety. Their heyday was in the '40s, when the growth of independent record-manufacturing plants eased the way of the storefront operator who simply wanted 500 pressings of "She Made It Hard for Him," cash up front, no questions asked. But archeologists of the blue disc can date this shady side of the record business farther back, to the mid-'30s, when companies like Hollywood Hot Shots and Racy produced records of sexed-up cowboy songs by members of the Sons of the Pioneers or the Beverly Hill Billies, along with smutty parodies of pop songs of the day, or nudge-nudge stand-up routines.

These records were chiefly made for the jukebox trade and were not sold, or at least not visible, in regular music stores. But Bluebird was a division of RCA Victor, a company of considerable age and impeccable standing. And here was that distinguished logo attached to songs about wieners and Vaseline. What was label manager Eli Oberstein *thinking?*

He was probably thinking: these will sell. The performances had an easy-rolling swing and a spontaneous informality, with cries of encouragement and Bob-Wills-style interjections: "Honey, your motor is red hot, yeah!" What it was, was hokum blues, an idiom African American artists had been developing for a decade. "Feels Good" was based on the hokum archetype, Tampa Red and Georgia Tom's "It's Tight Like That." "Let Me Play with It" shares the tune of Blind Willie McTell's "Let Me Play with Yo' Yo-Yo."

The Heart Breakers were not the first hillbilly musicians to run whooping down this alley. In the early '30s, Jimmie Davis, Gene Autry, and Cliff Carlisle regularly produced suggestive songs about high-steppin' mamas and shanghai roosters. "You can feel-a my legs, you can feel-a my thigh, if you feel my legs you've gotta ride me high," declared Autry in "Do Right Daddy Blues" (1931) in a last burst of bawdy bravado; a few months later, the only daddies he was singing about were silver-haired. In the same year, Victor, with an eye on the sort of record-buyers Autry would desert, coupled a pair of songs about enthusiastic girlfriends, "She's Killing Me" by the Nichols Brothers—"I took my baby right out in the sun, Then we both got hot and we had fun"—and "She Wouldn't Be Still"

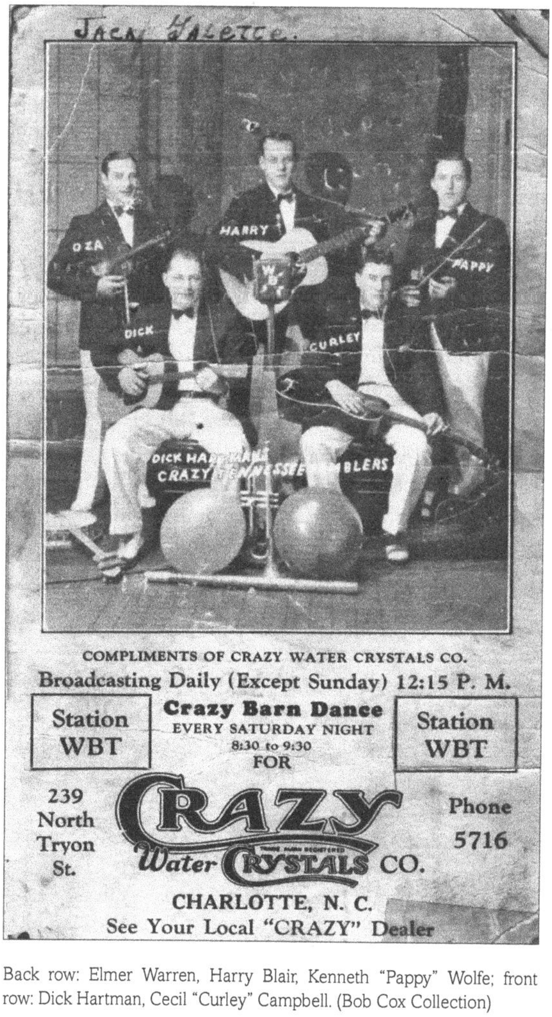

Back row: Elmer Warren, Harry Blair, Kenneth "Pappy" Wolfe; front row: Dick Hartman, Cecil "Curley" Campbell. (Bob Cox Collection)

"Betty Lou," 1936. (Courtesy of Thomas Quinn)

by the Pine Mountain Boys: "I been to the east and away out west, Since I met this gal, I haven't had any rest . . . She gave me a thrill, but she wouldn't be still."

What made the Heart Breakers different was that their songs were sung by a woman.

Women had made relatively few appearances in the first decade or so of recorded old-time music (➤70), and, when they did, were generally either decorous or self-effacing. Betty Lou was neither. The star of these playlets, she comes on like a randy hillbilly Betty Boop, jailbait in gingham. Actually, she was thirty-eight, a Salisbury, North Carolina, homemaker, and mother of three.

"I wrote most of the songs I recorded," Carrie Clontz Goodman, aka Betty Lou, told me. "Kind of bluesy, aren't they? The worst one I did, I'll hum a little of it for you," and she began not humming but singing "Fetch It on Down to My House": "Ain't so good-looking, that's understood, but boys all like me 'cause I do it so good." She remembered Oberstein (she called him Bernstein) coming down and making the records, and people listening to them at parties and on jukeboxes. She made a few personal appearances at schoolhouses with the Hartman crew, singing, dancing, and playing the 120-bass accordion. She had pictures taken of herself holding the big instrument and wearing a small bathing suit, so that it looked as if behind the accordion she was naked. "I always did crazy things."

Cecil "Curly" Campbell, the Heart Breakers' banjoist, thought the records were Oberstein's idea and believed they were withdrawn; evidently not straightaway, because they're not uncommon, and besides, there was a second session, four months later: not eight songs as before, but a dozen, including pieces like "I Want It," "Dick and I," and the tantalizingly titled "Cuban Appetizer," possibly not about *bocaditos* or *croquetas*. Perhaps, by then, Oberstein was feeling a chilly breeze from the head office, for only two numbers were released, "A Night in Carolina" and "My Southern Movements," both saucily sung but fractionally less on the button than the earlier recordings. With that, the curtains closed on the Heart Breakers, and the Bluebird hillbilly catalog was never so explicitly naughty again. (Though, a few months afterward, a Western Swing unit, the Modern Mountaineers, did sneak a no-foolin' obscenity on to a Bluebird record, of which more later [➤77].)

70

"THOSE RAMBLING BLUES"

Steelman Sisters
Melotone 6-11-69

Recorded in Hattiesburg, MS, July 23, 1936
Released in November 1936

In the 1930s, a new sound appeared on hillbilly records: the close-harmony female duet.

There had been female singing groups before, of course. In the late 1920s, the Okeh catalog boasted the three Giddens Sisters, the two Moore Sisters, and Ruth and Wanda Neal; Columbia, the two Bowman Sisters and the three Wisdom Sisters; Victor, the Palmer Sisters and Forman Sisters, both trios; Gennett, the Minneapolitan evangelist Helen Jepsen and her sister Ruth Donaldson. But none of these acts had a long recording career; from the early 1920s to the mid-'30s, the only women who did were Sara and Maybelle Carter and Rosa Lee Carson, "Moonshine Kate." The eight sister acts just mentioned made, altogether, fewer than two dozen discs.

(If the reader finds this surprising, some statistics may be in order. In the period spanned by this book, recordings in which women played a significant part—mostly as sister acts, in male–female duets, as soloists like Billie Maxwell [➤42], or as band vocalists like "Betty Lou" [➤69]—occupied not much more than 5 percent of the entire hillbilly disc library. Even when one includes all the women who took secondary roles, such as playing rhythm mandolin or ukulele in a family band, or furnishing a piano accompaniment for a male quartet, their contribution still falls short of 10 percent.)

Most of the early sister acts observed gender-appropriate norms of the time and the places in which they lived, by selecting either sacred material or old-time heart songs. (The Bowman Sisters' perky blues coupling of 1929, "Railroad Take Me Back"/"Old Lonesome Blues," is a rare exception.) By contrast, the Carter Family—many of whose records are female duets, with A. P. merely a guiding presence in the background—possessed a repertoire that was much wider and, at times, feistier.

Around the mid-'30s, records began to introduce sister acts of a different musical character. Out of the cast of the WLS National Barn Dance emerged the Overstake Sisters, known as the "Three Little Maids"; Mildred and Dolly Good, billed as the "Girls of the Golden West"; and the Flannery Sisters, Billie and Allie. The most successful of the three, the Girls of the Golden West, justified their billing both in their attire and with a long catalog of Western songs about cowboys and cowgirls, trails and prairies. Sartorially, the Overstakes and Flannerys preferred gingham modesty to cowgirl swagger and matched it with a mostly sweet and decorous repertoire of hillbilly local-color songs like "Carry Me Back to the Mountains" or "When the Flowers Are Blooming in the Springtime." But they were all united in their dedication to radio-friendly close harmony and a fondness for yodeling. They redefined one strain of female hillbilly music for most of a decade.

* * *

Nine months after their location session in Jackson, Mississippi, ARC–Brunswick returned to the state for another talent grab, this time in Hattiesburg. As noted earlier (➤68), the company could exploit a rich talent base in the Southwest, but its expectations in the other locations it visited, where there was no burgeoning idiom like Western Swing, are harder to define. Part of the purpose of these location sessions may have been to find regional acts that modeled themselves on national ones, recording director Art Satherley and his colleagues presumably reckoning that, as well as their local appeal, such acts might attract devotees of the well-known acts too. So, for example, if you admired the Delmore Brothers and literally couldn't get enough of their Bluebird discs, you might investigate

"Sis" (left) and "Shang" Steelman, with "Aubrey" on guitar, Mississippi, 1936. (Courtesy of Dale Snyder)

Vocalion carbon-copyists like the White Brothers or Andrews Brothers.

This may be why the Hattiesburg recording team chose the teenaged Steelman Sisters, whose guitar-accompanied close-harmony yodel songs echoed the manner, and in a couple of cases the repertoire, of recent female forerunners: "Lonesome Valley Sally" had been recorded by the Girls of the Golden West, and "I'm Drifting Back to Dreamland" by the Flannery Sisters. The first of their numbers to be recorded, which the Steelmans might have composed, was a swaggering piece written from a male point of view, "Those Rambling Blues."

When I hit the trail, it'll be so grand,
To knock about all over the land.
But after a while I'll miss you, old pal,
And I'll have to come back to see my gal.
I've got those ra-am—bli-ing blues . . .

So come on, Liza, don't be so blue,
You know I'm coming back to you.
You will always be my honey,
And you can always spend my money.

The Steelman Sisters' releases evidently did well enough to prompt ARC–Brunswick to record them again, in Birmingham, Alabama, in April 1937, but the four songs cut on that occasion remained unissued.

Mary Elizabeth "Sis" Steelman (1918–2005) and Vivian "Shang" Steelman (1920–2003), the daughters of Charles J. Steelman and Viola McLellan Steelman, grew up with their seven brothers in Hattiesburg, where the family ran a couple of grocery stores. Their career in music was probably brief, but for a while, around the time of their recordings, they did travel to perform. As Sis's daughter Vivian recalled in 2007, Charles and Viola "would take Momma and Shang to places to sing. They were very supportive of their daughters. Mamaw [Viola] played the piano, Momma played the guitar, Allen [an older brother] played the harmonica, Shang played the ukulele, Richard [a younger brother] played the guitar. . . . It was a little like a vaudeville show. Momma would be dressed like Minnie Pearl. They would sing, tell jokes, and do skits. They played off each other. . . . They sang at outdoor gatherings and county fairs. They would get paid a little money, and that would help the family out with food and other expenses."

In 1938, Charles Stillman moved to nearby Ocean Springs and opened a grocery business there, leaving some of his sons to mind the stores in Hattiesburg. Sis and Shang married, began to raise families, and left a music career behind. But Sis continued to sing and play her guitar for her children and grandchildren, and in her later years, according to family member Laurah Tate, she "sang so much in the nursing home that she [said] she was going to have to start charging. She said they were wearing her out."

★ ★ ★

Being "taken to places to sing" by their parents, and accompanied, in both senses, by some of their brothers, was probably the only way Sis and Shang Steelman could have performed in public. Women had always played a part in hillbilly music-making, but chiefly in family and community contexts; they were discouraged by convention from performing outside these safe areas, and in particular from following the life of a traveling musician. A woman on the road with a band risked her reputation, unless the band included kinsmen or other reliable persons who could defend it. Rosa Lee Carson, a teenager throughout the 1920s, always traveled with her father Fiddlin' John. Billie Maxwell and the Louisiana Cajun singer Cleoma Breaux Falcon had protective cordons of father, brothers, and husband. Rose Maddox was encircled by up to six brothers. Sara and Maybelle Carter had A. P., who was Sara's husband and Maybelle's brother-in-law. Texas Ruby had her partner Chubby Wise, Lulu Belle Wiseman her Scotty.

Hence the gender switch of "Those Rambling Blues": the only permissible way two young women could present a fantasy of "knocking about all over the land" was by pretending they were men.

71

"COURTIN' "/"V-8 BLUES"

Three Tobacco Tags
Bluebird B-6730

Recorded in Charlotte, NC, October 13, 1936
Released in February 1937

Reissued on *Get Your Head in Here* (BACM CD D 131) [both] • *Hillbilly Blues* (ASV Living Era CD AJA5361) ["V-8 Blues"]

Online: Spotify, YT ["V-8 Blues"]

By the mid-'30s, a fissure was opening in the vernacular division of the record business. The "race" (African American) catalogs, previously home to a wide variety of music, not limited to blues, were now more tightly managed spaces, reserved for men and women who could deftly shuffle and deal song subjects while playing by the strict rules of the Twelve Bar Club. Peetie Wheatstraw, Walter Davis, Washboard Sam, and Curtis Jones made scores of recordings that were melodically all but identical. Lonnie Johnson claimed he had copyrighted more than a hundred songs with the same tune.

In contrast, the hillbilly lists became baggier. In the 1920s, an artist could prioritize one kind of material throughout his or her recording life, like Chris Bouchillon with his humorous monologs. Now, the repertoire of a successful recording act had to be a carefully calculated pie chart, with segments of heart songs, hoedowns, sacred songs, yodeling, blues, comic songs, and an occasional sliver of uncategorizable weirdness.

The driver of change was radio. Hillbilly groups with radio shows knew promptly from their fan mail what their audience liked; and, since that proved to be a lot of different things, they became experts in versatility. African American artists, with little or no access to radio schedules, were under no such pressure from their customers; the pressure came instead from record producers, and probably also jukebox operators, for whom "race records" and "blues" were practically synonymous terms.

★ ★ ★

Foremost among the hillbilly purveyors of heart, holiness, and hilarity were the Three Tobacco Tags: North Carolinians Edgar Reid Summey (1903–75), Henry Luther Baucom (1902–67), and George Henry Wade (1905–58). In the late 1920s, Wade was employed at the Seminole cotton mill in Gastonia, and by 1931 he was playing with Baucom and Summey, fellow workers at the Seminole who had moved to the area more recently. The lineup was unusual: two mandolins, played by Baucom and Wade, and Summey's guitar.

The trio were signed by Victor in 1931, allegedly scouted by Gwyn Foster of the Carolina Tar Heels, a fellow Gaston Countian, who told them, "If you don't make the grade, you're nothing but plain old tobacco tags." Small tin tags, often in bright colors and with elaborate designs, were fixed to plugs of chewing tobacco as brand identifiers. Introduced in the 1870s, they were manufactured in millions, so that "tobacco tag" became an exemplar of throwaway. When Foster made his jibe, they had recently gone out of production. (Ninety years on, they are collectables.) Under this ironic billing, the trio made a record that a later songbook candidly described as "a dismal failure" and were not called back.

The following year they cut a couple of discs for Gennett's Champion label, which sold very poorly. By 1936, however, their time had come: their radio popularity rekindled Victor's interest, and over the next five years, various lineups of Tobacco Tags made eighty-six recordings for the Bluebird catalog, many of which were also licensed to Montgomery Ward's mail-order label.

★ ★ ★

In 1934, the *Gastonia Daily Gazette* ran a piece on the trio, bylined "(Contributed)," which I suspect was

(Courtesy of Marshall Wyatt and Hunter Holmes)

a euphemism for "sent to us by someone connected with the band." It throws an interesting light on what a publicist at the time thought were their strongest selling points.

> The Crazy Tobacco Tags, of whom all Gastonia is proud, have lived here among us for many years . . . rubbing elbows with the boys in the cotton mills and can tell you all about the many operations in converting cotton into the finest yarn. They are known among our church goers as good, clean Christian gentlemen, one of the boys filling the office of deacon in the church to which he belongs, and they therefore have a very broad acquaintance among their church associates. They also possess recognized musical ability and have been seen and heard by thousands in their personal appearances in churches, school houses, and theatres and have been heard by millions in their broadcasts over radio stations WBT and WPTF. (October 19, 1934)

"Good, clean Christian gentlemen" might not be the first epithet the listener would reach for while listening to songs like "The Teacher's Hair Was Red," with its uh-oh last verse:

> When the sled turned over
> And stood her on her head,
> Don't you remember, boys,
> The teacher's hair was red?

"Courtin'" and "V-8 Blues," the Tags' second, and well-received, Bluebird release, are somewhat milder numbers, but might still have been greeted with pursed lips by some of the boys' "church associates."

Texas honkytonk musicians access their female side. Among them are Floyd Tillman (back row, third from left) and, in front of him, Leo Raley. (OTM Collection, from the late Leo Raley)

(Author's Collection)

"Courtin'," a comic dialogue between "Luke" (Baucom) and "Jane" (Summey), is the same song as Ernest Stoneman's "The Mountaineer's Courtship" (1927), with its barrage of female questions: "When are you coming to see me?"—"When will we be married?" —"Who're you going to bring to the wedding?" To which the man replies, "Guess I'll bring my children . . . Jim, John, Sally, and the baby." In Stoneman's recording, the affianced woman makes no response to this news, but the Tags develop the dramatic situation. Jane responds, "Why, you deceitful old jarhead rascal, you! Here you've been a-foolin' me these last fifteen years!" and sings, "I 'spect we won't get married . . ." Then, tearfully, "Goodbye, honey!" "Ohh," replies her suitor, disappointed. Or perhaps not.

"Courtin'" is almost unique in twitching aside the curtain between us and the unrecorded comic playlets of '30s hillbilly music, staple items in the public repertoire of bands like the Tags and J. E. Mainer's Mountaineers. (There is another trace in the Tags' 1937 record "Tall and Handsome Comedy," with its double female impersonation.) A preview of a 1938 concert by the Tags at the Graham, North Carolina, courthouse trailed their new show "Married Bliss," a successor to an earlier piece called "Ain't Love Grand": "The characters are the same . . . except this time Jonah, Delphina, Percy and Beatrice are celebrating their first wedding anniversary"

Original tobacco tags.

(Burlington *Daily Times-News*, February 24). Such playlets gave male musicians the opportunity to put on frocks and women's voices (as in the curious, and contemporary, Southern craze for "womanless weddings"), while in others they could extend the parodizing to African Americans by blacking up: devices, now difficult or impossible to use, that once guaranteed merriment in a rural audience.

"V-8 Blues," written by Wade and Summey, redeploys the blues melody of the group's ambiguous 1931 Victor recording "Get Your Head in Here" in a jaunty cautionary tale about drink-driving, with the refrain "I got the V-8 blues, I got the V-8 blues . . . Shake, rattle, and ramble, I got the V-8 blues." Launched in 1932, the Ford company's most significant development since the Model A recommended a few years earlier by Oscar Ford (➤38), the V-8 was boosted by black record-makers like the Cedar Creek Sheik, who sang a different "V-8 Blues" for Bluebird four months before the Tags, and Buddy Moss, who promised to ride in one to his girlfriend's funeral. In comparison, the Tags' V-8 song is easygoing, uninvolved, a white-egg omelet, blues lite. Whether because of that, or the rube comedy of "Courtin'," this coupling was selected for issue in both the UK and India.

★ ★ ★

Somewhat over a year later, the Tags, having moved from WPTF in Raleigh to WRVA in Richmond, Virginia, were described by the Burlington paper, in their week-long coverage of the Graham concert mentioned above, as "the cleanest and funniest entertainment you ever saw." They were about to get cleaner. Within the next six months, George Wade would be eased out of the group, allegedly because of his propensity to bestow his favors on female fans and then skip town. He made a final set of recordings with a new band in September 1938 (one of the songs was titled "He Turned Around and Went the Other Way"), but his part in the Tags' history was obliterated from accounts in their subsequent songbooks.

Some of the group's uniqueness went with him. Who else in hillbilly music was thinking up numbers like "Lady Twinklepuss," a guitar-accompanied monolog about assignations in a medieval court? But Baucom and Summey carried on, recruiting fiddler and mandolinist Harvey Ellington and guitarist Bob Hartsell, soon replaced by Sam Pridgin, and these unnumbered Tobacco Tags continued their buoyant passage over the airwaves and on Bluebird Records. They are one of the acts Bob Coltman was thinking of when he wrote:

> Bluebird became so successful at sensing and creating public taste that one finds it difficult to think of 1930s country music without picturing that familiar buff-and-blue label and hearing in one's imagination the characteristic warm golden sound of the Bluebird artists, a sound which—an important marketing advance—won repeat customers not merely for individual artists, but apparently for the label itself.

Bluebird survived (with different-colored labels) until the late '40s; the Tobacco Tags lasted a little longer. They returned to WPTF during the war years, then to Richmond and the WRVA Old Dominion Barn Dance. They continued to fill engagements around Virginia into the early '50s, latterly with the WDVA Barn Dance out of Danville. The last trace I have found of them is on that show in November 1951, where the remaining founder members, now both approaching their fiftieth birthdays, are billed as "Looney Luke and Roley Poley Reid." It was probably not long afterward that the Tobacco Tags took a long look at their radio and personal-appearance circuit and decided to pull the plug.

72

"WONDERING"

Riverside Ramblers
Bluebird B-6926

Recorded in New Orleans, LA, February 22, 1937
Released in May/June 1937

Reissued on *The Hackberry Ramblers—Early Recordings: 1935–1950* (Arhoolie CD7050), *Cajun: Louisiane 1928–1939* (Frémeaux FA019)

Online: Spotify, YT

This may have been the first Cajun–country crossover hit. "Wondering, wondering, who's kissing you . . ." The yearning strains spiraled like blue smoke into the late-'30s sky from jukeboxes across the Southwestern United States. "I pray every night to the good Lord above, Please send back the Madame Queen that I really love . . ." It was sumptuously sad, the storytelling underscored by fiddling tremulous with heartache. Cajun honkytonk.

The original sound of Cajun music on record, as established in the late 1920s by Joseph Falcon, the Breaux family, Leo Soileau, and others, had been the combination of fiddle and accordion. There might be a guitar, or a *tit' fer* (triangle), but essentially it was duet music. By the mid-'30s, this had radically altered. Now, the dominant sound of French music in Louisiana was a stringband built to the design of the hillbilly combo: fiddle and guitars. The new idiom was spearheaded by the Hackberry Ramblers, recording for Bluebird, and Leo Soileau's groups on Decca, and their example was followed by Miller's Merrymakers, J. B. Fuslier, Happy Fats LeBlanc, and others. Joe Falcon apart, after 1934 there was hardly an accordion to be heard on Cajun records. (This would remain true until the '50s, when a new generation of Cajun accordionists, such as Iry LeJune, Austin Pitre, and Sidney Brown, reclaimed their place in the dancehalls and on records.)

The Hackberry Ramblers, most prolific of the '30s bands, generally sang in French. For English songs, they used another band name. They were broadcasting from the Montgomery Ward store in Lake Charles, the station held a contest for a new name for the group, and a listener, thinking of a popular brand of tires sold by the store, suggested "Riverside Ramblers." The personnel shifted around a little, but in February 1937 it consisted of Luderin Darbone (1913–2008), fiddle; Lennis Sonnier (1917–93), guitar; and Joe Werner (1909–78), who sang the English numbers (and some of the French ones), occasionally whistled, and played harmonica and guitar.

It was Werner who brought "Wondering" to the Ramblers. He later gave an account to a journalist that awarded himself all the credit—

> It was back in my courtin' days. One day I sat down and started picking away at the guitar and playing the harmonica and the tune fell together. I worked out the words the same way. It was in Paco's Café over in Rayne. I had the song and words before I left Paco's that night.

—but on another occasion he said he had learned it from a hobo guitar player in Rayne, which is more likely, because the song had been around for something like a decade. It seems to have been first recorded by Jack Golding, a singer on WSMK in Dayton, Ohio, who dropped by the Gennett studios on several occasions to record standard and novelty numbers, including covers of "bum" songs by "Mac" McClintock and Goebel Reeves. His first recording for the company, though, in 1928, was "Wondering." Werner flattens out and simplifies the melody, moves some of the words around, and adds others ("Madame Queen," not in Golding's lyric, was the nickname of Stephanie St. Clair, a notorious female gang leader in '30s Harlem), but it's clearly the same song.

(Ben Sandmel Collection)

Just Received New Records, Including

WONDERING

By Riverside Ramblers

Boudreaux's Piano Shop

RADIOS AND MUSICAL INSTRUMENTS
EXPERT RADIO REPAIRS
SALES, SERVICE AND SUPPLIES PHONE 1231-J
Wilfred Boudreaux, Prop. 608 Scott Road Lafayette, La.

Lafayette Daily Advertiser, July 24, 1937. (Author's Collection)

Not, to be blunt, that it *is* much of a song, as far as the words are concerned. The power of the recording is the emotion Werner invests in it, the feeling, so typical of Cajun music, of an inexplicable, irrecoverable loss. Here it is the loss of a lover, but we may choose to discern, in the fog of the singer's misery, the dim outline of that older, ancestral loss, the original Acadian homeland.

★ ★ ★

The Riverside Ramblers recorded again in September 1937, but by that time Werner had joined Happy Fats' Rayne-Bo Ramblers. A couple of months later he had moved on again and was recording for Decca with a group called the Louisiana Rounders. Then, during 1938, he returned to Bluebird and Happy Fats' band. In these years, he was perhaps the most distinctive voice of south Louisiana, the nearest that '30s Cajun music came to producing its own Crosby or Vallee.

Werner believed that his hit record could have more momentum in its wheels than just what the Riverside Ramblers had given it, and while he was with the Louisiana Rounders he recorded an "Answer to Wondering," the problem now sorted: "I'm so gay, since you've come back to stay . . ." It was a wrong move: the people who had loved "Wondering" didn't want so easy a resolution. If heartbreak could be so readily repaired, maybe it hadn't been so bad in the first place: in record-collectors' lingo, not a break but a hair crack.

★ ★ ★

More than a decade later, "Wondering" was a hit all over again, thanks to an up-and-coming country singer named Webb Pierce. "Maybe you've been wonderin' about 'Wondering,'" wrote H. I. Mitchell in the *Rayne Weekly Acadian* in February 1952, "—the song that holds fourth ranking on the Hillbilly Hit Parade, and which has been pouring out of juke boxes and radio stations over the country more recently in

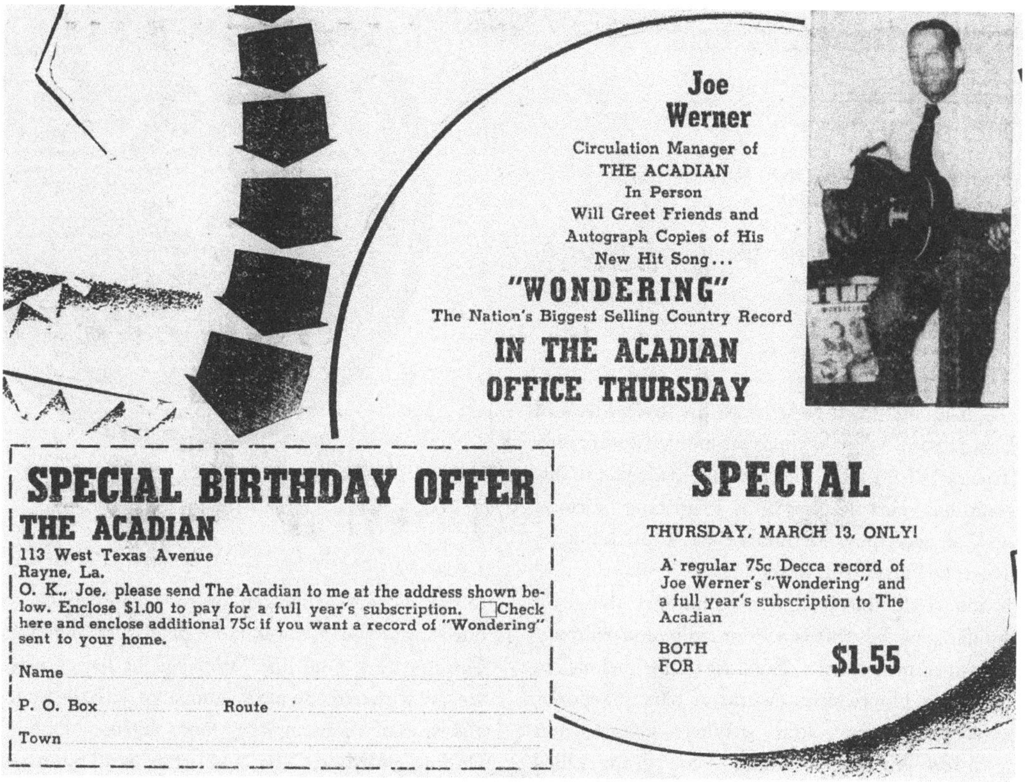

Fifteen years on, "Wondering" is a hit again (*Rayne Weekly Acadian*, March 13, 1952). (Author's Collection)

delicate waltz time via [a] recording of the Andrews Sisters." He then made his readers acquainted with "Joe Werner, author of the song hit," observing:

> Introducing you to Joe Werner is like introducing you to yourself. Probably no other man is as widely known throughout Acadia parish to grown-ups and young folks as Joe Werner, rural circulation manager of the Crowl[e]y Daily Signal. . . . For 4½ years, Joe was top entertainer on the Saturday Night Barn Dance over KSIG in Crowley. He sang "Wondering" in those years, too, for although the song has gained a tremendous popularity in past weeks, it's actually 18 years old. . . . (February 21, 1952)

Since Werner's name was printed on the record label as composer, he should have been making some money, especially after the Crowley paper announced, in mid-April, that Pierce's recording was now No. 1 on the Hillbilly Hit Parade. It would have been a good time for Werner to reconnect with his old fans; he had almost retired from music during the previous year, after his ten-year-old son Richard, who used to perform with him on radio, was killed in a road accident. In time, he did make a comeback, and maintained his local reputation into the '50s, appearing on KPLC-TV in Lake Charles, and lending his name to a column, "Along the Rural Routes," for the *Crowley Daily Signal*.

★ ★ ★

If Cajun music in the '30s was reshaped by the hillbilly music of the period, the process was not all one way. Cajun fiddlers like Leo Soileau, Luderin Darbone, and Doc Guidry left unmistakable fingerprints on the music of contemporary Southwestern stringbands. We can trace the thick blue lines of Cajun fiddling in the sound of Bill Nettles, who in the late '30s and '40s was prominent on the Southwest's answer to the Grand Ole Opry, the Louisiana Hayride; and then, a little later, in a Hayride performer who had the opportunity to absorb the sound of Cajun music and remodel it for the entire hillbilly audience—Hank Williams.

73

"THE LAST LETTER"

Rex Griffin
Decca 5383

Recorded in New York, NY, May 13, 1937
Released in summer 1937

Reissued on *The Last Letter* (Bear Family BCD15911)

Online: Spotify, YT

A man sits down to write to his lover. He is in despair. "Why do you treat me as if I were only a friend? What have I done that has made you so different and cold?" He has done everything he could think of, everything he thought she wanted, but it's no use: he knows he is losing her.

You could hardly find a commoner theme in popular song, but this is its first truly modern treatment in country music. "The Last Letter" belongs to the low-lit Hopperesque world of bars, jukeboxes, rented rooms, and solitary drinkers. It anticipates by a few years what would come to be called honkytonk music.

Honkytonk was urban; it bore the same relationship to old-time music as Chicago blues of the '40s and '50s did to antecedents in the Mississippi Delta—but with a difference. Honkytonk songs were less often based on old models because they were moving into new textual and emotional territory. The language of the ballad and the pre–World War I parlor song could not deal with honkytonk's newly uncovered themes of hedonistic partying and erotic disappointment. A fresh dialect was created, drawn from the vocabulary of mainstream popular song but given a honkytonk twist, like a street scene distorted by viewing it through a whiskey glass.

Take that startling line in the second verse: "I cannot offer you clothes that your young body craves." This is frank speaking as never before in country music, a rare moment of erotic physicality. Up to this point, any body mentioned in an old-time song would have been dead.

Part of the power of the recording lies in Rex Griffin's tone, the poignant melancholy of his voice. The situation the song depicts is real, and he evokes it with a pathos that is wholly credible. Few earlier singer-songwriters could have brought off this effect. Jimmie Rodgers, Griffin's obvious model, was either too ironic and distanced or too sentimental. No one else in the '30s was more plain-speaking. Take Griffin's stark final line, "Will you be happy when you are withered and old?" Compared with the honey and roses of a contemporary love song like "Nobody's Darling but Mine," "The Last Letter" is all bitterness and thorns.

★ ★ ★

Alsie "Rex" Griffin (1912–58) was from Gadsden, Alabama. In his late teens and early twenties, he sang on WAPI in Birmingham, first stop on a journey

Rex Griffin, ca. 1935. (Kevin Coffey Collection)

Emmett Miller. He signed this promotional picture for musician Claude Casey. (From the collection of the late Claude Casey)

across the terrain of Southern radio that would take him from Miami to Dallas. He joined Decca Records' hillbilly list, recording Rodgers-like blue yodels and original songs that hinted at a thoughtful, unclichéd writing style, as in the resigned hobo lament "I'm Just Passing Through." Thus for a couple of years, and then, in 1937, he recorded "The Last Letter." This and its reverse side "Over the River"—a mysterious song about a crossing over stormy waters, which prompts us to wonder whether the river is real or metaphorical—were the only sides made at the session, and his last recordings for almost two and a half years. Both facts are puzzling. Decca used recording dates efficiently and seldom recorded fewer than six or eight sides at a time; and Griffin was on a roll, his picture on the front of the company's hillbilly catalog, his discs selling well, this one his most successful yet.

Today, he is probably better known for his version of "Lovesick Blues," made a couple of years later, the source of Hank Williams's recording and every other version since. It describes a similar situation to that of "The Last Letter"—"I'm in love with a beautiful gal, but she don't care about me"—but here the singer is hardened to romantic disappointment, and his mood is almost jaunty. Besides, "Lovesick Blues" is colored by its history: literally, since it began life as a novelty blackface yodel, as in the 1925 and '28 recordings by Emmett Miller. (Griffin worked with Miller's vaudeville troupe in 1931 and may have learned the song directly from the boss.) Yodeling, however, though an often pleasing and sometimes ingenious device, is not readily compatible with serious emotional narrative. Griffin, an excellent yodeler, realized this and sang "The Last Letter" without it.

★ ★ ★

He signs off: "But to this world I will soon say my farewell at last . . . I will be gone when you read this last letter from me." In the words of the country music historian Kevin Coffey, "The Last Letter" is "essentially a suicide note set to music." Coffey detects "a fragile stoicism that was notably devoid of the cloying sentimentality that was so often the rule of the day" and identifies the woman who inspired it: "Griffin's first wife, Margaret, a gorgeous, dark-haired woman he'd met in Chattanooga who had been, by at least one account, a prostitute before her marriage to [him]. . . . [He] adored her and was devastated when their apparently volatile relationship ripped apart." According to his youngest brother, Buddy Griffin, he was never the same afterward.

★ ★ ★

Over the decades since its release, "The Last Letter" has become a country music standard, recorded by Jimmie Davis, the Blue Sky Boys, the Carter Family, Ray Price, Roy Acuff, Bob Wills, George Jones, Willie Nelson (a great admirer of the song), Waylon Jennings, and many others. Griffin continued to write, supported in later years by friends who recognized his gift, such as Ernest Tubb, but he never came up with anything to equal "The Last Letter."

When songwriters' early work proves to be their most potent, they sometimes have a hard time coming to terms with it. The music historian Arnold Shaw told a story about the African American singer and pianist Cecil Gant, who had a huge hit in the mid-'40s with his first recording, "I Wonder." Shaw met him a few years later while working for a music publisher. "I could tell that he was bugged by his inability to duplicate . . . 'I Wonder.' Through the years, I have seen this frustration and puzzlement in the eyes of publishers, writers, and artists, and it is a painful and unforgettable sight." Gant, like Griffin, spent some of his last years knocking at the doors of Nashville's record companies and music publishers. The two men probably never met, but had they done so, each might have recognized something in the other: the lost look of a man who has done something great and knows that he will never match it.

74

"HELLO STRANGER"

The Carter Family

Decca 5479

Recorded in New York, NY, June 17, 1937
Released on January 24, 1938

Reissued on *The Carter Family* (MCA MCAD-10088), *Hillbilly Blues* (ASV Living Era CD AJA5361)

Online: Spotify, YT

By the summer of 1937, the Carter Family—A. P., his wife, Sara, and sister-in-law Maybelle—had been making records for a decade. With 185 issuable sides behind them, they were one of the best-selling acts in old-time music, outstripping artists who had been going two, three, or even four years longer, such as Riley Puckett, Ernest Stoneman, Fiddlin' John Carson, Uncle Dave Macon, or Doc Roberts. Only Gene Autry and the ubiquitous Vernon Dalhart and Carson Robison could boast larger outputs.

But it wasn't just about the numbers. The Carters still *mattered*. Carson's career on disc was over, Roberts's too, and Dalhart's virtually so; Stoneman's had gone into hibernation, and Macon and Puckett had just a few sessions left; but the Carter Family, thanks in part to their nationwide exposure on TexMex border radio stations, held an evergreen appeal for record-buyers.

The group had ended their long association with Victor in 1935 and turned to Brunswick–ARC. In an industrious week of recording, they came up with forty marketable performances, but many were remakes of Victor sides like "Single Girl, Married Girl," "Keep on the Sunny Side," or "River of Jordan." Listeners may have detected the dull thuds of a group marking time.

Then, in 1936, the Carter Family signed with Decca, and it was as if the sun emerged from behind the clouds. The sixty recordings made during three long sessions in 1936–38 had a new richness, the blend of voices and instruments captured with warmth and depth, Maybelle's guitar front and center. A. P., evidently commissioned to do something bolder than recycle his back catalog, had accrued what would prove to be some of the most attractive pieces in their repertoire, among them "My Dixie Darling" (the first number they cut for Decca), "No Depression," "You've Been a Friend to Me," and "You Are My Flower." He also collected four songs that revealed what earlier recordings had only hinted at: their way with the blues.

★ ★ ★

Unlike Jimmie Rodgers, the Carter Family didn't have much truck with the blues. It may be the most important difference between them. Rodgers represents the man alone, with few ties or responsibilities, on the move, taking his fun where he finds it: any old place I hang my hat is home sweet home to me. He is a man living a blues life. The Carters, by contrast, stand for family, permanence, holding fast to the right: get behind me, Satan, and take those blues with you.

There had been blues titles in the Carters' earlier work—"Worried Man Blues," "East Virginia Blues," "Cannon Ball Blues," "Carter's Blues"—but only "Worried Man" had a blues form. The Decca recordings proved that there was a place in the Carters' world for actual blues numbers: not the strutting braggadocio Rodgers enacted in numbers like "Pistol Packin' Papa," or the wry jokefests of his blue yodels, but evocations of hard lives, as in "Coal Miner's Blues," or of the blue moods of wistfulness and loss, as in "Jealous Hearted Me," "Oh, Take Me Back," and "Hello Stranger."

"Hello, stranger—put your lovin' hand in mine . . . you are a stranger, but you're a pal of mine." These expressions of comradeship, of greeting an outsider, recall Henry Steele Commager's observation in *The American Mind*: "The American . . . reversed the whole history of language to make the term 'stranger' one of welcome." In a blues context, such

(OTM Collection)

almost Quaker-like sentiments seem surprising. But the Carters don't develop the theme: the next verse speaks up for the hard-working man as against the loafer, and the two that follow are about a sweetheart confined to prison. Then the first theme returns: "I'll see you when your troubles are like mine." Or does it? Is this an expression of sympathy and fellowship—or a prediction of a comeuppance? Does "I'll see you" mean just that, or does it carry a faint hint of challenge, like the "I'll see you" of a poker player?

The final verse resolves nothing: "Weepin' like a willow, mournin' like a dove . . . There's a girl up the country that I really love." No stranger, then. So what *is* this song about?

Well, it's a blues, and blues, by and large, place no premium on narrative coherence. As I remarked earlier (➤18) (and obviously there is some generalization here), blues do not tell stories. You want a story, read a dime novel. A blues operates more like a stand-up routine by a comedian with a short attention span, restlessly switching from topic to topic, creating a string of observations, sometimes aphorisms—"It takes a worried man to sing a worried song," as the Carters once sang—sometimes seemingly random snapshots of surrounding life, the shifts of subject prompted by verbal or mental, or possibly subconscious, associations and connections. Sometimes, there is no sequential logic at all.

While we may feel that "Hello Stranger" has puzzling discontinuities, we have no reason to think that A. P., who we assume laid at least an arranger's hand upon the song, saw it that way. *That*, he might have retorted, is how blues *are*. In any case, someone who could pass as fit for purpose the euphonious gibberish of "Wildwood Flower" ("twine with my mingles," "the pale and the leader") plainly wasn't troubled by texts that didn't make sense.

What raises "Hello Stranger" above this debate about meaning is the grace of the recording. The words are so well fitted to the tune, the speech rhythms so natural, that it's an aesthetic pleasure simply to sing them or listen to them. Sara and Maybelle deliver the song in a call-and-response pattern, Sara singing the first part of each line ("Hello, stranger—"), Maybelle the second ("—put your lovin' hand in mine"); it was the only time on all their recordings that they did this. Maybelle plays three exquisite choruses of finger-picked guitar. Finally, there is the arresting image of the song's name, fulfilling as it does a basic purpose of music: bringing people together, turning strangers into friends.

Perhaps that's why the title keeps turning up in the American song portfolio. It has been attached to a pleading love song by the rhythm 'n' blues crooner Titus Turner, a witty chat-up blues by Baby Boy Warren, a witless teen-pop number by Mickey & Sylvia, and, most memorably, Barbara Lewis's yearning "Hello Stranger" of 1963, in which "stranger" is used not in the Carters' sense but ironically, of a lover coming back after being gone too long.

Lesley Riddles. (Courtesy of Kip Lornell)

But in the mid-'30s, the title had another currency. Around the time the Carter Family were constructing a new repertoire for their Decca contract, radio listeners across the nation were tuning in every week to the NBC Red Network for the Jell-O Program with comedian Jack Benny. One of Benny's radio gang was a character called Schlepperman, played by Sam Hearn, a former dialect comedian and violinist on the vaudeville stage. And one of Schlepperman's trademark catchphrases was "Hello, stranger." Coincidence, or cultural diffusion?

Schlepperman's other favorite line, which he used as an excuse for just about anything, was "Jake sent me." As it happens, "Jake" was a family nickname for Sara Carter.

★ ★ ★

During the Carter Family's recording years, A. P. had a collaborator in the African American singer and guitarist Lesley Riddles, then living in Kingsport, Tennessee. While collecting songs in that city, A. P. heard Riddles, took a liking to him, and invited him over to Maces Springs, Virginia, to sing and play for the family. Soon Riddles was visiting the Carters frequently and often accompanied A. P. on safari. "I went out with A. P. about fifteen times to collect songs," he recalled years later. "A lot of the time I would help him remember the tune."

The Carters did not acquire many blues from these forays. "We never did get any songs from colored folks," said Riddles, but in some cases he himself was the family's source for a song, and he recognized his hand in "The Cannonball" (alias "Cannon Ball Blues") and "Bear Creek Blues." Either he was modest about his contribution to the Carters' repertoire and sound, or he genuinely didn't believe it had been very significant, but according to Sara, it was Riddles who unearthed most of the rich seam of blues they mined on their Decca recordings: the old Ma Rainey number "Jealous Hearted Me," "Oh, Take Me Back," and "Hello Stranger."

75

"COTTON MILL BLUES"

Lester (The Highway Man) [Lester "Pete" Bivins] Decca 5559

Recorded in Charlotte, NC, June 9, 1938
Released on July 1, 1938

Come all you people, I'll tell you somethin' true.
When you work in a cotton mill, what you got to do.
Get up before daylight,
You labor all day until it gets night . . .
Ashes to ashes and dust to dust,
Let the rich man live and the poor man bust.

When dinnertime comes you'll have to run;
They'll blow the whistle before you're done.
Payday comes, you ain't got a penny
When you pay your bills 'cause you got so many.
Sometimes you hear a racket like a peckerwood:
Merchants outside tryin' to sell their goods.
Merchants' hair's just about gray,
Studyin' how to get the poor man's pay.
Ashes to ashes and dust to dust,
Let the rich man live and the poor man bust . . .

Now when wintertime comes there's hell to pay.
You'll see the boss, you'll have to say,
"I want a load of wood and I want a ton of coal,
Take a dollar out a week or I'll go in the hole."
Have to buy [from] a merchant at some chain store;
You can't afford to pay any more.
You don't starve, I'm a son of a gun,
Cain't buy beans without any mon'—
Ashes to ashes and dust to dust,
Let the rich man live and the poor man bust.

You go to the store and the clerk won't speak;
You go downstairs, grab a little piece of meat.
You can work all week, you can work your best,
Can't buy your wife a ten-cent dress.
Ashes to ashes and dust to dust,
Let the rich man live and the poor man bust.

When Alan Lomax was assembling his *List of American Folk Songs on Commercial Records*, completed in 1942, "in order that the interested musician or student of American society may explore this unknown body of Americana with readiness," one of the most recent releases he picked was "Cotton Mill Blues" by "Lester (The Highway Man)," adding the comment "tells problems of cotton mill workers." In order to compile his list of 350 items, Lomax said, he had listened to "three thousand odd" discs, including many by musicians mentioned in this book, but he had seemingly not come across—because, if he had, he would surely have picked at least one of them—the textile-topical songs of David McCarn. This singer-guitarist's recording career had been brief (eleven issued sides for Victor in 1930–31) but his first release, "Cotton Mill Colic," was an original commentary, by turns humorous and acerbic, on the conditions of mill workers' lives in the North Carolina Piedmont. (In his youth, McCarn lived and worked in Belmont, and it's possible that he knew Wilmer Watts [➤13].) The recording had been moderately successful, selling over 4,800 copies and prompting two successors, and the first of these, "Poor Man, Rich Man (Cotton Mill Colic No. 2)," issued in early 1931, was the model, though Lomax was unaware of it, for the "Cotton Mill Blues" he approved a decade later.

The first thing to say about "Poor Man, Rich Man"/"Cotton Mill Blues" is that evidently not much had changed in seven years. If the earlier text's allusions to mill workers' poverty and near-starvation had not still been relevant, the later singer—we shall come to him shortly—would hardly have chosen the song. He even extends McCarn's catalog of deprivation, for the final verse, with its contemptuous store clerk and its husband unable to afford even a dime for his wife's dress, does not come from "Poor Man,

(OTM Collection, from Mrs. Maggie Bivins)

Rich Man." He also drops half a stanza of McCarn's text in which the composer waxes a little sententious about "the cotton mill people [who] make the world go round," and their love of "a little fun."

There is another difference between the two songs: just two words switched, but with a point. McCarn's refrain ended: "Let the poor man live and the rich man bust." In 1930, it would have had a revolutionary ring in the Piedmont, this message that poor people had a right to a decent life, even if it meant lightening the pockets of a few plutocrats. But "Lester" twists the slogan round, meeting McCarn's political optimism with a cynic's reply. "This is how the world really works, Dave: the rich get richer, the poor get screwed. 'Let the *rich man* live and the *poor man* bust.' That's the way to say it."

★ ★ ★

"Lester (The Highway Man)" was Decca's moniker for Lester Bivins of Shelby, North Carolina. He was born on May 16, 1903, in Cleveland County, which from the 1920s to the '50s was an important cotton producer and processor, with textile mills reputed to be the best paying in the South. By his mid-teens, Bivins was working as a doffer in a mill in Shelby, possibly Lily Mill, where his wife Maggie was working in 1930 and he himself later in the decade and into the '40s. (Earl Scruggs, who was born in Shelby in 1924, worked at the Lily Mill up until the day in December 1945 when he joined Bill Monroe's Blue Grass Boys.) Founded in 1903, Lily was a thread mill that also produced instruction books for weaving, crocheting, tatting, rug-hooking, and the like.

Shelby was a unionized town, and Bivins's revised revival of an anthem from seven years earlier would readily have found listeners who knew firsthand what the song was about and why it was worth reviving. But I see a further, and quite different, reason why this record was made. Here is a musician taking a known, recorded song (though he changed its title and claimed the composer credit) and performing it in overdrive, with a dynamic flat-picked guitar accompaniment McCarn could not have conceived. This was not peculiar to "Cotton Mill Blues": at the same session, Bivins similarly re-energized Charlie Poole's "The Highway Man" (1926) and the Allen Brothers' "Maybe Next Week Some Time" (1930). The year before, at a date for Bluebird (billed as "Lester Pete Bivins"), he had reworked Oscar Ford's "Married Life Blues" (➤38), two of Dock Walsh's banjo songs, and Frank Hutchison's "Coney Isle" and "Back in My Home Town," all introduced on disc in the mid-to-late 1920s. In each case, Bivins smashed the original template with his speed, his verve, and his flying-fingered guitar playing.

So Lester Bivins finds a place among a small group of significant players in '30s country music that might be called the upcyclers. Their métier was rolling out songs originally recorded a decade or so earlier, recharged by a more spirited tempo and a more modern accompaniment, and they bequeathed their approach to the first generation of bluegrass musicians. It's a practical demonstration of part of what I mean by rural rhythm.

You can spy this kind of reconstruction in some of the work of Cliff and Bill Carlisle or the Shelton Brothers, but the most notable upcyclers were J. E. Mainer's Mountaineers. At their Bluebird session of June 1936, for example, they recast a series of 1920s hillbilly hits like "The Old and Faded Picture" (i.e., "Picture on the Wall [➤15]), "Take

(OTM Collection, from Mrs. Maggie Bivins)

Me Home to the Sweet Sunny South," "Walk That Lonesome Valley," "Johnson's Old Grey Mule," "Goin' Down the River of Jordan," "Why Do You Bob Your Hair, Girls?," and "Watermelon on the Vine," doubtless conned from 78s by the Georgia Yellow Hammers, the Carter Family, Blind Alfred Reed, and the Skillet-Lickers.

A&R men like Eli Oberstein and Dave Kapp were surely aware of what was going on. They had been in the business long enough to know there had been earlier recordings of these songs. But the 1920s recordings had long disappeared from the catalogs and perhaps were beginning to fade from public memory—not so much so that they could be reintroduced as if brand new, but enough that they might be offered to record-buyers in a fresh format. (When, in 1939, an east Tennessee country swing band called the Dixieland Swingsters recorded one of the oldest hillbilly numbers, they wryly titled it "A New Dress for Ida Red.") Reliance on previously recorded material, once frowned upon by record producers, was no longer a problem: on the contrary, it seems to have been actively encouraged.

★ ★ ★

Bivins may have had a radio career in North Carolina; he certainly did when he crossed the state line south and joined WSPA in Spartanburg. As his widow, Maggie, recalled, most of his public appearances were at fiddlers' contests, in Shelby, Charlotte, or Spartanburg. In 1967, Lomax printed "Cotton Mill Blues" in *Hard Hitting Songs for Hard-Hit People*, naming Bivins as both composer and recordist. I wonder if he knew that the musician was not only still alive but also still playing. Around that time, the Bivinses resettled in the Myrtle Beach area, and in the '70s Lester's beaky-nosed face, bent over his guitar, can be spotted in newspaper photographs of local events like the Hilton Head Island Arts & Jazz Festival. He died on April 19, 1978.

76

"GUITAR BLUES"/"SWEET HAWAIIAN CHIMES"

The DeZurik Sisters (Caroline and Mary Jane)

Vocalion 04704, Conqueror 9252

Recorded in Chicago, IL, December 16, 1938
Released in 1939

Online: Spotify, YT

"I once had a mama, she make a freight train leave the rail—now I've got a gal, she make a tomcat heist his tail. I've got the guitar blues, just as blue as I can be . . ." When Cliff Carlisle recorded "Guitar Blues" in 1931, it was a standard-issue hillbilly blue yodel. Seven years on, a Midwestern cowgirl act picked it up and transformed it into a coruscating display of instrumental impressionism.

The only real instrument involved was a strummed acoustic guitar. Balanced upon it was a rococo construction of vocal effects: yodels, tweedles, growls, scat, birdcalls, falsetto imitations of steel-guitar licks. Some of the vocal trickery recalled the muted-trumpet effects of the Mills Brothers.

The other side of the record, barely less startling in its execution, was a new popular number, "Sweet Hawaiian Chimes," part composed by the Hawaiian guitarist Lani McIntire; it had been recorded eight months earlier by Bing Crosby with McIntire's Hawaiian group. The singers' crystalline harmony quivers with bell sounds and steel-guitar glissandi.

Nobody else in hillbilly music was doing anything remotely like this.

★ ★ ★

Mary Jane and Caroline DeZurik were from around Royalton, in Benton County, Minnesota. This is deep Garrison Keillor country. His imagined Mist County, he once revealed, is located somewhere round actual Stearns County, which borders Benton County on the west. Name-dropped real towns in the Lake Wobegon stories, such as St. Cloud and St. Wendel, are in Stearns County.

> One day they were singing as they did the housework, and Mary Jane picked up a guitar that her brother had recently bought and began plunking on it. . . . They found that they sang well together, and stuck to it. A short time later they won an amateur talent contest in Royalton, and were sent to St. Cloud, Minn., to enter another contest. It was there that radio talent scouts heard them and started them on their way. (*Moville* [Iowa] *Mail*, December 28, 1939)

They first broadcast over KSTP in St. Paul, but by the winter of 1936, when Mary Jane was just twenty and Caroline eighteen, they had graduated to WLS in Chicago, where they were featured on the Saturday Merry-Go-Round and the National Barn Dance. They were instant favorites with the WLS audience, evidenced by letters to the station's magazine *Stand By!* "The addition of the DeZurik Sisters makes the Barn Dance all the better," wrote a correspondent in March 1937. "We have never heard anyone yodel quite like them. More power to those two Minnesota gals!" In May, a listener asked, "Why not have the best part of the Barn Dance first? Put the DeZurik Sisters on and let them sing and yodel for everybody." "I never have heard better singing and yodeling than that of the DeZurik Sisters. We'd sit up all night just to hear them," enthused a fan in October. "I heard the DeZurik Sisters sing for the first time the other day," wrote another in January 1938. "I think they are the best yodelers I have ever heard."

They joined the National Barn Dance touring shows and in August 1940 were a hit at the Sheboygan County Fair, "called upon for numerous encores as they offered novelty songs, one upon another. Their apparently most popular contribution

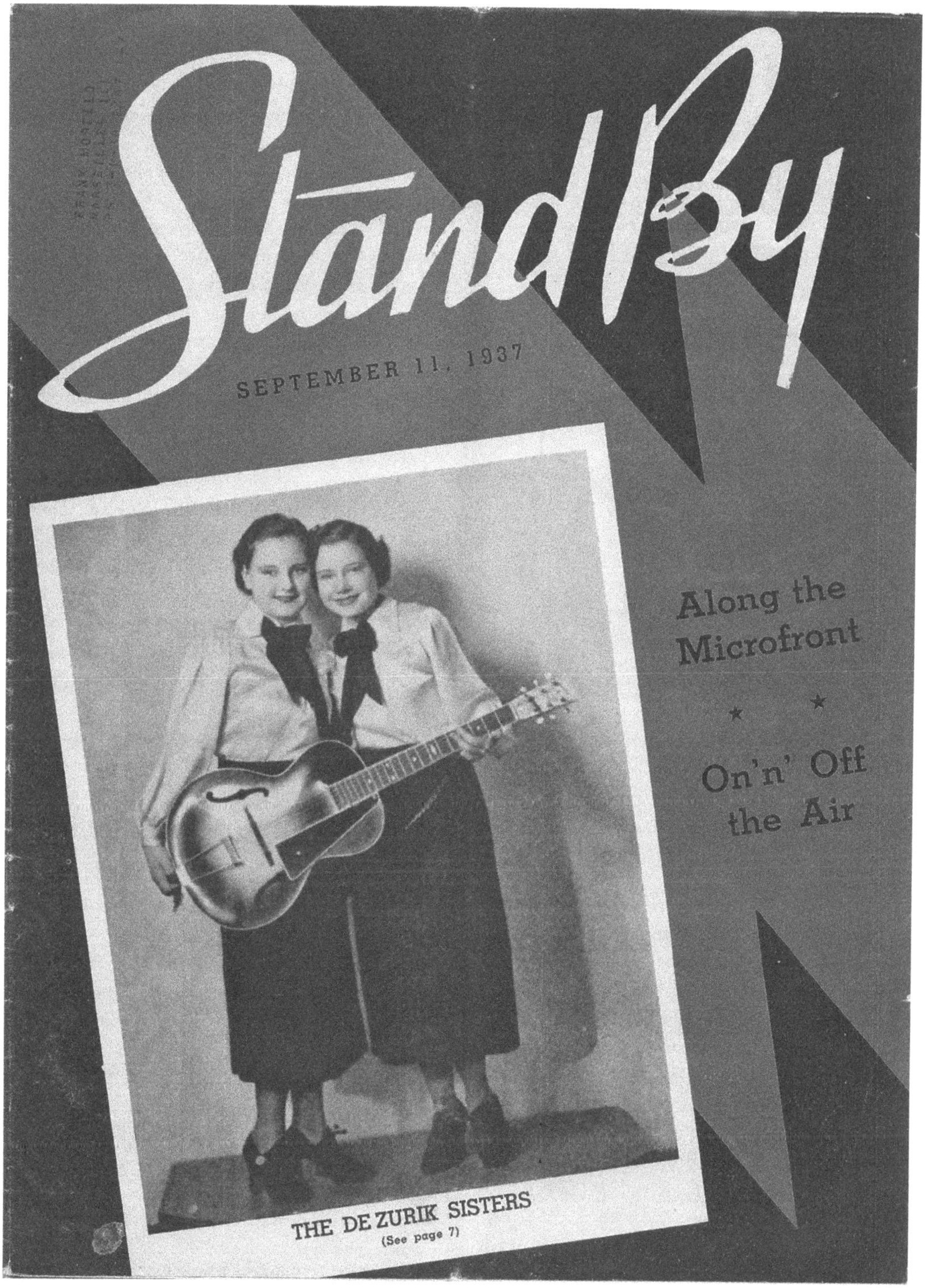

(Author's Collection)

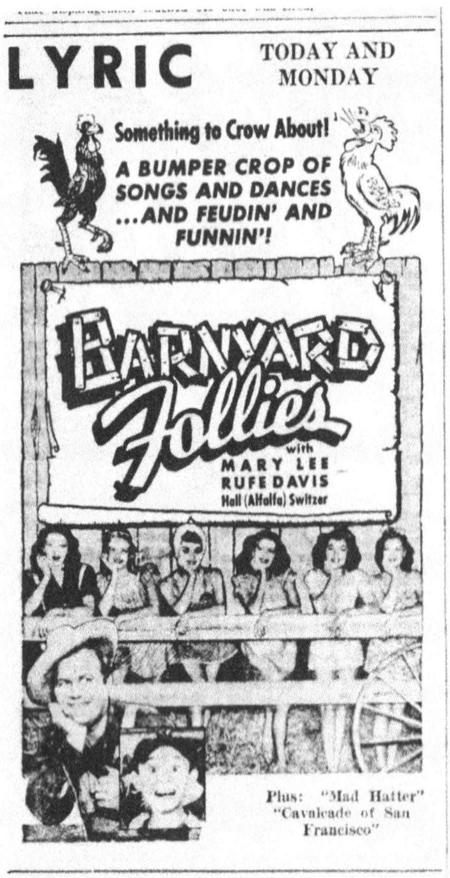

Big Spring [Texas] *Daily Herald*, February 9, 1941. (Author's Collection)

was a 'cackle song.'" That month, they were featured on the cover of *The Jamboree*, an early country music fanzine published in Frankton, Indiana. In October, *The Jamboree* reported that they had left for Hollywood to appear in the movie *Barnyard Follies*. Hollywood had decided that hillbilly movies were the next big thing, and weighed in with *Shine On, Harvest Moon* (1938) and *The Village Barn Dance* (1940), both featuring Lulu Belle and Scotty; *Grand Ole Opry* (1940) with Roy Acuff, the Weaver Brothers and Elviry, and Uncle Dave Macon; and *Country Fair* (1941), with Lulu Belle and Scotty again.

National Barn Dance artists, thrown into each other's company during the long radio shows and on tour, often formed romantic alliances. Eva Overstake of the Three Little Maids married Red Foley, while her sister and co-Maid Virginia had a brief marriage to guitarist and comedian Red Blanchard. Billie Flannery of the Flannery Sisters married Howard Black of the Hoosier Sod Busters, and Dolly Good of the Girls of the Golden West wed Tex Atchison of the Prairie Ramblers. Christine Endeback, "The Little Swiss Miss," married Jack Holden. Lulu Belle and Scotty turned their stage double act into the real thing, but the station didn't release the news at first, in case it lost them some of their fans. It was later revealed when Lulu Belle became pregnant, and the response was so warm (booties by every mail) that the station changed its policy.

So when, within a couple of months in summer 1940, Caroline DeZurik married Rusty Gill, singer and guitarist with the Sod Busters, and Mary Jane wed Augie Klein, who played accordion in the WLS house band the Rangers, the unions were proudly reported in the 1941 *WLS Family Album*. (Their younger sister, Eva, took the broad hint and married Ray Klein, Augie's younger brother and another accordionist.)

Since 1937, the DeZuriks had also been appearing on Checkerboard Time, a show sponsored by Ralston Purina. Working for chicken feed—literally, because Purina manufactured foods for farm animals, including Chick Startena—they were known as the Cackle Sisters. After a break in which they both started families, they signed up with Purina again in 1944 and took the act to Nashville and WSM. Some of their radio programs from this period survive, and they are remarkable, the sisters imitating whippoorwills or mandolins, and clucking, chirping, and crowing in harmony like Disneyfied chickens.

Mary Jane retired in 1946 but Caroline carried on, joined by another younger sister, Lorraine. Then Lorraine quit, and Caroline took the place of Patsy Montana as the female voice of the Prairie Ramblers—or the Polka Chips, as the Ramblers called themselves in a calculated idiom switch in the mid-'50s. In this guise, Caroline was for several years the voice of radio ads for Busch Bavarian Beer. Mary Jane died in 1981, Caroline and Lorraine in 2009.

Unsurprisingly, given the very particular nature of their act, they have had no followers. I hear something of their precision yodeling in the work of two women who were active in '40s Australian country music, Shirley Thoms and June Holms: both skillful vocal technicians, but with no leanings toward scat, steel-guitar mockery, or chicken noises. I think this is as it should be. The DeZurik Sisters stand alone, a wondrous oddity, unchallenged in their field—or perhaps I should say barnyard.

77

"TRUCK DRIVER'S BLUES"

Cliff Bruner and His Boys

Decca 5725

Recorded in Houston, TX, August 26, 1939
Released in September 1939

Reissued on *Cliff Bruner and His Texas Wanderers* (Bear Family BCD15932), *Western Swing: Texas 1928–1944* (Frémeaux FA032)

Online: Spotify, YT

Preparing for a summer 1939 Decca session at the Rice Hotel in Houston, bandleader Cliff Bruner turned for fresh material to a friend in the city, the steel-guitar player and songwriter Ted Daffan. He was in luck: Daffan had a bookful. On August 26, his first day of recording, Bruner cut eight songs, six of them written by Daffan. One of them was a melancholic medium-tempo blues number, sung by pianist Moon Mullican, with Cliff joining him on the refrains.

"Feelin' tired an' weary from my head down to my shoes . . . Never did have nothin', I got nothin' much to lose . . . Got a lowdown feelin', truck driver's blues." Moon sings for the dogged trucker, barreling along, trying to make time, looking forward to getting to town and drowning his troubles with a honkytonk gal. He plays a delectable blues chorus, while Bob Dunn's steel guitar mutters and grumbles behind the singing. It was a Yogi Berra record: short, strong, and memorable. It was called—what else?—"Truck Driver's Blues."

★ ★ ★

"What gave you the idea for that song?" Nick Tosches asked Daffan in a 1975 interview.

> I had to write original songs for a recording session . . . and I was searching frantically for a commercial idea. After dances we'd stop at these little roadside cafés, for hamburgers or chili, one thing or another, and I noticed the truck drivers always stopping in these cafés, and it occurred to me that if someone wrote them a song they would play it even if it wasn't very good. And so I wrote the song "Truck Driver's Blues," and they loved it. In fact, I've had hundreds of 'em ask me—*tell* me that I must've been a truck driver. Of course, I never had.
>
> I'd been trying to get it on record for about two years. I had auditioned the song to Dave Kapp, who was then A&R man in the country field for Decca. I was with the Bar-X Cowboys at

Cliff Bruner. (OTM Collection, from the late Cliff Bruner)

> that time, and we played it everywhere we went. It was a very popular request song, and requests from the truck drivers that attended our dances went all over the country and it finally got back to Dave Kapp, who had turned down the song in the first place, and he telegraphed to each of the bands that was recording here in Houston . . . to find the song about the truck driver. And Cliff Bruner got there first.

Beating, by a short head, his fellow Houston bandleader Leon Selph and the Shreveport policeman and honkytonk singer Buddy Jones.

> Then the truck drivers demanded that all over America, instead of just down South—ordinarily, country music in the '30s, the only sales was here in the South, the juke boxes. So this was a very big song, and as a result Arthur Satherley of Columbia flew down and signed me up as an artist on the strength of the song "Truck Driver's Blues."

Like the first writers of cotton-mill songs (➤51), Daffan had identified an occupational group that was known to everyone around him yet had never been featured in songs. In writing about truck drivers, realistically and with sympathy, he gave them stature, worth, a story of their own.

His song was covered by the Light Crust Doughboys (Vocalion, 1939) and subsequently recorded by Webb Pierce, Chet Atkins, Red Simpson, Asleep at the Wheel, and several more.

Ted Daffan. (OTM Collection)

Merle Haggard recorded a different song with the same title, and Marty Stuart another. Daffan's idea had thrown a new ingredient into the primordial soup of country music. Trucking songs became a subgenre of their own, from the Delmore Brothers' "The Dying Truckdriver" (1940), Dick Reinhart's "Truck Drivers' Coffee Stop" (1941), and Karl and Harty's "Truck Drivers' Sweetheart" (1942) to hit numbers of the '50s and '60s like "Truck Driving Man," "Truck Drivin' Queen," "Truck Driver's Nightmare," "Phantom 309," and the biggest of the trucking hits, Dave Dudley's "Six Days on the Road."

"Trucking songs and the subculture they reflect are in a way a symbiosis of railroad and cowboy folkways," argued Frederick E. Danker. "[M]any [trucking] songs extol the hardihood of men making it alone on long runs across the plains, deserts, and mountains. The trucker is frequently pictured as a heroic figure in the mold of the cowboy myth."

Don Pierce of Starday Records, a Nashville label that led the field in the '50s and '60s in trucking-song compilation albums, told Danker that Southerners liked trucking songs "because they can combine the main ingredients of country songs in one song: women, drinking, gambling, traveling, and death." He added that Southerners associated truck driving with "the old moonshine runs in souped-up cars"—shades of "The Fiddlin' Bootleggers" (➤17)—"and the tradition of the stock car races which grew out of them."

★ ★ ★

Spoiler alert: some trucking songs have nothing to do with big eighteen-wheelers. They refer to truckin', a dance craze originating in Harlem that became nationally popular in the mid-'30s. Or at least ostensibly they do, but several of them had considerable potential for being heard as something else again, such as "Can't Nobody Truck Like Me," "Keep on Truckin'," and "Everybody's Truckin'." In the last of these, when recorded by the Texas swing band the Modern Mountaineers (Bluebird, 1937), the vocalists audibly slip from "truckin'" to the obvious rhyme. This was almost certainly a recorded first, cut a year earlier than the record usually identified as the first to sneak in the f-word, Eddy Duchin and His Orchestra's "Ol' Man Mose."

★ ★ ★

Cliff Bruner's Texas Wanderers, ca. 1938: (left to right) Leo Raley, Dickie McBride, Cliff Bruner, Moon Mullican, J. R. Chatwell, Randall Raley, Hezzie Bryant, Bob Dunn. At the time he recorded "Truck Driver's Blues," Bruner had no regular band but recruited for the session his former colleagues Dunn, Mullican, Bryant, and probably McBride, plus banjoist Johnny Thames. (OTM Collection, from the late Leo Raley)

Cliff Bruner's six-piece band and its trucking song symbolize a crossroads moment in country music: the point where Texas swing, the music shaped by Milton Brown, Bob Wills, the Light Crust Doughboys, and the Hi-Flyers, begins to split into two directions, separate but always in each other's ears: Western Swing and honkytonk. In the conventional narrative of country music history, in 1939 honkytonk is still work in progress, waiting for the molding hands of Ernest Tubb, Webb Pierce, and Lefty Frizzell; but with its tight arrangements, carefully leashed improvisation, jazz instinct, and blues feeling, "Truck Driver's Blues" seems to me to be as good as a blueprint.

78

"NEW SAN ANTONIO ROSE"

Bob Wills and His Texas Playboys
Vocalion/Okeh 05694

Recorded in Saginaw, TX, April 16, 1940
Released in August 1940

Reissued on *The Essential Bob Wills 1935–1947* (Columbia/Legacy CK48958)

Online: Spotify, YT

"Deep within my heart lies a melody, a song of old San Antone . . ." The tune's come-hither swing, the lush arrangement, suggesting both the open spaces of a Western movie soundtrack and the scented closeness of a night in old Mexico . . . and above it all, Tommy Duncan, the Bing of Western Swing, remembering a night and a woman and evoking a city. Easy to see why this tune found its way onto every jukebox in the Southwest.

In fact, it did so twice.

Bob Wills and His Texas Playboys first recorded "San Antonio Rose" in November 1938. Frankie McWhorter described the occasion in his reminiscences, *Cowboy Fiddler in Bob Wills' Band*:

> The Colonel [producer Art Satherley] went back in the control room and the boys asked Bob what they were going to do. Bob said, "I don't have any idea. I'm going to play the bridge of 'The Spanish Two-Step' backwards, and Leon [McAuliffe], when I get through, you do anything you want to do and let's get out of here."
>
> They played it through for a time and the Colonel came running out of there with his eyes wide open, said, "Bob, what do you call that tune?" Bob said, "You know, we haven't named it. We were going to let you name it. This tune's especially for you and you can name it anything you want to." He said, "I'm going to call it 'San Antonio Rose.'"

It's a good story, but McWhorter didn't join the Playboys until more than twenty years afterward, so he can have heard it only secondhand. Perhaps by then it was band lore. Some of it we know to be wrong. "'Let's get out of here'" implies that Wills was hurrying to finish the session, and this was their last number; in fact, it was the first. But Al Stricklin—who *was* there, playing piano—did remember that Satherley named the tune, and Satherley himself later confirmed it. The reference to "Spanish Two Step," a tune the Playboys had recorded at their first session in 1935, also rings half-true, because the melody of "San Antonio Rose" is clearly based on it, but it wasn't "played backwards," whatever that might mean; just, as Stricklin says, "rewritten and modified."

This first "San Antonio Rose" was instrumental, apart from a few of Wills's trademark interjections. Issued in April 1939—coupled, aptly enough, with a song we have met before, "The Convict and the Rose" (➤23)—it sold well; according to Wills's biographer Charles R. Townsend, at that point it was "the nearest thing to a really big hit that Wills had ever had."

Al Stricklin didn't think much of it at first—"it was just another number to me"—but he gradually came to feel that it had "that little extra something."

> It made you feel the wind blowing and you could see the farmers struggling against the wind and drought and feeling like they were whipped but all of the time they knew they weren't because somewhere out there floating on the clouds beyond the burning sun was hope. The melody put that hope into the hearts of people.

Early in 1940, Irving Berlin, Inc., of New York declared an interest in publishing the number, if it could be fitted with lyrics. These were duly composed

The Texas Playboys at the Blue Moon Dance Pavilion in Tulsa, spring/summer 1939: (left to right) Herman Arnspiger, Leon McAuliffe (steel), Zeb McNally (alto), Everett Stover (trumpet), Joe Ferguson (tenor), Tubby Lewis (trumpet), Tiny Mott (tenor), Bob Wills, Smoky Dacus (drums), Jesse Ashlock (fiddle), Son Lansford (bass), Johnnie Lee Wills (banjo), Tommy Duncan, Al Stricklin (piano), Eldon Shamblin (guitar), O. W. Mayo. (OTM Collection)

by committee, the principal contributors being Wills, Duncan, and trumpeter Everett Stover. And what lyrics they are: insinuating, mysterious ("enchantment strange as the blue up above"), a sequence of images that doesn't quite amount to a narrative. The people at Berlin, Inc., couldn't figure it out, so they rewrote it as a conventional cowboy song, a decision that Wills's lawyer fought hard, and eventually successfully, to reverse.

The first "San Antonio Rose" had simply alternated the fiddles and Leon McAuliffe's steel guitar. In the revised version, titled "New San Antonio Rose," Wills, or perhaps Satherley, made the radical decision to dispense with both fiddles and steel: the vocal verse is sandwiched between a verse of reeds and rhythm and another that's split between the mariachi-style brass section and the reeds. "New San Antonio Rose" was an anomaly: a hillbilly record with no typically hillbilly lead instruments.

A year later, the band made a third version, reinstating the fiddles and steel. It probably represents more accurately how they played the song on stage—for instance, at the Grand Ole Opry on December 30, 1944, when the horns and drums offended hillbilly music conservatives—but the recording went unreleased at the time and had to wait sixty years to be heard.

★ ★ ★

Wills had enjoyed strong sellers before, but "New San Antonio Rose" would be his biggest record yet. It seems to have taken a few months to catch on, but in a roundup of the year's hits in the *San Antonio Express* on the last day of 1940, the reviewer noted, albeit somewhat sniffily: "In the string band section (which this column does not regularly review) Bob

Wills' NEW SAN ANTONIO ROSE made quite the biggest splash."

In the rival *San Antonio Light*, a few months later, record critic Renwicke E. Cary was more sympathetic: "Thrusting steadily upward in recent weeks, 'NEW SAN ANTONIO ROSE' has blossomed into one of the most popular recorded tunes in America today. It is not yet among the 10 biggest hits, and it may never be; but, according to sales indexes, it is just outside this charmed circle and still gaining favor" (March 9, 1941).

Cary went on to contribute his dime to the Bob Wills Myth Fund—"Compared with Bob's early lot in life, that of the most downtrodden Horatio Alger hero was a silver-spoon-in-the-mouth existence"—and to praise him for knowing his place: "[He] has become the idol of dance lovers in scores of small communities in Texas, Oklahoma, Arkansas and other states in this region. These people acclaimed him and he remained among them. He did not seek national fame, although apparently it has now come to him. . . . [I]t is through 'NEW SAN ANTONIO ROSE' that he reaches his greatest audience."

The hillbilly fanzine *The Jamboree* reported in its issue of October 25, 1941, that "Rose" "has just passed the 230,000 mark in sales." The record charted in that year and again in 1943. It helped that it was covered: on Bluebird by the Gray Gordon orchestra and, for the hillbilly list, by Roy Hall's Blue Ridge Entertainers; and on Decca by Texas Jim Lewis's Lone Star Cowboys (with Spade Cooley on fiddle) and, most significantly, by Bing Crosby, with another country-going-mainstream song on the reverse, Floyd Tillman's "It Makes No Difference Now," a coupling said to have sold a million. The song even gave its name, but nothing more, to a movie, *San Antonio Rose* (1941).

★ ★ ★

Not everyone was partial to the smell of the "Rose."

"Every once in a while," wrote Nina Laura Smith in her "Disc and Dial" column in the *Denton* [Texas] *Lass-O*,

> a hillbilly number with golden ears of corn sticking out all over the thing catches on amoung [*sic*] so-called sophfisticates [*sic*] and gets played more than the favorite popular tunes. Such an oddity is "San Antonio Rose." . . . But, even the most horrified jitterbugs will have to admit that in its way it has something and it isn't impossible for dancing of a sort. (November 29, 1940)

In his *Pampa* [Texas] *News* column "Tex's Topics" (November 18, 1940), Tex DeWeese commented sourly, "Life is still being made miserable for us by persons who delight in dropping a nickel into 'New San Antonio Rose' just to watch us wince." The same paper reported in August 1941 on a "memorable night" at the local station KPDN (owned by the *News*, and the location, some years earlier, of the first broadcasts by Woody Guthrie) when disc jockey Bob Morris first broke a station rule, that no record be played more than once on a request program, by spinning "New San Antonio Rose" three times, and then broke the disc in front of the mike, in what the paper described as "a gesture of consideration for the feelings of both those who loved to hear it over and over again and those who complained so vigorously at its to[o] frequent airing."

An anonymous commentator in the *Menard* [Texas] *News* joined the critics' circle: "This song . . . may baffle or even irritate fastidious rhetoricians, and its tune is strictly golden bantam." But the writer went on to make a sound point:

> New San Antonio Rose was evidence of a new factor in the U. S. song business. . . . It was a seller long before Tin Pan Alley heard it. For Texas has boomed mightily as a source and an outlet for popular music. The late guitar-toting Jimmie Rogers [*sic*] . . . helped start the boom, on Victor hillbilly records a dozen years ago. Now Victor's Bill Boyd, Columbia's Gene Autry, Bob Wills, Bonnie Blue Eyes and Patsy Montana sing to the nation the songs that Texas makes. And the Kapp brothers, who run Decca, see to it that Bing Crosby cro[o]ns the Texas sellers. . . .
>
> Most Southwest minstrelsy sticks to an ancient form: a 16-measure ballad, repeated over and over. But melodies have taken on a Tin Pan Alley cast, with embellishments which the Southwest takes to be "hot." (March 27, 1941)

Those hot embellishments are what collectors and music buffs value Western Swing for: the invention of hillbilly jazz. But this music has always had a sentimental side, too. Think of Wills's "Maiden's Prayer" or "Faded Love," Milton Brown's "My Precious Sonny Boy" or "The Waltz You Saved for Me," or the Light

A rare close-up of Bob Wills and his rhythm section at a dance, ca. 1938: (left to right) Bob Wills, Tommy Duncan, Johnnie Lee Wills, Smokey Dacus, Eldon Shamblin. (OTM Collection)

Crust Doughboys' "There's an Empty Cot in the Bunkhouse Tonight." Latterly, when much of the spirit of youthful inquiry and musical experiment that created hillbilly jazz had ebbed away, a large part of the legacy of Western Swing lay in these sweeter, slower songs, the oldies-but-goodies of the Texas retirement-home set.

But that was all in the future when the Texas Playboys cut "New San Antonio Rose." In 1940, there was a young, hungry audience for this music, and, within a couple of years, that audience would spread far beyond the Southwest, as the shipyards and munitions factories of wartime southern California gave jobs to thousands of incomers from Texas, Oklahoma, and Arkansas, economic migrants for whom, as the disc jockey Cliff Johnson, aka "Cactus Jack," remarked, "Bob Wills was like a little tin Jesus." Coming off shift, they crowded immense dance pavilions to jive to the Western brand of swing music dispensed by Wills, Spade Cooley, and Hank Penny, and then drift into a romantic, nostalgic swoon at "a song of old San Antone," a city that many of them would never live in again, perhaps never even revisit.

With that fanbase, and hits as solid as "New San Antonio Rose," which eventually sold a reputed 2 million copies, Wills became a force in the national, not just regional, disc business. The music trade paper *Metronome* confided to its readers in April 1941 that "this here Bob Wills is the best-selling Columbia records band at the moment." On the ballroom and dancehall circuit, he equaled or surpassed the drawing power of mainstream contemporaries like Benny Goodman, Artie Shaw, or the Dorsey Brothers. *Metronome* declared the Texas Playboys "some of the finest jazzmen you've ever heard," and other fine jazzmen hastened to join them. "We were on top," remembered Stricklin. "We were the honey for the buttered biscuits."

There have been hundreds of recordings of "[New] San Antonio Rose," by artists ranging from

Soon after he recorded "New San Antonio Rose," Wills appeared with Tex Ritter in *Take Me Back to Oklahoma*, released in November 1940. Wills and the Texas Playboys had five numbers in the movie, including "Bob Wills Special" and "Take Me Back to Tulsa." Sitting behind Ritter and Wills on the stagecoach is guitarist Eldon Shamblin. (OTM Collection)

Patsy Cline to the Norman Luboff Choir. Members of the Western Writers of America, voting for The Top 100 Western Songs, ranked it #49. In 1969, astronauts on Apollo 12 sang it to a listening Earth.

★ ★ ★

"New San Antonio Rose" was recorded sixteen years and ten months after Fiddlin' John Carson sang about the little old log cabin in the lane (➤1). You wouldn't think it possible. The two performances seem hardly to fit into the same universe, let alone into less than two decades. But in the same period, jazz had gone from King Oliver's Creole Jazz Band to Dizzy Gillespie, blues from Bessie Smith to boogie woogie, books from *Bambi* to *For Whom the Bell Tolls*, movies from *The Ten Commandments* and *Safety Last!* to *The Philadelphia Story* and *The Grapes of Wrath*. Country music still had far to go, but for now, "New San Antonio Rose" was the latest, freshest, and most eye-opening landmark on the map of rural rhythm.

The Development of Early Country Music: A Phonographic–Radiophonic–Sociohistorical Timeline

1900–20
Studio singers Billy Murray, Arthur Collins, Byron G. Harlan, and others, and banjoists Vess L. Ossman and Fred Van Eps, record many songs and tunes that will pass into the repertoire of the first generation of old-time recordists.

1909
November Edison makes cylinder recordings of banjoist Polk Miller and His Old South Quartette in Richmond, VA.

1910–30
Fiddlers' conventions and fiddling contests in many states confer local or regional celebrity on such players as Fiddlin' John Carson, Lowe Stokes, A. A. Gray, Clayton McMichen (GA), Whitmore Gaydon (AL), "Red" Gay (FL), Uncle Jimmy Thompson, Allen Sisson, John Dykes (TN), Ed Haley (KY), John Baltzell (OH), Uncle Joe Shippee (CT), Mellie Dunham (ME), Fiddlin' Sam Long (MO/OK), Eck Robertson, M. L. Franklin (TX), and many others.

1912–20
Hawaiian music, known in the US since the 1890s, enters the popular music mainstream. In 1913, Walter Kolomoku, with the Hawaiian Quintette, makes probably the first recordings of Hawaiian steel guitar, to be followed in 1915 by Frank Ferera. Touring Hawaiian troupes attract many guitarists to Hawaiian-style playing.

1916–22
New York–based professional violinists such as Don Richardson and Joseph Samuels make many records of tunes like "Turkey in the Straw" and "Arkansaw Traveler."

1920
January The Eighteenth Amendment, ratified a year earlier, goes into effect, initiating Prohibition.

1921
August Opening of WRR Dallas, first licensed radio station in Texas.

1922
March Opening of Atlanta stations WSB (owned by the *Atlanta Journal*) and WGM (owned by the *Atlanta Constitution*). WSB will be a major broadcaster of old-time music. • Opening of WLW Cincinnati, later home of the Boone County Jamboree.
April Opening of WBT Charlotte, later home of the Crazy Barn Dance.
May Opening of WBAP Fort Worth.
June Gennett makes sacred recordings at its Richmond, IN, studio by (and for) the Vaughan Quartet of Lawrenceburg, TN. • Opening of WFAA Dallas (owned by the *Dallas News*).
June–July What are considered the first recordings of instrumental old-time music are made by Southwestern fiddlers A. C. ("Eck") Robertson and Henry C. Gilliland, for Victor in New York.
July Opening of WHAS Louisville.

c. July First recordings of Sacred Harp music, by a group from Texas, for Brunswick in New York.
September First recordings by Ohio-based fiddler William B. Houchens (Gennett). • Opening of WOAI San Antonio, WLAP Louisville.
November Opening of WNAX Yankton, SD, later home of the Missouri Valley Barn Dance.

1923

January Opening of WMC Memphis (owned by the *Memphis Commercial Appeal*).
June The first disc recordings made in a Southern location, by Okeh in Atlanta, supervised by Ralph S. Peer, include old-time songs by Fiddlin' John Carson, danceband music, and African American gospel and blues.
July Release of Fiddlin' John Carson's "The Little Old Log Cabin in the Lane"/"The Old Hen Cackled and the Rooster's Going to Crow" (Okeh).
September First recordings by Ohio fiddler John Baltzell (Edison). • Birth of Hank Williams.
December First recordings by Henry Whitter (Okeh).

1924

March First recordings by Gid Tanner and Riley Puckett (Columbia). Company advertising promotes Southern fiddle and guitar music. • First recordings by Bascom Lamar Lunsford, A. A. Gray (Okeh).
March/April First recordings of a Southern old-time stringband of fiddle, banjo, and guitar, Fiddlin' John Carson and His Virginia Reelers (Okeh).
April Official opening of WLS Chicago (owned by Sears, Roebuck). The National Barn Dance begins a week later. • Samantha Bumgarner and Eva Davis are the first women to record old-time music (Columbia). • First recordings by George Reneau (assisted by popular singer Gene Austin) (Vocalion), Ernest Thompson (Columbia), Land Norris (Okeh).
May First recordings by Walter C. Peterson (Paramount) and Carson Robison, playing guitar for vaudeville artist Wendell Hall (Victor).
May–August Vernon Dalhart records "The Wreck of the Old 97" for Edison, Victor, and other labels, initiating a productive decade-long career as a recordist of hillbilly songs.
June First recordings by the Tweedy Brothers (Gennett), D. D. Hollis (Paramount).
July First recordings by Uncle "Am" Stuart, Uncle Dave Macon (Vocalion), including Macon's "Hill Billie Blues."
August First recordings by Fiddlin' Powers and Family (Victor), Roba Stanley, the Jenkins Family (Okeh).
October Okeh holds the first location recording session in Dallas.
c. October Columbia launches "Old Familiar Tunes" (15000-D) series.
November First recording of a cowboy song, "The Great Round Up," by Charles Nabell (Okeh). • First old-time record released in the UK is Gid Tanner and Riley Puckett's "Black-Eyed Susie" and Ernest Thompson's "Are You from Dixie?" (Regal).

1925

January Columbia holds its first Southern location recording session, in Atlanta. • First recordings by Kelly Harrell (Victor), Ernest V. Stoneman (Okeh), the Hill Billies (Okeh).
February First recordings by the McCravy Brothers (Okeh).
March Victor holds its first Southern location recording sessions, in Houston and New Orleans.
April Opening of WDOD Chattanooga, TN.
May Opening of KPRC Houston (affiliated with the *Houston Post*).
June Gennett launches 35-cent Champion label.
July First recordings by Clayton McMichen (Okeh), Charlie Poole (Columbia).
c. July Okeh launches "Old Time Tunes" (45000) series.
July/August Release of Vernon Dalhart's "The Death of Floyd Collins"/"Little Mary Phagan" (Columbia), which will sell over 300,000 copies.
August First recordings by Charlie Oaks (Vocalion), Carl T. Sprague (Victor). • Okeh records on location in Asheville, NC. • Opening of WNOX Knoxville (formerly WNAV). • Opening of KMA Shenandoah, IA, which will be an important Midwestern broadcaster of hillbilly music.
October Opening of WSM Nashville. • First recordings by Doc Roberts (Gennett).
November Fiddler Uncle Jimmy Thompson broadcasts for two hours over WSM. • First recordings by Bud Landress and Bill Chitwood (Brunswick). • Opening of WRVA Richmond, VA.
December Launch of WSM barn-dance program, effectively the birth of the Grand Ole Opry. • Ralph

S. Peer is made Okeh's general sales manager. • *The Talking Machine World* publishes article on "What the Popularity of Hill-Billy Songs Means in Retail Profit Possibilities."

1925–26

Development of Western Electric recording process leads to dramatic improvement in recorded sound and widens the scope of location recording.
Henry Ford's Old Time Orchestra revives old-time dances, playing both in public and on radio, and making records.

1926

February Ralph Peer leaves Okeh Records.
March *Radio Digest* features the Hill Billies.
April First recordings by Gid Tanner and His Skillet-Lickers and Smith's Sacred Singers (Columbia). The Skillet-Lickers' four releases from this Atlanta session will sell over half a million, and Smith's Sacred Singers' "Pictures from Life's Other Side"/ "Where We'll Never Grow Old" over a quarter of a million, establishing Atlanta as the company's primary Southern location for old-time music.
May First recordings by Otto Gray's Oklahoma Cowboy Band (Okeh).
August Opening of KWKH Shreveport, LA.
September First recordings by Frank Hutchison (Okeh). • Ralph Peer now working for Victor.
October First recordings by Lester McFarland and Robert A. Gardner ("Mac and Bob") (Vocalion). • Opening of KRLD Dallas.
November Columbia and Okeh amalgamate. • First recordings by McMichen's Melody Men, Burnett and Rutherford (Columbia). • Chris Bouchillon introduces "Talking Blues" (Columbia).
December Opening of WWVA Wheeling, WV.

Virgil O. Stamps and J. R. Baxter, Jr., create the Stamps–Baxter Music & Printing Co., publishing gospel songbooks and promoting S-B quartets.

1927

February Victor holds the first location recording session in Memphis. • First recordings by the Georgia Yellow Hammers, Carolina Tar Heels (Victor), Earl Johnson (Okeh). • Opening of WWNC Asheville.
March Dock Boggs makes his first recordings, including "Country Blues," "Down South Blues," and "Pretty Polly" (Brunswick).
April Clayton McMichen and associates record "A Fiddlers' Convention in Georgia"—Parts 1 and 2 (Columbia), the first hillbilly sketch record. • Leake County Revelers record "Wednesday Night Waltz"/ "Good Night Waltz" (Columbia), which will sell almost 200,000 copies. • Buell Kazee records "East Virginia" and other old-time ballads and banjo songs (Brunswick).
April/May Paramount initiates "Old Time Tunes" (3000) series.
May Charles Lindbergh flies from New York to Paris in the *Spirit of St. Louis*, an achievement celebrated on records by Vernon Dalhart and others.
July–August Gennett sets up a temporary studio in Birmingham to record mostly Alabama talent. It will be the company's only Southern location recording. • Victor records on location in the Taylor-Christian Building, 406 State St, Bristol, TN. First recordings by Jimmie Rodgers, the Carter Family.
August Victor holds the first location recording sessions in Charlotte, NC, and Savannah, GA.
September Okeh records on location in Winston-Salem, NC. • KVOO ("the Voice of Oklahoma"), which opened in Bristow in 1926, moves to Tulsa.
October Opening of WOBU Charleston, WV. • First recordings by G. B. Grayson and Henry Whitter (Gennett, Victor), the (Frank) Stamps Quartet (Victor), Lowe Stokes (Columbia).
November Tom Darby and Jimmie Tarlton record "Birmingham Jail"/"Columbus Stockade Blues" (Columbia), which will sell almost 200,000 copies. • First recordings by John McGhee and Frank Welling (Gennett). • Jimmie Rodgers records "Blue Yodel" (Victor).
December First recordings by Bradley Kincaid (Gennett).

Vocalion and Brunswick initiate old-time series (5000 and 100, respectively).

Sears, Roebuck's cheap labels Challenge and Conqueror begin issuing hillbilly recordings licensed from Gennett, Plaza, and other sources.

Publication of Ethel Park Richardson and Sigmund Spaeth's *American Mountain Songs* and Carl Sandburg's *The American Songbag*.

1928

January Emry Arthur makes the first recording of "I Am a Man of Constant Sorrow" (Vocalion).

February Brunswick–Vocalion holds its first location recording session, in Ashland, KY. First recordings by the Kessinger Brothers.

February–November Jack Kapp, recording director, holds Brunswick–Vocalion's first location recording sessions in Atlanta, Indianapolis, Dallas, New Orleans, Birmingham, and Memphis.

March Okeh holds the first location recording session in San Antonio.

March–April Victor holds first sessions by Jules V. Allen and Harry (Mac) McClintock.

April Accordionist-singer Joseph Falcon makes the first records of Louisiana Cajun music (Columbia).

June Carson Robison and Frank Luther make their first joint recordings. • Frankie Marvin begins recording Jimmie Rodgers covers for several labels. • WNOX Knoxville purchased by Sterchi Brothers.

August Songwriter Bob Miller debuts as a hillbilly recordist with "Eleven Cent Cotton Forty Cent Meat" (Columbia).

September–October Victor records on location in Nashville, the only session held there before 1945.

October Columbia holds the first location recording session in Johnson City, TN.

1928–29

The peak years for location recording sessions: Brunswick–Vocalion, Columbia, Okeh, and Victor log sixty-two trips to twenty-three cities, making over 4,000 recordings in all idioms.

1929

January Victor launches "Native American Melodies" (V-40000) series.

March W. T. Narmour and S. W. Smith record "Carroll County Blues"/"Charleston No. 1" (Okeh).

c. April Talent scout Harry Charles organizes the recording of old-time and "race" musicians for QRS in New York.

June Opening of WOPI Bristol, TN-VA.

July First recordings by Bill Cox (Gennett).

August Cameo, Pathé, and Plaza amalgamate as the American Record Company (ARC).

August–September Brunswick–Vocalion holds the first location recording session in Knoxville, TN.

September Jimmie Davis makes his first recordings for Victor.

October First recordings of black Louisiana French (Creole) music, by Douglas Bellar and Kirby Riley (Vocalion). • First recordings by Gene Autry (Victor). • Okeh records on location in Richmond, VA. • The Wall Street Crash.

December Release of Jimmie Rodgers's movie short *The Singing Brakeman*.

A notable year for touring hillbilly vaudeville acts such as the Pickard Family, Crockett's Kentucky Mountaineers, and the Blue Ridge Ramblers.

1930

February First recordings by Cliff Carlisle (Gennett). • Bob Miller publishes "Twenty-One Years," which will be one of his biggest hits.

April Ken Maynard, the first singing cowboy in movies, records for Columbia in Hollywood. • Warner Brothers acquires Brunswick.

May Victor changes name of V-40000 series to "Old Familiar Tunes & Novelties". • Allen Brothers record "Jake Walk Blues" (Victor).

July Opening of WIS Columbia, SC.

November–December Brunswick–Vocalion holds final location recording sessions in Atlanta, Knoxville, New Orleans, Dallas, and San Antonio.

December Okeh records on location in Jackson, MS.

1931

January Victor V-40000 series terminates, to be succeeded by a 23500 hillbilly series.

February The Colt Brothers (an Arthur Fields–Fred Hall group) record the hillbilly novelty "Eleven More Months and Ten More Days" (Melotone). The song will become an international best-seller.

April Warner Brothers–Brunswick launches the UK label Panachord, which will build the largest catalog of US hillbilly recordings. (It will be acquired by UK Decca in April 1932.) • Vernon Dalhart and Adelyne Hood visit the UK and record in London.

April/May–July Lifespan of Timely Tunes Records (Victor-owned 25-cent label).

May Death of Charlie Poole.

June Victor records on location in Louisville and instigates joint recording sessions by Jimmie Rodgers and the Carter Family.

October Last Columbia–Okeh location recording session, in Atlanta. • Gene Autry records "Silver Haired Daddy of Mine" (ARC).
December Formation of ARC–Brunswick Records (ARC–BRC).

1932
February Last Victor location recording sessions, in Dallas and Atlanta. In Dallas, Bob Wills and Milton Brown make their first recordings, as members of the Fort Worth Doughboys.
April Carson Robison and Frank Luther end a four-year recording partnership.
April–September Carson Robison and His Pioneers are in the UK, filling theater dates and making recordings and Pathé news shorts.
August Clayton McMichen records in New York with Jimmie Rodgers (Victor) and with his own Georgia Wildcats (Crown). • Opening of border radio station XER Villa Acuña, Mexico, owned by John R. Brinkley. It will be closed down in February 1933.
c. September Frank Luther forms Frank Luther Trio with his wife Zora Layman and Leonard Stokes.

Columbia "Old Familiar Tunes" (15000-D) series terminates.

The Iowa Barn Dance Frolic, which began on WOC Davenport, moves to WHO Des Moines.

The Hoosier Hop begins on WOWO Fort Wayne, IN.

Bob Miller is the nation's most prolific hillbilly recordist, making seventy recordings for four companies. (Carson Robison makes seventy-one but mostly in the UK.)

By now, the fiddle–banjo combination, crucial to early stringband music, is losing its importance, and the role of the guitar is becoming central in the ensemble.

1933
January Victor launches 35-cent Bluebird label. • WWVA Wheeling, WV, launches a country music program, the Jamboree.
April First recordings by The Vagabonds (Victor), Red Foley (ARC–BRC).
May Last recordings by, and death of, Jimmie Rodgers.
June Victor begins licensing recordings to Montgomery Ward store label. • Gene Autry records "The Death of Jimmie Rodgers" (ARC–BRC).
July First recordings by the Girls of the Golden West (Bluebird).
August Leon Chappelear and the Shelton brothers, as the Lone Star Cowboys, record "Deep Elm Blues" and "Just Because" (Bluebird), which prove to be long-term sellers and are much copied.
September WLS National Barn Dance carried by the NBC Blue Network.
October First recordings by W. Lee O'Daniel's Light Crust Doughboys and the Massey Family (The Westerners) (ARC–BRC).
December Repeal of the Eighteenth Amendment ends Prohibition. • Delmore Brothers record "Brown's Ferry Blues" (Bluebird). • First recordings by the Prairie Ramblers and Wilf Carter ("Montana Slim") (Bluebird).

Brunswick and Vocalion old-time series terminate.

First year since 1923 in which there are no Southern location recordings.

1933–35
New Deal agencies like the Civilian Conservation Corps (CCC) and Works Progress Administration (WPA) are created to alleviate unemployment.

1934
January Ernest V. Stoneman returns, after more than five years, to record for ARC–BRC. • First recordings by the Callahan Brothers (ARC–BRC).
February–March Bluebird makes the last recordings of Fiddlin' John Carson and Gid Tanner.
March The Crazy Water Crystals Co. of Mineral Wells, TX, launches the Crazy Barn Dance on WBT Charlotte. It will give exposure to the Monroe Brothers, Dixon Brothers, Mainer's Mountaineers, Dick Hartman's Tennessee Ramblers, the Three Tobacco Tags, and other hillbilly acts. Associated programs are broadcast from WSOC Charlotte, WWNC Asheville, NC, and WPTF Raleigh, NC.
April First recordings by Milton Brown and His Musical Brownies (Bluebird).

July After a three-year absence, Smith's Sacred Singers return to recording with Bluebird.
July/August Decca is launched as a 35-cent label, with old-time material in a "Hillbilly" (5000) series.
August First recordings by Bill Boyd and His Cowboy Ramblers (Bluebird), and by the Sons of the Pioneers, including "Tumbling Tumbleweeds" (Decca).
September KPRC Houston, WBAP Fort Worth, WFAA Dallas, and WOAI San Antonio form the Texas Quality Network and share programming. • Jimmie Davis records "Nobody's Darling but Mine" (Decca). • First recordings by Roy Newman and His Boys (Vocalion).
November First recordings by the Hoosier Hot Shots (ARC–BRC).
December Champion 15/16000 series terminates.

Okeh "Old Time Tunes" (45000) and Victor 23500 series terminate.

Bob Wills and His Texas Playboys begin broadcasting regularly from the Tulsa dancehall Cain's Academy on KVOO Tulsa.

1934–42
The center of gravity of hillbilly recording shifts westward with the rise of Texas swing music and the sales of records by Bob Wills, Milton Brown, the Light Crust Doughboys, etc.

The amplified steel guitar becomes an important instrument in Texas swing—developed by musicians like Bob Dunn, with Milton Brown and other leaders, and Leon McAuliffe, with Bob Wills—as well as in other idioms.

The "brother duet" becomes one of the staples of hillbilly broadcasting and recording.

Bluebird (owned by Victor), Vocalion (ARC–BRC), and Decca dominate the recording of hillbilly (and blues) music.

ARC-BRC holds location recording sessions in Jackson, MS, Augusta, GA, Hattiesburg, MS, Hot Springs, AR, Birmingham, Columbia, SC, and Memphis.

Jukeboxes account for a significant proportion of hillbilly record sales.

Many bands make electrical transcriptions for widespread radio use.

1935
January First recordings by Dick Hartman's Tennessee Ramblers and by fiddler Arthur Smith (Bluebird).
February First issue of the magazine *WLS Weekly*, Chicago. By March, the name has been changed to *Stand By!* (later *Stand By*). • First recordings by the Shelton Brothers (Decca).
June Decca acquires rights to Champion and reissues many recordings in the Champion 45000 series.
August First recordings by J. E. Mainer's Mountaineers, including "Maple on the Hill" (Bluebird). • Patsy Montana records "I Wanna Be a Cowboy's Sweetheart" (ARC–BRC). • First recordings by the Louisiana Cajun stringband the Hackberry Ramblers (Bluebird).
September First recordings by Bob Wills and His Texas Playboys (Vocalion).

Ralph Peer ends his association with Victor. The Carter Family, which he manages, leaves Victor and records for ARC–BRC.

Opening of border radio station XERA Villa Acuña, Mexico, owned by John R. Brinkley. It will be closed down in 1939.

1936
February First recordings by the Dixon Brothers, Monroe Brothers, Tune Wranglers (Bluebird).
April Death of Milton Brown.
June The Carter Family begins recording for Decca. • First recordings by the Blue Sky Boys (Bluebird).
October First recordings by Roy Acuff, including "Great Speckle[d] Bird" and "Wabash Cannon Ball" (ARC–BRC). • First recordings by Jimmie Revard and His Oklahoma Cowboys, Hank Snow, Ernest Tubb (Bluebird). • The Three Tobacco Tags make their first recordings for Bluebird.
October–January 1937 Carson Robison and His Pioneers make their second trip to the UK.

Tex Ritter begins his career in Western musical movies with *Song of the Gringo* and *Headin' for the Rio Grande*.

1937
February First recordings by Cliff Bruner's Texas Wanderers (Decca), Bob Skyles and His Skyrockets (Bluebird).

June First recordings by the Hi-Flyers, Nite Owls, Bill Nettles and His Dixie Blue Boys (ARC–BRC).
July Clayton McMichen's Georgia Wildcats make their first recordings for Decca.
September The Farm Security Administration is created to combat rural poverty. FSA photographers will capture iconic images of Southern music-making.
October First broadcast of the Renfro Valley Barn Dance from WLW Cincinnati.

Hank Williams and His Drifting Cowboys begin broadcasting regularly on WSFA Montgomery, AL.

1938
January First recordings by the Morris Brothers (Wiley and Zeke) (Bluebird).
February First issue of *Rural Radio* magazine, Nashville, TN.
April Adolph Hofner leaves Jimmie Revard band and begins recording for Bluebird. • Kyle Crichton's article "Thar's Gold in Them Hillbillies" in *Collier's* magazine offers an early national story about the history of blues and hillbilly recording, focusing on Ralph Peer.
September The Boone County Jamboree begins on WLW Cincinnati. • Bluebird moves its southeastern location recording site from Charlotte, NC, to Rock Hill, SC.
November Jimmie Davis records Floyd Tillman's composition "It Makes No Difference Now" (Decca).
December Release of the movie *Shine on Harvest Moon*, with Roy Rogers, Lulu Belle and Scotty.

Columbia Broadcasting System absorbs ARC–BRC, Columbia, Okeh, and Vocalion holdings.

The Carter Family begins broadcasting on XERA Villa Acuña, Mexico.

1939
March Bob Dunn's Vagabonds begin recording for Decca.
April–June Carson Robison and His Pioneers make their third trip to the UK.
May Vernon Dalhart returns to the studio for a last session (Bluebird).
June The Rouse Brothers record "Orange Blossom Special" (Bluebird).
July First issue of hillbilly fanzine *The Mountain Broadcast and Prairie Recorder*, New York, NY.
August Bluebird moves its southeastern location recording site to Atlanta.
September Rex Griffin records "The Lovesick Blues" (Decca).
October WSM Grand Ole Opry carried by NBC. • Bill Monroe and the Blue Grass Boys make their first Opry broadcast.
November UK label Panachord terminates.

1940
January First issue of hillbilly fanzine *The Jamboree*, Frankton, IN. • Release of the movie *The Village Barn Dance*, with Lulu Belle and Scotty, the Texas Wanderers, and Doris Day. • First broadcast of Gene Autry's Melody Ranch (originally Doublemint's Melody Ranch), a weekly variety program carried by CBS.
February Jimmie Davis records "You Are My Sunshine" (Decca).
April Bob Wills and His Texas Playboys record "New San Antonio Rose" (Vocalion). • Ernest Tubb begins recording for Decca. • First recordings by Ted Daffan's Texans (Vocalion/Okeh). • City fathers of Hamtramck, MI, attempt to ban the York Brothers' "Hamtramck Mama" (on the independent Universal label) from jukeboxes in the Detroit area.
April–May Woody Guthrie records two volumes of *Dust Bowl Ballads* (Victor).
June Release of the movie *Grand Ole Opry*, with Roy Acuff and Uncle Dave Macon.
October Release of the movie *Barnyard Follies*, with the DeZurik Sisters. • First recordings by Bill Monroe and His Blue Grass Boys (Bluebird).

The Missouri Valley Barn Dance begins on WNAX Yankton, SD.

1941
February Carson Robison records an album of square-dance music (Columbia).
April Ernest Tubb records "Walking the Floor Over You" (Decca). Johnny Lee Wills records "Milk Cow Blues" (Decca).
December US enters World War II.

1942

February Ted Daffan records "Born to Lose" (Okeh).

March Al Dexter records "Pistol Packin' Mama" (Okeh). • Elton Britt records "There's a Star Spangled Banner Waving Somewhere" (Bluebird), co-written by Bob Miller, which will be one of the biggest country hits of World War II.

July At the instigation of James Petrillo, president of the American Federation of Musicians, union musicians refuse to work with record companies.

October Bluebird hillbilly/blues series terminates.

★

Sources

Citations of books and articles are given in full on their first appearance but thereafter more briefly.

1 "THE LITTLE OLD LOG CABIN IN THE LANE"

Cohen, Norm. "Fiddlin' John Carson: An Appreciation and a Discography." *JEMF Quarterly* 10:4, no. 36 (Winter 1974): 138–50.

Coltman, Bob. "Look Out! Here He Comes . . . Fiddlin' John Carson: One of a Kind, & Twice as Feisty." *Old Time Music* 9 (Summer 1973): 16–21.

Green, Archie. "Hillbilly Music: Source and Symbol." *Journal of American Folklore* 78:309 (July–September 1965): 204–28.

Huber, Patrick. "A Hillbilly Barnum: Fiddlin' John Carson and the Modern Origins of His Old-Time Music in Atlanta." *Atlanta History* 46:1 (2004): 25–53.

Huber, Patrick. *Linthead Stomp: The Creation of Country Music in the Piedmont South*. Chapel Hill: University of North Carolina Press, 2008, 72–76, 88–92.

Mazor, Barry. *Ralph Peer and the Making of Popular Roots Music*. Chicago: Chicago Review Press, 2015, 49–56.

Peer, Ralph S. Interviews with Lillian Borgeson, Los Angeles, CA, January and May 1959.

Wiggins, Gene. *Fiddlin' Georgia Crazy: Fiddlin' John Carson, His Real World, and the World of His Songs*. Urbana: University of Illinois Press, 1987, 73–76, 220–30.

2 "SILLY BILL"/"OLD TIME CINDA"

Cohen, John, and Mike Seeger (eds.). *The New Lost City Ramblers Song Book*. New York: Oak Publications, 1964, 92.

Green, Archie. "Hillbilly Music: Source and Symbol," 211–14.

Wilson, Joe. Notes to *The Hill Billies* [LP] (County 405, 1974).

Wilson, Joe. "The Hill Billies: The Band That Named the Music." In Fred Bartenstein (ed.). *Roots Music in America: Collected Writings of Joe Wilson*. Knoxville: University of Tennessee Press, 2017, 107–12.

3 "WOMEN'S SUFFRAGE"

Green, Archie. "Hillbilly Music: Source and Symbol," 215–16.

Russell, Tony. "George Reneau: The First Knoxvillian on Record." In Tony Russell and Ted Olson, Notes to *Knox County Stomp: The Knoxville Sessions 1929–1930* [CD box-set] (Bear Family BCD 16097, 2016): 25–26.

Wolfe, Charles K. "George Reneau: A Biographical Sketch." *JEMF Quarterly* 15, no. 56 (Winter 1979): 205–7.

Thanks to Jack Neely, Professor George K. Schweitzer.

4 "THE DEATH OF FLOYD COLLINS"/"LITTLE MARY PHAGAN"

Benton, John, Bill Napper, and Bob Thompson. *The Floyd Collins Tragedy at Sand Cave*. Charleston, SC: Arcadia Publishing, 2017.

Dinnerstein, Leonard. *The Leo Frank Case*. New York: Columbia University Press, 1968.

Futrelle, Irene Spain. Quoted in Dorothy Horstman, *Sing Your Heart Out, Country Boy*. 2nd ed. Nashville: Country Music Foundation Press, 1986, 74.

Huber, Patrick. "The New York Sound: Citybilly Recording Artists and the Creation of Hillbilly Music, 1924–1932." *Journal of American Folklore* 127:504 (Spring 2014): 140–58.

Murray, Robert K., and Roger W. Brucker. *Trapped! The Story of Floyd Collins*. Rev. ed. Lexington: University Press of Kentucky, 1999.

Oney, Steve. *And the Dead Shall Rise: The Murder of Mary Phagan and the Lynching of Leo Frank*. New York: Pantheon Books, 2003.

Palmer, Jack. *Vernon Dalhart: First Star of Country Music*. Denver, CO: Mainspring Press, 2005.

Ward, Brian, and Patrick Huber. *A&R Pioneers: Architects of American Roots Music on Record*. Nashville: Country Music Foundation Press/Vanderbilt University Press, 2018, 149–50.

Wiggins, Gene. *Fiddlin' Georgia Crazy*, 33–38.

Wilgus, D. K., and Nathan Hurvitz. "'Little Mary Phagan': Further Notes on a Native American Ballad in Context." *Journal of Country Music* 4:1 (Spring 1973): 17–30.

Thanks to Bob and Lee Linn.

5 "WHEN THE WORK'S ALL DONE THIS FALL"

Allen, Jules V. *Cowboy Lore*. San Antonio: Naylor Printing, 1933, xiii.

Lomax, John A., and Alan Lomax. *Cowboy Songs and Other Frontier Ballads*. Rev. and enl. ed. New York: Macmillan, 1938, 74–76.

Russell, Tony. "Retelling the West: Jules Verne Allen, The Singing Cowboy." *The Old-Time Herald* 12:11 (June–July 2011): 8–17; 12:12 (August–September 2011): 34–40.

Sprague, Carl T. Quoted in John I. White. Notes to *Carl T. Sprague: Classic Cowboy Songs* [CD] (Bear Family BCD 15456, 1988).

White, John I. *Git Along, Little Dogies: Songs and Songmakers of the American West*. Urbana: University of Illinois Press, 1975, 85–87, 193–95.

6 "SENECA SQUARE DANCE"/"ECHOES OF THE OZARKS"

Tyler, Paul L. "Hillbilly Music Re-imagined: Folk and Country Music in the Midwest." *Journal of American Folklore* 127:504 (Spring 2014): 159–90.

[A trenchant and persuasive critique of the South-centric narrative of country music history.]

7 "WISH TO THE LORD I HAD NEVER BEEN BORN"

Aaron, Larry G. *Pittsylvania County, Virginia: A Brief History*. Charleston, SC: History Press, 2009, 84.

Danville, Virginia City Directory. Vol. 13 (1927). Asheville, NC: House of Directories, 1927, 9–10.

McDaniel, Lewis. Interview with the author, Ridgeway, VA, September 8, 1971.

Rorrer, Kinney. Quoted in "Charley La Prade: The Fiddler's Fiddler." *The Bee* [Danville, Virginia], April 16, 1975: 1B–2B.

8 "WHERE WE NEVER GROW OLD"/"PICTURES FROM LIFE'S OTHER SIDE"

Carpenter, Jerry. Correspondence with the author, 2015–16.

Fischer, Sarah. "Sing Praises unto the Lord." Unidentified Lawrenceville or Gwinnett County [Georgia] newspaper, November 16, 1994.
Wolfe, Charles K. "Frank Smith, Andrew Jenkins, and Early Commercial Gospel Music." *American Music* 1:1 (Spring 1983): 49–59.
Quotations from what I refer to as a "local paper" are taken from undated clippings from an unidentified newspaper, possibly the *Braselton* [Georgia] *News*.

9 "LET ME CALL YOU SWEETHEART"/"SWEET BUNCH OF DAISIES"

Coffey, Kevin. Correspondence with the author, May 2019.
Cohen, Norm. "Clayton McMichen: His Life and Music." *JEMF Quarterly* 11:3, no. 39 (Autumn 1975): 117–24.
Layne, Bert. "A Skillet-Licker's Memoirs." [Interview with Margaret Riddle.] *Old Time Music* 14 (Autumn 1974): 8.
McMichen, Clayton. "Clayton McMichen Talking." [Interview with Fred Hoeptner and Bob Pinson, July 7, 1959.] *Old Time Music* 1 (Summer 1971): 8–10; 2 (Autumn 1971): 13–15; 3 (Winter 1971/72): 14–15, 19; 4 (Spring 1972): 19–20, 30.
Malone, K. D. Interview with Jack Spence, Atlanta, GA, 2003.
Malone, K. D. Interview with Ron Penn, Warren Wilson College, Swannanoa, NC, July 24, 2003.
Malone, K. D. *My Best to You . . . Eighty Years as a Sideman*. Ed. Patricia A. Poos. Trafford, 2010.
Mathews, Burgin. "Kasper 'Stranger' Malone in His Own Words." *The Old-Time Herald* 11:12 (August–September 2009): 24–33.
I am grateful to Jack Spence and Kevin Coffey for sharing their K. D. Malone material.

10 "I'M A STERN OLD BACHELOR"

This essay is based on my article cited below.

Biggar, George C. "The Early Days of WLS & the National Barn Dance." *Old Time Music* 1 (Summer 1971): 11–13.
Daniel, Wayne. *Pickin' on Peachtree: A History of Country Music in Atlanta, Georgia*. Urbana: University of Illinois Press, 1990, 63–65.
Gennett, Robert P. Letter (1971). Online source untraced.
Kennedy, Rick. *Jelly Roll, Bix, and Hoagy: Gennett Studios and the Birth of Recorded Jazz*. Bloomington: Indiana University Press, 1994, 162.
Russell, Tony. "The World's Most Popular Radio Artist: Tuning in Again to Chubby Parker." *Old-Time Herald* 11:8 (December 2008–January 2009): 32–37.
Wolfe, Charles K. *Kentucky Country: Folk and Country Music of Kentucky*. Lexington: University Press of Kentucky, 1982, 47.

11 "GOING SLOW"/"SPARTANBURG BLUES"

Christopher, Homer C. Letter to the author, June 15, 1977.
Culver, Terry. Correspondence with the author, 2011.
Franklin, Ben. Correspondence with the author, 2011.
Russell, Tony. "Homer Christopher & The Rise & Fall of the Piano Accordion." *Old Time Music* 33 (Summer 1979–Spring 1980): 15–17.

12 "CARBOLIC RAG"/"STONE MOUNTAIN WOBBLE"

This essay is based on my article cited below.

Daniel, Wayne. Letter to Guthrie T. Meade, February 13, 1984. Meade Papers, Southern Folklife Collection, University of North Carolina at Chapel Hill. [Information from *Atlanta Journal*, 1927–29.]
Head, Eva. Letter to Bob Pinson, 1977.
Rattray, Bill. "Scottdale Boys." *Old Time Music* 1 (Summer 1971): 22.
Russell, Tony. Notes to *The Scottdale String Band: Old Folks Better Go to Bed* [CD] (Arhoolie CD 7054, 2014).

13 "CHAIN GANG SPECIAL"/"WALK RIGHT IN BELMONT"

Blackard, Malcolm V. "Wilmer Watts & The Lonely Eagles." *JEMF Quarterly* 5:4, no. 16 (Winter 1969): 126–40.
Carlin, Bob. *String Bands in the North Carolina Piedmont*. Jefferson, NC: McFarland, 2004, 143–45.
Cash, W. J. *The Mind of the South*. London: Thames & Hudson, 1971, 345.
Cope, Robert F., and Manly Wade Wellman. *The County of Gaston*. Gastonia, NC: Gaston County Historical Society, 1961.
Green, Archie. *Wobblies, Pile Butts, and Other Heroes: Laborlore Explorations*. Urbana: University of Illinois Press, 1993, 275–319.
Huber, Patrick. *Linthead Stomp*, 184, 349–50.
Huber, Patrick. Notes to *Gastonia Gallop* [CD] (Old Hat CD 1007, 2009).
Moss, Dot Wilson. Correspondence and phone conversations with the author, 1983–2008.
Nelson, Donald Lee. "'Walk Right in Belmont': The Wilmer Watts Story." *JEMF Quarterly* 9:3, no. 31 (Autumn 1973): 91–96.
Roscigno, Vincent J., and William F. Danaher. *The Voice of Southern Labor: Radio, Music, and Textile Strikes, 1929–1934*. Minneapolis: University of Minnesota Press, 2004, 84–85, 130–31.
Russell, Tony. "Stepstones [Watts & Wilson]." *Old Time Music* 40 (Winter 1984): 11, 14.
Russell, Tony. "Watts and Wilson." In *Field Manual FM 21-100: Paramount Records and Associated Labels. Volume 1 (1917–1927)* [Notes to LP box-set]. Third Man Records/Revenant Records, 2013, 260–61.
Stutts, John C. *"Picked up Here and There" and "Gleanings from the Gullies."* Haw River, NC: Author, c. 1919.
Wilson, Rick. Correspondence with the author, 2017–19.
Wolfe, Charles K. "The Tennessee Ramblers: Ramblin' On." *Old Time Music* 13 (Summer 1974): 5–12.

14 "GRAY EAGLE"/"FORKED DEER"

Lomax, Alan. *List of American Folk Songs on Commercial Records*. Washington, DC: Library of Congress, 1942, 8.
Meade, Guthrie. Notes to *Old Time Fiddle Band Music from Kentucky* [LPs] (Morning Star 45003–05, 1980).
Russell, Tony. "Kelly Harrell & the Virginia Ramblers." *Old Time Music* 2 (Autumn 1971): 9.
Smith, Harrison. Quoted in Tom Tsotsi and Pete Whelan, "Black Patti." *78 Quarterly* 11 (2000): 49.

15 "THE PICTURE ON THE WALL"/"MY CAROLINA GIRL"

Gulledge, Lloyd. "Moody, 300-Hymn Composer, Now Working on New Song." *Calhoun* [Georgia] *Times*, October 7, 1952.
Gulledge, Lloyd. "'Uncle Bud' Landress, Living in Quiet, Recalls Yesteryear." *Atlanta Journal & Constitution*, February 8, 1953.
Landress, Dixie. "I Remember Bud Landress." *Old Time Music* 30 (Autumn 1978): 16–17.
Meade, Guthrie, Dick Spottswood, and Douglas S. Meade. *Country Music Sources: A Biblio-Discography of Commercially Recorded Traditional Music*. Chapel Hill, NC: Southern Folklife Collection/University of North Carolina at Chapel Hill Libraries, 2002, 835.
Reeve, Chris, Janet, Peter, and Robin, and Jane Reeve Hosemann. Conversation with the author, Calhoun, GA, April 27, 2017.

Russell, Tony. Notes to *The Georgia Yellow Hammers and Associates Volumes 1–4* [CDs] (Document DOCD-8067–70, 2014).
Wiggins, Gene, with Tony Russell. "Hell Broke Loose in Gordon County, Georgia." *Old Time Music* 25 (Summer 1977): 9–21.
Warm thanks to Jane and Ed Weldon, Terresa and Mildred Dutton.

16 "YOU CAN'T MAKE A MONKEY OUT OF ME"

Cohen, Norm. "John T. Scopes and Evolution in Hillbilly Songs." *JEMF Quarterly* 6:4, no. 20 (Winter 1971): 174–81.
Doubler, Michael D. *Dixie Dewdrop: The Uncle Dave Macon Story*. Urbana: University of Illinois Press, 2018, 132–33.
Robinson, F. E., and W. E. Morgan. *Why Dayton? Of All Places?* Chattanooga, TN: Andrews Printery, 1925.
Scopes Festival. https://scopesfestival.com.
Smocovitis, Vassiliki Betty. "Singing His Praises: Darwin and His Theory in Song and Musical Production." *Isis* 100 (2009): 590–614.

17 "A CORN LICKER STILL IN GEORGIA"—PARTS 1 AND 2

Allen, Frederick Lewis. *Only Yesterday: An Informal History of the Nineteen-Twenties*. New York: Harper and Brothers, 1931, 245–69.
Dunning, John. *On the Air: The Encyclopedia of Old-Time Radio*. New York: Oxford University Press, 1998.
LaRose, Joe. "An Interview with Lowe Stokes." *Old Time Music* 39 (Spring 1984): 6–9.
Layne, Bert. "A Skillet-Licker's Memoirs." [Interview with Margaret Riddle.] *Old Time Music* 15 (Winter 1974/75): 24.
McMichen, Clayton. "Clayton McMichen Talking."
McMichen, Clayton. Interview with Lou Curtiss and Ken Swerilas, 1966.
Minton, John. *78 Blues*. Jackson: University Press of Mississippi, 2008, 158–210.
[Minton and I cover a little of the same ground, though our eyes tend to be drawn to different features. He also discusses, valuably and in detail, several of the non-"Corn Licker Still" sketches.]
Stevenson, Elizabeth. *Babbitts & Bohemians: The American 1920s*. New York: Macmillan, 1967, 198.
Ward, Brian, and Patrick Huber. *A&R Pioneers*, 139–40.
Thanks to Margaret Riddle.

18 "BLUE YODEL"

Parts of this essay are based on my article cited below.
Mazor, Barry. *Meeting Jimmie Rodgers*. New York: Oxford University Press, 2009.
Porterfield, Nolan. *Jimmie Rodgers: The Life and Times of America's Blue Yodeler*. Urbana: University of Illinois Press, 1979, 104–26.
Russell, Tony. "Playback: Blue Yodel (T for Texas)." *Classic Rock Country Music Magazine* 2 (2014): 32–34.

19 "COMBINATION RAG"

Bogan, Patrick Henry, Jr. "East Texas Serenaders." *Handbook of Texas Online*. http://www.tshaonline.org/handbook/online/articles/xge02.
Bredenberg, Nancy Fly. Notes to *The East Texas Serenaders 1927–1936* [LP] (County 410, 1977).
Hamman, Cloet. Interview with Bill C. Malone, Lindale, TX, July 5, 1978.
Hoeptner, Fred G. "The Western Style: The Story of an Early Fiddle Band." *Disc Collector* 17 (May 1961): 8–11.

20 "DAVY"/"GREENBACK DOLLAR"

Cohen, John, and Mike Seeger (eds.). *The New Lost City Ramblers Song Book*, 84.
Meade, Guthrie, Dick Spottswood, and Douglas S. Meade. *Country Music Sources*: 782, 796–97.
Perry Countian. Undated clipping, probably early May 1927.
Pevahouse, Jerry. Correspondence with the author, 2008–9.
Pevahouse, Jerry. Comment on Arts Center of Cannon County MusicSprings: Southern Music Sources "Weems String Band." YouTube, 2013.
Weems, Harold, and others. Interview with Richard Nevins, Perry County, TN, 1973.

21 "HANDY MAN"/"I TICKLED 'EM"

Barker, Tony. Correspondence with the author, 2019.
Brown, Virginia. Correspondence with the author, 2019.
Goldstein, Carolyn M. *Do It Yourself: Home Improvement in 20th-Century America*. Washington, DC: National Building Museum/New York: Princeton Architectural Press, 1998, 13–25.
Roud, Steve. Notes to *My Bonnie Lies Over the Ocean: British Songs in the USA* [CD box-set] (Nehi NEH3X1, 2015): 16.
Thanks to Anthony Pearson.

22 "HOG EYE"

Cohen, John, and Mike Seeger (eds.). *The New Lost City Ramblers Song Book*, 83.
Hager, Julia, and Jim Olin. "An Interview with Tip McKinney." *M. F. F. A. [Newsletter]* 2:3–4 (1975): 3–10. Reprinted in *The Devil's Box* 9:4 (December 1, 1975): 23–40.
McNeil, W. K. "Five Pre-World War II Arkansas String Bands: Some Thoughts on Their Recording Success." *JEMF Quarterly* 20, no. 74 (Fall/Winter 1984): 68–75.
McNeil, W. K. Notes to *Somewhere in Arkansas: Early Commercial Country Music Recordings from Arkansas: 1928–1932* [CD box-set]. Center for Arkansas and Regional Studies, 1997.
Randolph, Vance. *Roll Me in Your Arms: "Unprintable" Ozark Folksongs and Folklore. Volume I. Blow the Candle Out: "Unprintable" Ozark Folksongs and Folklore. Volume II*. Ed. G. Legman. Fayetteville: University of Arkansas Press, 1992, 401–2, 648.
Sandburg, Carl. *The American Songbag*. New York: Harcourt, Brace, 1927, 380, 410.
[Sandburg prints two distinct songs, both of which he associates with sailors.]

23 "THE BLUEFIELD MURDER"

Bluefield [West Virginia] *Daily Telegraph*. Various issues, January 10–February 23, 1926.
Rorrer, Kinney. *Rambling Blues: The Life and Songs of Charlie Poole*. Old Time Music Booklet 3. London: Old Time Music, 1982, 34, 60.
Thanks to Louise Yarbrough.

24 "A FIDDLER'S CONTEST"

Russell, Tony, and Ted Olson. Notes to *Knox County Stomp*: 29–33.
Wolfe, Charles K. "Early Country Music in Knoxville: The Brunswick Sessions & the End of an Era." *Old Time Music* 12 (Spring 1974): 19–31.
Wolfe, Charles K. "The Tennessee Ramblers: Ramblin' On."
Thanks to Eric Dawson, Bradley Reeves.

25 "RYE WALTZ"/"MEDLEY—SCOTTISCHE"

Culver, Kathy Skiles, and Jerry Culver. Correspondence with the author, 2008–9.

Homesley, Sterlin. "Texas Jazz Veterans: A Collection of Oral Histories." *Journal of Texas Music History* 6:1 (2006): 17–19.

26 "HALLELUJAH! I'M A BUM"/"THE BUM SONG"

Cohen, Ronald D. *Work and Sing: A History of Occupational and Labor Union Songs in the United States*. Crockett, CA: Carquinez Press, 2010, 18–23.

Kornbluh, Joyce L. (ed.). *Rebel Voices: An I. W. W. Anthology*. Ann Arbor: University of Michigan Press, 1964, 29–30, 65–72.

Lomax, Alan (ed.). *The Penguin Book of American Folk Songs*. Harmondsworth, Middlesex: Penguin Books, 1964, 129.

Renshaw, Patrick. *The Wobblies: The Story of Syndicalism in the United States*. London: Eyre & Spottiswoode, 1967.

Sandburg, Carl. *The American Songbag*, 184.

Young, Henry. *"Haywire Mac" and the "Big Rock Candy Mountain."* Unknown: Stillhouse Hollow Publishers, 1985.

27 "HOME AGAIN MEDLEY"

Linthicum, Chalmers D. Phone interview with the author, November 6, 1978.

28 "A RED-HEADED WIDOW WAS THE CAUSE OF IT ALL"/"DON'T GET ONE WOMAN ON YOUR MIND"

Thanks to Sarah Bryan, Peter Honig, Hal Pugh.

29 "STAY IN THE WAGON YARD"

Jordan, Dick. "King of the Ditty Singers." *Rural Radio* 1:11 (December 1938): 7.

30 "ELEVEN CENT COTTON FORTY CENT MEAT"—PARTS 1 & 2

Pugh, Ronnie. "The Political Balladry of Bob Miller." Paper given at the 21st Annual International Country Music Conference, Nashville, May 28, 2004. Published as "A Song for Every Plot." *Journal of Country Music* 24:2 (2005): 33–37.

Stevenson, Elizabeth. *Babbitts & Bohemians*.

31 "LINDY"/"LOUISE"

This essay is based on my article cited below.

Russell, Tony. "Proximity String Quartet." In Tony Russell and Ted Olson, Notes to *"Can You Sing or Play Old-Time Music?": The Johnson City Sessions 1928–1929* [CD box-set] (Bear Family BCD 16083, 2013): 36–37.

Thanks to Donna Blake, Joyce Butler Blake, Kenneth Butler.

32 "WHEN THE ROSES BLOOM FOR THE BOOTLEGGER"

Parts of this essay are based on my article cited below.

Russell, Tony. "Earl Shirkey and Roy Harper." In Tony Russell and Ted Olson, Notes to *"Can You Sing or Play Old-Time Music?"*: 51–53, 73–74.

33 "JUST OVER THE RIVER"/"BEAUTIFUL"

Parts of this essay are based on my article cited below.
Russell, Tony. "Garland Brothers & Grinstead." In Tony Russell and Ted Olson, Notes to *"Can You Sing or Play Old-Time Music?"*: 54–57.
Shaffer, Marguerite S. *See America First: Tourism and National Identity, 1880–1940.* Washington, DC: Smithsonian Institution Press, 2001, 4–6.
Thanks to Peggy Lawhon, Barbara Campbell Plumley, Ethel Garland Slusher.

34 "THE LOST CHILD"

Blech, Kerry. Correspondence with the author, 2018.
Carmer, Carl. *Stars Fell on Alabama.* London: Lovat Dickson & Thompson, 1935, 276.
Cauthen, Joyce H. *With Fiddle and Well-Rosined Bow: Old-Time Fiddling in Alabama.* Tuscaloosa: University of Alabama Press, 1989, 64, 122.
Cauthen, Joyce H. "The Legacy of a Neighborhood: Uncle Plez Carroll and Charlie Stripling." *The Old-Time Herald* 7:8 (Summer 2001): 18–22, 34.
Cauthen, Joyce H. "Charlie Stripling." www.encyclopediaofalabama.org/article/h-2473.
Cole, Ron. "Essential Hillbilly Commercial Recordings on 78s." *The Old-Time Herald* 11:4 (April–May 2008): 14–18. [Cole and his collaborators' list includes five other recordings discussed in this book: "Forked Deer," "Davy"/"Greenback Dollar," "Streak o' Lean—Streak o' Fat," and "The Nick Nack Song."]
Meade, Guthrie, Dick Spottswood, and Douglas S. Meade. *Country Music Sources*, 706.
Stripling, Charles and Ira. Interview with Bob Pinson, Kennedy, AL, September 2, 1963. Published as "Tapescripts: Interview with the Stripling Brothers." *JEMF Newsletter* 4:1, no. 9 (March 1968): 15–20.
Wolfe, Charles K. *The Devil's Box: Masters of Southern Fiddling.* Nashville: Country Music Foundation Press & Vanderbilt University Press, 1997, 171–82.

35 "WHO BROKE THE LOCK ON THE HEN-HOUSE DOOR?"/"SHE'LL BE COMIN' ROUND THE MOUNTAIN WHEN SHE COMES"

Cox, Bob L. *Forever a Hillbilly: Pictorial Old-Time Music Journey of Appalachian Fiddler Charlie Bowman.* Columbia, SC: BC Yesteryear Press, 2017, 93–139.
Kerr, Janet. "Lonnie Austin/Norman Woodlieff." *Old Time Music* 17 (Summer 1975): 7–10.
Russell, Tony. "H. M. Barnes' Blue Ridge Ramblers." *Old Time Music* 17 (Summer 1975): 11.

36 "WIMBUSH RAG"/"BARROW COUNTY STOMP"

Clark, Darlene Norris. Post to Clark Family Genealogy Forum, 1999.
Judelman, Craig. Notes to The Dust Busters with John Cohen, *Old Man Below* [CD] (Smithsonian Folkways SFW CD 40206, 2012).
King, Christopher. Correspondence with the author, 2018.
LaRose, Joe. Correspondence with the author, 2018.
Skelton, Lorie Vaughn. Correspondence with the author, 2018.
Vaughn, Billie Clark. Phone interview with the author, August 24, 2018.
Williams, Chris. Correspondence with the author, 2007, 2018–19.

37 "BIRMINGHAM JAIL"/"SIX MONTHS AIN'T LONG"

Foster, John. Letter to Charles K. Wolfe. Quoted in Tony Russell. *Country Music Originals: The Legends and the Lost.* New York: Oxford University Press, 2007, 94–96.

Wolfe, Charles K., and Tony Russell. "Melvin Robinette." *Old Time Music* 19 (Winter 1975/76): 4–7.

38 "HENRY FORD'S MODEL A"/"MARRIED LIFE BLUES"

Watkins, T. H. *The Great Depression: America in the 1930s*. Boston: Little, Brown, 1993, 30–31.
Thanks to Terry Ford, Paul Solarski.

39 "FLOP EARED MULE"/"LYNCHBURG TOWN"

Rorrer, Kinney. *Rambling Blues*, 44–45.
Rorrer, Kinney. Notes to *Charlie Poole with The Highlanders* [CD] (Tompkins Square TSQ 2875, 2013).

40 "LEVEE BREAKING BLUES"—PARTS I AND II

Smith, Bernard. Interview with the author, Atlanta, GA, October 11, 1977.

41 "OVER THE HILLS TO THE POORHOUSE"

Harkleroad, Haskell. Letter to Guthrie T. Meade, January 10, 1969. Meade Papers, Southern Folklife Collection, University of North Carolina at Chapel Hill.

42 "HAUNTED HUNTER"

Wolfe, Charles K. "Billie Maxwell: The First Singing Cowgirl." *Country & Western Spotlight* 21 (December 1979): 24–26.
Thanks to Allan Sutton for publishing the articles from the *El Paso Herald* on his website 78 Records, Cylinder Records & Vintage Phonographs. https://78records.wordpress.com/.

43 "LONELY COWBOY"—PARTS 1 & 2

Russell, Tony. "Retelling the West: Jules Verne Allen, The Singing Cowboy."

44 "SUGAR HILL"/"FRESNO BLUES"

Cohen, John, and Mike Seeger (eds.). *The New Lost City Ramblers Song Book*, 209.
Crockett, John H., Jr. (Johnny). Interview with Gene Earle and Norm Cohen, Santa Monica, CA, January 7, 1966.
Fleder, Rob. Notes to *Old-Time Mountain Guitar* [LP] (County 510, 1972).

45 "TIM BROOK"

Carver, Noble, with Ernie Lawson. *52 Years of Uncle Bozo (Noble Carver) of the Original Carver Family*. Burkesville, KY: Cumberland Publishing, 1965.
[Noble Carver's recollection of the recording session is accurate in several details, but it is difficult to account for the three-week discrepancy between the recording date he remembered and the one of September 6 given in Gennett files.]
"Molly and Tenbrooks [Laws H27]." In Robert B. Waltz and David G. Engle, *The Traditional Ballad Index*, 2019. www.fresnostate.edu/folklore/ballads/LH27.html.
Roud, Steve. Roud Folksong Index #RN2190. www.vwml.org/roudnumber/2190.

The two preceding sources summarize the scholarly literature. I am indebted to Neil V. Rosenberg for directing my attention to aspects of this song I would otherwise have overlooked.

46 "TENNESSEE COON HUNT"/"HEN CACKLIN' PIECE"

Garrett, Franklin M. *Atlanta and Environs: A Chronicle of Its People and Events, 1820s–1870s: Volume I.* Atlanta: University of Georgia Press, 2011, 843.

Mincey, Ernest B. Untitled article submitted to the *Gainesville* [Georgia] *News*. Written in Long Beach, CA, December 14, 1934.

Preddy, Beth. Correspondence with the author, 2019.

47 "WHERE THE SWEET MAGNOLIAS BLOOM"

Meade, Guthrie, Dick Spottswood, and Douglas S. Meade. *Country Music Sources*, 327.

Russell, Tony. "The Leake County Revelers: Waltz Kings of the Old South." *Old Time Music* 20 (Spring 1976): 26–35.

Russell, Tony, with Ausie B. Grigg. "Music in Arcadia: The Story of the Taylor-Griggs Louisiana Melody Makers." *Old Time Music* 24 (Spring 1977): 4–16. Reprinted in the *Caldwell* [Louisiana] *Watchman-Progress*, August 18, 1977, 9.

The unidentified "local newspaper" excerpt ("which made such a hit . . .") is from an undated clipping owned by Ausie B. Grigg.

48 "THREE MEN WENT A HUNTING"

Parts of this essay are based on my article cited below.

Cohen, John, and Mike Seeger (eds.). *The New Lost City Ramblers Song Book*, 184.

Lornell, Kip. *Virginia's Blues, Country, & Gospel Records 1902–1943: An Annotated Discography*. Lexington: University Press of Kentucky, 1989, 115–19.

Russell, Tony. "Byrd Moore & His Hot Shots." In Tony Russell and Ted Olson, Notes to *"Can You Sing or Play Old-Time Music?"*: 79–80.

Wolfe, Charles K. "Fiddlin' Powers and His Family." *Old Time Music* 42 (Winter 1985/86): 7–10.

Wolfe, Charles K. "Man of Constant Sorrow: Richard Burnett's Story 2." *Old Time Music* 10 (Autumn 1973): 5–9.

49 "DOWN ON PENNY'S FARM"

Parts of this essay are based on my article cited below.

Dunson, Josh, and Ethel Raim (eds.). *Anthology of American Folk Music*. New York: Oak Publications, 1973, 66–67.

Lockamy, Kathleen. Phone interview with the author, 2007.

Lockamy, Tom. Phone interviews and correspondence with the author, 2012–13.

Lomax, Alan, Woody Guthrie, and Pete Seeger. *Hard Hitting Songs for Hard-Hit People*. New York: Oak Publications, 1967, 34–35.

["Down on Roberts' Farm" was collected by Bascom Lamar Lunsford from Claude Reeves of Little River, Transylvania County, NC, who claimed to have written it, though its many similarities to "Down on Penny's Farm" make that doubtful.]

Loy, Mary Lockamy. Phone interviews with the author, 2007, 2013.

Russell, Tony. "The Bentley Boys." In Tony Russell and Ted Olson, Notes to *"Can You Sing or Play Old-Time Music?"*, 83–85.

Walker, Frank B. "Who Chose These Records?: A Look into the Life, Tastes, and Procedures of Frank Walker." [Interview with Mike Seeger, June 19, 1962.] In Josh Dunson and Ethel Raim (eds.), *Anthology of American Folk Music*, 8–17.

50 "THE FATE OF RHODA SWEETIN"

Blackard, Malcolm V. "Wilmer Watts & The Lonely Eagles."

51 "COTTON MILL GIRL"

PoliticalGraveyard.com. politicalgraveyard.com/geo/SC/merchant.html.
Sloan, David. Interview with the author, Union, SC, April 25, 2017, and subsequent correspondence.
Yeary, Vonda. Correspondence with the author, 2009–14.
Some of the research for this essay was done in collaboration with my friend Hunter Holmes. We were greatly assisted by Union County librarian Ola Jean Kelly.

52 "THE ROAMIN' MUSICIAN"

Meade, Guthrie, Dick Spottswood, and Douglas S. Meade. *Country Music Sources*, 54.

53 "THAT'S THE BLUE HEAVEN FOR ME/"SINCE I'VE GROWN SO USED TO YOU"

No references.

54 "STREAK O' LEAN—STREAK O' FAT"

Daniel, Wayne. "Georgia Fiddling Champion: A. A. Gray." *Old Time Music* 41 (Spring 1985): 9–13.
Russell, Tony. Notes to *John Dilleshaw (1929–1930)* [CD] (Document DOCD 8002, 1997).
Wolfe, Charles K. "The Legend of John Dilleshaw." *Old Time Music* 36 (Summer 1981): 12–16.

55 "SALVATION IS FOR ALL"

Boone, Edward. *Sunshine Sacred Specials*. Des Moines, IA: Boone Publishing, 1935, 78.
Bryson, Bill. *The Life and Times of the Thunderbolt Kid*. London: Doubleday, 2006, 209.
Roesink, Olive Boone. Phone interview with the author, June 17, 2006.

56 "THE BALD HEADED END OF THE BROOM"/"THE NICK NACK SONG"

Parts of this essay are based on my article cited below.
Nelson, Donald Lee. "Ridgel's Fountain Citians." *JEMF Quarterly* 8:3, no. 27 (Autumn 1972): 133–39.
Russell, Tony. "Ridgel's Fountain Citians." In Tony Russell and Ted Olson, Notes to *Knox County Stomp*, 37, 87–88.
Tudor, Betty. Interview with the author and Ted Olson, Knoxville, TN, May 26, 2015.
Thanks to Eric Dawson, Bradley Reeves.

57 "FORTY PER CENT"

Bastin, Bruce. Correspondence with the author, 2009.
Crow, Sybil Garner. Correspondence with the author, 2008–9.
Crow, Sybil Garner. Interview with the author and Hunter Holmes, Union, SC, October 24, 2013.

Meng, Donna. Correspondence with the author, 2008–9.

Robinson, Cathy Meng. Correspondence with the author, 2008–9.

Wiacek, Win. "Now Read This! Graphic Novel Reviews and Recommendations." www.comicsreview.co.uk/nowreadthis/2016/12/11/sidney-smiths-the-gumps/.

Yeary, Vonda. Correspondence with the author, 2009–14.

Some of the research for this essay was done in collaboration with my friend Hunter Holmes. We were greatly assisted by Union County librarian Ola Jean Kelly. Thanks also to Dean Mullaney (www.libraryofamericancomics.com) and David Sloan.

58 "I'VE GOT THE CHAIN STORE BLUES"

Lebhar, Godfrey M. *Chain Stores in America 1859–1962*. New York: Chain Store Publishing, 1963.

Wolfe, Charles K. "Lee Allen's Radio Days and Other Salty Dog Chronicles." *Old Time Music* 44 (Winter 1987/88): 9–11.

59 "MY FATHER DOESN'T LOVE ME"

Bowling, Dan. Correspondence with the author, 2017.

Kerr, Janet. Correspondence with the author, 2018.

McDaniel, Lewis. Interview with Janet Kerr and Kinney Rorrer, Ridgeway, VA, August 17, 1971.

McDaniel, Lewis. Interview with the author, Ridgeway, VA, September 8, 1971.

Rorrer, Kinney. Correspondence with the author, 2017–19.

60 "FLAT WHEEL TRAIN BLUES"—NOS. 1 & 2

"R. D. Gay, Sr., Well Known Tampan, Dies." *Tampa Tribune*, August 30, 1950.

"R. E. D. Gay Dies in Hospital Here." *Tampa Times*, August 29, 1950.

61 "GOT THE JAKE LEG TOO"

Baum, Dan. "Jake Leg: How the Blues Diagnosed a Medical Mystery." *The New Yorker* (September 15, 2003): 50–57. Reprinted in Norm Cohen (ed.). *All This for a Song*. Chapel Hill, NC: Southern Folklife Collection, 2009, 309–20.

Case, Robert [writer/producer/director]. *The Jake Leg Infamy*. Film shown at the North American College of Clinical Toxicology meeting, San Antonio, TX, September 2009. Available on YouTube.

Morgan, John P., and Thomas C. Tulloss. "The Jake Walk Blues: A Toxicologic Tragedy Mirrored in American Popular Music." *JEMF Quarterly* 13, no. 47 (Autumn 1977): 122–26. Reprinted from *Annals of Internal Medicine* 85:6 (December 1976): 804–8.

Morgan, John P., and Thomas C. Tulloss. "The Jake Walk Blues." *Old Time Music* 28 (Spring 1978): 17–24.

Russell, Tony. "Doc Bailey: Talent Scout, Winona." *Old Time Music* 20 (Spring 1976): 22–23, 25.

Shepherd, William G. "Kansas, by Ginger!" *Collier's*, July 26, 1930, 12–13, 48, 50.

Tyler, Clayton. Letter to the author, January 22, 1977.

Tyler, Clayton. Interview with the author, Kilmichael, MS, September 21, 1977.

Vitelli, Romeo. "The Ginger Jake Blues." https://drvitelli.typepad.com/providentia/2017/04/ginger-jake.html.

Thanks to Rich Remsberg.

62 "THE NIGHT HERDING SONG"

Adams, Ramon F. *The Old-Time Cowhand*. New York: Macmillan, 1948, 35.

Dobie, J. Frank. *Up the Trail from Texas*. New York: Random House, 1955, 66.

James, Will. *Lone Cowboy: My Life Story*. New York: Charles Scribner's Sons, 1930, 168.
Lomax, John A., and Alan Lomax. *Cowboy Songs and Other Frontier Ballads*, 60–61.
Miller, Kathi. "Singing Cowboy Swapped Stage for FW Law Office." *Fort Worth Star-Telegram*, January [exact date unknown], 1974.
Russell, Tony. "'Rough but Strikingly Melodious': British Responses to American Country Music in the 1930s." Paper given at the conference Transatlantic Routes of American Roots Music, University of Worcester, England, September 12, 2009.
Stephens, Harry. "The Night Herding Song" (including interview with John A. Lomax) (1946). *Cowboy Songs, Ballads, and Cattle Calls from Texas* [CD] (Rounder CD1512, 1999).
Woods, Woody. "Wake Up with a Smile." *Rural Radio* (February 1939): 10–11.

63 "ELEVEN MORE MONTHS AND TEN MORE DAYS"—PARTS 1 AND 2

Barna, Ryan. "Fred Hall (1898–1954): Creative Composer, Publisher, Radio, and Recording Artist." *VJM* 158 (Autumn 2010): 3–10.
Mencken, H. L. "Famine." Baltimore *Evening Sun*, January 19, 1931.
[It is often stated that Mencken called Arkansas "the apex of Moronia." It sounds characteristic, but I have found no evidence for it in the period's press.]
Mencken, H. L. "The Sahara of the Bozart" (1917). In *Prejudices: A Selection*. New York: Vintage Books, 1958, 81.
Sutton, Allan. "Synthetic Country: Arthur Fields, Fred Hall, and the Creation of the 'Hillbilly' Stereotype." www.mainspringpress.com/fieldshall.html. (No longer accessible.)

64 "WHEN KATIE COMES DOWN TO THE GATE"/"A LITTLE WHITE ROSE"

Crisp, David L. Correspondence with the author, 2012.
King, Christopher C. Correspondence with the author, 2012.
Murphy, Dale. Correspondence with the author, 2012.
Murphy, Judson. Account books, 1930–31.
Murphy, R. D. Interview with the author, Cross Keys, SC, October 23, 2013.
I am grateful to John Burton for putting me in touch with Dale Murphy.

65 "PROSPERITY IS JUST AROUND WHICH CORNER?"/"WHAT ARE YOU SQUAWKIN' ABOUT?"

Coltman, Bob. "Carson Robison: First of the Rural Professionals." *Old Time Music* 29 (Summer 1978): 5–13, 27.
Horstman, Dorothy. *Sing Your Heart Out, Country Boy*, 110–11. ["Life Gets Tee-Jus, Don't It?"]

66 "THAT'S MY RABBIT—MY DOG CAUGHT IT"

Hughes, Robert. *The Shock of the New*. BBC/Time-Life TV series transmitted by the BBC (1980)/PBS (1981).
Meade, Guthrie. Notes to *Old Time Fiddle Band Music from Kentucky*.
Nevins, Rich. Notes to *Kentucky Mountain Music*.
Wheeler, Lisa. "Georgia Pot Lickers 78 Sells for $10,126.05." *Goldmine* 31:22, issue 659 (October 28, 2005). http://isleofwrite.com/stories/GeorgiaPotLickers.pdf.

67 "CHINATOWN, MY CHINATOWN"

Cundell, Guy. Correspondence with the author, 2018.
[The passage cited is an edited portion of a more extensive commentary on this recording.]

Ginell, Cary. *Milton Brown and the Founding of Western Swing.* Urbana: University of Illinois Press, 1994.
Pinson, Bob. "The Musical Brownies." *Old Time Music* 1 (Summer 1971): 14–16.

68 "BANKHEAD BLUES"

Nations, Marshall. Correspondence with the author, 1972–73.
Russell, Tony. "Lincoln County Bluesmen: Mississippi Stringbands 2: The Nations Brothers." *Old Time Music* 10 (Autumn 1973): 12, 24.
Thanks to Gil Sewell, Gayle Dean Wardlow.

69 "FEELS GOOD"/"LET ME PLAY WITH IT"

Campbell, Cecil. Phone interview with the author, Charlotte, NC, September 17, 1978.
Goodman, Carrie Clontz. Phone interview with the author, Salisbury, NC, October 2, 1978.
Russell, Tony. Notes to *She's Selling What She Used to Give Away* [CD] (Bear Family BCD 17550, 2018).
Sutton, Allan. "'These Songs Glorify Depravity': John McClelland and the Birth of the Dirty-Record Industry." Post to 78 Records, Cylinder Records & Vintage Phonographs https://78records.wordpress.com/, June 2, 2020.
Wyatt, Marshall. Correspondence with the author, October 2017.

70 "THOSE RAMBLING BLUES"

Bellande, Ray. Correspondence with the author, 2006–7.
Coltman, Bob. "'Sweethearts of the Hills': Women in Early Country Music." *JEMF Quarterly* 14, no. 52 (Winter 1978): 161–80.
Russell, Tony. "Backtrack: Steelman Sisters." *Old Time Music* 29 (Summer 1978): 19.
Thanks to Laurah Sims, Dale Snyder, Vivian Hall Wall.

71 "V-8 BLUES"/"COURTIN'"

Coltman, Bob. "Across the Chasm: How the Depression Changed Country Music." *Old Time Music* 23 (Winter 1976/77): 6–12.
Springate, Megan E. "Some Brief Notes on the Tobacco Tag" (1997). https://works.bepress.com/meganspringate/4/.
Wyatt, Marshall. Correspondence with the author, January 2019.

72 "WONDERING"

Falcon, Wade. http://earlycajunmusic.blogspot.com/2017/02/wondering-riverside-ramblers.html. Posted February 1, 2017.
Falcon, Wade. http://earlycajunmusic.blogspot.com/2017/02/ayou-ayou-mon-petite-chien-pour-edete.html. Posted February 25, 2017.
Falcon, Wade. Correspondence with the author, February 7, 2018.
Falcon, Wade. http://earlycajunmusic.blogspot.com/2018/04/vingt-et-un-ans-twenty-one-years.html. Posted April 20, 2018.
Sandmel, Ben. Correspondence with the author, February 8, 2018.

73 "THE LAST LETTER"

Coffey, Kevin. Notes to *The Last Letter* [CD box-set] (Bear Family BCD 15911, 1996).

Garmon, M. D. "Rex Griffin—Country Music Legend." *Gadsden* [Alabama] *Times*, March 26, 1978: 4–5.
Shaw, Arnold. *Honkers and Shouters: The Golden Years of Rhythm and Blues*. New York: Collier Books, 1978, 92.

74 "HELLO STRANGER"

Commager, Henry Steele. *The American Mind: An Interpretation of American Thought and Character Since the 1880's*. New Haven, CT: Yale University Press, 1950, 16.
Lornell, Kip. "'I Used to Go Along and Help:' Leslie Riddles Remembers Songhunting with A. P." In John Atkins (ed.), *The Carter Family*. Old Time Music Booklet 1. London: Old Time Music, 1973, 34–35.

75 "COTTON MILL BLUES"

Bivins, Maggie. Phone interview with Bob Pinson, 1978.
Huber, Patrick. *Linthead Stomp*: 203–204.
Lomax, Alan. *List of American Folk Songs on Commercial Records*, 6.
Lomax, Alan, Woody Guthrie, and Pete Seeger. *Hard Hitting Songs for Hard-Hit People*, 123.

76 "GUITAR BLUES"/"SWEET HAWAIIAN CHIMES"

Coltman, Bob. "'Sweethearts of the Hills.'"
Daniel, Wayne. "Same Faces, Different Names: The DeZurik Sisters and The Cackle Sisters." hillbilly-music.com, undated.
Stand By!. Various issues. Chicago: Prairie Farmer, 1935–38.

77 "TRUCK DRIVER'S BLUES"

Coffey, Kevin. Notes to *Cliff Bruner and His Texas Wanderers* [CD box-set] (Bear Family BCD 15932, 1997): 20–21.
Danker, Frederick E. "Trucking Songs: A Comparison with Traditional Occupational Songs." *Journal of Country Music* 7:1 (January 1978): 78–86.
Ginell, Cary. Correspondence with the author, July 3, 2019.
Tosches, Nick. "Ted Daffan Interview." *Old Time Music* 30 (Autumn 1978): 6–8.

78 "NEW SAN ANTONIO ROSE"

Ginell, Cary. Correspondence with the author, December 8, 2017.
McWhorter, Frankie, with John R. Erickson. *Cowboy Fiddler*. Lubbock: Texas Tech University Press, 1992. Reprinted as *Cowboy Fiddler in Bob Wills' Band*. Denton: University of North Texas Press, 1997.
Radiobob805. "Bob Wills & The Story of San Antonio Rose with Interviews." YouTube, 2012.
Stricklin, Al, with John McConal. *My Years with Bob Wills*. San Antonio: Naylor, 1976, 78–79, 121–24.
Townsend, Charles R. *San Antonio Rose: The Life and Music of Bob Wills*. Urbana: University of Illinois Press, 1976, 118, 190–98.

For further discographical details of the recordings discussed in this book, see my *Country Music Records: A Discography, 1921–1942*. New York: Oxford University Press, 2004.

General Bibliography

In addition to the works cited in Sources, the following books and articles, though not drawn on for specific essays, have been valued teachers and companions through many years of study.

Gentry, Linnell. *A History and Encyclopedia of Country, Western and Gospel Music*. 2nd ed. Nashville: Clairmont, 1969.

Kingsbury, Paul, ed. *The Encyclopedia of Country Music*. New York: Oxford University Press, 1998.

Malone, Bill C. *Southern Music, American Music*. Lexington: University Press of Kentucky, 1979.

Malone, Bill C. *Country Music, U.S.A.* Austin: University of Texas Press for the American Folklore Society, 1968. Rev. ed. Austin: University of Texas Press for the American Folklore Society, 1985.

Malone, Bill C. *Don't Get Above Your Raisin': Country Music and the Southern Working Class*. Urbana: University of Illinois Press, 2002.

Malone, Bill C., and Tracey E. W. Laird. *Country Music USA*. 50th anniv. ed. Austin: University of Texas Press, 2018.

Malone, Bill C., and Judith McCulloh (eds.). *Stars of Country Music: Uncle Dave Macon to Johnny Rodriguez*. Urbana: University of Illinois Press, 1975.

Porterfield, Nolan. *Exploring Roots Music: Twenty Years of the* JEMF Quarterly. Lanham, MD: Scarecrow Press, 2003.

Richardson, Ethel Park, and Sigmund Spaeth. *American Mountain Songs*. New York: Greenberg, 1927.

Savoy, Ann Allen. *Cajun Music: A Reflection of a People*. Eunice, LA: Bluebird Press, 1984.

Shelton, Robert, and Burt Goldblatt. *The Country Music Story*. New York: Bobbs-Merrill, 1966.

Spaeth, Sigmund. *A History of Popular Music in America*. New York: Random House, 1948; London: Phoenix House, 1960.

Stambler, Irwin, and Grelun Landon. *The Encyclopedia of Folk, Country and Western Music*. 2nd ed. New York: St Martin's Press, 1983.

Tribe, Ivan M. *Mountaineer Jamboree: Country Music in West Virginia*. Lexington: University Press of Kentucky, 1984.

Van der Merwe, Peter. *Origins of the Popular Style*. Oxford: Oxford University Press, 1989.

Wolfe, Charles K. "Ralph Peer at Work: The Victor 1927 Bristol Sessions." *Old Time Music* 5 (Summer 1972): 10-15.

Wolfe, Charles K. *The Grand Ole Opry: The Early Years, 1925–35*. Old Time Music Booklet 2. London: Old Time Music, 1975.

Wolfe, Charles K. *Tennessee Strings: The Story of Country Music in Tennessee*. Knoxville: University of Tennessee Press, 1977.

Wolfe, Charles K. "Fiddlin' Powers and His Family." *Old Time Music* 42 (Winter 1985/86): 7–10.

Wolfe, Charles K. "A Lighter Shade of Blue: White Country Blues." In Lawrence Cohn (ed.), *Nothing but the Blues*. New York: Abbeville Press, 1993, 233–63.

Wolfe, Charles K., and Ted Olson (eds.). *The Bristol Sessions: Writings about the Big Bang of Country Music*. Jefferson, NC: McFarland, 2005.

Wolfe, Charles K., and Tony Russell. "Two Cow Girls on the Lone Prairie: The True Story of the Girls of the Golden West." *Old Time Music* 43 (Winter 1986/87): 6–13.

Index of Names

Page references in italics denote illustrations or captions

★

Index of Songs

Page references in bold denote the primary discussion of the song or tune
Page references in italics denote illustrations

Printed in the USA/Agawam, MA
February 10, 2022

788514.062